INSTRUCTOR'S MANUAL

Stern Neill *Louisiana State University*

Chris Pullig *Louisiana State University*

Barbara Ross *Louisiana State University*

William C. Black *Louisiana State University*

MULTIVARIATE DATA ANALYSIS

Fifth Edition

Joseph F. Hair, Jr.
Rolph E. Anderson
Ronald L. Tatham
William C. Black

Prentice
Hall

Prentice Hall, Upper Saddle River, New Jersey 07458

Acquisitions editor: *Whitney Blake*
Associate editor: *John Larkin*
Project editor: *Theresa Festa*
Manufacturer: *Integrated Book Technology, Inc.*

© 1999 by Prentice Hall, Inc.
Upper Saddle River, New Jersey 07458

Printed in the United States of America

10 9 8 7 6 5 4

ISBN 0-13-906025-1

Prentice-Hall International (UK) Limited, *London*
Prentice-Hall of Australia Pty. Limited, *Sydney*
Prentice-Hall Canada Inc., *Toronto*
Prentice-Hall Hispanoamericana, S.A., *Mexico*
Prentice-Hall of India Private Limited, *New Delhi*
Prentice-Hall of Japan, Inc., *Tokyo*
Editora Prentice-Hall do Brasil, Ltda., *Rio de Janeiro*

TABLE OF CONTENTS

INTRODUCTION

This manual has been designed to provide teachers using **Multivariate Data Analysis, 5th edition,** with supplementary teaching aids. The course suggestions made here are the result of years of experience teaching the basic content of this text in several universities. Obviously, the contents may be modified to suit the level of the students and the length of the term.

Multivariate data analysis is an interesting and challenging subject to teach. As an instructor, your objective is to direct your students' energies and interests so that they can learn the concepts and principles underlying the various techniques. You will also want to help your students learn to apply the techniques. Through years of teaching multivariate analysis, we have learned that the most effective approach to teaching the techniques is to provide the students with real world data and have them manipulate the variables using several different programs and techniques . The text is designed to facilitate this approach, making available two data sets for analysis. Moreover, accompanying sample output and control cards are provided to supplement the analyses discussed in the text.

ORGANIZATION OF THE CHAPTERS IN THE TEXT

The text is designed to help make your teaching as enjoyable and as simple as possible. First, the chapters have been organized into four sections. After the introduction to multivariate statistics in Chapter One, the first section, *Preparing for a Multivariate Analysis*, contains Chapter Two (Examining Your Data) and Chapter Three (Factor Analysis). Section Two, *Dependence Techniques*, contains Chapters Four through Eight, covering Multiple Regression, Discriminant Analysis, Multivariate Analysis of Variance, Conjoint Analysis and Canonical Correlation. Then Section Three, Interdependence Techniques, covers Chapters Nine (Cluster Analysis) and Ten (Multidimensional Scaling). Finally, Section Four, Advanced and Emerging Techniques, includes Chapter 11 (Structural Equation Modeling) and Chapter 12, Emerging Techniques in Multivariate analysis which discusses data mining, neural networks and resampling.

Each chapter begins with a "Chapter Preview" so students will understand the major concepts they are expected to learn. To facilitate understanding of the chapter material and as a ready reference for clarification, definitions of key terms are presented at the front of each chapter. The text is designed for those individuals who want to obtain a conceptual understanding of multivariate methods--what they can do, when they should be used, and how the results should be interpreted. Following this design, each chapter is structured in a step by step manner, including six steps. The end of each chapter includes an illustration of how to apply and interpret each technique. Basically, the approach is for the "data analyst," therefore, the math formulae and symbols are minimized. We believe it is the most practical, readable guide available to understanding and applying these otherwise complex statistical tools.

At the end of each chapter, a series of questions are provided to stimulate the student to evaluate what has been read and to translate this material into a workable knowledge base for use in future applications. To aid in gaining insights into a method's application, we have provided annotations of several articles illustrating the usefulness of a technique in solving "real world" problems. Care has been taken to select articles demonstrating the technique in as simple, but complete, a manner as possible.

ORGANIZATION OF THE MANUAL

This instructor's manual is designed to facilitate the preparation and conduct of classes, exams, and seminars. Materials included in the manual are organized by chapters in three major sections.

Section One:

(1) Chapter summaries: to refresh the instructor's memory without the necessity of re-reading the entire chapter prior to class. Each chapter summary is organized around four major sections. The objective of these sections is to identify particular issues that may be useful in organizing class discussion. The four sections are:

   a. **What** -- an overview, or brief description, of the technique.

   b. **Why** -- a description of the basic objectives of the technique.

   c. **When** -- identification of the types of problems the technique may be used to address.

   d. **How** -- description of the assumptions applicable to the technique, the data requirements for its use, the major points which are essential to the successful implementation of the research plan and the key points contained in the computer output needed for a complete and accurate interpretation of the results.

(2) Answers to the end-of-chapter questions: suggested answers to the questions that can form the basis for further elaboration if desired.

(3) Sample exam questions: while essay or short answer questions are probably preferable for examinations, many times multiple choice questions can be used as a method for assessing specific knowledge about the subject. To ease the burden of writing exam questions, multiple choice questions are provided for each chapter.

Section Two:

This section contains documentation on the three databases provided with the text. The first is the HATCO database used throughout the text as a basis for examples. The second database is the HATCO Missing Data database used in Chapter Two to illustrate data examination. The third database concerns sales training and is comprised of 80 respondents, representing a portion of data that was collected by academic researchers. Provided for each database is a brief description, a listing of the actual data and the SPSS and SAS control cards necessary for its creation. Also, a copy of the sales training database questionnaire is provided.

Section Three:

This final section provides sample computer output for the analyses in each chapter. The manual utilizes the HATCO data base (including the HATCO Missing Data database in chapter two) throughout the text for illustration of each technique. Included in this section are the computer outputs for each example used in the text. Listings of the output are annotated with comments to aid you in better discussing the output from an interpretive perspective. Actual outputs of the analyses are all from SPSS, except in the instances of Chapter 9 (some of the multidimensional scaling examples from a series of PC-based packages) and Chapter 11 (LISREL output from the LISREL package).

ACCOMPANYING COMPUTER DISKETTE

The understanding and interpretation of multivariate analysis is enhanced immeasurably by the ability of students to actually analyze data (e.g., derive research questions and execute the analysis) and/or examine actual computer output to ascertain what is the form and content of the results. To avoid any unnecessary duplication of effort on the part of the instructor, the instructor's manual is accompanied by an IBM-PC compatible disk which contains two types of files:

Data and Control Card Files:

The three data bases are on the disk as ASCII (or text) files for direct input as the "raw data" to either mainframe or PC applications. To assist the instructor in performing the analyses illustrated in the text, ASCII text files are also provided for all of the control cards documented in Appendix A of the text. Included are examples of programming the multivariate techniques in SAS (Statistical Analysis System, SAS Institute), SPSS (Statistical Package for the Social Sciences, SPSS Inc.), and LISREL (Scientific Software, Inc.).

Computer Outputs

If computer access is not available for a particular technique, files of the actual outputs (from SPSS, the MDS programs and LISREL) for each example from the text are also provided on the diskette. This enables you to provide students with the complete computer outputs even without actually running the programs.

Using the Files and Computer Output

The methods needed to extract the output and files from the computer disk are contained on the file README.TXT.

Internet Support

The authors have established a website entitled "Great Ideas in Teaching Multivariate Statistics" with the objective of providing a clearinghouse for instructional materials and a forum for discussions about pedagogical issues. Accessed through the Prentice-Hall website (www.prenhall.com), the website will offer supplementary materials for the text, such as links to additional datasets for use in class and we-based materials for each technique. We will also sponsor a mailing list MVSTAT that will focus on instructional issues in teaching multivariate techniques. We encourage any faculty member to contribute to the collection of materials, which can then be disseminated among all those interested in the subject area.

We envision this to be an evolutionary project, with its growth and focus guided primarily by its users and contributors. We hope that we can provide an easy and readily available forum for discussion and collaboration among interested faculty members.

SECTION ONE:

CHAPTER SUMMARIES,
ANSWERS TO THE END-OF-CHAPTER QUESTIONS
AND
SAMPLE MULTIPLE CHOICE QUESTIONS

CHAPTER ONE
INTRODUCTION TO MULTIVARIATE ANALYSIS

This presentation will approach the general idea of multivariate data analysis by attempting to answer the basic questions of "What?," "Why?," "When?," and "How?".

What is multivariate analysis?

1. Multivariate analysis, in this text, includes both multivariable techniques and multivariate techniques. The term "multivariate analysis" really stands for a family of techniques, and it is important that you realize this fact from the onset. The common characteristic is that multiple variables are used for the dependent and/or independent variables in the analysis. Each technique has its own special powers and unique instances of applicability. These will be revealed to you in detail in subsequent chapters in the text.

2. For now, it is only necessary that you realize in general terms the **special powers** represented by this family of analyses:

- *Description* - Some of the techniques have rather amazing abilities to describe phenomena. They can find patterns of relationships where the human eye and even univariate or bivariate statistics fail to do so.
- *Explanation* - Other techniques have special capabilities to explain or to help explain relationships. For instance, they can isolate the impact of one variable on another; show relative differences between the magnitude of impact for two or more variables; or even reveal how one set of variables impinges on another set.
- *Prediction* - Certainly every researcher desires the ability to predict, and multivariate techniques afford that promise. Certain multivariate analyses are explicitly designed to yield predictive modes with specific levels of accuracy.
- *Control* - Finally, certain multivariate techniques can be used for control. Of course, the techniques themselves will not institute control, but their application can help a researcher develop cause-and-effect relationships and models which will ultimately enhance their ability to control events to some degree.

3. There are **primary and secondary** uses of each of the multivariate techniques as well as cases in which they are not applicable. Given that you will be introduced to each one in the text chapters, perhaps it would be helpful to show the "fit" of each to the four abilities just enumerated. Figure 1 at the end of this section is a reference in this respect. In the Figure,"P" indicates a primary ability of the technique, while "S" represents a secondary ability. The "NA" means that the technique is not applicable for that purpose.

4. While multivariate analyses are descended from univariate techniques, the extension to multiple variables or variates introduces a number of issues which must be understood before examining each technique in detail.

- *The Role of the Variate* --Multivariate techniques differ from univariate techniques in that they employ a variate.

  ➢ Definition: a linear combination of variables with empirically determined weights.

  ➢ Variables are specified by the researcher, and the weights are assigned by the technique.

  ➢ Single value: When summed, the variate produces a single value which represents the entire set of variables. This single value, in addition to the specific contribution of each variable to the variate, is important in all multivariate techniques.

- *Specification of measurement scales* -- Each multivariate technique assumes the use of a certain type of data. For this reason, the type of data held by the researcher is instrumental in the selection of the appropriate multivariate technique. The researcher must make sure that he or she has the appropriate type of data to employ the chosen multivariate technique.

  ➢ Metric vs nonmetric: Data, in the form of measurement scales, can be metric or nonmetric.

    1. Nonmetric data are categorical variables describing differences in type or kind by indicating the presence or absence of a characteristic or property.

    2. Metric data are continuous measures reflecting differences in amount or degree in a relative quantity or distance.

- *Identification of measurement error*

  ➢ Definition: the degree to which the observed values in the sample are not representative of the true values in the population.

  ➢ Sources: several sources are possible, including data entry errors and the use of inappropriate gradations in a measurement scale.

  ➢ All variables in a multivariate analysis have some degree of measurement error, which adds residual error to the observed variables.

➤ <u>Need for assessment of both the validity and the reliability</u> of measures.

  1. *Validity* is the degree to which a measure accurately represents what it is supposed to.

  2. *Reliability* is the degree to which the observed variable measures the true value and is error free.

- ***Statistical significance and statistical power.*** Almost all of the multivariate techniques discussed in this text are based on ***statistical inference*** of a population's values from a randomly drawn sample of the population.

  ➤ <u>Specifying statistical error levels.</u> Interpretation of statistical inferences requires the specification of acceptable levels of error.

    1. *Type I error (alpha)* is the probability of rejecting the null hypothesis when it is actually true.

    2. *Type II error (beta)* is the probability of failing to reject the null hypothesis when it is actually false. Alpha and beta are inversely related.

  ➤ <u>Power</u>: the probability (1-beta) of correctly rejecting the null hypothesis when it should be rejected.

    1. *Specifying type II error (beta)* also specifies the power of the statistical inference test.

    2. Power is *determined by 3 factors*:
       - its inverse relationship with alpha
       - the effect size
       - the sample size.

    3. When *planning* research, the researcher should:
       - estimate the expected effect size
       - then select the sample size and the alpha level to achieve the desired power level.

    4. Upon *completion* of the analyses, the actual power should be calculated to properly interpret the results.

Why is there multivariate data analysis?

The need for multivariate analysis comes from the simple fact of life that just about everything is in some way interrelated with other things. Inflation, for instance, is related to taxes, interest rates, the money supply, oil prices, the business cycle, foreign wars, and a good deal more. Buyers' reactions to an advertisement are related to the price of the item, competitors, warranty terms, previous experiences with the product, conversations with neighbors, credibility of the actor used in the commercial, and season of the year.

To managers or persons responsible for making decisions within an organization, each decision is affected by many "variables." These variables are identifiable entities which have some impact or relationship to the focal topic. In addition to the main impact of these variables, the variables interact with each other as well. In short, a manager is faced with a complete system of complicated relationships in any single decision-problem.

Humans, by their very nature, strive to make some sense out of their environment. They seek some order to the chaos of interrelationships. There are many ways of attempting to achieve order. You can use intuition, logical systems such as set theory, or simplification. You could even choose to ignore the impacts of some variables. But most intelligent managers prefer to rely on some framework which is more accepted.

From these two situations--the myriad of interrelated variables and the need for an accepted framework--springs the need for multivariate analysis techniques. They are the means of achieving parsimonious descriptions, explanations, and predictions of reality.

When do you use multivariate analysis?

Essentially, multivariate analysis is appropriate whenever you have two or more variables observed a number of times. In fact, it is most common to have several variables observed a great many times, also known as a "data set." It is traditional to envision a data set as being comprised of rows and columns. The rows pertain to each observation, such as each person or each completed questionnaire in a large survey. The columns, on the other hand, pertain to each variable, such as a response to a question or an observed characteristic for each person.

Data sets can be immense; a single study may have a sample size of 1,000 or more respondents, each answering 100 questions. Hence the data set would be 1,000 by 100, or 100,000 cells of data. Obviously, the need for parsimony is very evident.

Multivariate techniques aid the researcher in obtaining parsimony by reducing the number of computations necessary to complete statistical tests. For example, when completing univariate tests, if an average were computed for each variable, 100 means would result, and if a correlation were computed between each variable and every other variable, there would be close to 5,000 separate values computed. In sharp contrast, multivariate analysis would require many less computations. For example, factor analysis might result in ten factors. Cluster analysis might yield five clusters. Multiple regression could identify six significant predictor variables. MANOVA might reveal 12 cases of significant differences. Multiple discriminant analysis perhaps would find seven significant variables. It should be evident that parsimony can be achieved by using multivariate techniques when analyzing most data sets.

How do you use multivariate data analysis techniques?

This text follows a structured approach to multivariate model building. The six steps defined in the following chapters should be viewed as guidelines for better understanding the process of applying each technique. The conceptual, as well as the empirical, issues for each technique are discussed. The following summary provides an overview of each of the six steps.

Step 1: Define the Research Problem, Objectives, and Multivariate Technique To Be Used.

Based on an underlying theoretical model, the researcher should define the research question(s). Depending on the type of question, the researcher should also identify the type of multivariate technique, dependence or interdependence, which is most appropriate.

Step 2: Develop the Analysis Plan

Each multivariate technique has an associated set of issues which are relevant to the design of an analysis plan. Sample sizes, scaling of variables, and estimation methods are common issues which must be evaluated by the researcher prior to data collection.

Step 3: Evaluate the Assumptions Underlying the Multivariate Technique

Once the data are collected, the researcher must evaluate the underlying assumptions of the chosen multivariate technique. All techniques have conceptual and statistical assumptions that must be met before the analysis can proceed.

Step 4: Estimate the Multivariate Model and Assess Overall Model Fit

Following a testing of the assumptions, a multivariate model is estimated with the objective of meeting specific characteristics. After the model is estimated, the overall model fit is compared to specified criteria. The model may be respecified for better fit if necessary.

Step 5: Interpret the Variate

Once an acceptable model is achieved, the nature of the multivariate relationship is investigated. Coefficients of the variables in the variate are examined. Interpretation may lead to model respecification. The objective is to identify findings that can be generalized to the population.

Step 6: Apply the Diagnostics to the Results

Finally, the researcher must assess whether the results are unduly affected by an single or small set of observations and determine the degree of generalizability of the results by validation methods. These two actions provide the researcher with support for the research findings.

Some General Guidelines For Multivariate Analysis

Further, six guidelines applicable to all multivariate analyses are given below. As you review each chapter, you will find that these issues are identified several times across a number of multivariate techniques. For this reason, these guidelines serve as a "general philosophy" for completing multivariate analyses.

- **Establish Practical Significance as Well as Statistical Significance**
  Not only must the researcher assess whether or not the results of a multivariate analysis are statistically significant, but he or she must also determine whether or not the results have managerial, or practical, implications for action.

- **Sample Size Affects All Results**
  The size of the sample will impact whether or not the results achieve statistical significance. Too little or too much power can be the result of sample sizes. Researchers should always assess the analysis results in light of the sample size.

- **Know Your Data**
  Multivariate analyses require rigorous examination of data. Diagnostic measures are available to evaluate the nature of sets of multivariate variables.

- **Strive for Model Parsimony**
  The researcher should evaluate those variables chosen for inclusion in the analysis. The objective is to create a parsimonious model which includes all relevant variables and excludes all irrelevant variables. Specification error (omission of relevant variables) and high multicollinearity (inclusion of irrelevant variables) can substantially impact analysis results.

- **Look at Your Errors**
  Often, the first model estimation does not provide the best model fit. Thus, the researcher should analyze the prediction errors and determine potential changes to the model. Errors serve as diagnostics for achieving better model fit.

- *Validate Your Results*
   The researcher should always validate the results. Validation procedures ensure the analyst that the results are not merely specific to the sample, but are representative and generalizable to the population.

Selecting a Multivariate Technique

Figure 1.2 in the text provides a general decision process with which to select the appropriate multivariate technique. In doing so, the analyst must address two issues: objective of the analysis and type of variables used. First, the analyst must evaluate the theoretical nature of the problem and determine if the objective is to assess a dependence relationship (predictive) or is an interdependence approach (structure seeking) needed. If the relationship is dependence based, the analyst must first determine the number of dependent variables. Second, the analyst must determine how the dependent variables will be measured. In selecting among the interdependence techniques, the analyst must define whether structure among variables, respondents or objects is desired.

FIGURE 1
MULTIVARIATE TECHNIQUES AND THEIR ABILITIES

Technique	Ability			
	Describe	Explain	Predict	Control
Multiple Regression	S	S	P	NA
Multiple Discriminant	S	S	P	NA
MANOVA	NA	S	S	P
Canonical Correlation	P	S	S	NA
Factor Analysis	P	S	NA	NA
Cluster Analysis	P	S	NA	NA
Multidimensional Scaling	S	P	S	NA
Conjoint Analysis	S	P	S	NA
Structural Equation Modeling	S	P	P	NA

Legend:

P: Primary ability
S: Secondary ability
NA: Not applicable

ANSWERS TO END-OF-CHAPTER QUESTIONS

(1)   IN YOUR OWN WORDS, DEFINE MULTIVARIATE ANALYSIS.

<u>Answer</u>

a.   The authors adopt a fairly inclusive description of the term. In so doing, they avoid becoming bogged down in the nuances of "multi-variable" and "multivariate." The distinction between these terms is made as follows:

<u>Multi-variable</u> - usually referring to techniques used in the simultaneous analysis of more than two variables.

<u>Multivariate</u> - to be considered truly multivariate, all the variables must be random variables that are interrelated in such ways that their different effects cannot easily be studied separately. The multivariate character lies in the multiple combinations of variables, not solely in the number of variables or observations.

(2)   NAME SEVERAL FACTORS THAT HAVE CONTRIBUTED TO THE INCREASED APPLICATION OF TECHNIQUES FOR MULTIVARIATE DATA ANALYSIS IN RECENT YEARS.

<u>Answer</u>

a.   The ability to conceptualize data analysis has increased through the study of statistical methods;

b.   Advances in computer technology which make it feasible to attempt to analyze large quantities of complex data;

c.   The development of several fairly sophisticated "canned" computer programs for carrying out multivariate techniques; and

d.   The research questions being asked are becoming more and more complex, and more sophisticated techniques for data analysis are needed.

(3) **LIST AND DESCRIBE THE MULTIVARIATE DATA ANALYSIS TECHNIQUES DESCRIBED IN THIS CHAPTER. CITE EXAMPLES FOR WHICH EACH TECHNIQUE IS APPROPRIATE.**

Answer

a. DEPENDENCE TECHNIQUES - variables are divided into dependent and independent.

(1) Multiple Regression (MR) - the objective of MR is to predict changes in a single metric dependent variable in response to changes in several metric independent variables. A related technique is multiple correlation.

(2) Multiple Discriminant Analysis (MDA) - the objective of MDA is to predict group membership for a single non-metric dependent variable using several metric independent variables.

(3) Multivariate Analysis of Variance (MANOVA) simultaneously analyzes the relationship of 2 or more metric dependent variables and several non-metric independent variables. A related procedure is multivariate analysis of covariance (MANCOVA) which can be used to control factors other than the included independent variables.

(4) Canonical Correlation Analysis (CCA) simultaneously correlates several metric dependent variables and several metric independent variables. Note that this procedure can be considered an extension of MR, where there is only one metric dependent variable.

(5) Conjoint Analysis (CA) - used to transform non-metric scale responses into metric form. It is concerned with the joint effect of two or more non-metric independent variables on the ordering of a single dependent variable.

(6) Structural Equation Modeling (SEM) - simultaneously analyzes several dependence relationships (e.g., several regression equations) while also having the ability to account for measurement error in the process of estimating coefficients for each independent variable.

b. <u>INTERDEPENDENCE TECHNIQUES</u> - all variables are analyzed simultaneously, with none being designated as either dependent or independent.

    (1)   <u>Factor Analysis</u> (FA) - used to analyze the interrelationships among a large number of variables and then explain these variables in terms of their common, underlying dimensions. The two major approaches are component analysis and common factor analysis.

    (2)   <u>Cluster Analysis</u> - used to classify a sample into several mutually exclusive groups based on similarities and differences among the sample components.

    (3)   <u>Multidimensional Scaling</u> (MDS) - a technique used to transform similarity scaling into distances in a multidimensional space.

(4)   EXPLAIN WHY AND HOW THE VARIOUS MULTIVARIATE METHODS CAN BE VIEWED AS A FAMILY OF TECHNIQUES.

<u>Answer</u>

The multivariate techniques can be viewed as a "family" of techniques in that they are all based upon constructing composite linear relationships among variables or sets of variables. The family members complement one another by accommodating unique combinations of input and output requirements so that an exhaustive array of capabilities can be brought to bear on complex problems.

(5)   WHY IS KNOWLEDGE OF MEASUREMENT SCALES IMPORTANT TO AN UNDERSTANDING OF MULTIVARIATE DATA ANALYSIS?

<u>Answer</u>

Knowledge and understanding of measurement scales is a must before the proper multivariate technique can be chosen. Inadequate understanding of the type of data to be used can cause the selection of an improper technique, which makes any results invalid. Measurement scales must be understood so that questionnaires can be properly designed and data adequately analyzed.

(6)   WHAT ARE THE DIFFERENCES BETWEEN STATISTICAL AND PRACTICAL SIGNIFICANCE? IS ONE A PREREQUISITE FOR THE OTHER?

<u>Answer</u>

Statistical significance is a means of assessing whether the results are due to change. Practical significance assesses whether the result is useful or substantial enough to warrant action. Statistical significance would be a prerequisite of practical significance.

(7)   WHAT ARE THE IMPLICATIONS OF LOW STATISTICAL POWER?   HOW CAN THE POWER BE IMPROVED IF IT IS DEEMED TOO LOW?

<u>Answer</u>

The implication of low power is that the researcher may fail to find significance when it actually exists. Power may be improved through decreasing the alpha level or increasing the sample size.

(8)   DETAIL THE MODEL-BUILDING APPROACH TO MULTIVARIATE ANALYSIS, FOCUSING ON THE MAJOR ISSUES AT EACH STEP.

<u>Answer</u>

Stage One: Define the Research Problem, Objectives, and Multivariate Technique to Be Used The starting point for any analysis is to define the research problem and objectives in conceptual terms before specifying any variables or measures. This will lead to an understanding of the appropriate type of technique, dependence or interdependence, needed to achieve the desired objectives. Then based on the nature of the variables involved a specific technique may be chosen.

Stage Two: Develop the Analysis Plan A plan must be developed that addresses the particular needs of the chosen multivariate technique. These issues include: (1) sample size, (2) type of variables (metric vs. non-metric, and (3) special characteristics of the technique.

Stage Three: Evaluate the Assumptions Underlying the Multivariate Technique All techniques have underlying assumptions, both conceptual and empirical, that impact their ability to represent multivariate assumptions. Techniques based on statistical inference must meet the assumptions of multivariate normality, linearity, independence of error terms, and equality of variances. Each technique must be considered individually for meeting these and other assumptions.

Stage Four: Estimate the Multivariate Model and Assess Overall Model Fit With assumptions met, a model is estimated considering the specific characteristics of the data. After the model is estimated, the overall model fit is evaluated to determine whether it achieves acceptable levels of statistical criteria, identifies proposed relationships, and achieves practical significance. At this stage the influence of outlier observations is also assessed.

Stage Five: Interpret the Variate With acceptable model fit, interpretation of the model reveals the nature of the multivariate relationship.

14

Stage Six: Validate the Multivariate Model The attempts to validate the model are directed toward demonstrating the generalizability of the results. Each technique has its own ways of validating the model.

SAMPLE MULTIPLE CHOICE QUESTIONS
(correct answers indicated by bolded letter)

Circle the letter of the item best answering the question.

1.   Multivariate analysis is difficult to define. Which of the below statements most adequately defines this type of analysis?

    a.   Examining relationships between or among more than two variables.
    b.   Simultaneously analyzing multiple measurements using statistical methods.
    c.   An analysis in which all variables must be random variables that are interrelated in such ways that their different effects cannot be easily studied separately.
    d.   Multivariate analysis is best defined as an extension of univariate analysis and/or bivariate analysis.

2.   There are eight specific techniques used in multivariate analysis. From the list below pick the two that can be classified under the dependence methods.

    a.   Factor analysis
    b.   Multiple discriminant analysis
    c.   Canonical analysis
    d.   Cluster analysis

3.   Multiple discriminant analysis is useful in situations where:

    a.   The total sample can be divided into groups based on descriptive variables.
    b.   The total sample can be divided into groups based on descriptive variables.
    c.   The total sample can be divided into groups based on dependent variables.
    d.   The total sample can be divided into groups based on a combination of independent and dependent variables.

4.   The different methods constituting the analysis of dependence can be categorized by two things. Pick the best two answers.

    a.   The number of dependent variables
    b.   The number of independent variables
    c.   The type of measurement scale employed by the variables
    d.   The number of relative variables

5. Canonical Correlation Analysis is best described as a:

   a. Nonmetric dependence method
   b. Nonmetric independence method
   c. Metric independence method
   d. Metric dependence method

6. Data analysis involves the basic nature of:

   a. Testing, evaluating, and gathering information.
   b. Assigning, labeling, and manipulating information.
   c. Partitioning, identifying, and measuring information.

7. Cluster analysis is used to:

   a. Transform consumer judgments of similarity or preference into distances represented in multidimensional space.
   b. Analyze the interrelationships among a large number of variables.
   c. Explore simultaneously the relationship among several independent variables.
   d. Develop meaningful subgroups of individuals or objects.

8. Measurements with a nominal scale involve:

   a. The most precise measurements available in data analysis.
   b. Showing the relation to the amount of the attribute possessed .
   c. Assigning numbers which are used to label subjects or objects.
   d. An absolute zero point.

9. If you had nonmetric or qualitative data, one would use:
   a. nominal scale
   b. interval scale
   c. ratio scale
   d. ordinal scale
   e. d or a
   f. b or c

10. An example of a multivariate technique that would be appropriate for use with a nonmetric dependent variable and a metric independent variable is:

   a. multiple discriminant analysis
   b. multiple regression analysis
   c. multivariate analysis of variance
   d. canonical correlation analysis

CHAPTER TWO
EXAMINING YOUR DATA

Similar to the style of Chapter One, this presentation will address the basic questions of "Why?," "What?," "When?," and "How?" as applied to examining your data prior to the application of a multivariate technique.

Why examine data?

1. To *gain a basic understanding of the data set*, including information about the relationships among the variables. The two approaches are:

- **Case-by-case evaluation** -- although necessary in the examination of response bias, this approach is time consuming and does not enable the researcher to get the "big picture."

- **Compilation of cases** -- this preferred method provides a more meaningful interpretation of the cases. Descriptive statistics, or data examination, provide the analyst with a means to present data descriptors in a manageable form. Examining a compilation of cases reduces individual observations to easily interpretable summaries. In addition, variable associations, or relationships, can be calculated from the raw data and represented simply in reduced form.

2. To ensure that the *statistical and theoretical underpinnings* of the chosen multivariate technique are upheld.

- Data examination enables the researcher to analyze the multivariate assumptions of normality, homoscedasticity, linearity, and independence of error terms. Each multivariate technique has underlying assumptions which will be highlighted in the following chapters.

3. **To analyze the impacts of uncertainties** inherent in data collection, including controllable and uncontrollable factors which may influence the data set.

- **Controllable factors** -- controlled by the researcher or analyst, such as the input of data. No matter how carefully the data is input, some errors will occur. For example, errors may result from incorrect coding or the misinterpretation of codes. Data examination provides the analyst an overview of the data, which will call attention to any impossible or improbable values requiring further attention.

- **Uncontrollable factors** -- characteristic of the respondent or the data collection instrument, may also be detected via data examination. For example, cases with a large number of missing values may be identified. In addition, outliers, or extreme cases, are designated in data examination techniques.

What is involved in examining data?

Data examination techniques vary from a simple visual examination of graphical representations to complex statistical analyses which address missing data problems and the assumptions underlying the multivariate technique. This chapter provides a detailed description of data examination in four phases:

- graphical representation analysis,
- evaluating missing data,
- identifying outliers
- assessing assumptions.

When do you examine your data?

Essentially, an analyst should examine every new data set and should re-examine any dataset being used for a new multivariate application. In fact, data examination is a necessary first step in any multivariate application. Not only does examination provide the analyst with a test of the underlying assumptions of the multivariate technique, but it also gives the analyst a better understanding of the nature of the data set.

Many techniques are available for examining data sets. Most statistical software packages offer techniques for the evaluation of data. Many packages refer to data examination as descriptive statistics. In addition to computer packages, data examination may also be computed by hand; however, the process is tedious and is not recommended given the computing power available.

How do you examine your data?

As outlined in the chapter, there are four phases of data examination:
1. **graphical examination** of the variables in the analysis,
2. evaluation of the possible causes and remedies for **missing data** in the variables in the analysis,
3. identification of **outliers**
4. assessment of the ability of the data to **meet the statistical assumptions** specific to the selected multivariate technique.

Phase 1: Graphical Examination of the Data

1. The nature of the variable can be evaluated by examining the shape of the distribution.

- *Histogram* -- the most common form of graphical representation of the data. It displays the frequency of occurrences of the data values (X axis) with the data categories (Y axis). Histograms can be used to examine any type of variable.

- *Stem and leaf diagram* -- similar to histograms, graphically displays the data distribution by frequencies and data categories, but also includes the actual data values. The stem is the root value to which each leaf is added to derive the actual data value.

2. Relationships between two or more variables may be examined by graphical plots.

- *Scatterplot* -- the most common form of graphical display for examining the bivariate relationships among variables. The scatterplot is a graph of data points, where the horizontal axis is one variable and the vertical axis is another variable. The variable observations can be many values, including actual values, expected values, and residuals. The patterns of the data points represent the relationship between the two variables (i.e. linear, curvilinear, etc...).

- *Scatterplot matrices* -- scatterplots computed for all combinations of variables. The diagonal of the matrix contains the histograms for each variable.

3. Testing for group differences requires examination of 1) how the values are distributed for each group, 2) if outliers are present in the groups, and 3) whether or not the groups are different from one another.

- *Box plot* -- a pictorial representation of the data distribution of each group. Each group is represented by a box, with the upper and lower boundaries of the box marking the upper and lower quartiles of the data distribution.

  ➢ Box length is the distance between the 25% percentile and the 75% percentile, such that the box contains the middle 50% of the values. The asterisk inside the box identifies the median.
  ➢ Lines or whiskers extending from each box represent the distance to the smallest and the largest observations that are less than one quartile range from the box (also marked by an X).
  ➢ Outliers (marked O) are observations which range between 1.0 and 1.5 quartiles away from the box.
  ➢ Extreme values are marked E and represent those observations which are greater than 1.5 quartiles away from the end of the box.

4. When the analyst wishes to graphically examine more than two variables, one of three types of multivariate profiles is appropriate.

- *Glyphs or Metroglyphs*: some form of circle with radii that correspond to a data value or a multivariate profile which portrays a bar-like profile for each observation
- *Mathematical transformation:* transformation of the original data into a mathematical relationship that can be displayed graphically.
- *Iconic representation:* pictorially represents each variable as a component of a whole picture. This most common form is a face, with each variable representing a different feature.

Phase 2: Evaluating Missing Data

1. Missing data can produce hidden biases in the analysis results and can also adversely affect the sample size available for analysis.

- Without remedy, any observation with missing data on any of the variables will be excluded from the analysis.

- Exclusion of too many variables due to missing data can substantially affect the sample size. We know that sample size will impact the power of any statistical tests and affect whether or not the results achieve statistical significance.

2. The analyst must identify the missing data process (reasons underlying missing data) before he or she can select a remedy, or appropriate course of action.

3. A missing data process may be of two kinds: a systematic event external to the respondent (ignorable) or any action on the part of the respondent which leads to missing values (unidentifiable).

- *Ignorable missing data* -- When the missing data process is known and is external to the respondent, and it can be accommodated in the research plan. Specific remedies are not needed since the allowances are inherent in the technique used.

  ➤ <u>Ignorable missing data operate at random</u>; the observed values are a random sample of the total set of values, observed and missing.

  ➤ <u>Examples of ignorable missing data:</u>
    1. observations in a population which are not included in the sample
    2. censored data (observations which are not complete because of their stage in the missing data process).

- *Unidentifiable* -- When the missing data are due to an action of the respondent, they are often unidentifiable and cannot be accommodated in the research design. In this case, the researcher evaluates the pattern of the missing data and determines the potential for remedy.

4. Assessing the degree of randomness will identify one of two types: missing at random (MAR) and missing completely at random (MCAR).

- *Missing at random (MAR)*: When the missing values of Y depend on X, but not on Y. This occurs when X biases the randomness of the observed Y values, such that the observed Y values do not represent a true random sample of all actual Y values in the population.

- *Missing completely at random (MCAR)*: When the observed values of Y are truly a random sample of all Y values.

- *Approaches for diagnosing the randomness of the missing data process*

  - ➤ <u>Significance tests for a single variable</u>: Form two groups, one group being those observations with missing data and another group being those observations with valid values, and test for significant differences between the two groups on any other variables of interest. If significant differences are found, a nonrandom missing data process is present, meaning that the missing data should be classified as MAR.

  - ➤ <u>Dichotomized correlations for a pair of variables</u>: For each of the two variables, replace each valid value with a value of one and each missing value with a value of zero, then compute correlations for the missing values of each variable. The correlations indicate the degree of association between the missing data on each variable pair. Low correlations denote randomness in the pair of variables. If all variable pairs have low correlations, the missing data can be classified as MCAR.

  - ➤ <u>Overall test of randomness</u>: Analyze the pattern of missing data on all variables and compare it to the pattern expected for a random missing data process. If no significant differences are found, the missing data can be classified as MCAR.

5. **Approaches are available for dealing with missing data that are selected based on the randomness of the missing data process.**

   - *Use of only observations with complete data.* When conducting analysis, the researcher would include only those observations with complete data.

     - ➤ <u>Default in many statistical programs</u>.
     - ➤ <u>Used only if the missing data are missing completely at random (MCAR)</u>; when used with data which are missing at random (MAR), the results are not generalizable to the population.

   - *Delete case(s) and / or variable(s).* The researcher would delete the case(s) and/or variable(s) exceeding a specified level from the analysis.

     - ➤ <u>Most effective for data which are not missing at random</u>, but is an alternative which can be used if the data are MAR or MCAR.

- *Imputation methods.* Imputation methods replace missing values with estimates based on the valid values of other variables and / or cases in the sample. Imputation methods should be used only if the data are MCAR.

  ➤ <u>Selecting values or observations to be used in the imputation process.</u>
    1. The complete case approach uses only data from observations that have no missing data.
    2. The all-available approach uses all available valid observations to estimate missing data, maximizing pairwise information.

  ➤ <u>Five imputation methods are available:</u>
    1. *Case substitution*: observations with missing data are replaced by choosing another nonsampled observation.
    2. *Mean substitution*: missing values for a single variable are replaced with the means value of that variable based on all responses.
    3. *Cold deck imputation*: missing values are replaced with a constant value derived from external sources or previous research.
    4. *Regression imputation*: missing values are replaced with predicted estimates from a regression analysis. Estimated values are based on their relationship with other variables in the data set.
    5. *Multiple imputation*: a combination of several methods, two or more methods of imputation are used to derive a composite estimate for the missing value.

- *Model-based procedures.* Model-based procedures incorporate missing data into the analysis, either through a process specifically designed for missing data estimation or as an integral portion of the standard multivariate analysis.

Phase 3: Identification of Outliers

1. **Outliers cannot be categorically characterized as either beneficial or problematic, but instead must be viewed within the context of the analysis and should be evaluated by the types of information that they may provide regarding the phenomenon under study.**

  - *Beneficial outliers* -- when they are indicative of characteristics in the population that would not be discovered in the normal course of analysis.
  - *Problematic outliers* -- when they are not representative of the population and are counter to the objectives of the analysis.

2. Outliers can be classified into four categories.

- *Outliers arising from a procedural error*. These outliers result from data entry errors or mistakes in coding. They should be identified and eliminated during data cleaning.

- *Outliers resulting from an extraordinary event with an explanation* These outliers can be explained. If found to be representative of the population, they should be kept in the data set.

- *Outliers resulting from an extraordinary event with no explanation*. These outliers can not be explained. Often, these observations are deleted from the data set.

- *Ordinary values that become unique when combined with other variables*. While these values can not be distinguished individually, they become very noticeable when combined with other values across other variables. In these cases, the observations should be retained unless specific evidence to the contrary is found.

3. Identification can be made from any of three perspectives: univariate, bivariate, or multivariate. If possible, multiple perspectives should be utilized to triangulate the identification of outliers.

- *Univariate detection*: examine the distribution of observations for a variable and select as outliers those values that fall at the outer ranges of the distribution.
- When standardized, data values which are greater than 2.5 may be potential outliers. (For large sample sizes, the value may increase to 3 or 4.)

- *Bivariate detection:* examine scatterplots of variable pairs and select as outliers those values that fall markedly outside the range of the other observations.

  ➢ Ellipse representing a confidence interval may be drawn around the expected range of observations on the scatterplot. Those values falling outside the range are potential outliers.

  ➢ Influence plot, where the point varies in size in proportion to its influence on the relationship and the largest points are potential outliers.

- *Multivariate detection*: assess each observation across a set of variables and select as outliers those values which fall outside a specified range specific to the statistical test employed.

  - ➢ Mahalanobis D^2 is commonly used in multivariate analyses to identify outliers. It is a measure of the distance in multidimensional space of each observation from the mean center of the observations.

  - ➢ Conservative values (i.e. .001) for the statistical tests should be set for identification of potential outliers.

4. Only observations truly unique from the population should be designated as outliers. The researcher should be careful of identifying too many observations as outliers.

- *Profiles* on each outlier should be generated and the data should be examined for the variable(s) responsible for generating the outlier. Multivariate techniques may also be employed to trace the underlying causes of outliers. The researcher should be able to classify the outlier in one of the four categories discussed above.

- *Unnecessary deletion* of outliers will limit the generalizability of the analysis. Outliers should be deleted from the analysis only if they are proven to be not representative of the population.

Stage 4: Testing the Assumptions of Multivariate Analysis

1. **Multivariate analyses require that the assumptions underlying the statistical techniques be tested twice: once for the individual variables and once for the multivariate model.**

   The following discussion relates only to assumptions underlying the individual variables. The assumptions for the variate for each technique will be discussed in the appropriate chapter.

2. **Normality: Each variable in the analysis must be normally distributed.**

   - *Most fundamental assumption* in multivariate analyses.

   - *Sufficient non-normality invalidates statistical tests* using the F and t statistics.

- *Visual checks*: The simplest way to evaluate the normality of a variable to is visually check a histogram or a normal probability plot.

  ➢ Histogram, the distribution should approximate a bell-shaped curve.

  ➢ Normal probability plot, the data points should closely follow the diagonal line.

- *Statistical tests*: The two most common are the Shapiro-Wilks and Kolmogorov-Smirnov tests.

- *Transformations*: When a distribution is found to be non-normal, data transformations should be computed.

- *Skewness*: Skewness values exceeding ± 2.58 are indicative of a non-normal distribution. Other statistical tests are available in specific statistical software programs.

3. Homoscedasticity: dependent variables should exhibit equal levels of variance across the range of predictor variables.

- *Common sources*: Most problems with unequal variances stem from either the type of variables included in the model or from a skewed distribution.

- *Impact*: Violation of this assumption will cause hypothesis tests to be either too conservative or too sensitive.

- *Identification:* graphical versus statistical.

  ➢ Graphical plot of residuals will reveal violations of this assumption.

  ➢ Statistical tests for equal variance dispersion relate to the variances within groups formed by nonmetric variables. The most common test is the **Levene test**, which is used to assess if the variances of a single metric variable are equal across any number of groups. When more than one variable is being tested, the **Box's M** test should be used.

- *Remedies*: Heteroscedastic variables can be remedied through data transformations.

4. Linearity: variables should be linearly related.

- *Identification*: Scatterplots of variable pairs are most commonly used to identify departures from linearity. Examination of the residuals in a simple regression analysis may also be used as a diagnostic method.

- *Nonlinearity*: If a nonlinear relationship is detected, the most direct approach is to transform one or both of the variables. Other than a transformation, a new variable representing the non-linear relationship can be created.

5. Prediction errors should not be correlated.

- ***Patterns in the error terms*** reflect an underlying systematic bias in the relationship.

- ***Residual plots*** should not contain any recognizable pattern.

- ***Violations of this assumption*** often result from problems in the data collection process.

6. Data transformations enable the researcher to modify variables to correct violations of the assumptions of normality, homoscedasticity, and linearity and to improve the relationships between variables.

- *Basis*: Transformations can be based on **theoretical or empirical** reasons.

- *Distribution shape*: The shape of the distribution provides the basis for selecting the appropriate transformation.

  - ➤ Flat distribution, the most common transformation is the inverse.

  - ➤ Positively skewed distributions are transformed by taking logarithms

  - ➤ Negatively skewed distributions are transformed by taking the square root.

  - ➤ Cone shaped distribution which opens to the right should be transformed using an inverse. A cone shaped distribution which opens to the left should be transformed by taking the square root.

  - ➤ Non-linear transformations can take many forms, including squaring the variable and adding additional variables termed polynomials.

- *General guidelines* for performing data transformations.

  ➤ Ratio of a variable's mean divided by its standard deviation should be less than 4.0.

  ➤ Select the variable with the smallest ratio from item 1.

  ➤ Transformations should be applied to the independent variables except in the case of heteroscedasticity.

  ➤ Heteroscedasticity can only be remedied by transformation of the dependent variable in a dependence relationship. If a heteroscedasticity relationship is also nonlinear, the dependent and perhaps the independent variables must be transformed.

  ➤ Transformations may change the interpretation of the variables.

Incorporating Nonmetric Data with Dummy Variables

When faced with nonmetric variables in the data the researcher may wish to represent these categorical variables as metric through the use of dummy variables. Any nonmetric variable with k groups may be represented as $k - 1$ dummy variables. There are two general methods of accomplishing this task.

- *Indicator coding* assigns a value of 1 to one group, for instance females, and zero to the comparison group (males).

- *Effects coding* assign a value of -1 to the comparison group while still using 1 to designate the other group.

30

(1) **LIST POTENTIAL UNDERLYING CAUSES OF OUTLIERS. BE SURE TO INCLUDE ATTRIBUTIONS TO BOTH THE RESPONDENT AND THE RESEARCHER.**

Answer

a. Respondent:
   1) Misunderstanding of the question
   2) Response bias, such as yea-saying
   3) Extraordinary experience

b. Researcher:
   1) Data entry errors
   2) Data coding mistakes

c. An extraordinary observation with no explanation.

d. An ordinary value that is unique when combined with other variables.

(2) **DISCUSS WHY OUTLIERS MIGHT BE CLASSIFIED AS BENEFICIAL AND AS PROBLEMATIC.**

Answer

a. Beneficial outliers are indicative of some characteristic of the population that would not have been otherwise known. For example, if only one respondent from a lower income group is included in the sample and that respondent expresses an attitude atypical to the remainder of the sample, this respondent would be considered beneficial.

b. Problematic outliers are not indicative of the population and distort multivariate analyses. Problematic outliers may be the result of data input errors, a respondent's misunderstanding of the question, or response bias. These extreme responses must be evaluated as to the type of influence exerted and dealt with accordingly.

(3) **DISTINGUISH BETWEEN DATA WHICH ARE MISSING AT RANDOM (MAR) AND MISSING COMPLETELY AT RANDOM (MCAR). EXPLAIN HOW EACH TYPE WILL IMPACT THE ANALYSIS OF MISSING DATA.**

Answer

a. Missing at Random (MAR): If the missing values of Y depend on X, but not on Y, the missing data are at random. This occurs when X biases the randomness of the observed Y values, such that the observed Y values do not represent a true random sample of all actual Y values in the population.

b. Missing Completely at Random (MCAR): When the observed values of Y are truly a random sample of all Y values.

c. When the missing data are missing at random (MAR), the analyst should only use a modeling-based approach accounting for the underlying processes of the missing data. When the missing data are missing completely at random (MCAR), the analyst may use any of the suggested approaches for dealing with missing data, such as using only observations with complete data, deleting case(s) or variable(s), or employing an imputation method.

(4) **DESCRIBE THE CONDITIONS UNDER WHICH A RESEARCHER WOULD DELETE A CASE WITH MISSING DATA VERSUS THE CONDITIONS UNDER WHICH A RESEARCHER WOULD USE AN IMPUTATION METHOD.**

Answer

The researcher must first evaluate the randomness of the missing data process. If the data are missing at random, deleting a case is the only acceptable alternative of the two. Data that are missing at random cannot employ an imputation method, as it would introduce bias into the results. Only cases with data missing completely at random would utilize an imputation method.

If the data are missing completely at random, the choice of case deletion versus imputation method should be based on theoretical and empirical considerations.

If the sample size is sufficiently large, the analyst may wish to consider deletion of cases with a great degree of missing data. Cases with missing data are good candidates for deletion if they represent a small subset of the sample and if their absence do not otherwise distort the data set. For instance, cases with missing dependent variable values are often deleted.

If the sample size is small, the analyst may wish to use an imputation method to fill in missing data. The analyst should, however, consider the amount of missing data when

32

selecting this option. The degree of missing data will influence the researcher's choice of information used in the imputation (i.e. complete case vs. all-available approaches) and the researcher's choice of imputation method (i.e. case substitution, mean substitution, cold deck imputation, regression imputation, or multiple imputation).

(5) **EVALUATE THE FOLLOWING STATEMENT, "IN ORDER TO RUN MOST MULTIVARIATE ANALYSES, IT IS NOT NECESSARY TO MEET ALL OF THE ASSUMPTIONS OF NORMALITY, LINEARITY, HOMOSCEDASTICITY, AND INDEPENDENCE."**

Answer

As will be shown in each of the following chapter outlines, each multivariate technique has a set of underlying assumptions that must be met. The degree to which a violation of any of the four above assumptions will distort data analyses is dependent on the specific multivariate technique. For example, multiple regression analysis is sensitive to violations of all four of the assumptions, whereas multiple discriminant analysis is primarily sensitive to violations of multivariate normality.

(6) **DISCUSS THE FOLLOWING STATEMENT, "MULTIVARIATE ANALYSES CAN BE RUN ON ANY DATA SET, AS LONG AS THE SAMPLE SIZE IS ADEQUATE."**

Answer

False. Although sample size is an important consideration in multivariate analyses, it is not the only consideration. Analysts must also consider the degree of missing data present in the data set and examine the variables for violations of the assumptions of the intended techniques.

SAMPLE MULTIPLE CHOICE QUESTIONS
(correct answers indicated by bolded letter)

Circle the letter of the item which best answers the question.

1. An analyst can examine the shape of the distribution of a variable through the use of:

    a. A box plot.
    b. A scatterplot.
    c. A stem-and-leaf diagram.
    d. A plot of the residuals.

2. From the list below, pick the item(s) which are **not** characteristic of a missing data process.

    a. Data entry errors.
    b. Respondent mis-interpretation of the question.
    c. Badly designed research questions.
    d. Respondent's refusal to complete an entire questionnaire.

3. To be considered ignorable, missing data <u>must</u> be:

    a. Censored data.
    b. Missing at random.
    c. Identifiable and able to be accommodated.
    d. Researcher imposed.

4. When missing data are missing at random, the following imputation method is most appropriate.

    a. Case substitution.
    b. Multiple imputation.
    c. Mean substitution.
    d. No imputation method should be used.

5. To examine the patterns of missing data and to determine if the missing data are distributed randomly, the following test is **not** appropriate:

    a. A comparison of the missing data with what would be expected if the missing data was totally randomly distributed.
    b. Analysis of the correlations between dichotomous variables.
    c. Comparison of the observations with and without missing data for each variable on the other variables
    d. A review of each case individually

6. The following item may be classified as characteristic of outliers:
   a. Identifiable as distinctly different from other observations.
   b. Categorized as neither beneficial, nor problematic.
   c. Influential observations which distort multivariate analyses.

7. Outliers are **not** the result of:
   a. Procedural errors.
   b. Extraordinary observations associated with a specific event.
   c. An unrepresentative sample.
   d. An ordinary value which is unique when combined with other variables.

8. The most fundamental assumption in multivariate analyses is:
   a. Independence of error terms.
   b. Linearity .
   c. Normality.
   d. Homoscedasticity.

9. The Box's M test is used to test for the assumption of:
   a. Independence of error terms.
   b. Linearity.
   c. Normality.
   d. Homoscedasticity.

10. All of the following statements are true, except:
    a. Heteroscedasticity can only be remedied by transformation of the independent variable.
    b. To conduct a transformation, the ratio of a variable's mean divided by its standard deviation should be less than 4.0.
    c. Simple transformations change the interpretation of the variables.
    d. When choosing between the transformation of two variables, the variable with the smallest ratio of a variable's mean divided by its standard deviation should be chosen.

CHAPTER THREE
FACTOR ANALYSIS

The following presentation will address the basic questions of "What?," "Why?," "When?," and "How?" as applied to Factor Analysis.

What is factor analysis?

1. Factor analysis *examines the interrelationships among a large number of variables* and then attempts to explain them in terms of their *common underlying dimensions*.

2. These common underlying dimensions are referred to as *factors*.

3. Factor analysis is a *summarization and data reduction technique* that does not have independent and dependent variables, but an interdependence technique in which all variables are considered simultaneously.

Why do we use factor analysis?

1. Factor analysis can meet the objectives of:

- *Data reduction*: factor analysis calculates scores, which represent a variable's interrelationship with the other variables in the data set, and substitutes these scores for the original variables, thereby reducing the size of the data set to equal the number of factors extracted.

- *Summarization:* factor analysis derives the underlying dimensionality or structure of a data set and allows the researcher to describe the data with a fewer, but representative, number of the original variables.

When do you use factor analysis?

Factor analysis is used when a) the analyst wishes to examine the underlying structure of a data matrix, or b) when analysts wish to understand the structure of the interrelationships among the variables in a data set, factor analysis is the appropriate analysis technique.

How do you use factor analysis?

Factor analyses follows the six-stage model-building process introduced in Chapter 1. The following are important points for each step of the process.

Stage 1: Objectives of Factor Analysis

1. Factor Analysis has three primary objectives.

- *Identification of the structure of relationships* among either variables or respondents.

- *Identification of representative variables* from a much larger set of variables for use in subsequent multivariate analyses.

- *Creation of an entirely new set of variables*, which are much smaller in number in order to partially or completely replace the original set of variables for inclusion in subsequent multivariate techniques.

Stage 2: Designing a Factor Analysis

1. There are two approaches to calculate the correlation matrix that determine the type of factor analysis performed:

- *R-type factor analysis*: input data matrix is computed from correlations between variables. This is the most common application of factor analysis.

- *Q-type factor analysis*: input data matrix is computed from correlations between individual respondents. This is quite similar to cluster analysis (Chapter 9).

2. Variables in factor analysis are generally metric. Dummy variables may be used in special circumstances.

3. The researcher should minimize the number of variables included in the analysis, but include a sufficient number of variables to represent each proposed factor (i.e. five or more).

4. Sample size is an important consideration in factor analyses.

- *The sample size should be 100 or larger.* Sample sizes between 50 and 100 may be analyzed but with extreme caution.

- The *ratio of observations to variables should be at least 5 to 1* to provide the most stable results.

Stage 3: Assumptions in Factor Analysis

---

1. The most basic assumption is that the set of variables analyzed are related.

- *Variables must be interrelated* in some way since factor analysis seeks the underlying common dimensions among the variables. If the variables are not related, then each variable will be its own factor.

    Example: if you had 20 unrelated variables, you would have 20 different factors. When the variables are unrelated, factor analysis has no common dimensions with which to create factors. Thus, some underlying structure or relationship among the variables must exist.

- The *sample should be homogenous* with respect to some underlying factor structure.

2. Factor analysis assumes the use of metric data.

- *Metric variables* are assumed, although dummy variables may be used (coded 0-1).

3. Factor analysis does not require multivariate normality.

- *Multivariate normality* is necessary if the researcher wishes to apply statistical tests for significance of factors.

4. The data matrix must have sufficient correlations to justify the use of factor analysis.

- *Rule of thumb:* substantial number of correlations greater than .30 are needed.

- *Tests of appropriateness*: anti-image correlation matrix of partial correlations, the Bartlett test of sphericity, and the measure of sampling adequacy (MSA).
  - ➤ Rule of Thumb: MSA exceeds .50 for overall and variable-specific tests.

Stage 4: Deriving Factors and Assessing Overall Fit

---

1. Two extraction methods: principal components and common factor analysis.

- *Principal components factor analysis* inserts 1's on the diagonal of the correlation matrix, thus considering all of the available variance.

  - ➤ Most appropriate when the concern is with **deriving a minimum number of factors to explain a maximum portion of variance in the original variables,** and the researcher knows the specific and error variances are small.

- *Common factor analysis* only uses the common variance and places communality estimates on the diagonal of the correlation matrix.

  - ➤ Most appropriate when there is a desire to **reveal latent dimensions** of the original variables and the researcher does not know about the nature of specific and error variance.

2. Determining the number of factors to extract should consider several criteria:

- *Latent Root criterion:* specifies a threshold value for evaluating the eigenvalues of the derived factors.

  - ➤ only factors with an <u>eigenvalues greater than 1</u> are significant and will be extracted. This is due to the notion that an individual variable contributes a value of 1 to the total eigenvalue, so an extracted factor should account for the variance of at least a single variable.

- *A Priori criterion* The researcher may know how many factors should be extracted. This criterion is useful if the researcher is testing previous research or specific hypotheses.

- *Percentage of Variance criterion* As factor analysis extracts each factor, the cumulative percent of variance explained is used to determine the number of factors. The researcher may desire to specify a necessary percentage of variance explained by the solution.

- *Scree Test criterion* A scree test is derived by plotting the eigenvalues of each factor relative to the number of factors in order of extraction.

  - ➢ Earlier extracted factors have the most common variance, causing rapid decline in amount of variance explained as additional factors extracted.

  - ➢ At some point, the amount of specific variance begins to overtake the common variance in the factors. A scree plot reveals this by a rapid flattening of the plot line.

  - ➢ While the factors contain mostly common variance the plot line will continue to decline sharply, but once specific variance becomes too large the plot line will become horizontal.

  - ➢ Point where the line becomes horizontal is the appropriate number of factors.

  - ➢ Scree test almost always suggests more factors than the latent root criterion.

- *Heterogeneity of the Respondents* In a heterogeneous sample, the first factors extracted are those which are more homogeneous across the entire sample. Those **factors which best discriminate among subgroups in the sample will be extracted later** in the analysis.

Stage 5: Interpreting the Factors

1. Interpretation is assisted through selection of a rotational method.

- *Rotation* redistributes the variance from earlier factors to later factors by turning the axes of the factors about the origin until a new position is reached. Rotation is used as an aid in explaining the factors by providing a more simple structure in the factor matrix. It will not change the amount of variance extracted or the number of factors extracted. There are two general types of rotation, orthogonal and oblique.

  - ➤ *Orthogonal rotation* maintains the axes at 90 degrees thus the factors are uncorrelated. There are three orthogonal approaches that operate on different aspects of the factor matrix.

    1. QUARTIMAX attempts to simplify the rows of the matrix so that variables load highly on a single factor. This tends to create a large general factor.

    2. VARIMAX simplifies the columns of the factor matrix indicating a clearer association and separation among variables and factors.

    3. EQUIMAX is a compromise between VARIMAX and QUARTIMAX in that it simplifies both the rows and columns.

  - ➤ *Oblique rotation methods* such as OBLIMIN (SPSS) and PROMAX (SAS) allow correlated factors.

2. Criteria for Practical and Statistical Significance of Factor Loadings

- *Magnitude for practical significance*: Factor loadings can be classified based on their magnitude:

  - ➤ *Greater than $\pm$ .30* -- minimum consideration level.

  - ➤ $\pm$ *.40* -- more important

  - ➤ $\pm$ *.50* -- practically significant (the factor accounts for 25% of variable's variance)

- *Power and statistical significance:* Given the sample size, the researcher may determine the level of factor loadings necessary to be significant at a predetermined level of power. For example, in a sample of 100 at an 80% power level, factor loadings of .55 and above are significant.

- *Necessary loading level* to be significant varies due to several factors:

  - ➢ Increases in the number of variables; decreases the level for significance.

  - ➢ Increases in the sample size; decreases the level necessary to consider a loading significant.

  - ➢ Increases in the number of factors extracted; increases the level necessary to consider a loading significant.

3. Interpreting a Factor Matrix:

- *Look for clear factor structure* indicated by significant loadings on a single factor and high communalities.

- ***Variables that load across factors or have low loadings or communalities may be candidates for deletion.***

4. Naming the factor is based on an interpretation of the factor loadings.

- *Significant loadings:* The variables that most significantly load on each factor should be used in naming the factors. The variables' magnitude and strength provide meaning to the factors.

- *Impact of the Rotation:* The selection of a rotation method affects the interpretation of the loadings.

  - ➢ Orthogonal rotation -- each variable's loading on each factor is independent of its loading on another factor.

  - ➢ Oblique rotation -- independence of the loadings is not preserved and interpretation then becomes more complex.

4. Respecification should always be considered. Some methods are:

- *Deletion of a variable(s)* from the analysis

- *Employing a different rotational method* for interpretation

- *Extraction of a different number of factors*

- *Employing a different extraction method*

Stage 6: Validating the Results

1. Validation assesses 1) the degree of generalizability of the findings and 2) the degree to which the results are influenced by individual cases.

- *Results should be replicable.* Confirmatory factor analysis is the most commonly used replication technique. Analyses can be run using a split sample or another new data set.

- The *factor structure should be stable* across additional analyses. Stability is highly dependent on sample size and the number of observations per variable.

- *The impact of outliers* should be determined by running the factor model with and without the influential observations.

Stage 7: Additional Uses of the Factor Analysis Results

Beyond the interpretation and understanding of the relationship among the variables, the researcher may wish to use the factor analysis results in subsequent analysis. Factor analysis may be used to reduce the data for further use by (1) the selection of a surrogate variable, (2) creation of a new variable with a summated scale, or (3) replacement of the factor with a factor score.

1. A surrogate variable that is representative of the factor may be selected as the variable with the highest loading.

2. All the variables loading highly on a factor may be combined (the sum or the average) to form a replacement variable.

- *Advantages of the summated scale:*
  Measurement Error is reduced by multiple measures.

  Taps all aspects or domains of a concept with highly related multiple indicators.

- *Basic Issues of Scale Construction:*

  ➤ A conceptual definition is the starting point for creating a scale. The scale must appropriately measure what it purports to measure to assure content or face validity.

  ➤ A scale must be unidimensional, meaning that all items are strongly associated with each other and represent a single concept.

  ➤ Reliability of the scale is essential. Reliability is the degree of consistency between multiple measurements of a variable. Test-retest reliability is one form of reliability. Another form of reliability is the internal consistency of the items in a scale. Measures of internal consistency include item-to-total correlation, inter-item correlation, and the reliability coefficient.

  ➤ Once content or face validity, unidimensionality, and reliability are established other forms of scale validity should be assessed. Convergent validity is the extent that two measures of the same concept are correlated. Discriminant validity is the extent that two measures of similar but different concepts are distinct. Nomological validity refers to the degree that the scale makes accurate predictions of other concepts.

3. Factor scores, computed using all variables loading on a factor, may also be used as a composite replacement for the original variable.

- *Factor scores are computed using all variables that load on a factor.*

- *Factor scores may not be easy to replicate.*

ANSWERS TO END-OF-CHAPTER QUESTIONS

---

(1)   WHAT ARE THE DIFFERENCES BETWEEN THE OBJECTIVES OF DATA SUMMARIZATION AND DATA REDUCTION?

Answer

The basic difference between the objectives of data summarization and data reduction depends upon the ultimate research question. In data summarization the ultimate research question may be to better understand the interrelationship among the variables. This may be accomplished by condensing a large number of respondents into a smaller number of distinctly different groups with Q-type factor analysis. More often data summarization is applied to variables in R-type factor analysis to identify the dimensions that are latent within a dataset. Data summarization makes the identification and understanding of these underlying dimensions or factors the ultimate research question.

Data reduction relies on the identification of the dimensions as well, but makes use of the discovery of the items that comprise the dimensions to reduce the data to fewer variables that represent the latent dimensions. This is accomplished either by the use of surrogate variables, summated scales, or factor scores. Once the data has been reduced to the fewer number of variables further analysis may become easier to perform and interpret.

.

(2)   HOW CAN FACTOR ANALYSIS HELP THE RESEARCHER IMPROVE THE RESULTS OF OTHER MULTIVARIATE TECHNIQUES?

Answer

Factor analysis provides direct insight into the interrelationships among variables or respondents through its data summarizing perspective. This gives the researcher a clear picture of which variables are highly correlated and will act in concert in other analysis. The summarization may also lead to a better understanding of the latent dimensions underlying a research question that is ultimately being answered with another technique. From a data reduction perspective, the factor analysis results allow the formation of surrogate or summated variables to represent the original variables in a way that avoids problems associated with highly correlated variables. In addition, the proper usage of scales can enrich the research process by allowing the measurement and analysis of concepts that require more than single item measures.

(3) **WHAT GUIDELINES CAN YOU USE TO DETERMINE THE NUMBER OF FACTORS TO EXTRACT? EXPLAIN EACH BRIEFLY.**

Answer

The appropriate guidelines utilized depend to some extent upon the research question and what is known about the number of factors that should be present in the data. If the researcher knows the number of factors that should be present, then the number to extract may be specified in the beginning of the analysis by the *a priori criterion.* If the research question is largely to explain a minimum amount of variance then the *percentage of variance criterion* may be most important.

When the objective of the research is to determine the number of latent factors underlying a set of variables a combination of criterion, possibly including the a priori and percentage of variance criterion, may be used in selecting the final number of factors. The *latent root criterion* is the most commonly used technique. This technique is to extract the number of factors having eigenvalues greater than 1. The rationale being that a factor should explain at least as much variance as a single variable. A related technique is the *scree test criterion.* To develop this test the latent roots (eigenvalues) are plotted against the number of factors in their order of extraction. The resulting plot shows an elbow in the sloped line where the unique variance begins to dominate common variance. The scree test criterion usually indicates more factors than the latent root rule. One of these four criterion for the initial number of factors to be extracted should be specified. Then an initial solution and several trial solutions are calculated. These solutions are rotated and the factor structure is examined for meaning. The factor structure that best represents the data and explains an acceptable amount of variance is retained as the final solution.

(4) **HOW DO YOU USE THE FACTOR-LOADING MATRIX TO INTERPRET THE MEANING OF FACTORS?**

Answer

The first step in interpreting the factor-loading matrix is to identify the largest significant loading of each variable on a factor. This is done by moving horizontally across the factor matrix and underlining the highest significant loading for each variable. Once completed for each variable the researcher continues to look for other significant loadings. If there is simple structure, only single significant loadings for each variable, then the factors are labeled. Variables with high factor loadings are considered more important than variables with lower factor loadings in the interpretation phase. In general, factor names will be assigned in such a way as to express the variables loading most significantly on the factor.

(5)   HOW AND WHEN SHOULD YOU USE FACTOR SCORES IN CONJUNCTION WITH OTHER MULTIVARIATE STATISTICAL TECHNIQUES?

Answer

When the analyst is interested in creating an entirely new set of a smaller number of composite variables to replace either in part or completely the original set of variables, then the analyst would compute factor scores for use as such composite variables. Factor scores are composite measures for each factor representing each subject. The original raw data measurements and the factor analysis results are utilized to compute factor scores for each individual. Factor scores may replicate as easily as a summated scale, therefore this must be considered in their use.

(6)   WHAT ARE THE DIFFERENCES BETWEEN FACTOR SCORES AND SUMMATED SCALES? WHEN ARE EACH MOST APPROPRIATE?

Answer

The key difference between the two is that the factor score is computed based on the factor loadings of all variables loading on a factor, whereas the summated scale is calculated by combining only selected variables. Thus, the factor score is characterized not only by the variables that load highly on a factor, but also those that have lower loadings. The summated scale represents only those variables that load highly on the factor.

Although both summated scales and factor scores are composite measures there are differences that lead to certain advantages and disadvantages for each method. Factor scores have the advantage of representing a composite of all variables loading on a factor. This is also a disadvantage in that it makes interpretation and replication more difficult. Also, factor scores can retain orthogonality whereas summated scales may not remain orthogonal. The key advantage of summated scales is that by including only those variables that load highly on a factor the use of summated scales makes interpretation and replication easier. Therefore, the decision rule would be that if data are used only in the original sample or orthogonality must be maintained, factor scores are suitable. If generalizability or transferability is desired then summated scales are preferred.

(7)   WHAT IS THE DIFFERENCE BETWEEN Q-TYPE FACTOR ANALYSIS AND CLUSTER ANALYSIS?

Answer

Both Q-Type factor analysis and cluster analysis compare a series of responses to a number of variables and place the respondents into several groups. The difference is that the resulting groups for a Q-type factor analysis would be based on the intercorrelations between the means and standard deviations of the respondents. In a typical cluster analysis approach, groupings would be based on a distance measure between the respondents' scores on the variables being analyzed.

(8) WHEN WOULD THE RESEARCHER USE AN OBLIQUE ROTATION INSTEAD OF AN ORTHOGONAL ROTATION? WHAT ARE THE BASIC DIFFERENCES BETWEEN THEM.

Answer

In an orthogonal factor rotation, the correlation between the factor axes is arbitrarily set at zero and the factors are assumed to be independent. This simplifies the mathematical procedures. In oblique factor rotation, the angles between axes are allowed to seek their own values, which depend on the density of variable clusterings. Thus, oblique rotation is more flexible <u>and</u> more realistic (it allows for correlation of underlying dimensions) than orthogonal rotation although it is more demanding mathematically. In fact, there is yet no consensus on a best technique for oblique rotation.

When the objective is to utilize the factor results in a subsequent statistical analysis, the analyst may wish to select an orthogonal rotation procedure. This is because the factors are orthogonal (independent) and therefore eliminate collinearity. However, if the analyst is simply interested in obtaining theoretically meaningful constructs or dimensions, the oblique factor rotation may be more desirable because it is theoretically and empirically more realistic.

SAMPLE MULTIPLE CHOICE QUESTIONS

Circle the letter of the item which best answers the question.

1. The primary purpose of factor analysis is:

    a. to transform unidimensional expressions of relationships into multidimensional expressions of the same relationships.
    b. to study the effect of multiple independent variables measured on two or more dependent variables simultaneously.
    c. to analyze the relationship between a single dependent variable and several independent variables.
    d. data reduction and summarization of characteristics.

2. Factor analysis can identify the:

    a. extraneous variable(s), and subsequent regression variables.
    b. canonical roots, and the residual variance.
    c. separate dimensions, and determine factor loadings.
    d. chance classifications of the sample size.

3. Raw data variables for factor analysis are generally assumed to be of:

    a. metric measurement and qualitative.
    b. metric measurement and quantitative.
    c. nonmetric measurement and nominal.
    d. nonmetric measurement and ordinal.

4. Factor analysis is most preferable with sample signs containing

    a. 10 or less observations.
    b. 25 or less observations.
    c. 50 or less observations.
    d. 100 or more observations.

5. Two basic models the analyst can utilize to obtain factor solutions are the:

    a. linear model and the collinear model.
    b. discriminant model and the centroid model.
    c. common factor model and the component model.
    d. monotone model and the preference model.

6. Variance in factor analysis consists of:

   a. common variance.
   b. specific variance.
   c. error variance.
   d. residual variance.
   e. interaction variance.
   f. a, b, c, only
   g. d, e only
   h. a, b, e only

7. Two ways to rotate factors in factor analysis are:

   a. oblique rotation, orthogonal rotation
   b. factor rotation, main rotation
   c. orthogonal rotation, centroid rotation
   d. linear rotation, parameter rotation

8. Unrotated factor solutions always achieve the objective of:

   a. data reduction
   b. data summarization
   c. bivariate reduction
   d. treatment reduction

9. The most commonly used technique in factor extraction is called the:

   a. priori criterion
   b. percentage of variance criterion
   c. scree test criterion
   d. latent root criterion

10. In testing the significance of factor loadings, the larger the sample size

    a. the larger the loading to be considered significant.
    b. the smaller the loading to be considered significant.
    c. the larger the residual variance.
    d. the smaller the residual variance.

CHAPTER FOUR
MULTIPLE REGRESSION ANALYSIS

The following presentation will address the basic questions of "What?," "Why?," "When?," and "How?" as applied to Multiple Regression Analysis.

What is multiple regression analysis?

1. Multiple regression analysis is the most widely-used *dependence technique*, with applications across all types of problems and all disciplines.

2. Multiple regression analysis has **two possible objectives**:

   - *prediction* -- attempts to predict a change in the dependent variable resulting from changes in multiple independent variables.

   - *explanation* -- enables the researcher to explain the variate by assessing the relative contribution of each independent variable to the regression equation.

3. This is accomplished by a statistical procedure called **ordinary least squares (OLS)** which minimizes the sum of squared prediction errors (residuals) in the equation.

Why do we use multiple regression analysis?

1. Multiple regression analysis is the technique of choice when **the research objective is to predict a statistical relationship or to explain underlying relationships among variables.**

2. We also use multiple regression analysis because it enables the researcher **to utilize two or more metric independent variables in order to estimate the dependent variable.**

When do you use multiple regression analysis?

1. Multiple regression may be used any time the researcher has *theoretical or conceptual justification* for predicting or explaining the dependent variable with the set of independent variables.

2. Multiple regression analysis is applicable in almost any business decision-making context. Common applications include models of:

- business forecasting
- consumer decision-making or preferences
- new products

- firm performance
- consumer attitudes
- quality control

How do you use multiple regression analysis?

Multiple regression analyses follow six stages. The following are important points for each step of the process.

Stage 1: Objectives of Multiple Regression

1. **Multiple regression analysis is appropriate for two types of research problems: prediction and explanation.**

- *Prediction* -- predict a dependent variable with a set of independent variables. As such, two objectives are associated with prediction:
  - ➢ Maximization of the overall predictive power of the independent variables in the variate.
  - ➢ Comparison of competing models made up of two or more sets of independent variables to assess the predictive power of each.

- *Explanation* -- explain the degree and character of the relationship between dependent and independent variables. As such, three objectives are associated with explanation:
  - ➢ Determination of the relative importance of each independent variable in the prediction of the dependent variable.
  - ➢ Assessment of the nature of the relationships between the predictors and the dependent variable. (i.e. linearity)
  - ➢ Insight into the interrelationships among the independent variables and the dependent variable. (i.e. correlations)

2. Multiple regression analysis is appropriate for statistical relationships, not functional relationships.

- *Statistical relationships* assume that more than one value of the dependent value will be observed for any value of the independent variables. An average value is estimated and error is expected in prediction.

- *Functional relationships* assume that a single value of the dependent value will be observed for any value of the independent variables. An exact estimate is made, with no error.

3. The selection of dependent and independent variables for multiple regression analysis should be based primarily on theoretical or conceptual meaning.

- *Selecting the dependent variable*: dictated by the research problem, with concern for measurement error, or whether the variable is an accurate and consistent measure of the concept being studied.

- *Selecting the independent variables:* The inclusion of an independent variable must be guided by the theoretical foundation of the regression model and its managerial implications. A variable that by chance happens to influence statistical significance, but has no theoretical or managerial relationship with the dependent variable is of no use to the researcher in explaining the phenomena under observation. Researchers must be concerned with specification error, or the inclusion of irrelevant variables or the omission of relevant variables.

4. The researcher must seek parsimony in the regression model.
>The fewest independent variables with the greatest contribution to the variance explained should be selected.

Stage 2: Research Design of a Multiple Regression Analysis

1. The sample size used will impact the statistical power and generalizability of the multiple regression analysis.

- The *power* (probability of detecting statistically significant relationships) at specified significance levels is related to sample size

  - Small samples (less than 20 observations), will detect only very strong relationships with any degree of certainty.

  - Large samples (1000 or more observations) will find almost any relationship statistically significant due to the over sensitivity of the test.

- The *generalizability of the results* is directly affected by the ratio of observations to independent variables.

  - Minimum level is 5 to 1 (i.e. 5 observations per independent variable in the variate).

  - Desired level is 15 to 20 observations for each independent variable.

2. Most regression models for survey data are random effects models.

In a random effects model, the levels of the predictor are selected at random and a portion of the random error comes from the sampling of the predictors.

3. When a non-linear relationship exists between the dependent and the independent variables or when the analyst wishes to include nonmetric independent variables in the regression model, transformations of the data should be computed.

- *Non-linear relationships:*
  - Arithmetic transformations (i.e. square root or logarithm) and polynomials are most often used to represent non-linear relationships.

- *Moderator effects:*

  ➤ reflect the changing nature of one independent variable's relationship with the dependent variable as a function of another independent variable.

  ➤ represented as a compound variable in the regression equation.

  ➤ moderators change the interpretation of the regression coefficients. To determine the total effect of an independent variable, the separate and the moderated effects must be combined.

- *Nonmetric variable inclusion:*
  ➤ Dichotomous variables, also known as dummy variables, may be used to replace nonmetric independent variables.

  ➤ The resulting coefficients represent the differences of group means from the comparison group and are in the same units as the dependent variable.

Stage 3: Assumptions in Multiple Regression Analysis

1. **Multiple regression analysis assumes the use of metric independent and dependent variables. In special cases, such as logistic regression, the dependent variable may be dichotomous.**

2. **A statistical linear relationship must exist between the independent and dependent variables.**

   - *Implied relationship*: Regression attempts to predict one variable from a group of other variables. When no relationship between the criterion variable and predictor variables exists, there can be no prediction. Therefore, the researcher must feel that some relationship will be found between the single criterion variable and the predictor group of variables.

   - *Linearity:* In order to justify the use of multiple regression analysis, the anticipated relationship should be linear. If a curvilinear relationship is anticipated between the criterion variable and one or more of the predictor variables, a number of data transformations may be used to regain a linear relationship.

- *Statistical relationship:* Since the single criterion variable will have a number of different values over the range of values for the predictor variables, the resulting relationship will be one of averages, or a statistical relationship.

2. Homoscedasticity -- constant variance of the dependent variable.

- The assumption of a statistical relationship means that the dependent variable will have a number of different values at each level of the independent variables.

- Assumption is that the *variance of the dependent variable values will be equal*. Thus, for each level of the independent variable, the dependent variable should have a constant variance. When the distributions are not equal, we have a condition referred to as **heteroscedasticity.**

- If variances are unequal, they may be corrected through data transformations.

3. Uncorrelated error terms.

- Any errors encountered in multiple regression analysis are expected to be completely random in nature and not systematically related.

- The researcher should expect the same chance of random error at each level of prediction.

4. Normality -- dependent and independent variables are normally distributed.

- The data distribution for all variables is assumed to be the *normal distribution*. A normal distribution is <u>necessary for the use of the F and t statistics</u>, since sufficiently large violations of this assumption invalidate the use of these statistics.

- *Diagnostics* for normality are:
    - histograms of the residuals (bell shaped curve)
    - normal probability plots (diagonal line)
    - skewness
        1. Shapiro-Wilks test
        2. Kolmogorov-Smirnov test

- If *violations of normality* are found, there are data transformations that may restore normality and allow the use of the variable(s) in the regression equation.

5. Multicollinearity -- multiple regression works best with no collinearity among the independent variables.

- The presence of collinearity or multicollinearity *suppresses the R^2 and confounds the analysis of the variate.* This correlation among the predictor variables prohibits assessment of the contribution of each independent variable.

- *Tolerance value or the variance inflation factor (VIF)* can be used to detect multicollinearity.

- Once detected, the analyst may choose one of four options:
    - ➢ omit the correlated variables,
    - ➢ use the model for prediction only,
    - ➢ assess the predictor-dependent variable relationship with simple correlations,
    - ➢ use a different method such as Bayesian regression.

Stage 4: Estimating the Regression Model and Assessing Overall Fit

---

1. Model selection -- accomplished by any of several methods are available to aid the researcher in selecting or estimating the best regression model.

- *Confirmatory specification* The <u>analyst specifies the complete set of independent variables</u>. Thus, the analyst has total control over variable selection.

- *Sequential search approaches* Sequential approaches <u>estimate a regression equation with a set of variables and by either adding or deleting variables until some overall criterion measure is achieved</u>. Variable entry may be done in a forward, backward, or stepwise manner.

    - ➢ <u>Forward method</u> begins with no variables in the equation and then adds variables that satisfy the F-to-enter test. Then the equation is estimated again and the F-to-enter of the remaining variables is calculated. This is repeated until the F-to-enter test finds no variables to enter.

    - ➢ <u>Backward elimination</u> begins with all variables in the regression equation and then eliminates any variables with the F-to-remove test. The same repetition of estimation is performed as with forward estimation.

    - ➢ <u>Stepwise estimation</u> is a **combination of forward and backward methods**. It begins with no variables in the equation as with forward estimation and then adds variables that satisfy the F test. The equation is estimated again and additional variables that satisfy the F test are entered. At each re-estimation stage, however, the variables already in the equation are also examined for removal by the appropriate F test. This repetition continues until both F tests are not satisfied by any of the variables either in or out of the regression equation.

- *Combinatorial Methods*

  ➢ The combinatorial approach <u>estimates regression equations for all subset combinations of the independent variables</u>. The most common procedure is known as all-possible-subsets regression.

  ➢ Combinatorial methods <u>become impractical for very large sets of independent variables.</u> For example, for even 10 independent variables, one would have to estimate 1024 regression equations.

2. The variate must meet the assumptions of linearity, constant variance, independence and normality along with the individual variables in the analysis.

3. Assessment of the regression model fit is in two parts: examining overall fit and analyzing the variate.

- *Examine the overall model fit.*

  ➢ Examine the variate's ability to predict the criterion variable and assess how well the independent variables predict the dependent variable.

  ➢ <u>Several statistics exist for the evaluation of overall model fit</u>

    1. *Coefficient of determination (R^2)*

       ▪ The coefficient of determination is a <u>measure of the amount of variance in the dependent variable explained by the independent variable(s)</u>. A value of one (1) means perfect explanation and is not encountered in reality due to ever present error. A value of .91 means that 91% of the variance in the dependent variable is explained by the independent variables.

       ▪ The amount of variation explained by the regression model <u>should be more than the variation explained by the average.</u> Thus, R^2 should be greater than zero.

60

- R^2 is impacted by two facets of the data:

    I.   **the number of independent variables relative to the sample size.** (see sample size discussion earlier) For this reason, analysts should use the <u>adjusted coefficient of determination</u>, which adjusts for inflation in R^2 from overfitting the data.

    II.   **the number of independent variables included in the analysis.** As you increase the number of independent variables in the model, you increase the R^2 automatically because the sum of squared errors by regression begins to approach the sum of squared errors about the average.

2. *Standard error of the estimate*
- Standard error of the estimate is another measure of the accuracy of our predictions. It represents an estimate of the standard deviation of the actual dependent values around the regression line.
- Since this is a measure of variation about the regression line, the smaller the standard error, the better.

3. *F-test*
- The F-test reported with the R^2 is a significance test of the R^2. This test indicates whether a significant amount (significantly different from zero) of variance was explained by the model.

- *Analyze the variate.*

    ➤ The <u>variate is the linear combination of independent variables</u> used to predict the dependent variables. Analysis of the variate relates the respective contribution of each independent variable in the variate to the regression model.

        The researcher is informed as to which independent variable contributes the most to the variance explained and may make relative judgments between/among independent variables (using standardized coefficients only).

    ➤ <u>Regression coefficients are tested for statistical significance.</u>

    1. The intercept (or constant term) should be tested for appropriateness for the predictive model. If the constant is not significantly different from zero, it cannot be used for predictive purposes.

2. The estimated coefficients should be tested to ensure that across all possible samples, the coefficient would be different from zero.

3. The size of the sample will impact the stability of the regression coefficients. The larger the sample size, the more generalizable the estimated coefficients will be.

4. An F-test may be used to test the appropriateness of the intercept and the regression coefficients.

4. The researcher should examine the data for influential observations.

- *Influential observations, leverage points, and outliers* all have an effect on the regression results. The objectives of this analysis are to determine the extent and type of effect.

- *One of four conditions* gives rise to influential observations:
  - an error in observation or data entry,
  - a valid but exceptional observation, which is explainable by an extraordinary situation,
  - an exceptional observation with no likely explanation, or
  - an ordinary observation on its individual characteristics, but exceptional in its combination of characteristics.

- *Detection of problem cases* is accomplished with:
  - examine residuals
    1. studentized residuals > 2 (+ or -)
    2. dummy variable regression (n + 1 df)
    3. partial regression plots

  - identify leverage points
    1. with two predictor variables, plot the two variables as the axes of a two-dimensional plot
    2. with three or more variables, use the hat matrix. Leverage values: $p > 10$ and $n > 50$ then use $2p/n$, $p < 10$ or $n < 50$ then use $3p/n$

  - examine single case diagnostics, such as DFBETA, Cook's distance, and DFFIT.

- With justifiable reasoning, the observation(s) may be discarded and the regression equation estimated again. If deletion is not warranted, then more "robust" estimation techniques must be used.

Stage 5: Interpreting the Regression Variate

1. In interpreting the regression variate, the researcher evaluates the estimated regression coefficients for their explanation of the dependent variable and evaluates the potential impact of omitted variables.

- *Standardized regression coefficients (beta coefficients)*

    ➢ Regression coefficients must be standardized (i.e. computed on the same unit of measurement) in order to be able to directly compare the contribution of each independent variable to explanation of the dependent variable.

    ➢ Beta coefficients (the term for standardized regression coefficients) enable the researcher to examine the relative strength of each variable in the equation.

    ➢ For prediction, regression coefficients are not standardized and, therefore, are in their original units of measurement.

- *Partial correlations*

    ➢ Partial correlation: correlation between each independent variable and the dependent variable with the effects of the other independent variables removed.

    > **'Part Correlation':** removes the effect of the remaining independent variables from the independent side of the equation.

    > **'Partial Correlation':** removes their effect from both sides of the regression equation. This correlation provides the researcher with a more pure correlation between the dependent and independent variables.

    ➢ T-values indicate the significance of the partial correlation of each variable. This may be compared against the researcher's a priori standard for significance.

63

2. Multicollinearity is a data problem that can adversely impact regression interpretation by limiting the size of the R-squared and confounding the contribution of independent variables. For this reason, two measures, tolerance and VIF, are used to assess the degree of collinearity among independent variables.

- *Tolerance* is a measure of collinearity between two independent variables or multicollinearity among three or more independent variables. It is the proportion of variance in one independent variable that is not explained by the remaining independent variables.

  ➢ Each independent variable will have a tolerance measure and each of measure <u>should be close to 1</u>. A tolerance of less than .5 indicates a collinearity or multicollinearity problem.

- *Variance inflation factor (VIF)* is the reciprocal of the tolerance value and measures the same problem of collinearity.

  ➢ VIF values of <u>just over 1.0 are desirable</u>, with the floor VIF value being 1.0. A VIF value of 1.007 would be considered very good and indicative of no collinearity.

Stage 6: Validation of the Results

---

1. The researcher must ensure that the regression model represents the general population (generalizability) and is appropriate for the applications in which it will be employed (transferability).

- *Collection of additional samples or split samples*
  ➢ The regression model or equation may be tested on a new or split sample. No regression model should be assumed to be the final or absolute model of the population.

- *Calculation of the PRESS statistic*
  ➢ Assesses the overall predictive accuracy of the regression by a series of iterations, whereby one observation is omitted in the estimation of the regression model and the omitted observation is predicted with the estimated model. The residuals for the observations are summed to provide an overall measure of predictive fit.

- *Comparison of regression models*
  - ➤ The adjusted R-square is compared across different estimated regression models to assess the model with the best prediction.

2. Before applying an estimated regression model to a new set of independent variable values, the researcher should consider the following,

- *Predictions have multiple sampling variations*, not only the sampling variations from the original sample, but also those of the newly drawn sample.

- *Conditions and relationships should not have changed materially* from their measurement at the time the original sample was taken .

- *Do not use the model to estimate beyond the range of the independent variables in the sample.* The regression equation is only valid for prediction purposes within the original range of magnitude for the prediction variables. Results can not be extrapolated beyond the original range of variables measured since the form of the relationship may change.

  - ➤ Example: If a predictor variable is the number of tires sold and in the original data the range of this variable was from 30 to 120 tires per month, then prediction of the dependent variable when 200 tires per month are sold is invalid. We are outside the original range of magnitude; we do not know the form of the relationship between the predictor variable and the criterion variable. At 200 tires per month the relational form may become curvilinear or quadratic.

APPENDIX 4A
ADVANCED DIAGNOSTICS FOR
MULTIPLE REGRESSION ANALYSIS

Overview

Appendix 4A reviews additional diagnostic procedures available to the research analyst to assess the underlying assumptions of multiple regression analysis. The following discussion includes the assessment of multicollinearity and the identification of influential observations. Although these concepts are particularly important in multiple regression analysis, these terms will be referred to in later chapters.

Assessing Multicollinearity

Multicollinearity can be diagnosed in a two step process:

Step one: Identify all condition indices above 30. The condition index represents the collinearity of combinations of variables in the data set.

Step two: For all condition indices above 30, identify variables with variance proportions above .50%.

- The *regression coefficient variance-decomposition matrix* shows the proportion of variance for each regression coefficient attributable to each eigenvalue (condition index).

- A collinearity problem is present when a *condition index identified in part one accounts for a substantial proportion of variance (.90 or above)* for two or more coefficients.

Identifying Influential Observations

Influential observations may be identified in a *four step* process.

Step 1: Examine the residuals.

- *Studentized residuals* identify observations that are outliers on the dependent variable. With large sample sizes, studentized residuals of greater than $\pm$ 2.0 are substantial.

- *Dummy-variable regression* may also be used to identify outliers on the dependent variable when the researcher has at least N + 1 (where N is the sample size) degrees of freedom available. A dummy variable is added for each observation, the model is re-estimated, and those dummy variables with significant coefficients are outliers.

- *Partial regression plots* visually portray all individual cases. Outliers can be identified as those cases that impact the regression slope and the corresponding regression equation coefficients.

Step 2: Identify leverage points from the predictors.

- *Hat matrix* represents the combined effects of all independent variables for each case and enables the researcher to identity multivariate leverage points.

  - ➢ Diagonal of the matrix represents the distance of the observation from the mean center of all other observations on the independent variables.

  - ➢ Interpretation: Large values indicate that the observations carry disproportionate weight in determining the dependent variable.

  - ➢ Threshold values: When the number of predictors is greater than 10 and the sample size exceeds 50, a value is large if it exceeds **2p/n** (where p is the number of predictors and n is the sample size); otherwise, use **3p/n.**

- *Mahalanobis distance*, as discussed in Chapter 2, is also used to identify outliers.

Step 3: Identify single case influential observations.

- *Studentized deleted residual* (the studentized residual for observation i when observation i is deleted from calculation of the regression equation) may be used to identify extremely influential, individual observations. Values greater than $\pm$ 2.0 indicate an influential case.

- *DFBETA* reflects the relative change in the regression coefficient when an observation is deleted. For small or medium sample sizes, values greater than 1.0 may be considered influential; for large sample sizes, values exceeding $2 \div \sqrt{n}$ are influential.

- *COVRATIO* is similar to DFBETA, but is different in that it considers all coefficients collectively rather than individually. Values of the COVRATIO - 1 which exceed $\pm$ 3p $\div$ n are indicative of influential observations.

- **Cook's distance** measures the influence of an observation based on the size of changes in the predicted values when the case is omitted (residuals) and the observation's distance from the other observations (leverage). Values greater than 1.0 should be considered influential.

- **DFFIT** measures the degree by which fitted values change when the case is deleted. Values exceeding 2 * square root of (p/n) are indicative of influential observations.

Step 4: Select and accommodate influential observations.

- **Use of multiple measures:** The above steps should converge on the identification of observations that may adversely affect the analyses. The researcher should never classify an observation based on a single measure, but should always conduct a number of diagnostics to identify truly influential observations.

- **Remedy**: Once identified, influential observations may be deleted where justified. If the researcher is unable to delete the observations, a more robust estimation technique should be used.

ANSWERS TO END-OF-CHAPTER QUESTIONS

(1) **HOW WOULD YOU EXPLAIN THE "RELATIVE IMPORTANCE" OF THE PREDICTOR VARIABLES USED IN A REGRESSION EQUATION?**

Answer

Two approaches: (a) beta coefficients and (b) the order that variables enter the equation in stepwise regression. Either approach must be used cautiously, being particularly concerned with the problems caused by multi-collinearity.

With regard to beta coefficients, they are the regression coefficients that are derived from standardized data. Their value is basically that we no longer have the problem of different units of measure. Thus, they reflect the impact on the criterion variable of a change of one standard deviation in any predictor variable. They should be used only as a guide to the relative importance of the predictor variables included in your equation, and only over the range of sample data included.

When using stepwise regression, the partial correlation coefficients are used to identify the sequence in which variables will enter the equation and thus their relative contribution.

(2) **WHY IS IT IMPORTANT TO EXAMINE THE ASSUMPTION OF LINEARITY WHEN USING REGRESSION?**

Answer

The regression model is constructed with the assumption of a linear relationship among the predictor variables. This gives the model the properties of additivity and homogeneity. Hence coefficients express directly the effect of changes in predictor variables. When the assumption of linearity is violated, a variety of conditions can occur such as multicollinearity, heteroscedasticity, or serial correlation (due to non-independence or error terms). All of these conditions require correction before statistical inferences of any validity can be made from a regression equation.

Basically, the linearity assumption should be examined because if the data are not linear, the regression results are not valid.

(3) **HOW CAN NONLINEARITY BE CORRECTED OR ACCOUNTED FOR IN THE REGRESSION EQUATION?**

Answer

Nonlinearity may be corrected or accounted for in the regression equation by three general methods. One way is through a direct data transformation of the original variable as discussed in Chapter 2. Two additional ways are to explicitly model the nonlinear relationship in the regression equation through the use of polynomials and/or interaction terms. Polynomials are power transformations that may be used to represent quadratic, cubic, or higher order polynomials in the regression equation. The advantage of polynomials over direct data transformations in that polynomials allow testing of the type of nonlinear relationship. Another method of representing nonlinear relationships is through the use of an interaction or moderator term for two independent variables. Inclusion of this type of term in the regression equation allows for the slope of the relationship of one independent variable to change across values of a second dependent variable.

(4) **COULD YOU FIND A REGRESSION EQUATION THAT WOULD BE ACCEPTABLE AS STATISTICALLY SIGNIFICANT AND YET OFFER NO ACCEPTABLE INTERPRETATIONAL VALUE TO MANAGEMENT?**

Answer

Yes. For example, with a sufficiently large sample size you could obtain a significant relationship, but a very small coefficient of determination--too small to be of value.

In addition, there are some basic assumptions associated with the use of the regression model, which if violated, could make any obtained results at best spurious. One of the assumptions is that the conditions and relationships existing when sample data were obtained remain unchanged. If changes have occurred they should be accommodated before any new inferences are made. Another is that there is a "relevant range" for any regression model. This range is determined by the predictor variable values used to construct the model. In using the model, predictor values should fall within this relevant range. Finally, there are statistical considerations. For example, the effect of multicollinearity among predictor variables is one such consideration.

(5) WHAT IS THE DIFFERENCE IN INTERPRETATION BETWEEN THE REGRESSION COEFFICIENTS ASSOCIATED WITH INTERVAL SCALED PREDICTOR VARIABLES AS OPPOSED TO DUMMY (0,1) PREDICTOR VARIABLES?

Answer

The use of dummy variables in regression analysis is structured so that there are (n-1) dummy variables included in the equation (where n = the number of categories being considered). In the dichotomous case, then, since n = 2, there is one variable in the equation. This variable has a value of one or zero depending on the category being expressed (e.g., male = 0, female = 1). In the equation, the dichotomous variable will be included when its value is one and omitted when its value is zero. When dichotomous predictor variables are used, the intercept (constant) coefficient (b_o) estimates the average effect of the omitted dichotomous variables. The other coefficients, b1 through bk, represent the average differences between the omitted dichotomous variables and the included dichotomous variables. These coefficients (b_1-b_k) then, represent the average importance of the two categories in predicting the dependent variable.

Coefficients b_o through b_k serve a different function when metric predictors are used. With metric predictors, the intercept (b_o) serves to locate the point where the regression equation crosses the Y axis, and the other coefficients (b_1-b_k) indicate the effect on the predictor variable(s) on the criterion variable (if any).

(6) WHAT ARE THE DIFFERENCES BETWEEN INTERACTIVE AND CORRELATED PREDICTOR VARIABLES? DO ANY OF THESE DIFFERENCES AFFECT YOUR INTERPRETATION OF THE REGRESSION EQUATION?

Answer

Interactive predictor variable is a term used to describe a situation where two predictor variables' functions intersect within the relevant range of the problem. The effect of this interaction is that over part of the relevant range one predictor variable may be considerably more important than the other; but over another part of the relevant range the second predictor variable may become the more important. When interactive effects are encountered, the coefficients actually represent averages of effects across values of the predictors rather than a constant level of effect. Thus, discrete ranges of influence can be misinterpreted as continuous effects.

When predictor variables are highly correlated, there can be no real gain in adding both of the variables to the predictor equation. In this case, the predictor with the highest simple correlation to the criterion variable would be used in the predictive equation.

Since the direction and magnitude of change is highly related for the two predictors, the addition of the second predictor will produce little, if any, gain in predictive power.

When correlated predictors exist, the coefficients of the predictors are a function of their correlation. In this case, little value can be associated with the coefficients since we are speaking of two simultaneous changes.

(7) **ARE INFLUENTIAL CASES ALWAYS TO BE OMITTED? GIVE EXAMPLES OF WHEN THEY SHOULD AND SHOULD NOT BE OMITTED?**

Answer

The principal reason for identifying influential observations is to address one question: Are the influential observations valid representations of the population of interest? Influential observations, whether they be "good" or "bad," can occur because of one of four reasons. Omission or correction is easily decided upon in one case, the case of an observation with some form of error (e.g., data entry).

However, with the other causes, the answer is not so obvious. A valid but exceptional observation may be excluded if it is the result of an extraordinary situation. The researcher must decide if the situation is one which can occur among the population, thus a representative observation. In the remaining two instances (an ordinary observation exceptional in its combination of characteristics or an exceptional observation with no likely explanation), the researcher has no absolute guidelines. The objective is to assess the likelihood of the observation occurring in the population. Theoretical or conceptual justification is much preferable to a decision based solely on empirical considerations.

SAMPLE MULTIPLE CHOICE QUESTIONS
(correct answers indicated by bolded letter)

Circle the letter of the item which best answers the question.

1.   Multiple regression analysis is a:

   a.   metric statistical technique used to analyze the relationship between a single independent variable and several dependent variables.
   b.   nonmetric statistical technique used to analyze the relationship between a single dependent variable and several independent variables.
   c.   metric statistical technique used to analyze the relationship between a single dependent variable and several independent variables.
   d.   procedure which involves obtaining a set of weights for the dependent and independent variables to provide the maximum simple correlation.

2. Multiple regression analysis can be used to:

   a.   predict the values of one variable from the values of others.
   b.   examine the strength of association between the single dependent variable and the one or more independent variables.
   c.   determine the appropriateness of using the regression procedure with the problem.
   d.   remove the effect of any uncontrolled independent variables on the dependent variables.
   e.   answers a, b only
   f.   answers c, d only
   g.   answers a, b, c, only

3.   One way to determine the appropriateness of our predictive model is through:

   a.   the examination of the coefficients of the dummy variables.
   b.   the examination of the errors in prediction.
   c.   looking at the relative size of the sample in comparison to the population size.
   d.   the transformation of the data to the appropriate formula $(X_1 - X) \div 8$

4.   When the variance of the error terms appears constant over a range of x values the data are said to be:

   a.   colluminar
   b.   linear
   c.   homoscedastic
   d.   standardized

5. The coefficient of determination is used:

    a.   to assess the relationship between the dependent and the independent variables.
    b.   as a guide to the relative importance of the predictor variables.
    c.   as a prediction in estimating the size of the confidence interval.
    d.   to test the different coefficients of each independent variable.

6. The two most common approaches to regression analysis are:
    a.   backward elimination, parameter elimination
    b.   stepwise forward estimation, backward elimination
    c.   the interval scale, ratio scale
    d.   multiple discriminant analysis, background elimination.

7. The coefficients resulting from standardized data are called:
    a.   alpha coefficients
    b.   variable coefficients
    c.   beta coefficients
    d.   freedom coefficients

8. The method of elimination of the variables from the regression model is done through a:
    a.   correlation matrix
    b.   confidence level measurement
    c.   residual plot
    d.   determination of the standard deviation of the data

9. In testing the normality of error term distribution one can use three procedures. The simplest method is:
    a.   testing the criterion variables for slack
    b.   construction of histograms
    c.   measure the variance of the plot of residuals
    d.   looking at the appropriateness of the F-statistic

10. Backward elimination involves:

    a.   looking at each variable for consideration in the model prior to the inclusion of the variable into the developing equation.
    b.   computing a regression equation with all the variables, and then going back and deleting those independent variables which are most significant.
    c.   examining the partial correlation coefficients.
    d.   examining the t-value for the original variables in the equation.

CHAPTER FIVE
MULTIPLE DISCRIMINANT ANALYSIS
AND LOGISTIC REGRESSION

Chapter Five discusses two multivariate techniques, multiple discriminant analysis and logistic regression, each appropriate when encountering a research question with a categorical dependent variable and several metric dependent variables. The following presentation will first address the basic questions of "What?" "Why?" "When?" and "How?" as applied to Multiple Discriminant Analysis. This is followed by a brief overview of the logistic regression and a discussion of the differences and similarities of the two techniques.

What is multiple discriminant analysis?

1. Discriminant analysis is a dependence technique that forms *variates* (linear combinations of metric independent variables), which are used to predict the classification of a categorical dependent variable.

2. Classification is accomplished by a statistical procedure, which derives discriminant functions, or variates of the predictor variables, which **maximize the between-group variance and minimize the within-group variance on the discriminant function score(s).**

3. The **null hypothesis is that the two or more group means are equal** on the discriminant function(s), thus a significant model would indicate that the group means are not equal.

4. Further analysis of the variate **reveals between which groups and by which independent variables there are significant differences.**

Why do we use multiple discriminant analysis?

1. Researchers use multiple discriminant analysis to help them understand:
   - group differences on a set of independent variables
   - the ability to correctly classify statistical units into groups or classes
   - the relative importance of independent variables in the classification process

When do you use multiple discriminant analysis?

1. Multiple discriminant analysis may be considered a type of profile analysis or an analytical predictive technique that is most appropriate when there is a single categorical dependent variable and multiple metric independent variables.

2. The appropriate applications are those in which respondents are profiled and/or classified into groups. Common applications include:

- assessing credit risk
- profiling market segments
- predicting failures (firm, product, etc.)
- selecting returns for IRS audits

How do you use multiple discriminant analysis?

Multiple discriminant analyses follow the six stages in model building. The following are important points for each step of the process.

Stage 1: Objectives of Discriminant Analysis

---

1. Discriminant analysis may address a number of common objectives:

- determine the *statistical significance of differences* between the average score profiles on a set of variables for two (or more) a priori defined groups.

- identify the *independent variables accounting most for the differences* in the average score profiles of the two or more groups.

- establish *procedures for classifying statistical units* (individuals or objects) into groups on the basis of their scores on a set of independent variables.

- establish the *number and composition of the dimensions of discrimination* between groups that are formed from the set of independent variables.

Stage 2: Research Design of a Multiple Discriminant Analysis

---

1. The dependent variable selected for use in the analysis must be categorical and the categories must be mutually exclusive and exhaustive.

- *Number of categories*: Any number of categorical groups can be developed. However, the basis for group division must be theory, previous knowledge, intuition, or some other technique (e.g., cluster analysis). Discriminant analysis is not an exploratory procedure that is used to define groups.

- *Two group dependent variable*: If the analyst is only concerned with the two extreme groups, a polar extremes approach which omits all middle categories may be used.

2. Selection of the independent variables for use in the analysis may be based on previous research, a theoretical model, or intuition.

3. Sample size may influence the results.

- *With very large sample sizes, indiscriminant variables may yield a significant difference between groups.* This occurs because as the sample size increases, the gross amount of overlap between the groups remains the same; thus, the percentage of overlap between the groups declines, resulting in a statistically significant difference between the groups, but no practical difference.

- *Examination of the group histograms* will provide the researcher with evidence that sample size effects may be operating.

4. Discriminant analysis is very sensitive to the ratio of sample size to the number of predictor variables.

- A *20 to 1 ratio* of the sample size to the number of independent variables is needed to maintain the integrity of discriminant analysis. This means that for every independent variable used, there should be twenty respondents.

- For *smaller samples or lower ratios* of independent variables to sample size, the researcher must keep an especially sharp eye on the assumptions and the stability of the discriminant function.

5. Discriminant analysis is also sensitive to the sample sizes of each group.

- At minimum, *smallest group size must exceed the number of independent variables*.

- Each group should have *at least 20 observations*.

- *Groups of similar relative size* avoid adverse effects on estimation and classification.

6. The sample should be divided into an estimation sample and a validation sample.

- Data used to derive the discriminant function can not also be used to validate the function. If the researcher uses all of the available data to derive the discriminant function, then the validation of that function on the same data is upwardly biased.

- By dividing the sample into two parts, the validation sample is not biased and also possesses the same properties as the analysis sample. Division of the sample is most often equal (i.e. 50% estimation / 50% validation); however, there is no rule specifying a certain division.

- A proportional stratified sampling procedure is used to select the observations in the validation sample. Thus, the sizes of the groups will be proportionate to the total sample distribution.

Stage 3: Assumptions in Multiple Discriminant Analysis

1. **Discriminant analysis requires nonmetric dependent variables and multiple metric independent variables.**

   - The dependent variable must be *categorical, with at least two groups*.

2. **Discriminant analysis assumes multivariate normality of the independent variables.**

   - The data distribution for the independent variables is assumed to be the *normal distribution*, a requirement for use of the F test.

3. **Discriminant analysis assumes unknown, but equal dispersion and covariance structures (matrices) for the groups as defined by the dependent variable.**

   - This assumption is necessary for the *maximization of the ratio of variance between groups to the variance within groups*. Unequal covariance matrices can have an adverse affect on classification.

   - Equality is assessed by the *Box's M test for homogeneity* of dispersion matrices.

   - Based on the problem's origin, *remedies for violations* of this assumption may be:
     - ➢ increasing sample size,
     - ➢ computing group-specific covariance matrices,
     - ➢ using quadratic classification techniques.

4. Discriminant analysis is adversely affected by collinearity of the independent variables.

- When selecting independent variables with a stepwise method, multicollinearity may *impede inclusion of certain variables* in the variate and impact interpretation.

5. Discriminant analysis implicitly assumes that all relationships are linear.

- Nonlinear relationships can be remedied with the appropriate transformations.

6. Outliers adversely impact the classification accuracy of discriminant analysis.

- The analyst should complete diagnostics for *influential observations, and outliers* not representative of the population should be deleted.

Stage 4: Estimation of the Discriminant Model and Assessing Overall Fit

1. To derive discriminant functions, the researcher must choose a computational method. Two methods from which to choose: simultaneous and stepwise methods.

- *Simultaneous* -- all of the independent variables, regardless of discriminatory power, are used to compute the discriminant function(s).

  ➢ Best use: when the researcher has some theoretical reason to include all of the independent variables.

- *Stepwise* -- independent variables are chosen one at a time on the basis of their discriminating power. Through a series of "step" iterations similar to stepwise regression, only those variables providing the unique discriminatory power will be included in the analysis.

  ➢ Best use: when the researcher has a large number of independent variables and wishes to select the best combination of predictor variables.

2. After the discriminant function is computed, the researcher must assess its level of statistical significance.

- *Criteria:* Wilks' lambda, Hotelling's trace, Pilliai's criteria, Roy's greatest characteristic root, Mahalanobis' distance, and Rao's V measures.

- *Significance level*: The conventional criterion of .05 or beyond is most often used.

- *3 or more groups*: If the dependent variable has three or more groups, analysts must:

  > carefully evaluate the statistical significance of each discriminant function.

  > some discriminant functions may not contribute significantly to overall discriminatory power.

3. Overall fit of the discriminant function may be assessed by constructing classification matrices.

- *Group sizes*: When developing a classification matrix, the analyst must decide whether or not the observed group sizes in the sample are representative of the group sizes in the population. The default assumption is that the population group sizes are assumed to have an equal chance of occurring.

- *Cutting Score*: Used to construct a classification matrix. The optimal cutting score (critical Z value) is dependent on whether or not the sizes of the groups are equal or unequal. Individual discriminant scores for the observations in the validation, or holdout, sample are compared to the cutting score and thereby classified into a group.

- *Interpretation*:
  > diagonal of the classification matrix represent the number of respondents correctly classified.
  > off-diagonal values represent the incorrect classifications.
  > Percentage correctly classified for is shown for **each group and overall.** The overall percentage correctly classified is shown at the bottom.

4. The acceptable level of predictive, or classification, accuracy of the discriminant function may be assessed via comparison to several criteria.

- *Chance criteria* -- the hit ratio may be compared to the percentage of respondents who would be correctly classified by chance, with the following chance criteria available:

    ➢ Equal chance criterion: When the sample sizes of the groups are equal, percentage of correct classification by chance is equal to 1 divided by the number of groups.

    ➢ Maximum chance criterion: Percentage of correct classification by chance is based on the sample size of the largest group. To accurately predict based on this criterion, the hit ratio should exceed the percentage equal to the proportional size of the largest group in the sample.

    ➢ Proportional chance criterion: When the sample sizes of the groups are unequal, percentage of correct classification by chance is equal to the sum of the proportion of respondents in each group squared.

    ➢ Classification accuracy should be at least one fourth greater than that achieved by chance.

- *Press's Q statistic* -- A statistical test that computes a value based on the number of correct classifications, the total sample size and the number of groups and compares this value to a critical value (chi-square value for 1 degree of freedom at the desired confidence level).

    ➢ Sensitive to sample size. Large samples are more likely to show significance than small sample sizes of the same classification rate.

Stage 5: Interpretation of the Variate

---

1. Examine the discriminant functions to determine the relative importance of each independent variable in discriminating between groups by one of the following methods:

- *Discriminant weights* -- The sign and magnitude of discriminant weights (also called discriminant coefficients) represent the relative contribution of each variable to the function.

- *Discriminant loadings* -- measure the simple linear correlation between each independent variable and the discriminant function.

  - ➤ Reflect the variance shared by the independent variables and the discriminant function.

  - ➤ Can be interpreted like factor loadings when assessing the relative contribution of each independent variable to the discriminant function.

- *Partial F values* -- Used when the stepwise method is selected, partial F values reflect the relative contribution of each independent variable to the discriminant function. Larger F values indicate greater discriminating power.

2. Interpretation of two or more discriminant functions is somewhat more complicated. The analyst must now determine the relative importance of the independent variables across all the discriminant functions.

- *Rotation*: Simplifies the profiling of each discriminant function. Rotations, similar to those done in factor analysis, do not change the structure of the solution, but make the functions easier to interpret.

- *Variable Importance Across Multiple Functions*: The relative importance of each independent variable across all significant discriminant functions can be determined with:

  - ➤ Potency Index is a composite or summary measure which indicates which independent variables are most discriminating across all discriminant functions.

  - ➤ Stretching the vectors is one approach used to identify the relative importance of independent variables. Vectors are created by drawing a line from the origin to a point representing each discriminant loading multiplied by its respective univariate F value. The length of the vector is indicative of the relative importance of each variable in discriminating among the groups.

1. **Accomplished by splitting the original data set, collecting a new data set, or using group profiling.**

   - *Split sample*: The data set is split into two parts: an analysis sample and a holdout sample. The discriminant functions are derived from the analysis sample and the results are validated with the holdout sample. This procedure may be completed several times by randomly dividing the total sample into analysis and holdout samples. The hit ratios obtained from the various analyses can be averaged.

   - *New sample*: A new data set is gathered. The discriminant functions derived from a previous sample are validated with new data.

   - *Profiling group differences:* Groups are profiled on the independent variables in order to ensure their correspondence to the conceptual bases of the model. Group may also be profiled on other independent variables not included in the analysis. This approach provides external validity to the findings.

Logistic Regression: Regression with a Binary Dependent Variable

1. Applications

   - Logistic regression (LR), also know as logit analysis, is appropriate when the dependent variable dichotomous (nonmetric binary), making it equivalent to a two-group discriminant analysis.

   - LR is preferable to discriminant analysis in the two-group case as it does not require the strict assumptions of multivariate normality and equal variance.

1. Similarities to Discriminant Analysis

   - Predicts group membership for each observation, with the logistic variate predicting the probability of group membership and then actual group membership predicted from the probability (over 50% = yes, under 50% = no).

- Requires an estimation and validation sample to best assess predictive accuracy.

Differences with Discriminant Analysis

- Assumed relationship between the logistic variate and the dependent variable is an S-shaped or logistic curve. It has the unique characteristic of becoming asymptotic to the probability limits (0 and 1), but never crosses these values.

- Estimated through the process of maximum likelihood estimation.

- Coefficients of the independent variables are interpreted much like regression coefficients, with direct statistical tests (Wald test) for their statistical significance.

- Goodness of fit can be measured with "pseudo R^2" values, much like the coefficient of determination in multiple regression.

ANSWERS TO END-OF-CHAPTER QUESTIONS

(1) HOW WOULD YOU DIFFERENTIATE BETWEEN MULTIPLE DISCRIMINANT ANALYSIS, REGRESSION ANALYSIS, AND ANALYSIS OF VARIANCE?

<u>Answer</u>

Basically, the difference lies in the number of independent and dependent variables and in the way in which these variables are measured. Note the following definitions:

<u>Multiple discriminant analysis</u> (MDA) - the single dependent (criterion) variable is nonmetric and the independent (predictor) variables are metric.

<u>Regression Analysis</u> - both the single dependent variable and the multiple independent variables are metric.

<u>Analysis of Variance</u> (ANOVA) - the multiple dependent variables are metric and the single independent variable is nonmetric.

(2) WHEN WOULD YOU EMPLOY LOGISTIC REGRESSION RATHER THAN DISCRIMINANT ANALYSIS? WHAT ARE THE ADVANTAGES AND DISADVANTAGES OF THE DECISION?

<u>Answer</u>

Both discriminant analysis and logistic regression are appropriate when the dependent variable is categorical and the independent variables are metric. In the case of a two group dependent variable either technique might be applied, but only discriminant analysis is capable of handling more than two groups. When the basic assumptions of both methods are met, each gives comparable predictive and classificatory results and employ similar diagnostic measures. Logistic regression has the advantage of being less affected than discriminant analysis when the basic assumptions of normality and equal variance are not met. It also can accommodate non-metric dummy coded variables as independent measures. Logistic regression is limited though to the prediction of only a two-group dependent measure. Thus, when more than two groups are involved, discriminant analysis is required.

(3) **WHAT CRITERIA COULD YOU USE IN DECIDING WHETHER TO STOP A DISCRIMINANT ANALYSIS AFTER ESTIMATING THE DISCRIMINANT FUNCTION(S)? AFTER THE INTERPRETATION STAGE?**

Answer

a.   Criterion for stopping after derivation. The level of significance must be assessed. If the function is not significant at a predetermined level (e.g., .05), then there is little justification for going further. This is because there is little likelihood that the function will classify more accurately than would be expected by randomly classifying individuals into groups (i.e., by chance).

b.   Criterion for stopping after interpretation. Comparison of "hit-ratio" to some criterion. The minimum acceptable percentage of correct classifications usually is predetermined.

(4) **WHAT PROCEDURE WOULD YOU FOLLOW IN DIVIDING YOUR SAMPLE INTO ANALYSIS AND HOLDOUT GROUPS? HOW WOULD YOU CHANGE THIS PROCEDURE IF YOUR SAMPLE CONSISTED OF FEWER THAN 100 INDIVIDUALS OR OBJECTS?**

Answer

When selecting individuals for analysis and holdout groups, a proportionately stratified sampling procedure is usually followed. The split in the sample typically is arbitrary (e.g., 50-50 analysis/hold-out, 60-40, or 75-25) so long as each "half" is proportionate to the entire sample.

There is no minimum sample size required for a sample split, but a cut-off value of 100 units is often used. Many researchers would use the entire sample for analysis and validation if the sample size were less than 100. The result is an upward bias in statistical significance which should be recognized in analysis and interpretation.

(5) **HOW DO YOU DETERMINE THE OPTIMUM CUTTING SCORE?**

Answer

a.   For equal group sizes, the optimum cutting score is defined by:

$$Z_{CE} = \frac{Z_A + Z_B}{N}$$

Z_{CE} = critical cutting score value for equal size groups
Z_A = centroid for group A
Z_B = centroid for Group B
N = total sample size

b.   For unequal group sizes, the optimum cutting score is defined by:

$$Z_{CU} = \frac{N_A Z_B + N_B Z_A}{N_A + N_B}$$

Z_{CU} = critical cutting score value for unequal size groups
N_A = sample size for group A
N_B = sample size for Group B

(6) HOW WOULD YOU DETERMINE WHETHER OR NOT THE CLASSIFICATION ACCURACY OF THE DISCRIMINANT FUNCTION IS SUFFICIENTLY HIGH RELATIVE TO CHANCE CLASSIFICATION?

Answer

Some chance criterion must be established. This is usually a fairly direct function of the classifications used in the model and of the sample size. The authors then suggest the following criterion: the classification accuracy (hit ratio) should be at least 25 percent greater than by chance.

Another test would be to use a test of proportions to examine for significance between the chance criterion proportion and the obtained hit-ratio proportion.

(7) HOW DOES A TWO-GROUP DISCRIMINANT ANALYSIS DIFFER FROM A THREE-GROUP ANALYSIS?

Answer

In many cases, the dependent variable consists of two groups or classifications, for example, male versus female or high versus low. In other instances, more than two groups are involved, such as a three-group classification involving low, medium and high classifications. Discriminant analysis is capable of handling either two groups or multiple groups (three or more). When two classifications are involved, the technique is referred to as two-group discriminant analysis. When three or more classifications are identified, the technique is referred to as multiple discriminant analysis (MDA).

(8) WHY SHOULD AN RESEARCHER STRETCH THE LOADINGS AND CENTROID DATA IN PLOTTING A DISCRIMINANT ANALYSIS SOLUTION?

Answer

Plots are used to illustrate the results of a multiple discriminant analysis. By using the statistically significant discriminant functions, the group centroids can be plotted in the reduced discriminant function space so as to show the separation of the groups. Plots are usually produced for the first two significant functions. Frequently, plots are less than satisfactory in illustrating how the groups differ on certain variables of interest to the researcher. In this case stretching the discriminant loadings and centroid data, prior to plotting the discriminant function, aids in detecting and interpreting differences between groups. Stretching the discriminant loadings by considering the variance contributed by a variable to the respective discriminant function gives the researcher an indication of the relative importance of the variable in discriminating among the groups. Group centroids can be stretched by multiplying the approximate F-value associated with each of the discriminant functions. This stretches the group centroids along the axis in the discriminant plot that provides more of the accounted-for variation.

(9) HOW DO LOGISTIC REGRESSION AND DISCRIMINANT ANALYSES EACH HANDLE THE RELATIONSHIP OF THE DEPENDENT AND INDEPENDENT VARIABLES?

Answer

Discriminant analysis derives a variate, the linear combination of two or more independent variables that will discriminate best between the dependent variable groups. Discrimination is achieved by setting variate weights for each variable to maximize between group variance. A discriminant (z) score is then calculated for each observation. Group means (centroids) are calculated and a test of discrimination is the distance between group centroids.

Logistic regression forms a single variate more similar to multiple regression. It differs from multiple regression in that it directly predicts the probability of an event occurring. To define the probability, logistic regression assumes the relationship between the independent and dependent variables resembles an S-shaped curve. At very low levels of the independent variables, the probability approaches zero. As the independent variable increases, the probability increases. Logistic regression uses a maximum likelihood procedure to fit the observed data to the curve.

(10) WHAT ARE THE DIFFERENCES IN ESTIMATION AND INTERPRETATION BETWEEN LOGISTIC REGRESSION AND DISCRIMINANT ANALYSIS?

Answer

Estimation of the discriminant variate is based on maximizing between group variance. Logistic regression is estimated using a maximum likelihood technique to fit the data to a logistic curve. Both techniques produce a variate that gives information about which variables explain the dependent variable or group membership. Logistic regression may be comfortable for many to interpret in that it resembles the more commonly seen regression analysis.

SAMPLE MULTIPLE CHOICE QUESTIONS
(correct answers indicated by bold letter)

Circle the letter of the item which best answers the question.

1. Multiple discriminant analysis is a statistical technique which involves:

    a.   ordinal and metric dependent variables
    b.   ratio and quantitative dependent variables
    c.   nominal and qualitative dependent variables
    d.   interval and nonmetric dependent variables

2. Multiple discriminant analysis is an appropriate analytical technique for using:

    a.   a categorical dependent variable and several nonmetric independent variables.
    b.   a metric dependent variable and several metric independent variables.
    c.   an ordinal dependent variable and several nonmetric independent variables.
    d.   a categorical dependent variable and several metric independent variables.

3. By averaging the discriminant scores in a particular analysis, one can arrive at what is called a:

    a.   standard analysis
    b.   centroid
    c.   cutting score
    d.   high ratio

4. One assumption in deriving discriminant functions is the:

    a.   abnormality of the distributions and a positive centroid.
    b.   unequal costs of misclassifications.
    c.   normality of the distributions and unknown depression and covariance structures.
    d.   normality of the distributions and known high-low ratio.

5. One objective for applying discriminant analysis is:

   a. to determine if statistically significant differences exist between the high ratios of the defined priori groups.

   b. to determine which independent variables account for the most difference in the average score profiles of the groups being analyzed.

   c. to determine the model which possesses the property of additivity and homogeneity, with the highest R^2 value.

   d. to determine the correlations between a single dependent variable and several independent variables.

6. The three stages of discriminant analysis include:

   a. rotation, correlation, and application.

   b. extraction, derivation, and projection.

   c. derivation, calibration, and interpretation.

   d. analyzing, predicting, and rotation.

7. The simultaneous method is:

   a. a computational method utilized in deriving discriminant functions.

   b. useful when the analyst wants to consider a relatively large number of independent variables for inclusion.

   c. necessary in order to clarify the usefulness Mahalanobis D statistic.

   d. useful in developing a classification matrix that discriminates significantly.

8. The maximum chance criterion should be used when the sole objective:

   a. is to estimate the hold-out samples.

   b. is to maximize the percentage correctly classified.

   c. is to interpret the magnitude of the standardized discriminant weights.

   d. to measure the linear correlation between independent variables.

9. Discriminant loadings are most commonly used to:

   a. examine the sign and magnitude of the standardized discriminant weights.

   b. develop a classification matrix to assess the predictions of the function.

   c. evaluate the group differences.

   d. measure the simple linear correlation between each independent variable and the discriminant function.

10. The interpretation phase of discriminant analysis involves the three methods of:

   a. standardized discriminant weights, discriminant structure correlations, and partial F-values.
   b. chance models, cutting score determination, and stepwise method.
   c. simultaneous method, discriminant structure, and partial F-values.
   d. deviation, validation, and standardization.

CHAPTER SIX
MULTIVARIATE ANALYSIS OF VARIANCE

The following presentation will address the basic questions of "What?," "Why?," "When?," and "How?" as applied to multivariate analysis of variance (MANOVA).

What is multivariate analysis of variance?

1. Multivariate analysis of variance (MANOVA) is used to assess *group differences across multiple metric dependent variables simultaneously*. It derives its name from its ability to perform a series of univariate analysis of variance (ANOVA) tests while maintaining a specified overall error rate for all tests combined.

2. The null hypothesis is that the *vectors of dependent variable means* are equal across groups formed by the categorical independent variable(s).

3. The *number of independent variables and the number of categories in each* defines the number of group vectors to examine.

- *single independent variable* -- each value of the independent variable becomes a group for which a vector of dependent variable means are calculated.

- *two or more independent variables* -- each combination of independent variable values forms a separate group for which the vector of dependent variable means is calculated.

Why do we use multivariate analysis of variance?

1. MANOVA is the technique of choice when a researcher wishes to *predict two or more metric dependent variables with multiple categorical independent variables*. It is misleading to think that it would be simpler to run multiple ANOVAs instead of using MANOVA.

2. By using MANOVA, the researcher avoids an inflated error level that occurs when alpha is not controlled during multiple ANOVA analyses. Therefore, MANOVA accomplishes the task of *multiple significance tests without a loss of control of the error level*. This provides the researcher a much more reliable and valid result.

When do you use multivariate analysis of variance?

MANOVA is the appropriate statistical technique when the researcher wishes to control for the experiment wide error rate or to test for differences among a combination of dependent variables.

How do you use multivariate analysis of variance?

Multivariate analysis of variance follows the six stage model building perspective.

Stage 1: Objectives of Multivariate Analysis of Variance

1. The following three types of questions are appropriate objectives for MANOVA

- *Multiple Univariate Research Questions*: The researcher identifies a number of separate dependent variables that are to be analyzed separately, but needs some control over the experiment wide error rate. MANOVA is used to assess whether an overall difference is found between groups; then the separate univariate tests are employed to address each dependent variable.

- *Structured Multivariate Research Questions*: The researcher gathers data having two or more dependent measures that have specific relationships between them. A common type of structured question would be a repeated measure design.

- *Intrinsically Multivariate Research Questions:* The researcher wishes to address how a set of dependent measures differs as a whole across groups. The collective effect of several variables is of interest, not the individual effects.

2. Only those dependent variables having a sound conceptual or theoretical basis should be selected for inclusion in the analysis.

- *Inclusion of irrelevant variables* may adversely affect the resulting conclusions of an analysis. This is especially so when the researcher's objective is to learn about the collective effect.

Stage 2: Issues in the Research Design of MANOVA

1. The sample size in each cell must be greater than the number of dependent variables included in the analysis.

2. Treatments in a factorial design should be selected based on the research question.

- *Treatments* (independent variables) will be specified in the design of the experiment.

- *Blocking factors* are treatments added after the analysis design. These treatments enable the researcher to further segment the respondents in order to obtain greater within-group homogeneity and to reduce the mean square within source of variance.

3. Examine interaction effects before main effects with multiple independent variables.

- Interactions are how one independent variable affects (interacts with) another independent variable. The interaction is represented by differing patterns of dependent variable means for combinations of the values of two or more independent variables.

- *Impact of significant interaction:* When a significant interaction is present, the interaction effect must be interpreted before any possible main effects.

- *Types of interactions:* nonparallel, ordinal interaction (acceptable) or a disordinal interaction (unacceptable).

  - ➢ Ordinal: the effects of a treatment are not equal across all levels of another treatment, but the magnitude is always the same direction

  - ➢ Disordinal: effects of one treatment are positive for some levels and negative for other levels of the other treatment

- *Diagnosis:* Interactions may be found by plotting the means of each dependent variable for each combination of two or more independent variables. Post hoc tests may be used to assess the significance of the differences (Scheffe's or contrast test).

- *Interpretation of significant interactions:* Ordinal interactions may be interpreted (when the results are conceptually acceptable) and the effects of each treatment may be described. Significant disordinal interactions require the re-design of the study; the main effects cannot be interpreted.

4. The researcher must decide on the use of a covariate.

- *Covariate* is a metric independent variable that is regressed on the dependent variables to eliminate its effect before using the dependent variable in the analysis. Thus, covariates remove effects on the dependent variable before assessing any main effects from the independent variables. Covariates are not entered into MANOVA as independent variables (factors) because they are metric and we would lose too much information if they were made categorical.

- *Use of covariate* to either
  - eliminate some systematic error outside the control of the researcher, which may bias the results, or
  - account for differences in the responses due to unique characteristics of the respondents.

- *Nature of covariate*: Highly correlated with the dependent variable, but not correlated with the independent variables.

- *Number of covariates* included in the analysis should be less than (.10 * sample size) - (number of groups - 1).

- *Requirements for Use of a Covariate:*
  - Must have some relationship with the dependent measures.
  - Must have a homogeneity of regression effect, meaning that they have equal effects on the dependent variable across groups.

Stage 3: Assumptions of Multivariate Analysis of Variance

---

1. The dependent variables must follow a multivariate normal distribution.

- *Multivariate normality* assumes that the joint effect of two variables is normally distributed.

- *Testing for multivariate normality:* Since there is no test for multivariate normality, the researcher should conduct univariate analyses with the idea that univariate normality is indicative of multivariate normality.

- *Nonnormal dependent variables* should be transformed.

2. The variance-covariance matrices must be equal for all treatment groups.

- *Equality of variance* assumed across the dependent variables for each group.

- *Box test* may be used to test equality of covariance matrices.

- *Violation of this assumption* has minimal impact if the groups are of approximately equal size.

3. The observations must be independent.

- Each observation or subject's response must be independent from all others. If any situation arises in which some connection is made between observations and not accounted for in the procedures, significant biases can occur.

- Violation of this assumption is the most serious. If violations are detected, the researcher can combine observations with a group and analyze the group's average score instead of the scores of separate respondents. In addition, if a violation occurs, the researcher may employ a covariate to account for the dependence.

4. A large sample size may increase the sensitivity to assumption violations.

- *Impact of large samples*: The equal variance-covariance matrix test most likely will be violated with a very large sample size. As an alternative, examine F statistic and Chi square for additional information.

- As a *rule-of-thumb*, there should be at least one Chi-square for each degree of freedom. While this is only a rule-of-thumb, ratios in this area will normally perform well with MANOVA.

5. Dependent variables must be linearly related and exhibit low multicollinearity.

- *Nonlinear relationship:* if detected among the dependent variables, an appropriate transformation should be conducted.

- *Multicollinearity* among the dependent variables indicates redundancy and decreases statistical efficiency.

6. MANOVA is especially sensitive to outliers and their impact on Type 1 error.

Stage 4: Estimation of the MANOVA Model and Assessing Overall Fit

1. Criteria to assess multivariate differences across groups: Roy's greatest characteristic root, Wilks' lambda, Hotellings' trace and Pillai's criterion.

- *Pillai's criterion or Wilks' lambda* are the most immune to violations of the assumptions and maintain the greatest power, while *Roy's gcr* is most powerful if all assumptions are met.

- *Pillai's criterion* is more robust if the sample size is small, unequal cell sizes are present, or homogeneity of covariances is violated.

2. The level of power of a statistical test is based on the alpha level, the effect size of the treatment and the sample size of the groups.

- *Power is inversely related to alpha.* If the alpha level is set too conservatively, the power of the test may be too low for valid results to be identified.

- *Effect size is directly related to the power* of the statistical test for a given sample size. The larger the effect size, the greater the power of the test (i.e. the greater the standardized differences between groups, the more probable that the statistical test will identify a treatment's effect if it exists).

- *Increasing the sample size increases the power* by reducing sampling error. However, sample sizes greater than 150 per group do not contribute greatly to increasing the power of the test. In fact, in very large sample sizes, the power of the test may become too sensitive, identifying almost any difference as significant.

Stage 5: Interpretation of Results

1. Interpreting MANOVA results involves three stages: interpretation of the covariate, determination of which dependent variables exhibited differences across groups, and identification of which groups differed on the dependent variate or a single dependent variable.

- *Interpreting the Covariates* by evaluating the effectiveness of including a covariate. This may be done by running the analysis with and without covariates. To be considered effective, the covariate should improve the statistical power of the tests and reduce with-in group variance.

- *Assessment of the dependent variable* is done through statistical tests to determine which dependent variables contribute the most to overall group differences. These tests may be **post hoc tests** and **a priori tests**.

  ➤ Post hoc tests are the most common post hoc procedures and include *Scheffe's test, Tukey's honestly significant difference method, Tukey's extension of the Fisher least significant difference approach, Duncan's multiple range test*, and the *Newman-Kuels test*.

    1) Since post hoc tests examine every possible combination of groups, these **methods suffer from low power.** The Scheffe test is most conservative with respect to type 1 error.

  ➤ A priori tests. The analyst specifies which group comparisons are to be made instead of testing all possible combinations. Thus, a priori tests are **more powerful than post hoc tests.**

    2) *Context for use*: A priori tests are most appropriate when the analyst has conceptual bases which support the selection of specific comparisons. *A priori* comparisons should not be used as an exploratory technique.

- *Identification of differences between groups* by *post hoc* or *a priori* statistical tests.

  ➤ Single dependent variable contribution assessment has the potential to inflate Type 1 error when running several consecutive *a priori tests* (univariate tests).

  ➤ Adjustment for potential Type 1 error inflation involves the use of the *Bonferroni inequality* or a *stepdown analysi*s.

99

Stage 6: Validation of the Results

1. Replication is the primary means of validation of MANOVA results.

- **Exact replication may be difficult** in certain research contexts (such as survey research).

- *Covariate usage* is dictated when the researcher is knowledgeable of characteristics of the population which may affect the dependent variables.

2. Significant MANOVA results do not necessarily support causation.

- *Causation* is based on several criteria must be met before the researcher can suggest causation. Causation can never be proved.

ANSWERS TO END-OF-CHAPTER QUESTIONS

(1)   WHAT ARE THE DIFFERENCES BETWEEN MANOVA AND DISCRIMINANT ANALYSIS?   WHAT SITUATIONS BEST SUIT EACH MULTIVARIATE TECHNIQUE?

In a way, MANOVA and discriminant analysis are mirror images. The dependent variables in MANOVA (a set of metric variables) are the independent variables in discriminant analysis. The single non-metric dependent variable of discriminant analysis becomes an independent variable in MANOVA. Moreover, both use the similar methods in forming the variates and assessing statistical significance between groups.

Use of one technique over the other primarily depends upon the research objective. Discriminant analysis employs a single non-metric variable as the dependent variable. The independent metric variables are used to form variates that maximize differences between groups formed by the dependent variable. The objective is to determine the independent variables that discriminate between groups. In MANOVA, the set of metric variables now act as dependent variables and the objective becomes finding groups of respondents that exhibit differences on the set of dependent variables.

(2)   DESIGN A TWO-WAY MANOVA EXPERIMENT. WHAT ARE THE DIFFERENT SOURCES OF VARIANCE IN YOUR EXPERIMENT? WHAT WOULD THE INTERACTION TEST TELL YOU?

<u>Answer</u>

a.   Requirements for two-way MANOVA
    1) Two (or more) metric dependent variables
    2) Two (or more) non-metric experimental (treatment) variables. The experimental design is a 2 x 2 (n x n) matrix of independent non-metric variables.
    3) Subjects are assigned at random, but in equal numbers to each of the cells.
    4) Statistics are calculated for each cell:
        a) totals for both (all) dependent variables
        b) sums of squares for both (all) dependent variables
        c) sums of products of dependent variables
    5) Marginals are computed

b.   There are four sources of variance:
    1) between columns (treatments)
    2) between rows (factors)
    3) interactions between factors and treatments
    4) residual error

c. In factorial designs (n x n) the interaction test would aid in discovering an interaction effect. In other words, the joint effect of treatment variables in addition to the individual main effects on the dependent variable(s).

(3) BESIDES THE OVERALL, OR GLOBAL, SIGNIFICANCE, THERE ARE AT LEAST THREE APPROACHES TO DOING FOLLOW-UP TESTS: (A) USE OF SCHEFFE' CONTRAST PROCEDURES; (B) STEP-DOWN ANALYSIS, WHICH IS SIMILAR TO STEPWISE REGRESSION IN THAT EACH SUCCESSIVE F-STATISTIC IS COMPUTED AFTER ELIMINATING THE EFFECTS OF THE PREVIOUS DEPENDENT VARIABLES; AND (C) EXAMINATION OF THE DISCRIMINANT FUNCTION(S). NAME THE PRACTICAL ADVANTAGES AND DISADVANTAGES OF EACH OF THESE APPROACHES.

Answer

a. Scheffe' Contrast procedures

1) Tests for differences between groups on any dependent variable.

2) These procedures ensure that the probability of any Type I error across all comparisons will be held to $d = .05$ (or at the level specified by the researcher). A disadvantage in using the Scheffe' test is that it requires the use of the gcr distribution. If the Scheffe' test is to be used, then the most appropriate overall test would be the gcr-statistic in MANOVA.

b. Step-Down Analysis

1) Similar to F-tests but allows for correlation among dependent variables.

2) Analogous to step-wise regression in concept. May overlook a significant dependent (independent) variable due to its high correlation with another dependent (independent) variable.

c. Multiple Discriminant Analysis of the SSCP matrix

1) The relative importance of each independent variable can be identified by deriving correlations between each original dependent variable and the discriminant function.

2) Major areas of differences between groups can be identified.

(4) HOW IS STATISTICAL POWER AFFECTED BY STATISTICAL AND RESEARCH DESIGN DECISIONS? HOW WOULD YOU DESIGN A STUDY TO ENSURE ADEQUATE POWER?

Answer

The primary factors affecting power can be assessed prior to a study, estimated effect size, desired alpha level, the number of dependent variables, and sample size. To ensure adequate power, the researcher should estimate the effect size and the needed sample size to achieve the desired level of power given the alpha required. In the design of the study, the researcher should consider the use of as few dependent variables as possible, especially if they are correlated.

(5) DESCRIBE SOME DATA ANALYSIS SITUATIONS IN WHICH MANOVA AND MANCOVA WOULD BE APPROPRIATE IN YOUR AREAS OF INTEREST. WHAT TYPES OF UNCONTROLLED VARIABLES OR COVARIATES MIGHT BE OPERATING IN EACH OF THESE SITUATIONS?

Answer

There are a wide variety of applications possible in the areas of psychology and education. Examples of the use of these techniques in these two fields may be found in the selected readings at the end of the chapter. A wide variety of applications are also possible in the area of marketing. One type of experiment which might be carried out in advertising research would be to test the effects of two broadcast communications media at three different times of the day on consumer knowledge and intention to buy simultaneously. Covariates in such an experiment might include sex, age, or education level of the respondents. These could be controlled for after the experiment if these variables did indeed have an effect on the outcome of the test.

Another type of experiment might be to test the effect of a point of purchase display (present or absent) against newspaper advertising. Two cities could be selected which possess similar demographic profiles. The local newspaper in one city only would carry ads about the specific product. Some stores would be selected in each city for the point of purchase displays and some selected for observation without the displays. Dependent variables to be observed might include levels of traffic on the aisles containing the product and the proportion of purchases containing the item of interest. Covariates might include frequency of shopping trips and readership of both newspapers. Similar problems of interest might occur in any discipline where experimental design is of concern.

SAMPLE MULTIPLE CHOICE QUESTIONS
(correct answers indicated by bolded letter)

Circle the letter of the item which best answers the question.

1. Multivariate Analysis of Variance is a statistical technique which can be used to study the effect of:

    a.   one independent variable on one dependent variable.
    b.   multiple independent variables measured on two or more dependent variables
    c.   two or more dependent variables on one independent variable simultaneously.
    d.   multiple independent variables measured on two or more dependent variables

2. Multivariate Analysis of Variance used in conjunction with covariance analysis is helpful to remove:

    a.   the effect of any autocorrelation.
    b.   the effect of any bivariate factor tendencies.
    c.   the effect of any uncontrolled independent variables on the independent variables.
    d.   the effect of any nonlinear interaction effects.

3. MANOVA makes use of:

    a.   only metric independent variables and metric dependent variables.
    b.   only nonmetric independent variables but metric dependent variables.
    c.   only metric independent variables but nonmetric dependent variables.
    d.   only nonmetric independent variables and nonmetric dependent variables.

4. When using Univariate Analysis of Variance the true population differences can be estimated from:

    a.   only looking at the whole population.
    b.   only looking at the centroid.
    c.   only looking at the population standard deviation.
    d.   only a sample group.

5. The primary function of an experimental design is to serve as:

    a.   a hypothesis for the experiment in general.
    b.   an analysis sample taken from the whole population.
    c.   the dummy variables used in the regression analysis.
    d.   a control mechanism to provide more confidence in your relationships among variables.

6. In "analysis of variance" designs:

    a.   metric dependent variables are used with metric independent variables.
    b.   metric independent variables are used with nonmetric independent variables.
    c.   nonmetric independent variables are used with nonmetric dependent variables.
    d.   nonmetric dependent variables are used with nonmetric independent variables.

7. Random effects designs assume the groups being studied are a random sample from a larger population with a:

    a.   known mean and variance.
    b.   unknown standard deviation and mean.
    c.   unknown mean and known variance.
    d.   unknown mass and variance.

8. When one is testing the significance of difference among three or more treatment groups, he must use:

    a.   only the Hotelling's T2 statistic.
    b.   both the Hotelling's T2 statistic and the Mahalanobis D2 statistic.
    c.   only the Mahalanobis D2 statistic in conjunction with Wilk's lambda.
    d.   the Wilk's lambda.

9. When one has two or more factors, each at two or more levels, he has what is known as a:

    a.   full factorial design.
    b.   bivariate factorial design.
    c.   fixed-effect factorial design.
    d.   random effect factorial design.

10. Residual or error variance should be:

    a.   not normally distributed, with unequal error variance among the cells.
    b.   normally distributed, with dependent variables.
    c.   normally distributed, with equal error variance among the cells.
    d.   bimodally distributed, with dependent variables.

Additional Notes:

CHAPTER SEVEN
CONJOINT ANALYSIS

The following presentation will address the basic questions of "What?," "Why?," "When?," and "How?" as applied to Conjoint Analysis.

What is conjoint analysis?

1. **Objective**: Conjoint analysis is a decompositional dependence technique that infers the importance of attributes used by the consumer in the decision-making.

2. **Difference from other dependence techniques:** It is in direct contrast to the other dependence techniques in that the values for the independent variables are prespecified by the researcher, who creates objects and, from the consumers' responses, infers the elements used in the thought process.

3. **Difference from other decompositional techniques**: This also differs from the other decompositional technique we have discussed, multi-dimensional scaling (MDS), in that in MDS the objects are existing objects (products, persons, etc.) that are evaluated.

4. **Type of results:** Conjoint does not try to determine the dimensions upon which a decision is made, rather the dimensions are specified a priori and conjoint attempts to determine each dimension's influence (and also each level of each dimension) in the decision process.

5. **Level of results:** Conjoint results are obtained for each respondent in the sample.

Why and when do we use conjoint analysis?

Conjoint analysis is the technique of choice when the objective is any of the following:

- Define the object or concept with the optimum combination of features.
- Show the relative contributions of each attribute and each level of each attribute to the overall evaluation of the object.
- Use estimates of purchaser or customer judgments to predict market shares among objects with differing sets of features (other things held constant).
- Isolate groups of potential customers who place differing importance on the features in order to define high and low potential segments.
- Identify marketing opportunities by exploring the market potential for feature combinations not currently available.

How do you use conjoint analysis?

Conjoint analyses follow the same six stages of all multivariate techniques discussed in the text. The following are important points for each step of the design process

---

Stage 1: The Objectives of Conjoint Analysis

---

1. Conjoint Analysis has two primary objectives.

- *Determine attributes' contribution* to determining consumer preferences.

- *Create a valid model of consumer preference judgments* that will predict consumer acceptance of any combination of attributes.

2. The total worth of the object defines the specificity of the model.

- *All positive and negative attributes* which impact (add to or detract from) the overall worth of the product / service should be included in the model.

- *Limited to making statements pertaining to the variables and levels used in the analysis.* We can not interpolate between variables or levels of variables. In its most general form of partworth utilities, the conjoint procedure uses categorical relationships between variables so there is no assumption of a linear relationship.

- *Assumption is that the model contains all the needed dimensions* to make the choice (i.e., inclusion of all determinant attributes), so the researcher must ensure that the specified attributes define the total worth of the products.

3. Determinant factors can be specified and are limited to what we specify as the basis for decision.

- *Implicit is that the researcher can specify the dimensions or variables upon which a decision is based,* and even further that the dimensions we specify are the only dimensions used.

- *Conjoint analysis requires some a priori basis for selection of variables.* The justification may be theoretical or derived from other research, such as a survey to determine the appropriate variables to include.

Stage 2: The Design of a Conjoint Analysis

1. Selecting a Conjoint Methodology

- **Several alternative methodologies have been developed to complement the "traditional" approach** given the increasing number of applications for conjoint analysis.

  - ➤ <u>traditional conjoint</u>: suitable for up to nine attributes with an additive model and analysis performed at the individual level
  - ➤ <u>adaptive conjoint</u>: accommodates up to 30 attributes while still using an additive model estimated at the individual level
  - ➤ <u>choice-based conjoint</u>: estimates additive and interactive effects, but only can employ up to six attributes and must be estimated at the aggregate level

2. Designing Stimuli Involves Specifying Both Factors and Levels of Each Factor

A researcher must specify a **factor** for each variable to be included in the conjoint analysis. Moreover, each possible value for the factor, known as a **level**, must also be specified. For example, color may be defined as a factor, with the levels of red, blue and green.

- **Factors and levels must be actionable and communicable.**

  - ➤ *They must be precise and perceptually distinct.* In other words, the descriptions of either factors or levels must be singular, concrete concepts which illicit the same interpretation from all respondents. A particular problem is describing more emotional (affective) or sensory attributes and their levels.
  - ➤ *They must be easily understood by respondents.* They must also be stated in very tangible terms. Both must be capable of being verbalized or written in order to be operationalized in conjoint analysis.

- **Dimensionality and the number of factors (attributes.)**

  - ➤ *The number of factors used in the analysis must balance the needs of complexity and specificity.* Including too many factors results in too complex a design, which requires consumers to make endless hypothetical preference judgments and researchers to complete intricate analyses. However, too few variables in the design will not provide the level of specificity needed to bring any validity to the model

  - ➤ *Unidimensionality is required of all variables used in conjoint analysis.* Variables that are multidimensional may lead to interpretation problems. One respondent may respond to the variable with low importance, while another considers the same variable with high importance because the two respondents were considering two different dimensions of the same variable.

1) Just as found in other multivariate techniques, the independent variables should not have any substantial degree of collinearity. Collinearity typically results from the basic character of the variable itself, not from the levels of a variable.

2) The solutions are to:
   - eliminate one of the attributes
   - create "superattributes" which are combinations of the correlated variables
   - use a modified form of experimental design which is "nearly" orthogonal, but eliminates the offending attribute combinations
   - constrain the estimation of model coefficients to a prespecified relationship

➢ **Price is a unique factor**

Price is a "natural" factor due to its importance in defining value, but has the unique characteristics of being highly intercorrelated with other attributes since it is already being "traded off" in determining value (more of attribute relates to higher cost). This does not negate its use, but the researcher must be aware of the complications that may arise. Moreover, specific estimation models are available

● **Specifying the Levels of each Factor**

➢ *Balance in number of levels*: The researcher should balance the number of levels across variables. Unequal levels across variables may adversely impact the consumer's perception of relative importance of the variables.

➢ *Reasonable and believable:* The number of levels for each variable should reflect the most reasonable levels expected by the consumer. Levels outside the range of believability only weaken the model and provide spurious results.

➢ *Complexity of design:* As you increase the number of variables and the levels of each variable, you will rapidly reach a very complex design. The researcher should use only the necessary variables and required levels for each variable.

3. The researcher must determine whether an additive or an interactive composition rule is appropriate.

- *Additive model* with no interactions is normally assumed. This type of model is widely used in consumer research and simplifies the implementation process. The **interactive composition rule** allows for certain combinations of levels to differ from their addititve total (either greater or less than), similar to the interaction term in ANOVA/MANOVA.

- *All consumers are assumed to use the same choice rule.* Conjoint does not make allowances for multiple choice rules (composition rules) in the same data set. When a conjoint analysis is to be performed the researcher must establish a priori the choice rule to used for the entire group.

4. The researcher must determine how the levels of a factor are related.

- *Each type of relationship can be specified separately*; however, such a choice would produce less efficient and less reliable estimates. The researcher must consider the trade-offs of selecting a type of relationship that is most like the preference formations of consumers and of producing reliable estimates. The choices are:

    ➤ *Linear* – a linear relationship is assumed between the coefficients for each level, which must be ordered
    ➤ *Quadratic* – a curvilinear relationship (either concave or convex) is assumed among ordered levels
    ➤ *Part-worth* – each level has a uniquely estimated coefficient

5. The researcher must select a presentation method. The three most popular forms of presentation are:

- *Full Profile*: By far the most widely used, full profile presents to the respondent a series of hypothetical objects, each derived from a combination of a level from each specified independent variable. It has the advantage of being more representative of the actual decision making process followed by respondents.

- *Tradeoff*: Tradeoff considers each pair of attributes and asks respondents to indicate the preference order for each combination of attribute levels. While attempting to approximate the consumer's true nature, it too often presents an artificial decision making context.

- *Pairwise comparison*: Pairwise comparison of profiles with a complete or reduced set of attributes allows the respondent to make simple judgments about the profiles.

6. In data collection, the researcher must select a means to create the stimuli. The two basic approaches are:

- *Factorial design: all combinations of levels are utilized.* This design is *many times impractical*, unless the researcher is interested in a very small number of variables and levels. It must be used when trade-off matrices are the presentation method.

- *Fractional factorial design: a sample of the combinations are employed.* This design is used most often, primarily with pairwise or full profile presentation methods. It is essential for researchers interested in larger numbers of variables and levels. The *number of stimuli is dependent on the composition rule.* Among the most important issues in creating this type of design are:

  - Optimality – based on the *orthogonality* (independence of attributes) and *balance* (number of times each level appears)

  - Unacceptable stimuli – any stimuli whose combination of levels creates a stimuli violating the criteria of reasonableness and believability. They can be dealt with by creating another fractional design that hopefully does not have any unacceptable stimuli. A second approach is to create a *"nearly orthogonal"* design eliminating the unacceptable stimuli. Such a design should be measured for *design efficiency* (its degree of orthogonality).

  - Bridging designs – appropriate when the number of stimuli are very large, this method employs different sets of stimuli which have some stimuli in common. The common stimuli are then used to pool the differing sets in the estimation process.

7. The researcher must select a measure of preference.

- *Dependent on choice of presentation method.*
  - Trade-off method: employs only ranking data

  - Pairwise comparison method and the full-profile method: either rating or ranking.

8. The researcher must choose a means to administer the stimuli.

- *Administration*: successfully performed by person, mail or telephone with the proper planning and technical support.

Stage 3: Assumptions of Conjoint Analysis

1. Testing of Statistical Assumptions

- *Least restrictive of the dependence techniques.* Most of the tests performed in other multivariate techniques are unnecessary.

- **Theory driven design.**

  - ➢ Conjoint analysis is extremely dependent on the conceptual assumptions underlying the design.

Stage 4: Estimating the Conjoint Model and Assessing Overall Fit

1. Estimation technique must be appropriate for the type of data collected.

- *Rank order data* requires the use of a modified analysis of variance technique designed for ordinal data.

2. Must assess the overall fit of the model at both the individual and the aggregate levels.

- *Individual level*: The correlations between a person's actual response and his / her predicted response should be tested for statistical significance.

- *Validation profiles*: In order to test for overfitting of the model, researchers should plan for a validation sample of stimuli. To do so, the researcher employs more stimuli than necessary to fit the model and uses the extra data to test model accuracy.

Stage 5: Interpreting the Results

1. Analysis begins with a comparison of each variable and then an examination of the levels of each variable.

- The results of conjoint analysis provide information pertaining to each variable as a whole and to each level of each variable. A comparison between variables may be performed and then an examination of the levels of each variable. In this manner, the researcher begins to understand the relative influence of each variable and the relative influence of each level for each variable.

2. In most cases, disaggregate analysis should be used to interpret conjoint results.

- *Level of analysis*: All of the measures mentioned above are provided for each respondent in the sample (disaggregate) and also for the sample as a whole (aggregate). *Unless the researcher has reason to assume the population is homogeneous with respect to the factors being measured, disaggregate analysis is most appropriate.*

3. Next, interpret the relative importance of each attribute and each level of each attribute.

- *Importance of variable/factor:* For each respondent, conjoint analysis determines an importance value for each variable used in the analysis.

  ➤ <u>Percentage value</u> based on a range of zero to 100 percent. When summed, the importance values for all variables will total 100 percent.

- *Importance of level*: There is also a utility value for each level of each variable, providing a measure of the influence of <u>each level</u> of each variable.

  ➤ <u>Expressed in raw form (utility) with a sign indicating the relationship (positive or negative) with the dependence variable.</u> A large negative value would mean that this level of the variable was associated with lower levels of preference, while a positive value increases preference.

  ➤ <u>Partworth utilities are expressed as differences from the overall average utility</u> (similar in concept to the intercept term in regression analysis).

Stage 6: Validation of the Conjoint Results

1. The researcher should internally and externally validate conjoint analysis results.

- *Internal validation*: the researcher confirms that the choice of composition rule is most appropriate. This is usually completed in a pretest.

- *External validation*: corresponds to a test of sample representativeness. The sample should always be evaluated for population representation.

Stage 7: Applying Conjoint Analysis Results

1. The three most common applications of conjoint results are:

- *Segmentation* is the grouping of individuals with similar part-worths or importance values.

- *A marginal profitability analysis* aids in the product design process by predicting the viability of each hypothetical product, given the cost of each product and its expected market share and sales volume.

- *Choice simulators* enable the researcher to predict consumer response to market questions. For example, the market shares among any set of products can be estimated. Any number of product sets can be evaluated, varying in both the type and number of products in a set. In any application, the researcher provides the market stimuli and the simulator predicts consumer response.

Alternative Conjoint Methodologies

1. **Current research in conjoint analysis is focused on two new methodologies: adaptive or hybrid conjoint for large numbers of factors and choice-based conjoint for more realistic choice tasks.**

2. **Adaptive or Hybrid Conjoint: Dealing with a Large Number of Factors**

   - A combination of the self-explicated (see below) and part-worth model, initial responses from the respondent are used to eliminate some stimuli and focus on those *most important to that respondent*. Most often performed in a computerized version (such as ACA by Sawtooth Software).

   - Self-explicated approaches are also available, where the respondent provides factor importance and level desirability ratings, which are then combined.

3. **Choice-Based Conjoint: Adding Another Form of Realism**

   Differs from the other approaches in that instead of evaluating a single stimulus. The respondent selects one stimulus from a set of stimuli (known as a choice set). This is thought to be a more realistic task, as consumers normally choose one product from among several. The consumer also has the option of not choosing any stimulus from the set if they are all unacceptable.

   - **Unique characteristics of choice-based conjoint**

       - Stimuli Design: the choice set allows for stimuli to be judged in a more consistent manner, especially in regard to comparability
       - Estimation Technique: usually estimated with multinomial logit models, which are particularly useful in estimating interaction effects
       - Must be estimated at the aggregate level, since no single respondent could provide enough information to estimate individual-level models
       - Still in its formative stages, with limited access to computer programs

116

ANSWERS TO END-OF-CHAPTER QUESTIONS

(1)   ASK THREE OF YOUR CLASSMATES TO EVALUATE CHOICE COMBINATIONS BASED ON THESE VARIABLES AND ON LEVELS RELATIVE TO THE CHOICE OF A TEXTBOOK FOR A CLASS AND SPECIFY THE COMPOSITIONAL RULE YOU THINK THEY WILL USE.

Depth:
    a. Goes into great depth on each subject.
    b. Introduces each subject in a general overview.

Illustrations:
    a. Each chapter includes humorous pictures.
    b. Illustrative topics are presented.
    c. Each chapter contains graphics to illustrate the numeric issues.

References:
    a. Each chapter includes specific references for topics covered.
    b. General references are included at the end of the textbook.

HOW DIFFICULT WAS IT FOR RESPONDENTS TO HANDLE THE WORDY AND SLIGHTLY ABSTRACT CONCEPTS THEY WERE ASKED TO EVALUATE? HOW WOULD YOU IMPROVE ON THE DESCRIPTIONS OF THE FACTORS OR LEVELS? WHICH PRESENTATION METHOD WAS EASIER FOR THE RESPONDENTS?

Answer

Students will have a difficult time with abstract notions presented as general concepts. You can point out that for the factor: Illustrations, the three levels are not really levels, e.g. a book could have both humorous illustrations and graphics to illustrate numeric topics. Students must be careful that levels of an attribute are truly discrete levels.

The pairwise design is sometimes seen as easier to evaluate simply because the information on each concept pair is easier to process. A goal should be to make the concepts easy to perceive regardless of which design is used.

A final concern: just because levels of a factor are discrete and precise does not mean the respondent will always be capable of dealing with the information. Some people try to quantify abstract concepts only to further confuse the respondent. For example, describing the thickness of a hand lotion in terms of viscosity does not help the average respondent.

You can just let them pour the lotion at different viscosities without defining a quantification for thickness.

(2)   USING EITHER THE DIFFERENCES MODEL OR A CONJOINT PROGRAM, ANALYZE THE DATA FROM THE PRECEDING EXPERIMENT. EXAMINE THE INTERACTIONS.

Answer

You must look for interactions on a respondent by respondent basis. When stress$=0$ or R-square $= 1$, you need not look. However, when stress is not 0 and regression is not 1, it does not mean that you necessarily have an interaction. Unfortunately, with some respondents, lack of attention or consistent evaluation procedures produces poor fits that can not be explained as interaction. A crude but effective way to look for interactions is the method shown in the text. An example follows for a 3 level factor with a 2 level (with one other 2 level factor as in problem 1).

	No Interaction			Interaction	
	A1	A2		A1	A2
B1	1+4=5	7+10=17	B1	1+4=5	9+12=21
B2	2+5=7	8+11=19	B2	2+5=7	8+11=19
B3	3+6=9	9+12=21	B3	3+6=9	7+10=17

Just looking at the linear component shows:

$$5+21=9+17 \quad \text{and} \quad 5+17<9+21$$

So there is likely only a simple interaction between A & B.

(3)   DESIGN A CONJOINT ANALYSIS EXPERIMENT WITH AT LEAST FOUR VARIABLES AND TWO LEVELS OF EACH VARIABLE THAT IS APPROPRIATE TO A MARKETING DECISION. IN DOING SO, DEFINE THE COMPOSITIONAL RULE YOU WILL USE, THE EXPERIMENTAL DESIGN FOR CREATING STIMULI, AND THE ANALYSIS METHOD. USE AT LEAST FIVE RESPONDENTS TO SUPPORT YOUR LOGIC.

Answer

The student can use any number of rules found in the literature (threshold, multiplicative, etc.) but will typically find that the simple linear additive model gives a good starting point. In addition to its naive simplicity, it lends itself to classical experimental designs for administration and interpretations. The student should quickly see (as pointed out in the example problems in this manual) that with rank order data, the number of solutions are bounded and easily estimated. For those respondents for whom the model fits, the analysis task equates to just classifying the respondents into the appropriate pattern of coefficients. If the student uses a scale for obtaining evaluations in the experiment, then the rank order assumptions of MANOVA are not necessary, as the data can be assumed to not clearly represent only order of choice. If inspection of the data from a design based on a linear model suggests another decision model was used by the respondent, it is usually easier to augment the original design rather than start over. The linear model is a good starting point to suggest the direction for augmentation (which may not be obvious before the initial linear experiment).

(4) **WHAT ARE THE PRACTICAL LIMITS OF CONJOINT ANALYSIS IN TERMS OF VARIABLES OR TYPES OF VALUES FOR EACH VARIABLE? WHAT TYPE OF CHOICE PROBLEMS ARE BEST SUITED TO ANALYSIS WITH CONJOINT ANALYSIS? WHICH ARE LEAST WELL SERVED BY THE USE OF CONJOINT ANALYSIS?**

Answer

1. Conjoint analysis is limited in terms of both the type and number of attributes that can be used to describe the choice objects. Perhaps more limiting is the fact that only tangible and easily communicated attributes are feasible, since other attributes are not easily accommodated in either of the presentation methods. Moreover, the number of attributes is usually limited to less than ten, such that a choice object must be characterized on a small number of dimensions.

2. Conjoint analysis is best suited to examining the choice of hypothetical objects which have easily quantifiable characteristics. Moreover, the product must be viewed as comprised of separate attributes and not really valued by "the whole is greater than the sum of its parts" axiom.

   It is ill-suited to examine existing objects (since it is hard to describe them in simple terms) and objects which have intangible attributes (e.g., sensory-based attributes or "images" which convey an emotional appeal).

5.   HOW WOULD YOU ADVISE A MARKET RESEARCHER TO CHOOSE AMONG THE THREE TYPES OF CONJOINT METHODOLOGIES? WHAT ARE THE MOST IMPORTANT ISSUES TO CONSIDER, ALONG WITH EACH METHODOLOGY'S STRENGTHS AND WEAKNESSES?

The choice of a conjoint methodology revolves around three basic characteristics of the proposed research: (1) the number attributes, (2) level of analysis and (3) the permitted model form. Traditional conjoint analysis is characterized by a simple additive model containing up to nine factors for each individual. The adaptive conjoint method, also an additive model, can accommodate up to 30 factors for each individual. A choice-based conjoint method employs a unique form of presenting stimuli in sets rather than one-by-one. It also differs in that it directly includes interaction and must be estimated at the aggregate level. Choice of a method should be made based on the number of factors and the need to represent interaction effects.

SAMPLE MULTIPLE CHOICE QUESTIONS

Circle the letter of the item which best answers the question.

1.   Conjoint measurement attempts to:

    a.   find scales that relate the predictor variables to the response variable using a selected composition rule.
    b.   determine the underlying dimensions of the predictor and response variables.
    c.   group the respondents according to their similarity or dissimilarity
    d.   none of the above

2.   In conjoint analysis, the predictors can be

    a.   metric
    b.   nonmetric
    c.   both metric and nonmetric
    d.   none of the above

3.   Which of the following is <u>not</u> an assumption of conjoint analysis?

    a.   there is a common composition rule for all respondents in the experiment
    b.   the variables and their levels are easily communicated
    c.   there is stability of evaluation across all variables and all levels of variables
    d.   there is no measurement error

4.   Which of the following is <u>not</u> a key issue in designing a conjoint analysis experiment?

    a.   the number of variables
    b.   the style of presentation
    c.   the complexity of the variables
    d.   the research setting

5.   A _____ is one of the object's attributes which has several _____ or values.

    a.   stimulus   factors
    b.   factor   levels
    c.   part worth   factors
    d.   stimulus   interaction terms
    e.   none of the above

6. The _____ method of presentation of the objects is presumed to be most realistic.

   a. trade-off
   b. full profile
   c. both are equally realistic
   d. realism is not a consideration in presentation methods

7. The part-worth relationship which is most similar to the relationships found in past multivariate techniques is:

   a. separate
   b. quadratic
   c. linear
   d. non-linear
   e. conjoint not comparable in this regard

8. The most appropriate use of a conjoint analysis choice simulator is for:

   a. assessing the importance of new attributes
   b. incorporating new choice objects into the estimation of the part-worths
   c. assessing preferences for a specified set of objects
   d. defining segments of consumers with similar part-worth profiles
   e. all of the above are appropriate uses for choice simulators
   f. none of the above are appropriate uses for choice simulators

9. Conjoint analysis is most closely like which of these multivariate techniques?

   a. factor analysis
   b. analysis of variance (ANOVA)
   c. cluster analysis
   d. discriminant analysis
   e. multidimensional scaling

10. Which of the following is not a feature which distinguishes conjoint analysis from other multivariate techniques?

    a. can predict non-linear as well as linear relationships
    b. predicts relationships for each respondent
    c. can be estimated in which each level of a variable has no relationship to other levels
    d. a and b only
    e. a and c only
    f. b and c only

CHAPTER EIGHT
CANONICAL CORRELATION ANALYSIS

The following presentation will address the basic questions of "What?," "Why?," "When?," and "How?" as applied to canonical correlation analysis.

What is canonical correlation analysis?

1. Canonical correlation seeks the **weighted linear composite (combination) for each variate (sets of dependent or independent variables)** to maximize the overlap in their distributions.

2. **Labeling of dependent and independent is arbitrary,** since this procedure is looking for relationships and not causation.

3. Canonical correlation attempts to derive the linear composite for each side of the equation such that the correlation is maximized. **The goal is to maximize the correlation and not the variance extracted as in most other techniques.**

Why do we use canonical correlation analysis?

Canonical correlation analysis (CCA) is the "mother" multivariate model. By this, we mean that canonical correlation analysis is the model from which most other multivariate techniques can be derived. While this generalizability leads to application in almost any situation, it also brings with it a lack of specificity in interpreting results that has limited its usefulness in many situations.

When do you use canonical correlation analysis?

CCA is best suited as a descriptive technique which can define structure in both the dependent and independent variates simultaneously. Therefore, situations where a series of measures are used for both dependent and independent variates are a logical choice for application of CCA. Canonical correlation also has the ability to define structure in each variate (i.e., multiple variates representing orthogonal dimensions) which are derived to maximize their correlation. Thus, canonical correlation combines an element of exploratory data analysis within a dependence technique.

How do you use canonical correlation analysis?

Canonical correlation analyses follow a six stage model building perspective. The following are important points for each step of the process.

Stage 1: Objectives of Canonical Correlation Analysis

---

1. Three common objectives of canonical correlation analysis are:

- *Determine the magnitude of the relationships* that may exist between two sets of variables

- *Derive a variate(s)* for each set of criterion and predictor variables such that the variate(s) of each set is maximally correlated

- *Explain the nature of whatever relationships* exist between the sets of criterion and predictor variables

---

Stage 2: Designing a Canonical Correlation Analysis

---

1. Small sample sizes may have an adverse affect on canonical correlation analysis.

- *Recommended number of observations required per variable* included in the analysis is 10. Thus, if the analysis includes 8 variables (dependent and independent), the sample size should be no less than 80.

2. The selection of variables to be included in the analysis must be based on conceptual or theoretical bases.

- *Inclusion of irrelevant variables or the deletion of relevant variables* may adversely affect the entire canonical solution.

- *All dependent and all independent variables must be interrelated* to be included in the analysis.

- *The composition of the dependent and the independent variates* is critical to producing practical results.

Stage 3: Assumptions in Canonical Correlation Analysis

1. CCA employs multiple metric/nonmetric variables for either dependent or independent variables.

2. CCA assumes a linear relationship between any two variables and between variates.

- *Variable Linearity:* The correlation coefficient between any two variables is based on a linear relationship. If the relationship is nonlinear, an appropriate transformation should be performed.

- *Variate Linearity*: The variates are assumed to be linearly related. If the variates are nonlinear, the relationship will not be captured by canonical correlation analysis.

3. Each variable does not have to have a normal distribution, but multivariate normality is necessary to perform statistical inference testing.

- *Non-normal variables* can be used if the distributional form does not decrease the correlation with other variables.

- *Multivariate normality* is necessary for statistical testing, thus the researcher is encouraged to transform non-normal variables.

4. CCA is sensitive to homoscedasticity to the extent that it decreases the correlation between variables.

5. Multicollinearity in either variate confounds interpretation of canonical results.

1. The maximum number of canonical variate functions that can be extracted from the sets of variables equals the number of variables in the smallest data set, independent or dependent.

2. Canonical variates are extracted in a series of iterative steps. At each step, the factor which accounts for the maximum amount of residual variance in the set of variables is selected.

- *First factor selected accounts for the greatest variance* in the set of variables.

- *Successive factors are derived from residual variance* leftover from earlier factors.

- *First pair of canonical variates has the highest intercorrelation possible* between the two sets of variables.

- *Successive pairs of variates are orthogonal and independent* of all other variates derived from the same data set.

- *Canonical correlation squared (CC^2)* represents the amount of variance in one canonical variate that is accounted for by the other canonical variate (also called canonical roots or eigenvalues).

3. Canonical correlation maximizes variance shared and not variance extracted.

- *Objective of CCA* is to seek the **maximum correlation** or shared variance between the two sides of the equation. Canonical correlation is a descriptive procedure and not predictive. We are not looking for causal-type relationships, only correlational relationships.

4. Criteria for selecting the canonical functions to be interpreted: level of statistical significance of the function, the magnitude of the canonical correlation, and the redundancy measure for the percentage of variance accounted for from the two data sets.

- *Significance tests* -- indicate the significance of the canonical correlation and are judged against the researcher's a priori significance level. The minimum acceptable level for canonical correlation interpretation is .05.

  ➢ **The most widely used test is the F statistic** based on Rao's approximation.

- *Magnitude of the canonical relationship* -- is a measure of the size of the canonical correlations. No general guidelines have been established for the interpretation of this measure. Assessment of this measure is normally based on the contribution of the findings to better understand the research problem under study.

  ➢ <u>Redundancy index</u> is an average R^2 for canonical correlation. This measure is a summary of the ability of a set of predictor variables to account for the variation in the set of criterion variables. It is interpreted in much the same way as multiple regression's R^2 statistic, with a larger number being desired.

Stage 4: Deriving the Canonical Functions and Assessing Overall Fit

---

1. Three methods are commonly used to determine the relative importance of each of the original variables in the canonical relationships: canonical weights, canonical loadings, and canonical cross-loadings.

- *Canonical weights* The weights are examined regarding their sign and magnitude. A relatively larger weight contributes more to the function and a weight with a negative sign displays an inverse relationship with other variables.

  ➢ <u>Caution</u> must be followed in the presence of multicollinearity, which may cause a weight to be small and this may be interpreted as meaning the variable does not contribute much to the function.

  ➢ <u>Stability of the weights</u> from one sample to another should be assessed. Instability occurs when canonical correlation derives a solution for a particular sample of independent and dependent variable sets that is not generalizable to other populations/samples.

- *Canonical loadings* -- a direct assessment of each variable's contribution to its respective canonical variate. The larger the loading, the more important it is in deriving the canonical variate. It is the correlation between the original variable and its canonical variate, interpreted much the same as a **factor loading**.

  ➤ Variability may occur, as with canonical weights, in the canonical loadings from one sample to another.

- *Canonical cross-loadings* -- a measure of the correlation of each original dependent variable with the independent canonical variate.

  ➤ Direct assessment of the relationship between each dependent variable and the independent variate.

  ➤ Provide a more pure measure of the dependent-independent variable relationship and are the preferred approach to interpretation.

Stage 6: Validation and Diagnosis

---

1. Common validation methods include splitting the original data set, collecting a new data set, or testing the sensitivity of the results to removal of a variable.

- *Splitting the original data set or collecting a new data set* both compare another data set and the results to the original analysis.

- *Removing a dependent or an independent variable* from the analysis allows the researcher to assess the sensitivity and stability of the canonical correlation results.

2. Limitations of CCA which impact the results and interpretation of the analysis are:

- *CCA reflects only the variance shared* by the linear composites of the sets of variables, not the variance extracted from the variables.

- *Canonical weights are subject to a great deal of instability.*

- *Canonical weights are derived to maximize the correlation* between linear composites, not the variance extracted.

128

- *Interpretation of the canonical variates may be difficult as there are no aids for interpretation such as rotation of variates as seen in factor analysis*, since they are calculated to maximize the relationship.

- *Difficult to identify meaningful relationships between the subsets of independent and dependent variables* because precise statistics have not yet been developed to interpret canonical analysis and we must rely on inadequate measures such as loadings or cross-loadings.

• ANSWERS TO END-OF-CHAPTER QUESTIONS

(1)   UNDER WHAT CIRCUMSTANCES WOULD YOU SELECT CANONICAL CORRELATION ANALYSIS INSTEAD OF MULTIPLE REGRESSION AS THE APPROPRIATE STATISTICAL TECHNIQUE?

Answer

Canonical correlation analysis is a multivariate statistical technique which facilitates the study of interrelationships among sets of multiple criterion variables and multiple predictor variables. Multiple regression predicts a single criterion variable from a set of multiple independent variables. The number of dependent variables determines the procedure.

(2)   WHAT THREE CRITERIA SHOULD YOU USE IN DECIDING WHICH CANONICAL FUNCTIONS SHOULD BE INTERPRETED? EXPLAIN THE ROLE OF EACH.

Answer

a.   Level of statistical significance

The level of significance of a canonical correlation which is generally considered to be the minimum for interpretation is the .05 level. However, researchers frequently must accept lower levels. (The .05 and .01 levels have become standard because of the availability of tables.)

b.   Magnitude of the Canonical Relationships

The decision is usually made based on the contribution of the findings toward a better understanding of the research problem being studied. It seems logical that the guidelines used for significant factor loadings might be useful with canonical correlations.

c.   Redundancy measure of shared variance

Provides a summary measure of the ability of a set of predictor variables (taken as a set) to explain variation in the criterion variables (taken one at a time). Analogous to the R2 of multiple regression.

(3)   HOW WOULD YOU INTERPRET A CANONICAL CORRELATION ANALYSIS?

Answer

There are several methods available for interpreting canonical analysis. The authors recommend the use of cross-loadings. This involves correlating each of the original observed dependent variables directly with the independent canonical variate. Both SAS and SPSS provide cross-loadings as optional output. A second approach is the calculation of canonical loadings. Referred to sometimes as structure correlations, canonical loadings measure the simple linear correlation between an original observed variable in the dependent or independent set and the set's canonical variate. A third method (least preferred by the authors), is the use of canonical weights. This traditional approach involves examining the sign and magnitude of the canonical weight assigned to each variable in computing the canonical functions. Variables with larger weights contribute more. Those with opposite signs exhibit inverse relationships, etc. Canonical weights are interpreted much like beta weights in regression.

(4)   WHAT IS THE RELATIONSHIP BETWEEN THE CANONICAL ROOT, THE REDUNDANCY INDEX, AND MULTIPLE REGRESSION'S R^2?

Answer

The redundancy index is the equivalent of computing the squared multiple correlation coefficient between the predictor variables and each variable in the criterion set.

It is analogous to multiple regression's R^2 statistic, and its value as an index is similar. The higher the redundancy index, the greater the explanatory power of the canonical model.

(5)   WHAT ARE THE LIMITATIONS ASSOCIATED WITH CANONICAL CORRELATION ANALYSIS?

Answer

The following limitations exist:

a. The canonical correlation reflects the variance shared by the linear composites of the sets of variables, and not the variance extracted from the variables;

b. Canonical weights derived in computing canonical functions are subject to a great deal of instability;

c. Canonical weights are derived to maximize the correlation between linear composites, not to maximize the variance extracted; and

d. It is difficult to identify meaningful relationships between the subsets of independent and dependent variables because precise statistics have not yet been developed to interpret canonical analysis and we must rely on inadequate measures such as loadings and cross-loadings.

(6) WHY HAS CANONICAL CORRELATION ANALYSIS BEEN USED MUCH LESS FREQUENTLY THAN THE OTHER MULTIVARIATE TECHNIQUES?

Answer

Canonical correlation analysis (CCA) has been used much less frequently than the other multivariate techniques because:

Some researchers view CCA as a less rigorous technique since CCA places the fewest restrictions on the types of data on which it operates and is viewed as a last-ditch effort to be used when all other higher level techniques have been exhausted.

Interpretation of CCA is very subjective and requires a certain amount of skill and experience in evaluating and interpreting the canonical weights, loadings, and cross-loadings. It is very difficult to identify meaningful relationships between the subsets of independent and dependent variables because precise statistics have not yet been developed to interpret canonical analysis and must rely on inadequate measures such as loadings or cross-loadings.

SAMPLE MULTIPLE CHOICE QUESTIONS
(correct answers indicated by bolded letter)

Circle the letter of the item which best answers the question.

1. Canonical Correlation Analysis is a multivariate statistical model which makes use of:

    a. metric independent variables and nonmetric dependent variables.
    b. metric dependent variables and nonmetric independent variables.
    c. nonmetric independent variables and nonmetric dependent variables.
    d. metric independent variables and metric dependent variables.

2. Canonical Correlation Analysis facilitates the study of interrelationships among sets of:

    a. multiple independent variables and multiple dependent variables.
    b. single dependent variables and multiple independent variables.
    c. multiple dependent variables with single independent variables.
    d. multiple criterion variables with multiple dependent variables.

3. Canonical Correlation Analysis gives which important output information?

    a. a significant centroid
    b. redundancy measure
    c. standard deviation
    d. Wilk's lambda statistic

4. To determine the relative importance of each of the original variables in deriving canonical relationships, one looks at:

    a. canonical weights
    b. canonical loadings
    c. canonical cross loadings
    d. all of the above
    e. none of the above

5. The canonical correlation reflects the variance shared by the:

    a. linear composites of the sets of variables
    b. equal variance-covariance cells
    c. uncontrolled influences of the denominator
    d. nonmetric variables in the equations

6.   Successive pairs of canonical variates are based on:

   a.   composite association
   b.   linear correlation
   c.   bivariate analysis
   d.   residual variance

7.   The most accurate, but least available way to examine the statistical significance of variables in canonical correlation is done through:

   a.   canonical weights
   b.   canonical loadings
   c.   discriminant loadings
   d.   cross-canonical loadings

8.   Canonical weights are derived to:

   a.   maximize the variance that is extracted.
   b.   maximize the co-variance that is extracted.
   c.   maximize the correlation between linear composites
   d.   minimize the co-variance that is extracted.

9.   If one has five independent variables and three dependent variables, the maximum number of canonical functions that can be extracted is:

   a.   five
   b.   eight
   c.   two
   d.   three

10.   To overcome the inherent bias and uncertainty in using canonical roots as a measure of shared variance:

   a.   a correlation index has been proposed.
   b.   a redundancy index has been proposed.
   c.   a predictor index has been proposed.
   d.   a value index has been proposed.

CHAPTER NINE
CLUSTER ANALYSIS

The following presentation will address the basic questions of "What?," "Why?," "When?," and "How?" as applied to Cluster Analysis.

What is cluster analysis?

1. Cluster analysis *classifies objects or variables on the basis of the similarity* of the characteristics they possess.

2. Cluster analysis seeks to *minimize within-group variance and maximize between-group variance*.

3. The result of cluster analysis is a number of *heterogeneous groups with homogeneous contents*.

Why do we use cluster analysis?

1. Cluster analysis is the technique of choice when the objective is one of the following:

- *Data reduction*: reduces the information from an entire population or sample to information about specific, smaller subgroups. The result is a more concise, understandable description of the observations with minimal loss of information.

- *Hypotheses development*: enables development of hypotheses about the nature of the data or examination of previously stated hypotheses.

- *Classification*: sample respondents may be profiled, or classified into similar demographic, psychographic, or consumption pattern groups.

When do you use cluster analysis?

Cluster analysis is used any time the analyst wishes to group individuals or objects. As such, cluster analysis is currently used in a wide variety of disciplines, including the hard and soft sciences.

How do you use cluster analysis?

Cluster analyses follow the six stages of all multivariate techniques discussed previously.

Stage 1: Objectives of Cluster Analysis

1. While the primary objective of cluster analysis is to partition a set of objects into two or more groups based on the similarity of the objects on a set of specified characteristics, other uses of cluster analysis include exploratory analysis to develop a classification system and generating hypotheses and confirmatory analysis to test a proposed structure.

Stage 2: Research Design in Cluster Analysis

1. Results from cluster analysis are only as good as the variables included in the analysis.

- *Irrelevant variables* will have a substantive detrimental effect on the results.

- *Each variable should have a specific reason for being included.*

- *The variable should be excluded* if the researcher can not identify why it should be included in the analysis.

2. Cluster analysis is very sensitive to outliers in the dataset; therefore, the researcher should conduct a preliminary screening of the data.

- *Outliers* are either observations which are truly nonrepresentative of the population or observations which are representative of an undersampling of an actual group in the population.

- *A graphic profile diagram* may be used to identify outliers.

- *Outliers should be assessed for their representativeness* of the population and deleted if they are unrepresentative.

136

3. The researcher must specify the interobject similarity measure and the characteristics defining similarity among the objects clustered.

- *Correlational measures* represent similarity by the analyzing patterns across the variables. These measures do not consider the magnitude of the variable values, only the patterns, and thus are rarely used.

- *Distance measures* represent similarity as the proximity of observations to each other across the variables. These measures focus on the magnitude of the values, by classifying as similar those cases closest to each other.

  ➤ Euclidean distance, which is the length of the hypotenuse of a right triangle formed between the points, is the most commonly used measure.

  ➤ Standardization:

  1) Preferred measure -- Mahalanobis distance, which standardizes the data and also sums the pooled within-group variance-covariance matrices, compensating for intercorrelation among the variables.
  2) Used when the range or scale of one variable is much larger or different from the range of others.

- *Association measures* are used to represent similarity among objects measured by nonmetric terms (nominal or ordinal measurement). Often simple association measures are used to determine the degree of agreement or disagreement between a pair of cases.

Stage 3: Assumptions in Cluster Analysis

---

1. Data may be metric, nonmetric, or a combination of both.

- *All scales of measurement may be used.* But note that the use of a combination of data types will make the interpretation of the cluster analysis very tentative. The researcher should be cautious interpreting these conditions.

2. Cluster analysis assumes that the sample is truly representative of the population.

- *Outliers* which are not representative of the population should be deleted.

3. Multicollinearity among the variables may have adverse effects on the analysis.

- *Multicollinearity* causes the related variables to be weighted more heavily, thereby receiving improper emphasis in the analysis.

- One or more of the **highly collinear variables** should be deleted or use a distance measure, such as Mahalanobis distance, which compensates for this correlation.

4. Naturally-occurring groups must be present in the data.

- Cluster analysis assumes that partitions of observations in mutually exclusive groupings do exist in the sample and population.

- Cluster analysis cannot confirm the validity of these groupings. This role must be performed by the researcher by

  ➢ ensuring that theoretical justification exists for the cluster analysis, and

  ➢ perform follow-up procedures of profiling and discriminating among groups

---

Stage 4: Deriving Clusters and Assessing Overall Fit

---

1. Hierarchical clustering has two approaches: agglomerative or divisive methods.

- *Agglomerative clustering* starts with each observation as a cluster and with each step combines observations to form clusters until there is only one large cluster.

- **Divisive method** begins with one large cluster and proceeds to split into smaller clusters items that are the most dissimilar.

2. There are five measures of forming clusters in hierarchical clustering:

- *Single linkage* -- based on the shortest distance between objects
- *Complete linkage* -- based on the maximum distance between objects
- *Average linkage* -- based on the average distance between objects
- *Ward's method* -- based on the sum of squares between the two clusters summed over all variables
- *Centroid method* -- based on the distance between cluster centroids. The centroid method requires metric data and is the only method to do so.

3. Nonhierarchical clustering assigns all objects within a specified distance of the cluster seed to that cluster instead of the tree building process of hierarchical clustering. Nonhierarchical clustering has three approaches:

- *sequential threshold* -- based on one cluster seed at a time selected and membership in that cluster fulfilled before another seed is selected

- *parallel threshold* -- based on simultaneous cluster seed selection and membership threshold distance adjusted to include more or fewer objects in the clusters

- *optimizing* -- same as the others except it allows for membership reassignment of objects to another cluster based on some optimizing criterion

4. While there is no set rule as to which type of clustering to use, it is suggested that both hierarchical and nonhierarchial clustering algorithms be used.

- *First stage* -- a hierarchical cluster analysis is used to generate and profile the clusters.

- *Second stage* -- a nonhierarchical cluster analysis is used to "fine tune" the cluster membership with its switching ability. In this case, the centroids from hierarchical clustering are used as the seeds for nonhierarchical clustering.

5. There is no generally accepted single procedure for determining the number of clusters to extract. This decision should be guided by theory and the practicality of the results.

Several items in the output are available to help the analyst determine how many clusters to extract. Some of the most common methods used include the following:

- *clustering coefficient* -- a measure of the distance between two objects being combined. The actual values will depend on the clustering method and measure of similarity used.

  ➤ Coefficient size indicates the homogeneity of objects being merged. Small coefficient indicates fairly homogeneous objects are being merged, while a large coefficient is the result of very different objects being combined.

  ➤ Large increase (absolute or percentage) in the clustering coefficient is an indication of the joining of two diverse clusters, which denotes that a possible "natural grouping" existed before the clusters were joined. This then becomes one potential cluster solution.

  ➤ Researcher must then examine the possible solutions identified from the results and select one as best supportive of the research objectives. The solution's appropriateness must be confirmed with additional analyses.

- *dendrogram* -- pictorial representation of the clustering process which identifies how the observations are combined into each cluster. As the lines joining clusters become longer, the clusters are becoming increasingly more dissimilar.

- *vertical icicle* -- pictorially represents the number of objects across the top and the number of clusters down the side. The blanks represent clusters and the X's indicate the members per cluster.

  ➤ Examination of this diagram for an equal number of members in each cluster is an indication of the number of clusters to be selected.

6. When cluster solution reached, examine the structure of each cluster and determine whether or not the solution should be respecified.

7. Respecification may be needed if widely varying cluster sizes or clusters with only one to two observations are found.

Stage 5: Interpretation of the Clusters

1. Cluster centroids on each variable are a common basis of interpretation.

- *Cluster centroids* represent the average score for each group. These scores may be used to assign labels to the clusters.

- *Statistical tests* (F statistic and significance level of each variable) are provided to denote significant differences across the clusters. Only significant variables should be considered in interpreting and labeling the clusters.

- *Profiling* of the clusters may be computed with discriminant analysis, by utilizing those variables which were not used in the cluster analysis.

Stage 6: Validation and Profiling of the Clusters

1. Validation involves analyzing the cluster solution for representativeness of the population and for generalizability.

Among the available methods are:

- *New, separate sample* is cluster analyzed and compared

- *Split the sample* into two groups and cluster analyze each separately.

- *Obtain cluster centers* from one group and use them with the other groups to define clusters.

2. Profiling involves assessing how each cluster differs from the other clusters on relevant descriptive dimensions.

- Only *variables not used in the cluster analysis* are used in profiling. Often, variables used in this step are demographics, psychographics, or consumption patterns.

- *Discriminant analysis* is technique often used.

3. Predictive or criterion validity of the clusters may be tested by selecting a criterion variable that is not used in the cluster analysis and testing for its expected variability across clusters.

ANSWERS TO END-OF-CHAPTER QUESTIONS

(1) WHAT ARE THE BASIC STAGES IN THE APPLICATION OF CLUSTER ANALYSIS?

Answer

a. Partitioning - the process of determining if and how clusters may be developed.

b. Interpretation - the process of understanding the characteristics of each cluster and developing a name or label that appropriately defines its nature.

c. Profiling - stage involving a description of the characteristics of each cluster to explain how they may differ on relevant dimensions.

(2) WHAT IS THE PURPOSE OF CLUSTER ANALYSIS AND WHEN SHOULD IT BE USED INSTEAD OF FACTOR ANALYSIS?

Answer

Cluster analysis is a data reduction technique whose primary purpose is to identify similar entities from the characteristics they possess. Cluster analysis identifies and classifies objects or variables so that each object is very similar to others in its cluster with respect to some predetermined selection criteria.

As you may recall, factor analysis is also a data reduction technique and can be used to combine or condense large numbers of people into distinctly different groups within a larger population (Q factor analysis).

Factor analytic approaches to clustering respondents are based on the intercorrelations between the means and standard deviations of the respondents resulting in groups of individuals demonstrating a similar response pattern on the variables included in the analysis. In a typical cluster analysis approach, groupings are devised based on a distance measure between the respondent's scores on the variables being analyzed.

Cluster analysis should then be employed when the researcher is interested in grouping respondents based on their similarity/dissimilarity on the variables being analyzed rather than obtaining clusters of individuals who have similar response patterns.

(3)   WHAT SHOULD THE RESEARCHER CONSIDER WHEN SELECTING A SIMILARITY MEASURE TO USE IN CLUSTER ANALYSIS?

Answer

The analyst should remember that in most situations, different distance measures lead to different cluster solutions; and it is advisable to use several measures and compare the results to theoretical or known patterns. Also, when the variables have different units, one should standardize the data before performing the cluster analysis. Finally, when the variables are intercorrelated (either positively or negatively), the Mahalanobis distance measure is likely to be the most appropriate because it adjusts for intercorrelations and weighs all variables equally.

(4)   HOW DOES THE RESEARCHER KNOW WHETHER TO USE HIERARCHICAL OR NONHIERARCHICAL CLUSTER TECHNIQUES? UNDER WHICH CONDITIONS WOULD EACH APPROACH BE USED?

Answer

The choice of a hierarchical or nonhierarchical technique often depends on the research problem at hand. In the past, hierarchical clustering techniques were more popular with Ward's method and average linkage being probably the best available. Hierarchical procedures do have the advantage of being fast and taking less computer time, but they can be misleading because undesirable early combinations may persist throughout the analysis and lead to artificial results. To reduce this possibility, the analyst may wish to cluster analyze the data several times after deleting problem observations or outlines.

However, the K-means procedure appears to be more robust than any of the hierarchical methods with respect to the presence of outliers, error disturbances of the distance measure, and the choice of a distance measure. The choice of the clustering algorithm and solution characteristics appears to be critical to the successful use of CA.

If a practical, objective, and theoretically sound approach can be developed to select the seeds or leaders, then a nonhierarchical method can be used. If the analyst is concerned with the cost of the analysis and has an a priori knowledge as to initial starting values or number of clusters, then a hierarchical method should be employed.

Punj and Stewart (1983) suggest a two-stage procedure to deal with the problem of selecting initial starting values and clusters. The first step entails using one of the hierarchical methods to obtain a first approximation of a solution. Then select candidate number of clusters based on the initial cluster solution, obtain centroids, and eliminate outliers. Finally, use an iterative partitioning algorithm using cluster centroids of preliminary analysis as starting points (excluding outliers) to obtain a final solution.

Punj, Girish and David Stewart, "Cluster Analysis in Marketing Research: Review and Suggestions for Application," _Journal of Marketing Research_, 20 (May 1983), pp. 134-148.

(5) HOW CAN YOU DECIDE HOW MANY CLUSTERS TO HAVE IN YOUR SOLUTION?

Answer

Although no standard objective selection procedure exists for determining the number of clusters, the analyst may use the distances between clusters at successive steps as a guideline. In using this method, the analyst may choose to stop when this distance exceeds a specified value or when the successive distances between steps make a sudden jump. Also, some intuitive conceptual or theoretical relationship may suggest a natural number of clusters. In the final analysis, however, it is probably best to compute solutions for several different numbers of clusters and then to decide among the alternative solutions based upon a priori criteria, practical judgment, common sense, or theoretical foundation.

(6) WHAT IS THE DIFFERENCE BETWEEN THE INTERPRETATION STAGE AND THE PROFILING STAGE?

Answer

The interpretation stage involves examining the statements that were used to develop the clusters in order to name or assign a label that accurately describes the nature of the clusters.

The profiling stage involves describing the characteristics of each cluster in order to explain how they may differ on relevant dimensions. Profile analysis focuses on describing not what directly determines the clusters but the characteristics of the clusters after they are identified. The emphasis is on the characteristics that differ significantly across the clusters, and in fact could be used to predict membership in a particular attitude cluster.

(7) HOW DO RESEARCHERS USE THE GRAPHICAL PORTRAYALS OF THE CLUSTER PROCEDURE?

Answer

The hierarchical clustering process may be represented graphically in several ways; nested groupings, a vertical icicle diagram, or a dendogram. The researcher would use these graphical portrayals to better understand the nature of the clustering process. Specifically, the graphics might provide additional information about the number of clusters that should be formed as well as information about outlier values that resist joining a group.

SAMPLE MULTIPLE CHOICE QUESTIONS

Circle the letter of the item which best answers the question.

1.   Cluster analysis is used for:

    a.   hypothesis testing of differences among groups of observations
    b.   identify the similarities among the observations of a sample
    c.   assess the characteristics of the sample most important in defining similarities among the sample
    d.   define "natural groupings," if any, among observations based on their characteristics

2.   Euclidean or Mahalanobis distances are among the most common measures of:

    a.   linkage methods
    b.   hierarchical algorithms
    c.   interobject similarity
    d.   nonhierarchical algorithms

3.   The agglomerative procedure most likely to produce equal size clusters is:

    a.   Ward's method
    b.   single linkage
    c.   centroid method
    d.   complete linkage

4.   The process of combining observations in a stepwise process until only a single cluster remains is:

    a.   divisive procedure
    b.   sequential threshold procedure
    c.   parallel threshold procedure
    d.   agglomerative procedure

5.   An objective of cluster analysis is to:

    a.   define a relationship between group membership and characteristics of the observations
    b.   define similarity based on a series of characteristics of the observations
    c.   develop a representative profile of the population in terms of characteristics
    d.   identify the most distinguishing characteristics of the sample

6. Cluster analysis is best seen as a data reduction technique when it:

    a. defines the sample in a small number of clusters
    b. represents similarity in a single multivariate measure
    c. identifies the most distinguishing characteristics of the differences among clusters
    d. a and c
    e. none of the above, is not a data reduction technique

7. In the absence of absolute guidelines, the number of clusters selected to represent the "natural groupings" of the sample are determined by:

    a. theoretical or conceptual guidelines
    b. measures of internal consistency
    c. practical considerations
    d. only can make the decision based on all of these measures

8. The validation stage involves:

    a. ensuring that the cluster solution is representative of the population
    b. assessing the accuracy of the similarity measure used
    c. determining that significant differences do exist between the clusters based on the characteristics used to define similarity
    d. all of the above

9. The linkage technique that minimizes the effects of extreme observations is:

    a. complete linkage
    b. Ward's method
    c. single linkage
    d. average linkage

10. Which of the following is of most concern when using a nonhierarchcial technique?

    a. the measure of similarity
    b. the linkage method
    c. the specification of seed points
    d. construction of the dendogram

Additional Notes:

CHAPTER TEN
MULTIDIMENSIONAL SCALING

The following presentation will address the basic questions of "What?," "Why?," "When?," and "How?" as applied to multidimensional scaling.

What is multidimensional scaling?

1. Multidimensional scaling (MDS) is essentially an **exploratory technique** designed to identify the evaluative dimensions employed by respondents and represent the respondents' perceptions of objects spatially.

2. These visual representations are referred to as **spatial maps**.

3. Two objectives of the visual display:

- *Portrayal of the perceptual dimensions* used by the respondents when evaluating the stimuli. From this, we have a better understanding of the similarities and dissimilarities between objective and perceptual dimensions.

- *Assessment of individual objects* for their perceptual location and their relative location to other objects.

Why do we use multidimensional scaling?

Its primary strength is its decompositional nature. MDS does not require the specification of the attributes used in evaluation. Rather, it employs a global measure of evaluation, such as similarity among objects, and then infers the dimensions of evaluation that constitute the overall evaluation. In this manner it "decomposes" the overall evaluation into dimensions.

This strength also gives rise to its primary disadvantage: the inability to precisely define the perceptual dimensions of evaluation. The researcher must attempt to identify these dimensions with additional analyses. In many cases identification can be made, but it is possible that MDS will result in perceptual dimensions that cannot be identified in terms of existing attributes.

When do you use multidimensional scaling?

Multidimensional scaling is best used as an exploratory tool in identifying the perceptual dimensions used in the evaluation of a set of objects. Its use of only global judgments and ability to be "attribute-free" provide the researcher with an analytical tool minimizing the potential bias from improper specification of the attributes characteristic of the objects.

How do you use multidimensional scaling?

Multidimensional scaling analyses follow a six stage model building perspective.

```
╔══════════════════════════════════════════════════════════════╗
║  Stage 1: Objectives of Multidimensional Scaling Analysis     ║
╚══════════════════════════════════════════════════════════════╝
```

1. Multidimensional scaling has two primary objectives:

- *Identify unrecognized dimensions* affecting behavior.

- *Obtain comparative evaluations of objects* when the specific bases of comparison are unknown or undefinable.

2. Multidimensional scaling is defined through three decisions: selection of the objects to be evaluated, choice of similarity or preference data, and choice of individual or group level analysis.

- *Selection of objects* -- All *relevant objects* must be included in the analysis. The omission of relevant objects or the inclusion of irrelevant objects will greatly influence the results. Relevancy is determined by the research questions.

- *Choice of similarity or preference data* -- The researcher must evaluate the research question and decide whether he or she is interested in respondents' evaluations of how similar one object is to another or of how a respondent feels (like / dislike) about one object compared to another.

150

- *Aggregate versus disaggregate analysis* -- the researcher must decide whether he or she is interested in producing output on a per subject basis or on a group basis.

    ➤ Aggregate analysis creates a single map for the group, resulting in an analysis of the "average respondent."

    ➤ Disaggregate analysis examines each respondent separately, creating a separate perceptual map for each respondent.

    ➤ Recommendation: disaggregate method of analysis due to representation problems in attempting to combine respondents for aggregate analysis.

Stage 2: Research Design of Multidimensional Scaling Analysis

1. **Assessing similarity is the most fundamental decision in perceptual mapping, with two approaches available: the decompositional (attribute-free) and compositional (attribute-based) approaches.**

    - *Decompositional*: measures the overall impression or evaluation of an object, or a global measure of similarity, and then derives spatial positions in multidimensional space to reflect these perceptions.

        ➤ Advantages:
            1. Requires only that respondents give overall perceptions of objects; they are not required to detail the attributes used in evaluation.
            2. Each respondent gives a full assessment of similarities among all objects, therefore maps can be developed for each respondent or aggregated to a composite map.
        ➤ Disadvantages:
            1. Research has no objective basis provided by the respondent which identifies the dimensions of evaluation.
            2. Solutions require substantial researcher judgment.

- *Compositional*: measures an impression or evaluation for each combination of specific attributes, combines the set of specified attributes in a linear combination, and derives evaluative dimensions for object positioning.

  - ➤ Advantages:
    1. Explicit descriptions of the dimensions underlying the perceptual space.
    2. Able to represent both attributes and objects on a single perceptual map.

  - ➤ Disadvantages:
    1. The similarity between objects is limited to only the attributes which are rated by the respondents
    2. The research must assume some method of combining these attributes to represent overall similarity. This chosen method may or may not represent the respondent's thinking.
    3. The data collection effort is substantial.
    4. Results are not available for the individual respondent.

2. The analyst must ensure that the objects selected for analysis do have some basis of comparison.

Just asking respondents for comparative responses between objects does not mean that underlying evaluative dimensions exist.

3. The number of objects must be determined while balancing two issues: a greater number of objects to ensure adequate information for higher dimensional solutions versus the increased effort demanded of the respondent as the number of objects increases.

- *Rule of thumb: more than four objects for each derived evaluative dimension*. Thus, at least five objects are required for a one dimensional perceptual map.

- *Violating the rule of thumb*: having less than the suggested number of objects for a given dimensionality causes an *inflated estimate of fit* and may adversely impact validity of the resulting perceptual maps.

4. Multidimensional scaling produces metric output for both metric and nonmetric input.

- *Input measures of similarity may be metric or nonmetric*. The results from both types are very similar, meaning that the researcher's choice is dependent mostly on the preferred mode of data collection.

5. Choice of using either similarity or preference data based on research objectives.

- *Similarity data* -- represent perceptions of attribute similarities of the specified objects, but do not offer any direct insights into the determinants of choice among the objects.

  ➤ Comparability of objects: Since similarities data investigate the question of which stimuli are the most similar and which are the most dissimilar, the analyst must be able to assume that all pairs of stimuli may be compared by the respondents.

  ➤ Three procedures for data collection:

    1. comparison of paired objects -- rank or rate similarity of all object pair combinations
    2. confusion data -- subjective clustering of objects
    3. derived measures -- scores given to stimuli by respondents

- *Preference data* -- reflect the preference order among the set of objects, but are not directly related to attributes, since we are not able to demonstrate the correspondence among attributes and choice.

  ➤ Nature of preference data: arrange the stimuli in terms of dominance relationships. The stimuli are ordered according to the preference for some property of the stimuli.

  ➤ Data collection modes:
    1. direct ranking -- objects ranked from most preferred to least preferred
    2. paired comparisons (when presented with all possible pair combinations, the most preferred object in each is chosen)

- *Combination approach*: Methods are available for combining the two approaches, but in each instance the analyst must assume the inference can be made between attributes and preference without being directly assessed.

Stage 3: Assumptions of Multidimensional Scaling Analysis

1. Not all respondents will perceive a stimulus to have the same dimensionality.

A dimension of the stimuli that one respondent feels is quite important may be of little consequence to another. All respondents will not use the same dimensions for evaluating stimuli.

2. Not all respondents will attach the same level of importance to a dimension, even if all respondents perceive the dimension.

Although two respondents may be aware of an attribute of a product, they may not both attach equal importance to this dimension. Thus, respondents may view different dimensions as important.

3. Respondents' dimensions and level of importance will change over time.

While it would be very convenient for marketers if respondents would always use the same decision process with the same stimuli dimensions, this is not the case. Over time, respondents will assign different levels of importance to the same dimensions of a stimuli or may even change the dimensions of the stimuli that they evaluate completely. Changes in respondents' lives are reflected in their evaluation of stimuli.

Stage 4: Deriving the MDS Solution and Assessing Overall Fit

NOTE: Given the wide number of techniques encompassed under the general technique of perceptual mapping, we are unable to discuss each separately. The instructor is encouraged to examine the annotated computer outputs for the various techniques in the third section of the instructor's manual, which gives a brief description of the major elements of each method. The following discussion will center on general issues in perceptual mapping.

154

1. How does MDS determine the optimal positioning of objects in perceptual space?

- *Five step procedure*: Most MDS programs follow a five step procedure which involves selection of a configuration, comparison to fit measures, and reduction of dimensionality.

- *Primary criterion for determining an optimal position* is the preservation of the ordered relationship between the original rank data and the derived distances between points.

- *Degenerate solutions*: The researcher should be aware of degenerate solutions, which are inaccurate perceptual maps. Degenerate solutions may be identified by a circular pattern of objects or a clustered pattern of objects at two ends of a single dimension.

2. How is the number of dimensions to be included in the perceptual map determined?

- *Tradeoff of best fit with the smallest number of dimensions possible.* Interpretation of more than three dimensions is difficult.

- *Three approaches for determining the number of dimensions:*

  ➤ Subjective evaluation: The researcher evaluates the spatial maps and determines whether or not the resulting configuration looks reasonable.

  ➤ Stress measurement: measures the proportion of variance in the data that is not accounted for by the model. It is the opposite of the fit index.

    1. Desire a low stress index, since stress is minimized when the objects are placed in a configuration such that the distances between the objects best matches the original distances.

    2. Scree plot of stress index: The stress measure for models with varying numbers of dimensions may be plotted to form a scree plot as in factor analysis. The interpretation of this plot is the same, where the analyst looks for the bend in the plot line.

  ➤ Overall fit index: a squared correlation index which indicates the amount of variance in the data that can be accounted for by the model. This is a measure of how well the model fits the data. Desired levels of the fit index are similar to those desired when using regressions R^2.

- *Parsimony*: parsimony should be sought in selecting the number of dimensions. The stress measure and the overall fit index react much the same as R^2 in regression. As you add dimensions, the fit index always improves and stress always decreases. Thus, the analyst must make a trade-off between the fit of the solution and difficulty of interpretation due to the number of dimensions.

3. With preference data, three additional issues are 1) estimation of the ideal point explicitly or implicitly, 2) use of an internal or external analysis, and 3) portrayal of ideal point.

- *Ideal point estimation*: ideal points (preferred combination of perceived attributes) may be determined by explicit or implicit estimation procedures.

  ➢ <u>Explicit estimation</u>: respondents are asked to identify or rate a hypothetical ideal combination of attributes

  ➢ <u>Implicit estimation</u>: an ideal combination of attributes is empirically determined from respondents' responses to preference measure questions

- *Internal versus external analysis*

  ➢ <u>Internal analysis</u> develops spatial maps solely from preference data.

  ➢ <u>External analysis</u> fits ideal points based on preference data to a stimulus space developed from similarities data.

  ➢ <u>Recommendation</u>: external analysis performed due to computational difficulties with internal analysis and since perceptual space (preference) and evaluative space (similarities) may not contain the same dimensions with the same salience.

- *Vector or point representation of ideal point* -- ideal point is the most preferred combination of dimensions.

  ➢ <u>Point representation</u> is location of most preferred combination of dimensions from the consumer's standpoint.

  ➢ <u>Vectors</u> are lines extended from the origin of the graph toward the point which represents the combination of dimensions specified as ideal.

  ➢ <u>Difference in representation</u>: with a point representation, deviance in any direction leads to a less preferred object, while with a vector, less preferred objects are those located in the opposite direction from which the vector is pointing.

156

Stage 5: Interpreting the MDS Results

1. For decompositional methods, the analyst must identify and describe the perceptual dimensions. Procedures for identification of dimensions may be objective or subjective.

- *Subjective procedures*: the researcher or the respondent visually inspects the perceptual map and identifies the underlying dimensions. This is the best approach when the dimensions are highly intangible or affective / emotional.

- *Objective procedures*: formal methods, such as PROFIT, are used to empirically derive underlying dimensionality from attribute ratings.

2. When using compositional methods, the analyst should compare the perceptual map against other measures of perception for interpretation.

- *Perceptual map positions* are totally defined by the attributes specified by the researcher.

Stage 6: Validating the MDS Results

1. Validation will help ensure generalizability across objects and to the population.

- *Split-samples or multi-samples* may be utilized to compare MDS results.

- *Only the relative positions of objects can be compared* across MDS analyses. Underlying dimensions across analyses cannot be compared.

- *Bases of comparisons across analyses*: visual or based on a simple correlation of coordinates.

Multi-approach method: applying both decompositional and compositional methods to the same sample and looking for convergence.

CORRESPONDENCE ANALYSIS

Correspondence analysis (CA) is another form of perceptual mapping that involves the use of contingency or cross-tabulation data. Its application is becoming widespread within many areas, both practitioner and academic. The following sections detail some of the unique aspects of correspondence analysis.

Stage 1: Objectives of Correspondence Analysis

1. Correspondence analysis will accommodate both nonmetric data and nonlinear relationships.

- *Contingency tables* are used to transform nonmetric data to metric form.

- *Dimensional reduction* is performed in a manner similar to factor analysis.

- *Performs perceptual mapping* where categories may be represented in multi-dimensional space.

Stage 2: Research Design of Correspondence Analysis

1. Correspondence analysis requires only a rectangular data matrix of nonnegative data.

- Rows and columns do not have predefined meanings, but represent responses to categorical variables.

- The categories for a row or column may be a single variable or a set of variables.

Stage 3: Assumptions of Correspondence Analysis

1. Unlike other multivariate techniques, correspondence analysis does not have a strict set of assumptions. The researcher need only be concerned with including all relevant attributes.

Stage 4: Deriving CA Results and Assessing Overall Fit

1. Correspondence analysis derives a single representation of categories (both rows and columns) in the same multi-dimensional space.

2. The researcher must identify the number and importance of the dimensions.

   • *Eigenvalues* are provided to aid the researcher in determining the appropriate number of dimensions to select and in evaluating the relative importance of each dimension.

Stage 5: Interpreting CA Results

1. The degree of similarity among categories is directly proportional to the proximity of categories in perceptual space.

   Although much debate centers around the issue, proximities should only be compared within rows or within columns.

Stage 6: Validation of the Results

1. Generalizability of the results may be confirmed by split-sample or multi-sample analyses.

2. The researcher should also assess the sensitivity of the analysis to the addition or deletion of certain objects and / or attributes.

(1)   **HOW DOES MDS DIFFER FROM OTHER INTERDEPENDENCE TECHNIQUES (CLUSTER AND FACTOR ANALYSIS)?**

<u>Answer</u>

Multidimensional scaling (MDS) is a family of techniques which helps the analyst to identify key dimensions underlying respondents' evaluations of objects. MDS techniques enable the researcher to represent respondents' perceptions spatially; that is, to create visual displays that represent the dimensions perceived by the respondents when evaluating stimuli (e.g., brands, objects).

MDS differs from cluster and factor analysis in that it provides a visual representation of individual and group respondents' perceptions of the object(s), while cluster and factor analysis provide a classification of objects or variables so that each object is very similar to others in its cluster.

(2)   **WHAT IS THE DIFFERENCE BETWEEN PREFERENCE DATA AND SIMILARITIES DATA, AND HOW DOES IT IMPACT THE RESULTS OF MDS PROCEDURES?**

<u>Answer</u>

In obtaining preference data from respondents, the stimuli are ordered in terms of the preference for some property. When collecting similarities data, the researcher is trying to determine which items are most similar to each other and which are most dissimilar. Preference data allow the researcher to view the location of objects in a spatial map when distance implies differences in preference.

The choice of input data is important to the researcher when using MDS since an individual's perception of objects in a preference context may be different from that in a similarity context. For instance a particular dimension may be very useful in describing the differences between two objects but is of no consequence in determining preferences. Therefore, two objects could be perceived as different in a similarities-based map but similar in a preference-based spatial map. In employing MDS the researcher should identify which type of output information is needed before deciding on the form of input data. For example, if a company is interested in determining how similar/dissimilar their product is to all competing products, then similarities data would be required. However, if the researcher is interested in respondent's preferences for one brand over another, then preference data is required.

(3)   HOW ARE IDEAL POINTS USED IN MDS PROCEDURES?

Answer

Ideal points may be used to represent the most preferred combination of perceived attributes (i.e., an ideal product), or may be used to define relative preference so that products further from the ideal should be less preferred. In determining ideal points, the researcher may use either explicit or implicit estimation.

Explicit estimation involves having the respondents rate a hypothetical ideal on the same attributes on which the other stimuli were rated. There are several procedures for implicitly positioning ideal points. One method is to locate the ideal point as close as possible to the most preferred object and as distant as possible from the least preferred object. Implicit estimation positions an ideal point in a defined perceptual space such that the distance from the ideal conveys changes in preference.

(4)   HOW DO METRIC AND NON-METRIC MDS PROCEDURES DIFFER?

Answer

Nonmetric methods assume ordinal input and metric output, and the distance output by the MDS procedure may be assumed to be approximately internally scaled.

Metric methods assume that input as well as output are metric, which allows the researcher to strengthen the relationship between the final output dimensionality and the input data.

(5)   HOW CAN THE ANALYST DETERMINE WHEN THE "BEST" MDS SOLUTION HAS BEEN OBTAINED?

The objective of the analyst should be to obtain the best fit with the smallest number of dimensions, which requires a trade-off between the fit of the solution and the number of dimensions. Interpretation of solutions derived in more than three dimensions is extremely difficult and is usually not worth the improvement in fit.

The analyst may also use an index of fit to determine the number of dimensions. The index of fit (or R-square) is a squared correlation index that can be interpreted as indicating the proportion of variance of the disparities that can be accounted for by the MDS procedure. Measures of .60 or better are considered acceptable; the higher the R-square, the better the fit.

161

A third approach is to use a measure of stress. Stress measures the proportion of the variance of the disparities that is not accounted for by the MDS model.

(6) HOW DOES THE RESEARCHER GO ABOUT IDENTIFYING THE DIMENSIONS IN MDS? COMPARE THIS PROCEDURE WITH THAT FOR FACTOR ANALYSIS.

Answer

1. The analyst can adopt several procedures for identifying the underlying dimensions:

(a)   Respondents may be asked to interpret the dimensionality subjectively by inspecting the maps.

(b)   If the data were obtained directly, the respondents may be asked (after stating the similarities and/or preferences) to identify the characteristics most important to them in stating these values. The set of characteristics can then be screened for values that match the relationships portrayed in the maps.

(c)   The subjects may be asked to evaluate the stimuli on the basis of research-determined criteria (usually objective values) and researcher perceived subjective values. These evaluations can be compared to the stimuli distances on a dimension-by-dimension basis for labeling the dimensions.

(d)   Attribute or ratings data may be collected in the original research to assist in labeling the dimensions. Specific programs, such as PROFIT (PROPerty FITting), are available for this specific purpose.

2. The procedure for labeling the dimensions in MDS is much more subjective and requires additional skill and experience in analyzing the results. While the labeling of factors is also met with its share of subjectivity, the researcher may rely on "rules of thumb" for use in determining which items load on which factor, the number of factors to extract, and the naming of factors.

(7) COMPARE AND CONTRAST CORRESPONDENCE ANALYSIS TO THE MDS TECHNIQUES.

Correspondence analysis is a compositional perceptual mapping technique which relies on the association among nominally scaled variables. Measures of similarity are based on the chi-square metric derived from a crosstabulation table. It has the unique feature of spatially representing both objects and attributes on the same spatial map.

(8)   DESCRIBE HOW "CORRESPONDENCE" OR ASSOCIATION IS DERIVED FROM A CONTINGENCY TABLE.

Correspondence analysis allows the representation of the rows and columns of a contingency table in joint space. Using the totals for each category an expected value is calculated for each cell. Then the difference between the expected and actual is calculated. Using this value a chi-square statistic is formed for each cell as the squared difference divided by the expected value. The chi-square values can be converted to similarity measures by applying the opposite sign of their difference. The similarity measure provides a standardized measure of association that can be plotted in an appropriate number of dimensions (number of rows or columns minus one).

SAMPLE MULTIPLE CHOICE QUESTIONS

Circle the letter of the item which best answers the question.

1. Multidimensional scaling is used for:
    a. differentiating multivariate from univariate variables.
    b. testing the hypothesis that the group means of two or more groups are equal.
    c. analyzing the interrelationships among a large number of variables, and then explaining these variables in terms of their common, underlying factors.
    d. transforming unidimensional expressions of relationships into multidimensional expressions of these same relationships.

2. The data that was gathered by having subjects evaluate stimuli and order them in preference according to some property is called:

    a   factor data
    b. preference data
    c. predictor data
    d. treatment data

3. In MDS, if we locate the point which represents the most preferred combination of perceived attributes, one would have a spatial representation of a subject's

    a. ideal stimuli
    b. component stimuli
    c. main stimuli
    d. optimal stimuli

4. Multidimensional scaling is an:

    a. interdependence method
    b. dependence method
    c. classification method
    d. collinear method

5. Multidimensional scaling categorizes variables according to the:

    a. level of measurement assessed for input and output.
    b. aggregate versus disaggregate data.
    c. interval versus external data.
    d. a, b, c, only
    e. none of the above

164

6. In MDS, nonmetric methods assume the use of:

    a.   ordinal input
    b.   metric output
    c.   nominal input
    d.   nonmetric output
    e.   c, d only
    f.   a, b only

7. In MDS, metric methods assume the use of:

    a.   nonmetric input and nonmetric output.
    b.   metric input and metric output.
    c.   nominal input and ordinal output
    d.   factor input and trace output.

8. One procedure for gathering preference data is to rate each stimuli on a(n):

    a.   implicit scale
    b.   explicit scale
    c.   disjoint scale
    d.   factor scale

9. _____ is the perceptual mapping technique based on the association of nominal data.

    a.   correspondence analysis
    b.   individual difference analysis (INDSCAL)
    c.   property fitting (PROFIT)
    d.   internal preference analysis
    e.   external preference analysis

10. Which of the following is not an assumption of MDS?

    a.   all respondents will perceive objects in the same dimensionality
    b.   respondents place different levels of importance on the dimensions of an object
    c.   perceptions are not stable over time
    d.   all of the above are assumptions of MDS

Supplemental Notes:

CHAPTER ELEVEN
STRUCTURAL EQUATION MODELING

The following presentation will address the basic questions of "What?," "Why?," "When?," and "How?" as applied to structural equation modeling.

What is structural equation modeling?

1. Structural equation modeling (SEM) *combines two different aspects of multivariate analysis*: the estimation of multiple interrelated dependence relationships (similar to separate regression equations) while employing multiple indicators for a single independent or dependent variable (similar to factor analysis).

2. This merging of multivariate techniques results in a unique analysis method which can *integrate measurement error in the estimation of dependence relationship*s, thus providing a more valid assessment of relationships. Given this increased capacity for analytical precision, theoretical rationale and justification plays a critical role in structural equation model formulation and testing.

3. The analyst *must think in terms of interrelated relationships*, most often depicted in what are termed path models. In doing so, constructs become the basic elements for which the analyst can define one or more indicators (variables used to measure the construct). Through the indicators, the concept of measurement error is introduced into model estimation.

Why do we use structural equation modeling?

Structural equation modeling has been proposed to be the appropriate technique for true theory testing due to two key aspects. Most distinctive is its ability to incorporate measurement error into the estimation of relationships between constructs. This allows for the researcher to identify the "true" relationship after measurement error is accounted for. It also allows for constructs to be represented by several measures (indicators), thus providing the researcher with a more realistic and valid means of construct operationalization.

When do you use structural equation modeling?

Structural equation modeling can be used with any type of dependence relationship, but is most suited to the estimation of a series of simultaneous equations with multiple indicator constructs. Such situations can arise both in applied and academic research. SEM is not the tool of only academic research, but any user should note the complexity of the analysis whatever the application.

How do you use structural equation modeling?

Structural equation modeling follows a seven stage model building approach that differs slightly from the six stage process used in previous chapters.

Stage 1: Developing a Theoretically Based Model

---

1. Structural equation modeling (SEM) must be guided by theory.

- **Theory-driven**: It is imperative that the analyst only employ structural equation modeling (SEM) when theory guides the analysis. It is a confirmatory technique which has little use in exploratory analysis.

- *Control of the analysis:* SEM does not have "default" values or such features as "stepwise" procedures which can assist in model specification. Instead, the analyst must totally specify the model form and then test it with the data.

- *Sources of theory:* Theory may be based on empirical research from academic or commercial sources or derived from practical experience. The critical element is that the analyst specifies the relationships and then empirically tests them against the data provided.

2. Specification error (the omission of one or more key predictive variables) is the most critical error in developing theoretically based models.

- *Specification error* will bias the assessment of the importance of the other predictor variables in the model.

- *Avoiding specification error*: The researcher should include all variables which are of practical concern to the research model being tested. However, the researcher must also keep in mind that models containing in excess of 20 constructs are difficult to manage.

Stage 2: Constructing a Path Diagram of Causal Relationships

1. Path diagrams identify exogenous and endogenous constructs and the relationships among these constructs.

- *Exogenous construct*: a construct from which structural relationships originate (i.e. constructs which only have arrows originating from them).

- *Endogenous construct*: a construct which is based on the inputs of one or more constructs (i.e. a construct which has one or more arrows leading into it). Endogenous constructs may also be determinants for other endogenous constructs.

- *Representation:* Relationships among constructs are represented by arrows.

  ➤ <u>Straight arrows</u> indicate a direct causal relationship from one construct to another.

  ➤ <u>Curved line</u> between constructs indicates a correlation.

2. Two assumptions underlie path diagrams.

- *Completeness*: All causal relationships are specified in the path diagram. The researcher should theoretically justify all included and omitted paths between constructs.

- *Linearity:* The relationships among the constructs are assumed to be linear.

Stage 3: Converting the Path Diagram into a Set of Structural and Measurement Models

1. The researcher must:

- **define the structural equations linking the constructs (structural model),**

- **specify the variable(s) which will be used to measure the constructs (measurement model)**

- **identify the matrices which define the hypothesized correlations among constructs.**

  - ➤ *Structural model* -- defines the relationships between constructs (exogenous and endogenous) in the multiple dependence equations.

    1. Each endogenous construct is the dependent variable in a separate equation.

    2. For each equation, the independent variables are all constructs at the end of the arrows leading into the endogenous construct. These independent variables may be exogenous or endogenous constructs.

  - ➤ *Measurement model* -- identifies the individual variables which are used to measure exogenous and endogenous constructs.

    1. Specification: Since SEM is a confirmatory analysis, the researcher has complete control over variables used to describe each construct.

    2. Reliability of the indicators (variables used to measure each construct) should be either empirically estimated in model estimation or specified as fixed.

       - Single item measure must "fix" reliability based on previous research or established scales with known reliabilities
       - Two-stage analysis whereby the measurement model is estimated first, then the reliabilities of constructs are "fixed" and the structural model is estimated

> *Correlations among constructs and indicators*

1. Exogenous constructs are often correlated, representing a shared influence on the endogenous constructs.

2. Endogenous constructs should not be correlated, since a correlation would confound interpretation.

3. Indicators may be correlated in special situations, but are recommended for use only in certain situations, such as a longitudinal study where there are known effects from the measurement or data collection process.

Stage 4: Choosing the Input Matrix Type and Estimating the Proposed Model

1. **Correlations versus Covariances: The focus of SEM is on the pattern of relationships across respondents. For this reason, SEM utilizes matrices, not individual observations, as input data. The researcher must select either a correlation or a covariance matrix.**

   - *Covariances* are the input data upon which SEM was originally formulated and is the preferred data for theory testing.

   - *Correlations* are permissible when the analyst is interested only in the patterns among constructs and not in the total explanation of a construct. Correlations are preferred input for confirmatory factor analysis.

   - *Computation*: The most widely used means of computing correlations and covariances is the Pearson product-moment correlation, which assumes metric measurement.

2. **Sample size is important to the estimation and interpretation of SEM results.**

   - *Sample size ratio:* The sample size should be large enough to include 5 observations for each estimated parameter.

- **<u>Minimum sample size:</u>** At a minimum to ensure appropriate use of the maximum likelihood estimation, the sample size should be 100.

- **Large sample sizes:** Sample sizes greater than 400-500 risk getting all goodness-of-fit measures which indicate poor fit due to over sensitivity in detecting differences in the data.

- *Optimal:* The optimal, or critical sample size is 200.

- *Impact:* Sample size provides the basis for estimating sampling error, a critical element in maximum likelihood estimation.

3. The researcher must select a computer program for estimation procedures.

- **LISREL** (LInear Structural RELations) is the most widely used program.

- *Other programs are available:* EQS, COSAN, CALIS (SAS),and AMOS (SPSS)

Stage 5: Assessing the Identification of the Structural Model

---

1. The structural model must be identified.

- *Identification:* satisfies number of equations versus number of unknowns. An identification problem exists when the proposed model is unable to generate unique estimates.

- *Symptoms of an identification problem include*: very large standard errors for one or more coefficients, inability of the program to invert the information matrix, wildly unreasonable estimates or impossible estimates, and high correlations (.90 or greater) among estimated coefficients.

- *Testing for identification problems*: the researcher may re-estimate the model with different starting values or fix a single coefficient to its estimated value and re-estimate the equation. A large variation in overall model fit may be an indication of identification problems.

- *Three common sources of identification problems:* large number of estimated coefficients relative to the number of covariances or correlations (which leads to a small degrees of freedom), the use of reciprocal effects (i.e. two-way causal arrows), or the failure to fix the scale of a construct.

- *Remedy*: To solve identification problems, the researcher should define more constraints on the model. An overidentified model is the objective.

Stage 6: Evaluating Goodness-of-Fit Criteria

1. Use of nonmetric or metric dependent and independent variables.

- *Types of variables*: Both metric or nonmetric variables can be used for either independent or dependent variables.

- *Correlation calculation*: The only requirement is that the correlations or covariances be calculated with the appropriate measurement scale in mind.

2. The most critical assumption of SEM is multivariate normality.

- *Violations* of multivariate normality can seriously bias the model results.

- *Testing* for multivariate normality can be undertaken by the methods discussed for other multivariate techniques.

3. SEM assumes independent observations, random sampling of respondents, and linearity of all relationships.

4. SEM assumes constant variance (homoscedasticity) and no collinearity.

- In order to meet the restrictions of linear dependence relationships, the observations must have a constant error variance and not be highly correlated.

5. The results should be examined for offending estimates.

- *Offending estimates* are estimated coefficients in either the structural or measurement models that exceed acceptable limits.

- *Common examples*: negative error variances (also known as Heywood cases) or nonsignificant error variances for any construct, standardized coefficients exceeding or very close to 1.0, or very large standard errors.

6. Goodness of fit is assessed from multiple perspectives, including overall model fit, measurement model fit, and structural model fit.

- *Chi Square:* the chi square value indicates the degree of correspondence between the input matrix and the predicted matrix based on the specified model. The chi square is sensitive to increases in sample size, such that model assessment must be evaluated not only on overall model fit, but also on the sample size.

- *Overall model fit* can be assessed by three types of measures:

    1. <u>Absolute fit measures:</u> assess only overall model fit (both structural and measurement models collectively) with no adjustment for the degree of overfitting.

    2. <u>Incremental fit measures:</u> compares the proposed model to a comparison model specified by the researcher.

    3. <u>Parsimonious fit measures:</u> compares models with differing numbers of estimated coefficients, with the intent of determining the amount of fit achieved by each estimated coefficient.

    4. <u>Three most common measures used to assess fit</u>:

        - *Chi square*: a measure of overall model fit, for which a nonsignificant value is desired (nonsignificance means that the predicted matrix is <u>not</u> different from the input matrix).
        - *AGFI:* the adjusted goodness of fit measure is a relative fit measure, adjusting the chi square value for the degrees of freedom in the proposed model. Values should exceed .90.
        - *RMSR*: the root mean square residual is the average prediction error between the input matrix and its predicted values. It is stated in terms of the input matrix (e.g., the average correlation prediction error if correlations are the input data).

174

- *Measurement model fit* represents the degree of measurement error in using the specified indicator variables to represent to model constructs. If measurement error is low, the structural relationships are closer to the actual correlations/covariances in the input matrix. If measurement error is high, the input matrix is said to be attenuated and the observed relationship (correlations or covariances) includes this error.

  - ➢ Construct Reliability: The primary measure of fit in the measurement model is the reliability of a construct, which indicates the degree to which the indicator variables are internally consistent (i.e., measure the same unobserved construct). Values should exceed the recommended threshold of .70.

  - ➢ Measurement model loadings: the analyst should make sure that all loadings in the measurement model are statistically significant. Non-significant indicator variables should be examined for possible deletion.

  - ➢ Indicator reliability: the squared multiple correlation values for each indicator. The value should exceed .70.

- *Structural model fit* is represented by the statistical significance of each structural coefficient (t-values for each estimated coefficient, including the correlations among constructs). To compare among the effects for each relationship, the analyst may examine the standardized solution, similar to beta coefficients in regression analysis.

  - ➢ Structural coefficients: the estimated coefficients for each hypothesized relationship between constructs can be tested for statistical significance

  - ➢ Structural equation fit: similar to the R^2 measure in regression, these measures portray the degree of explanation for each dependence relationship

7. Comparison of nested or competing models is best way to determine the best fitting model.

- *Nested models (same number of constructs)*: The difference in chi-square values for two competing models can be tested for statistical significance.

- *Competing model (differing number of constructs):* Parsimonious fit measures must be used, as the chi-square test is not appropriate.

- *Basis of comparison:* The effect of adding or deleting a causal path is tested by making model comparisons.

Step 7: Interpreting and Modifying the Model

1. Once the model is acceptable, the researcher should consider model modifications which may improve theoretical explanation or the goodness-of-fit of the model.

- *Modification indices* are calculated for each parameter which is not estimated. These indices represent the reduction in the overall model chi square that would occur if the relationship was specified in the model. Values above 3.84 are considered significant and are candidates for inclusion.

- *Examination of the residuals* of the predicted covariance or correlation matrix may also indicate areas where the model may obtain improved fit. These residuals represent prediction error from a pair of indicators. Residual values of greater than +2.58 are statistically significant at the .05 level.

- *Theory* should always be the basis for model respecifications, with empirical evidence supported conceptually before being considered for inclusion in the proposed model.

- *Cross-validation* with a new sample is essential for model respecifications.

(1) WHAT ARE THE SIMILARITIES OF STRUCTURAL EQUATION MODELING TO THE MULTIVARIATE TECHNIQUES DISCUSSED IN EARLIER CHAPTERS?

Answer

Structural equation modeling (SEM) incorporates two of the multivariate techniques we have discussed in earlier chapters: multiple regression and factor analysis. The estimation of dependence relationships in SEM is quite similar to multiple regression, although SEM adds the ability to estimate interrelated relationships. Factor analysis is incorporated in SEM in the measurement model, which is actually nothing more than a factor analysis wherein the loadings of each variable are specified a priori instead of each variable having a loading on each factor (construct).

(2) WHY SHOULD A RESEARCHER NEED TO ASSESS MEASUREMENT ERROR AND INCORPORATE IT INTO THE ANALYSIS?

The ability to incorporate measurement error into the estimation procedures has both statistical and practical benefits. From a statistical perspective, the estimation process is made more efficient and valid if the known degree of measurement error can be accommodated in the estimation of the structural relationships. Since we can reasonably expect to encounter measurement error in almost every measure we collect, its inclusion makes theory testing more rigorous and ultimately a more valid assessment of the proposed model.

From a practical perspective, the recognition of measurement error provides the basis for incorporating multiple measures for any single construct. Since we know that the latent (unobserved) construct can be better measured with several consistent, but fallible, indicators, a means of including measurement error in estimation allows for the develop of better multi-item measures of the construct. Again, this improves our ability to adequately assess the proposed model.

(3) BASED ON THE DEFINITION OF THEORY USED IN THIS TEXT, DESCRIBE "THEORIES" THAT MIGHT BE OF INTEREST AMONG ACADEMIC AND INDUSTRY ANALYSTS.

A theory is a set of interrelated propositions describing a phenomenon of study (individual behavior, strategies of a firm, a process or set of actions, etc.). In this regard, theory is any set of proposed relationships having a consistent and justifiable rationale. While academicians would like to think that they are the exclusive province of theories, practitioners can just as readily propose a "theory" in terms of a set of interrelated relationships.

Students should be encouraged to propose theories in terms of relationships, focusing on the interrelationships among propositions and how completely these relationships describe the situation of interest.

(4) **SPECIFY A SET OF CAUSAL RELATIONSHIPS AND THEN REPRESENT THEM IN A PATH DIAGRAM.**

Once the relationships have been specified, the path diagram can easily be constructed to portray the proposed model of multiple relationships. In developing the path diagram, remember two key points:

1. Exogenous constructs only originate arrows (indicating a relationship among constructs), while endogenous constructs must have at least one incoming arrow and may have one or more outward arrows.

2. A correlation between constructs, depicting the interdependency of the constructs, is represented by a curved two-headed arrow.

(5) **WHAT ARE THE CRITERIA BY WHICH THE RESEARCHER SHOULD DECIDE IF A MODEL HAS ACHIEVED AN ACCEPTABLE LEVEL OF FIT?**

There are more measures of fit than it is possible to enumerate in this answer and even in this text. However, when assessing a proposed model, the analyst can assess goodness of fit from three perspectives:

1. Overall model fit: perhaps the most closely examined area, numerous measures have been proposed, each of which can be classified into one of three types: (1) measures of absolute fit; (2) incremental fit measures and (3) parsimonious fit measures.

2. Measurement model fit: while the primary assessment is of the reliability of the constructs based on their indicators, the analyst must also consider other aspects of the measurement model, including unidimensionality of the construct as specified and modifications to the measurement model by the exclusion of certain indicators.

3. Structural model fit: the most direct measure of structural model fit is represented in the tests of statistical significance for each structural coefficient. The

larger the percentage of hypothesized coefficients that are significant, the greater the support for the proposed model. Model respecifications can be suggested through examination of the modification indices.

(6) USING THE PATH DIAGRAM FROM QUESTION 4 (OR ONE PREPARED FOR THIS QUESTION), SPECIFY AT LEAST TWO ALTERNATIVE MODELS WITH THE THEORETICAL RATIONALE.

Once the path model has been specified, competing models can be formulated by either adding or deleting structural relationships between constructs. The purpose of this question is to make students conceptualize the competing models rather than rely on empirical guidance, such as the modification indices.

(7) WHAT IS MEANT BY HIGHER-ORDER CONFIRMATORY FACTOR ANALYSIS? WHEN SHOULD IT BE USED AND WHAT CAN IT TELL YOU THAT OTHER FACTOR ANALYSES WILL NOT?

Higher-order confirmatory factor analysis is the specification of a second-order factor model, which posits that estimated first order factors are actually subdimensions of a broader higher-order construct. A higher-order factor should be specified when theoretically the first-order constructs represent the facets of dimensions of a more general higher-order construct. In estimating a higher-order factor the researcher can see more than just the correlations among the first order factors. Structural relationships between the first-order dimensions and the higher-order factor are demonstrated in the process.

SAMPLE MULTIPLE CHOICE QUESTIONS
(correct answer is in bold)

Circle the letter of the item which best answers the question.

1.   A _____ is not measured directly, but instead is operationalized through one or variables hypothesized to be representative of its basic meaning.

       a.   indicator variable
       b.   manifest variable
       c.   latent construct
       d.   structural coefficient
       e.   modification index

2.   The portion of structural equation modeling most similar to factor analysis is the:

       a.   structural model
       b.   measurement model
       c.   confirmatory model
       d.   exogenous construct
       e.   nested model

3.   Dependence relationships are specified and estimated in the:

       a.   structural model
       b.   measurement model
       c.   confirmatory model
       d.   exogenous construct
       e.   nested model

4.   A(n) _____ construct is one which has no determinants in the proposed model.

       a.   latent
       b.   manifest
       c.   endogenous
       d.   independent
       e.   exogenous

5.   A(n) _____ model is one which should be strived for since it will generate unique parameter estimates.
   a.   just-identified
   b.   fully specified
   c.   over-identified
   d.   saturated
   e.   a or d

6.   The fundamental measure of measurement model fit is:

   a.   construct variance
   b.   parsimonious fit measure
   c.   degrees of freedom
   d.   reliability
   e.   nonsignificant residuals

7.   Structural equation modeling is most well-suited for:

   a.   exploratory rather than confirmatory analysis
   b.   confirmatory rather than exploratory analysis
   c.   equally well suited for both types of analysis
   d.   cannot be answered without knowledge of the theory underlying the analysis

8.   The input data type preferred for theory testing is:

   a.   covariance matrix
   b.   correlation matrix
   c.   correlation matrix adjusted for measurement error
   d.   does not matter, structural equation modeling handles both equally well

9.   The measures of fit that relate the overall model fit to the number of estimated parameters are termed:

   a.   absolute fit measures
   b.   parsimonious fit measures
   c.   incremental fit measures
   d.   all fit measures take the number of estimated parameters into account
   e.   none of the fit measures take the number of estimated parameters into account; this is one of the principal criticisms of this technique

10   Which of the following is an incorrect statement regarding structural equation modeling (SEM)?

a.   SEM incorporates measurement error into the estimation of dependence relationships

b.   A nonsignificant overall fit statistic (the overall chi square) indicates that the model fits the data well

c.   SEM models have the ability to find the "best" set of estimated coefficients such that the theory being tested is confirmed/validated conclusively.

d.   Causation cannot be assured through the use of SEM

e.   All of the above are true

CHAPTER TWELVE
EMERGING TECHNIQUES IN MULTIVARIATE ANALYSIS

This chapter provides a perspective on the changes occurring due to increased technological abilities and the abundance of information available to organizations. New applied techniques that are closely related to multivariate analysis are evolving that need to be understood. These techniques include data warehousing and mining, neural networks, and resampling.

Data Warehousing and Data Mining

1. What is Data Warehousing?

- **Data warehousing is the facilitating mechanism for decision support systems (DDS), storing an organization's data in a single, integrated data base.**

- **Operating a data warehouse encompasses seven basic phases:**

  - ➤ *Data acquisition* from internal as well as external sources

  - ➤ *Data integration*, maintaining consistency by matching characteristics, attributes, and level of aggregation

  - ➤ *Data cleaning*, to ensure quality

  - ➤ *Metadata creation*, a complete description of the data element including attributes, source transformation etc.

  - ➤ *Data input*, new data must be imported into the warehouse at periodic intervals

  - ➤ *Data warehousing*, organization and processing of the database

  - ➤ *Decision support*, OLAP (on-line analytical processing) or user directed applications.

- **Information must be characterized on at least three dimensions:**

  ➤ **Operational versus analytical data** – operational data relate to the day-to-day operations, while analytical data have been processed to be in suitable form for data mining

  ➤ **Primitive versus aggregative** – primitive data is in the form collected, while aggregative data has been summarized

  ➤ **Metadata** – a special form of data, metadata is "data about data" and relates the characteristics of the data for data warehousing and datamining purposes

2. What is Data Mining?

- **Data mining is the process of extracting information from large databases.**

- **Data mining may involve both exploration and confirmation techniques.**

  ➤ *Queries* may be done in structured query language (SQL) or by on-line analytical processing (OLAP). Either may allow the researcher to "drill down" through the database examining interesting patterns and relationships

  ➤ *Visualization techniques* display multidimensional portrayals of associations.

  ➤ *Association rules* quantify the occurrence of two events. Confidence is the likelihood of event A happening when B occurs. Support is the percentage of time that the joint event occurs out of the total population

  ➤ *Decision trees* are sequential partitioning of the dataset in order to maximize differences on a dependent variable

  ➤ *Neural networks* try to learn by repeated trials how to best organize itself to achieve maximum prediction.

  ➤ *Genetic Algorithms* is also a learning based model based on a biological analogy of natural selection. Beginning with several possible solutions to a problem, survivors of each generation of solutions lead to an acceptable final solution.

Neural Networks

1. What are Neural Networks?

- Neural networks are a non-linear predictive model that learns through training. Analogous to the human brain neural networks can address many of the same issues as many multivariate techniques.

- A key element in a neural network is learning by which output errors (prediction or classification) are fed back into the system and adjusted accordingly.

- The most basic element in a neural network is a node, a self-contained processing unit that acts in parallel with other nodes in the neural network.

    ➤ *Nodes* accept a number of weighted inputs from other sources.
    ➤ An activation function processes the inputs and generates an output value, which is sent to the next node in the system.

- The neural network is a sequential arrangement of three basic types of nodes or layers: **input nodes, output nodes, and intermediate (hidden) nodes**.

- Neural networks are unique from other multivariate techniques in that they are designed to "learn" or "correct" based on its errors. The process occurs by making initial estimates for the values at each node. These are then compared and differences noted. Backpropogation is the process whereby the prediction error works backwards through the system, recalibrating the weights to minimize the error.

2. How would you estimate a Neural Network Model?

In estimating a neural network model there are five fundamental issues: (1) data preparation, (2) defining the model structure, (3) estimating the model, (4) evaluating the model results, and (5) model validation.

- **Data preparation** includes splitting the original sample into an appropriate calibration or training sample and a separate validation sample and examination of new data. A rule of thumb for sample size in the calibration sample is to have ten to thirty cases for each estimated weight. Examination of data should still be conducted for skewness, nonnormality, outliers, and missing data

- **Defining the model structure is** mainly a decision concerning the number of hidden layers to employ. Although multiple hidden layers may improve estimation, the consensus is to use only one or two layers at most.

- **The primary goal of the model estimation** process is to achieve the best possible model. It is important to avoid suboptimal solutions and reach the global optimal solution.

- **Evaluating a neural network** model consists primarily of assessing the level of prediction or classification of the output variables.

- **Model validation** is done to ensure that the optimum model is as generalizable as possible. This is done by employing a new sample of cases, providing different starting points for the weights, rearranging the order of the cases in the calibration sample, and/or varying the number of nodes.

Resampling

---

1. What is Resampling?

- Resampling discards the assumed sampling distribution of a parameter and calculates the actual empirical distribution from hundreds or thousands of samples. These samples are drawn repeatedly from the original sample in a manner shown to best reflect the actual population from which the original sample is drawn.

- Resampling techniques such as the jackknife and bootstrap methods enhance the ability to examine the actual distribution of the estimated parameters instead of relying on the assumed distribution.

2. Methods of Resampling

- The *jackknife method* computes n subsets $(n = $ sample size) by subsequently eliminating one case from each sample.

- The *bootstrap method* derives its sample by sampling with replacement from the original sample.

3. Applications of Resampling

Why would researchers employ resampling techniques? The statistical theory underlying resampling has made remarkable progress in the recent past and these techniques do have sound statistical bases. Should they replace our traditional approaches to employing sampling error in making statistical inference tests? Only the researcher can answer this question on a case-by-case basis. But where the data perhaps reflects problems that impact statistical inference and the traditional remedies are not possible or sufficient, then resampling techniques should be considered as viable alternatives.

ANSWERS TO END-OF-CHAPTER QUESTIONS

(1)   DEFINE THE ROLES DATA MINING AND DATA WAREHOUSING PLAY IN TODAY'S RESEARCH ENVIRONMENT?

Answer

Given the explosion of information available from both internal and external sources, organizations and researchers are faced with opportunities and tasks of both data management and analysis like never before. Data warehousing and data mining are complimentary elements in the improvement of data access for decision making. Data warehousing is the facilitating mechanism for decision support systems, storing an organization's data in a single integrated database and providing a historical perspective. Data mining is the search for relationships and data patterns in large databases. This search may include drilling down through layers of data to explore relationships in more detail.

(2)   EXPLAIN THE LOGIC UNDERLYING DECISION TREES AND HOW THEY MIGHT BE USED IN ADDRESSING A RESEARCH PROBLEM.

Answer

Decision trees are a sequential partitioning of the dataset in order to maximize differences on a categorical dependent variable. The process begins by identifying the independent variable that best explains the split of the categories of the dependent variables. This split is then followed by the next most explanatory variable. This process continues until there are no longer any significant splits. Decision trees would be applicable in any situation where the researcher could form a dependent variable category and use multiple independent categorical variables.

(3)   EXPLAIN HOW NEURAL NETWORKS LEARN AND TRAIN THEMSELVES. WHY CAN'T MULTIVARIATE TECHNIQUES DO THE SAME?

Answer

Neural network models take the first case, inputs the data, and makes an initial decision based on the weights. The prediction error is assessed, and then the model makes its best effort to modify the weights to improve prediction and then moves onto the next case. This cycle repeats itself for each case in the training phase, when the model can be used on a separate sample to assess its external validity. This type of complex learning process is unavailable in current multivariate techniques.

(4) WHAT ARE THE MAJOR DIFFERENCES BETWEEN THE RESAMPLING TECHNIQUES OF BOOTSTRAPPING AND THE JACKKNIFE?

Answer

The key difference between the two methods is whether the repeated samples used to calculate the distribution of a parameter is drawn with or without replacement. The jackknife method computes n subsets (n = sample size) by sequentially eliminating one case from each sample. Thus each sample has a sample size of n-1 and differs only by the single omitted case in each sample.

The bootstrap method derives its sample by sampling with replacement from the original sample. By replacing observations, the researcher is able to draw as many samples as needed and not worry about duplication except by chance.

(5) DESCRIBE HOW GENETIC ALGORITHMS WORK. WHAT ARE THEIR ADVANTAGES AND DISADVANTAGES?

Answer

Genetic algorithms mimic an evolutionary process. It starts with a number of possible solutions to a problem. These solutions compete with one another, and then the best solutions are selected and combined to provide the basis for further solutions. Over time the process weeds out inferior solutions and results in overall improvement. The key advantage is that genetic algorithms generally converge on the optional solution. The drawbacks are that the process may take many generations and a large number of individuals.

(6) DESCRIBE THE DIFFERENCES IN PROCEDURES BY WHICH A PARAMETRIC METHOD AND A NONPARAMETRIC (RESAMPLING) METHOD ESTIMATE CONFIDENCE INTERVALS.

Answer

Nonparametric (resampling) approaches discard the assumed sampling distribution of a parameter and calculates the actual distribution of the parameter. In doing so, nonparametric methods are capable of directly calculating the confidence interval. Parametric methods assume a distribution for the sample. Based on this distribution, usually a normal distribution, and classical statistical theory a confidence interval is estimated.

Additional Notes:

SECTION TWO:

DATABASE DESCRIPTIONS

HATCO Database

Description

This data bank is a hypothetical set of data generated by the authors to meet the assumptions required in the application of multivariate techniques. The data bank consists of 100 observations on 14 separate variables. It is assumed that the data were obtained from the Hair, Anderson, Tatham Company (HATCO). HATCO is interested in identifying the attitudes and attributes that characterize industrial customers and their perceptions of HATCO. The data provided in the database will enable HATCO to develop a profile of the type of customers most likely to be satisfied and buy the most from HATCO, as well as the characteristics typifying customers using each type of buying situation and buying process employed. A detailed discussion of the variables is provided in Chapter One of the text.

Control Cards

Listing of files for both SPSS and SAS that read the data and define the variable/value labels are provided in hard copy form in this section and on the data diskette. Appendix A in the text also lists the control cards necessary to perform all of the multivariate analysis examples in the text.

Creating the SPSS Data File

```
DATA LIST  /ID 4-6 X1 10-12 X2 16-18
   X3 21-24 X4 28-30 X5 34-36 X6 40-42
   X7 45-48 X8 51 X9 54-57 X10 61-63
   X11 66 X12 69 X13 72 X14 75.
FORMATS ID X1 X2 X4 X5 X6 X10 (F3.1).
FORMATS X3 X7 X9 (F4.1).
FORMATS X8 X11 X12 X13 X14 (F1.0).
VARIABLE LABELS  ID 'ID'
  /X1 'Delivery Speed'
  /X2 'Price Level'
  /X3 'Price Flexibility'
  /X4 'Manufacturer Image'
  /X5 'Service'
  /X6 'Salesforce Image'
  /X7 'Product Quality'
  /X8 'Firm Size'
  /X9 'Usage Level'
  /X10 'Satisfaction Level'
  /X11 'Specification Buying'
  /X12 'Structure of Procurement'
  /X13 'Type of Industry (SIC)'
  /X14 'Type of Buying Situation' .
VALUE LABELS  X8 0 'Small' 1 'Large'
  /X11 0 'Specification Buying' 1 'Total Value Analysis'
  /X12 0 'Decentralized' 1 'Centralized'
  /X13 0 'Firm Type One' 1 'Firm Type Two'
  /X14 1 'New Task' 2 'Modified Rebuy' 3 'Straight Rebuy' .
BEGIN DATA
  1  4.1  .6  6.9  4.7  2.4  2.3  5.2  0  32.0  4.2  1  0  1  1
  2  1.8  3.0  6.3  6.6  2.5  4.0  8.4  1  43.0  4.3  0  1  0  1
  3  3.4  5.2  5.7  6.0  4.3  2.7  8.2  1  48.0  5.2  0  1  1  2
  .  .   .   .   .   .   .   .   .   .   .   .  .  .  .
  .  .   .   .   .   .   .   .   .   .   .   .  .  .  .
```

A complete listing of the dataset is provided at the end of this Appendix

```
   .  .  .  .  .  .  .  .  . . . .
  .  .  .  .  .  .  .  . .    . . . .
 98  2.0  2.8  5.2  5.0  2.4  2.7  8.4  1  38.0  3.7  0  1  0  1
 99  3.1  2.2  6.7  6.8  2.6  2.9  8.4  1  42.0  4.3  0  1  0  1
 100 2.5  1.8  9.0  5.0  2.2  3.0  6.0  0  33.0  4.4  1  0  0  1
END DATA .
 SAVE OUTFILE='HATCO.SAV'.
```

Creating the SAS Data File

```
DATA HATCO;
INPUT ID 4-6 X1 10-12 X2 16-18 X3 21-24
    X4 28-30 X5 34-36 X6 40-42 X7 45-48
    X8 51 X9 54-57 X10 61-63
    X11 66 X12 69 X13 72 X14 75;
LABEL ID 'ID'
X1 'Delivery Speed'
X2 'Price Level'
X3 'Price Flexibility'
X4 'Manufacturer Image'
X5 'Service'
X6 'Salesforce Image'
X7 'Product Quality'
X8 'Firm Size'
X9 'Usage Level'
X10 'Satisfaction Level'
X11 'Specification Buying'
X12 'Structure of Procurement'
X13 'Type of Industry'
X14 'Type of Buying Situation';
CARDS;
   1  4.1  .6  6.9  4.7  2.4  2.3  5.2  0  32.0  4.2  1  0  1  1
   2  1.8  3.0  6.3  6.6  2.5  4.0  8.4  1  43.0  4.3  0  1  0  1

   .  .  .  .  .  .  .  .  .    .  .  .
  .  .  .  .  .  .  .  .  .   . . . .
```

A complete listing of the dataset is provided at the end of this Appendix
```
  .  .  .  .  .  .  .  .  .  . . . .
  .  .  .  .  .  .  .  .  .   . . . .
 99  3.1  2.2  6.7  6.8  2.6  2.9  8.4  1  42.0  4.3  0  1  0  1
 100 2.5  1.8  9.0  5.0  2.2  3.0  6.0  0  33.0  4.4  1  0  0  1
PROC FORMAT
    VALUE X8  0='Small' 1='Large'
    VALUE X11 0='Specification Buying' 1='Total Value Analysis'
    VALUE X12 0='Decentralized' 1='Centralized'
    VALUE X13 0='Firm Type One' 1='Firm Type Two'
    VALUE X14 1='New Task' 2='Modified Rebuy' 3='Straight Rebuy';
```

HATCO Database (X$_1$ to X$_{14}$)

1	4.1	.6	6.9	4.7	2.4	2.3	5.2	0	32.0	4.2	1	0	1	1
2	1.8	3.0	6.3	6.6	2.5	4.0	8.4	1	43.0	4.3	0	1	0	1
3	3.4	5.2	5.7	6.0	4.3	2.7	8.2	1	48.0	5.2	0	1	1	2
4	2.7	1.0	7.1	5.9	1.8	2.3	7.8	1	32.0	3.9	0	1	1	1
5	6.0	.9	9.6	7.8	3.4	4.6	4.5	0	58.0	6.8	1	0	1	3
6	1.9	3.3	7.9	4.8	2.6	1.9	9.7	1	45.0	4.4	0	1	1	2
7	4.6	2.4	9.5	6.6	3.5	4.5	7.6	0	46.0	5.8	1	0	1	1
8	1.3	4.2	6.2	5.1	2.8	2.2	6.9	1	44.0	4.3	0	1	0	2
9	5.5	1.6	9.4	4.7	3.5	3.0	7.6	0	63.0	5.4	1	0	1	3
10	4.0	3.5	6.5	6.0	3.7	3.2	8.7	1	54.0	5.4	0	1	0	2
11	2.4	1.6	8.8	4.8	2.0	2.8	5.8	0	32.0	4.3	1	0	0	1
12	3.9	2.2	9.1	4.6	3.0	2.5	8.3	0	47.0	5.0	1	0	1	2
13	2.8	1.4	8.1	3.8	2.1	1.4	6.6	1	39.0	4.4	0	1	0	1
14	3.7	1.5	8.6	5.7	2.7	3.7	6.7	0	38.0	5.0	1	0	1	1
15	4.7	1.3	9.9	6.7	3.0	2.6	6.8	0	54.0	5.9	1	0	0	3
16	3.4	2.0	9.7	4.7	2.7	1.7	4.8	0	49.0	4.7	1	0	0	3
17	3.2	4.1	5.7	5.1	3.6	2.9	6.2	0	38.0	4.4	1	1	1	2
18	4.9	1.8	7.7	4.3	3.4	1.5	5.9	0	40.0	5.6	1	0	0	2
19	5.3	1.4	9.7	6.1	3.3	3.9	6.8	0	54.0	5.9	1	0	1	3
20	4.7	1.3	9.9	6.7	3.0	2.6	6.8	0	55.0	6.0	1	0	0	3
21	3.3	.9	8.6	4.0	2.1	1.8	6.3	0	41.0	4.5	1	0	0	2
22	3.4	.4	8.3	2.5	1.2	1.7	5.2	0	35.0	3.3	1	0	0	1
23	3.0	4.0	9.1	7.1	3.5	3.4	8.4	0	55.0	5.2	1	1	0	3
24	2.4	1.5	6.7	4.8	1.9	2.5	7.2	1	36.0	3.7	0	1	0	1
25	5.1	1.4	8.7	4.8	3.3	2.6	3.8	0	49.0	4.9	1	0	0	2
26	4.6	2.1	7.9	5.8	3.4	2.8	4.7	0	49.0	5.9	1	0	1	3
27	2.4	1.5	6.6	4.8	1.9	2.5	7.2	1	36.0	3.7	0	1	0	1
28	5.2	1.3	9.7	6.1	3.2	3.9	6.7	0	54.0	5.8	1	0	1	3
29	3.5	2.8	9.9	3.5	3.1	1.7	5.4	0	49.0	5.4	1	0	1	3
30	4.1	3.7	5.9	5.5	3.9	3.0	8.4	1	46.0	5.1	0	1	0	2
31	3.0	3.2	6.0	5.3	3.1	3.0	8.0	1	43.0	3.3	0	1	0	1
32	2.8	3.8	8.9	6.9	3.3	3.2	8.2	0	53.0	5.0	1	1	0	3
33	5.2	2.0	9.3	5.9	3.7	2.4	4.6	0	60.0	6.1	1	0	0	3
34	3.4	3.7	6.4	5.7	3.5	3.4	8.4	1	47.0	3.8	0	1	0	1
35	2.4	1.0	7.7	3.4	1.7	1.1	6.2	1	35.0	4.1	0	1	0	1
36	1.8	3.3	7.5	4.5	2.5	2.4	7.6	1	39.0	3.6	0	1	1	1
37	3.6	4.0	5.8	5.8	3.7	2.5	9.3	1	44.0	4.8	0	1	1	2
38	4.0	.9	9.1	5.4	2.4	2.6	7.3	0	46.0	5.1	1	0	1	3
39	.0	2.1	6.9	5.4	1.1	2.6	8.9	1	29.0	3.9	0	1	1	1
40	2.4	2.0	6.4	4.5	2.1	2.2	8.8	1	28.0	3.3	0	1	1	1
41	1.9	3.4	7.6	4.6	2.6	2.5	7.7	1	40.0	3.7	0	1	1	1
42	5.9	.9	9.6	7.8	3.4	4.6	4.5	0	58.0	6.7	1	0	1	3
43	4.9	2.3	9.3	4.5	3.6	1.3	6.2	0	53.0	5.9	1	0	0	3
44	5.0	1.3	8.6	4.7	3.1	2.5	3.7	0	48.0	4.8	1	0	0	2
45	2.0	2.6	6.5	3.7	2.4	1.7	8.5	1	38.0	3.2	0	1	1	1
46	5.0	2.5	9.4	4.6	3.7	1.4	6.3	0	54.0	6.0	1	0	0	3
47	3.1	1.9	10.0	4.5	2.6	3.2	3.8	0	55.0	4.9	1	0	1	3
48	3.4	3.9	5.6	5.6	3.6	2.3	9.1	1	43.0	4.7	0	1	1	2
49	5.8	.2	8.8	4.5	3.0	2.4	6.7	0	57.0	4.9	1	0	1	3
50	5.4	2.1	8.0	3.0	3.8	1.4	5.2	0	53.0	3.8	0	1	1	3
51	3.7	.7	8.2	6.0	2.1	2.5	5.2	0	41.0	5.0	1	0	0	2
52	2.6	4.8	8.2	5.0	3.6	2.5	9.0	1	53.0	5.2	0	1	1	2
53	4.5	4.1	6.3	5.9	4.3	3.4	8.8	1	50.0	5.5	0	1	0	2
54	2.8	2.4	6.7	4.9	2.5	2.6	9.2	1	32.0	3.7	0	1	1	1
55	3.8	.8	8.7	2.9	1.6	2.1	5.6	0	39.0	3.7	1	0	0	1
56	2.9	2.6	7.7	7.0	2.8	3.6	7.7	0	47.0	4.2	1	1	1	2
57	4.9	4.4	7.4	6.9	4.6	4.0	9.6	1	62.0	6.2	0	1	0	2
58	5.4	2.5	9.6	5.5	4.0	3.0	7.7	0	65.0	6.0	1	0	0	3
59	4.3	1.8	7.6	5.4	3.1	2.5	4.4	0	46.0	5.6	1	0	1	3
60	2.3	4.5	8.0	4.7	3.3	2.2	8.7	1	50.0	5.0	0	1	1	2
61	3.1	1.9	9.9	4.5	2.6	3.1	3.8	0	54.0	4.8	1	0	1	3
62	5.1	1.9	9.2	5.8	3.6	2.3	4.5	0	60.0	6.1	1	0	0	3
63	4.1	1.1	9.3	5.5	2.5	2.7	7.4	0	47.0	5.3	1	0	1	3
64	3.0	3.8	5.5	4.9	3.4	2.6	6.0	0	36.0	4.2	1	1	1	2
65	1.1	2.0	7.2	4.7	1.6	3.2	10.0	1	40.0	3.4	0	1	1	1
66	3.7	1.4	9.0	4.5	2.6	2.3	6.8	0	45.0	4.9	1	0	0	2
67	4.2	2.5	9.2	6.2	3.3	3.9	7.3	0	59.0	6.0	1	0	0	3
68	1.6	4.5	6.4	5.3	3.0	2.5	7.1	1	46.0	4.5	0	1	0	2

69	5.3	1.7	8.5	3.7	3.5	1.9	4.8	0	58.0	4.3	1	0	0	3
70	2.3	3.7	8.3	5.2	3.0	2.3	9.1	1	49.0	4.8	0	1	1	2
71	3.6	5.4	5.9	6.2	4.5	2.9	8.4	1	50.0	5.4	0	1	1	2
72	5.6	2.2	8.2	3.1	4.0	1.6	5.3	0	55.0	3.9	1	0	1	3
73	3.6	2.2	9.9	4.8	2.9	1.9	4.9	0	51.0	4.9	1	0	0	3
74	5.2	1.3	9.1	4.5	3.3	2.7	7.3	0	60.0	5.1	1	0	1	3
75	3.0	2.0	6.6	6.6	2.4	2.7	8.2	1	41.0	4.1	0	1	0	1
76	4.2	2.4	9.4	4.9	3.2	2.7	8.5	0	49.0	5.2	1	0	1	2
77	3.8	.8	8.3	6.1	2.2	2.6	5.3	0	42.0	5.1	1	0	0	2
78	3.3	2.6	9.7	3.3	2.9	1.5	5.2	0	47.0	5.1	1	0	1	3
79	1.0	1.9	7.1	4.5	1.5	3.1	9.9	1	39.0	3.3	0	1	1	1
80	4.5	1.6	8.7	4.6	3.1	2.1	6.8	0	56.0	5.1	1	0	0	3
81	5.5	1.8	8.7	3.8	3.6	2.1	4.9	0	59.0	4.5	1	0	0	3
82	3.4	4.6	5.5	8.2	4.0	4.4	6.3	0	47.0	5.6	1	1	1	2
83	1.6	2.8	6.1	6.4	2.3	3.8	8.2	1	41.0	4.1	0	1	0	1
84	2.3	3.7	7.6	5.0	3.0	2.5	7.4	0	37.0	4.4	1	1	0	1
85	2.6	3.0	8.5	6.0	2.8	2.8	6.8	1	53.0	5.6	0	1	0	2
86	2.5	3.1	7.0	4.2	2.8	2.2	9.0	1	43.0	3.7	0	1	1	1
87	2.4	2.9	8.4	5.9	2.7	2.7	6.7	1	51.0	5.5	0	1	0	2
88	2.1	3.5	7.4	4.8	2.8	2.3	7.2	0	36.0	4.3	1	1	0	1
89	2.9	1.2	7.3	6.1	2.0	2.5	8.0	1	34.0	4.0	0	1	1	1
90	4.3	2.5	9.3	6.3	3.4	4.0	7.4	0	60.0	6.1	1	0	0	3
91	3.0	2.8	7.8	7.1	3.0	3.8	7.9	0	49.0	4.4	1	1	1	2
92	4.8	1.7	7.6	4.2	3.3	1.4	5.8	0	39.0	5.5	1	0	0	2
93	3.1	4.2	5.1	7.8	3.6	4.0	5.9	0	43.0	5.2	1	1	1	2
94	1.9	2.7	5.0	4.9	2.2	2.5	8.2	1	36.0	3.6	0	1	0	1
95	4.0	.5	6.7	4.5	2.2	2.1	5.0	0	31.0	4.0	1	0	1	1
96	.6	1.6	6.4	5.0	.7	2.1	8.4	1	25.0	3.4	0	1	1	1
97	6.1	.5	9.2	4.8	3.3	2.8	7.1	0	60.0	5.2	1	0	1	3
98	2.0	2.8	5.2	5.0	2.4	2.7	8.4	1	38.0	3.7	0	1	0	1
99	3.1	2.2	6.7	6.8	2.6	2.9	8.4	1	42.0	4.3	0	1	0	1
100	2.5	1.8	9.0	5.0	2.2	3.0	6.0	0	33.0	4.4	1	0	0	1

HATCO Missing Data Database

Description

This datafile has the same structure and layout as the HATCO datafile described in the previous section. However, this datafile contains missing data suitable for analysis by the techniques described in Chapter Two. If an instructor wishes to provide students with exposure to missing data identification and treatment, then this dataset can be used.

Control Cards

Listing of files for both SPSS and SAS that read the data and define the variables/value labels are the same as described for the HATCO datafile. Appendix A in the text lists the control cards necessary to perform all of the multivariate analysis examples discussed in the text.

The Sales Training Database

Description

The sales training database is provided as an alternative to the HATCO database. Unlike the HATCO data, which are multivariate normally distributed and contain no missing values, wild codes, etc., the sales training database is more "realistic." The data represent "typical" survey data in marketing. The level of measurement for the scale responses is assumed to be an "equally appearing interval" of measure, thus regression based techniques are assumed to be appropriate for use in analysis. The sales training data were collected via a mail questionnaire which was sent to 80 sales training managers at various firms throughout the United States (see the survey questionnaire later in this section). The questionnaire is divided into four sections:

Section One: Addresses the usage of various training methods by the respondent's firm. There are 17 methods. The respondent rates all methods on a five-point scale for present frequency of use in five years. These variables are labeled A1 thru A34.

Section Two: Concerns the effectiveness of training methods. Again, a five-point scale is used to elicit respondent's ratings concerning the effectiveness of the 17 methods in achieving certain training objectives: (a) acquire knowledge, (b) retention of what is learned, (c) change in attitude, (d) development of interpersonal skills, (e) development of problem solving skills, and (f) participant acceptance. These variables are label B1 thru B96.

Section Three: Concerns the ratings of the effectiveness of a training program using several different approaches: (a) reactions, (b) learning, (c) behavior on the job, and (d) results. The managers were asked to rate both the importance of these dimensions and the frequency with which they use these evaluative criterion. These variables are labeled C1 thru C34.

Section Four: Includes demographic data. Variable D1 is the industry category. There are four broad categories represented in the data: (a) retail/wholesale/services/, (b) consumer goods manufacturers, (c) industrial goods manufacturers, and (d) financial/insurance/real estate. Also included are D2 – annual sales, D3 – number of employees, D4 – number of salespersons, D5 – number of training department employees, and D6 – whether or not the training department subscribes to training trade journals (coded "0" = NO and "1" = YES).

1. Please respond to the following questions with regard to the training programs in your organization. For each method, please circle the number corresponding to how frequently the method is currently used and how frequently you predict it will be used five years from now.

FREQUENCY
0 - Never
1 - Seldom
2 - Sometimes
3 - Often
4 - Almost always

METHODS	Present Frequency		Frequency In 5 Years	
Conference or Discussion Method	0 1 2 3 4	A1	0 1 2 3 4	A18
Lecture Method (with questions)	0 1 2 3 4		0 1 2 3 4	
Case Study	0 1 2 3 4		0 1 2 3 4	
TV-Lecture	0 1 2 3 4		0 1 2 3 4	
Film Viewing	0 1 2 3 4		0 1 2 3 4	
Videotape or Video Disk Presentation	0 1 2 3 4		0 1 2 3 4	
Interactive Video	0 1 2 3 4		0 1 2 3 4	
Role Playing (no recordings made)	0 1 2 3 4		0 1 2 3 4	
Role Playing with Videotape Feedback	0 1 2 3 4		0 1 2 3 4	
Behavioral Modeling	0 1 2 3 4		0 1 2 3 4	
Computer-Assisted Instruction (CAI)	0 1 2 3 4		0 1 2 3 4	
Business Games	0 1 2 3 4		0 1 2 3 4	
Business Games (computer assisted)	0 1 2 3 4		0 1 2 3 4	
Sensitivity Training (t groups)	0 1 2 3 4		0 1 2 3 4	
Home Study	0 1 2 3 4		0 1 2 3 4	
Reading Lists	0 1 2 3 4		0 1 2 3 4	
In-Basket Technique	0 1 2 3 4	A17	0 1 2 3 4	A34

NOTE: The alpha-numeric codes to the right of the scales (in the margin) are the variable notations for the particular item used in the computer output. Variable labels are included at the end of the questionnaire for the SPSS program. There is also a file on the database diskette containing the SPSS data list file statements and the variable and value labels listings. All you need do is transfer this file to the beginning of your SPSS program and the correct labels will be printed on your output. This will aid in interpretation without the necessity of referring to this manual.

2. We are trying to determine the effectiveness of several different training methods in their ability to achieve 6 objectives. These objectives are:

A. Acquisition of Knowledge - ability to learn new information
B. Retention of What is Learned - ability to remember and use the information/skills that were presented during previous training sessions
C. Change in Attitude - alter or change existing beliefs
D. Development of Interpersonal Skills - improve effectiveness in dealing with other workers, supervisors and customers
E. Development of Problem-Solving Skills - improve effectiveness in problem-solving skills
F. Participant Acceptance - degree to which person willingly accepts and gets involved in tra'ing experience.

Please respond to the following questions with regard to the training programs in your organization. If your organization does not use these methods we would still like for you to rate the methods based on how effective you believe they may be. Circle the number that corresponds to the effectiveness of each of the following training methods in accomplishing each training objective.

EFFECTIVENESS RATINGS
1 - Not effective
2 - Limited effectiveness
3 - Moderately effective
4 - Quite effective
5 - Highly effective

TRAINING OBJECTIVES (A-C above)

METHODS	A. Acquire Knowledge	B. Retention of what is Learned	C. Change in Attitude
Conference or Discussion Method	1 2 3 4 5 B1	1 2 3 4 5 B17	1 2 3 4 5 B33
Lecture Method (with questions)	1 2 3 4 5	1 2 3 4 5	1 2 3 4 5
Case Study	1 2 3 4 5	1 2 3 4 5	1 2 3 4 5
TV-Lecture	1 2 3 4 5	1 2 3 4 5	1 2 3 4 5
Film Viewing	1 2 3 4 5	1 2 3 4 5	1 2 3 4 5
Videotape Presentation	1 2 3 4 5	1 2 3 4 5	1 2 3 4 5
Role Playing (no recordings made)	1 2 3 4 5	1 2 3 4 5	1 2 3 4 5
Role Playing with Videotape Feedback	1 2 3 4 5	1 2 3 4 5	1 2 3 4 5
Behavioral Modeling	1 2 3 4 5	1 2 3 4 5	1 2 3 4 5
Computer-Assisted Instruction (CAI)	1 2 3 4 5	1 2 3 4 5	1 2 3 4 5
Business Games	1 2 3 4 5	1 2 3 4 5	1 2 3 4 5
Business Games (computer assisted)	1 2 3 4 5	1 2 3 4 5	1 2 3 4 5
Sensitivity Training (t groups)	1 2 3 4 5	1 2 3 4 5	1 2 3 4 5
Home Study	1 2 3 4 5	1 2 3 4 5	1 2 3 4 5
Reading Lists	1 2 3 4 5	1 2 3 4 5	1 2 3 4 5
In-Basket Technique	1 2 3 4 5 B16	1 2 3 4 5 B32	1 2 3 4 5 B48

2. Continued

EFFECTIVENESS RATINGS
1 - Not effective
2 - Limited effectiveness
3 - Moderately effective
4 - Quite effective
5 - Highly effective

TRAINING OBJECTIVES (D-F)

METHODS	D. Development of Interpersonal Skills		E. Development of Problem-Solving Skills		F. Participant Acceptance	
Conference or Discussion Method	1 2 3 4 5	B49	1 2 3 4 5	B65	1 2 3 4 5	B81
Lecture Method (with questions)	1 2 3 4 5		1 2 3 4 5		1 2 3 4 5	
Case Study	1 2 3 4 5		1 2 3 4 5		1 2 3 4 5	
TV-Lecture	1 2 3 4 5		1 2 3 4 5		1 2 3 4 5	
Film Viewing	1 2 3 4 5		1 2 3 4 5		1 2 3 4 5	
Videotape Presentation	1 2 3 4 5		1 2 3 4 5		1 2 3 4 5	
Role Playing (no recordings made)	1 2 3 4 5		1 2 3 4 5		1 2 3 4 5	
Role Playing with Videotape Feedback	1 2 3 4 5		1 2 3 4 5		1 2 3 4 5	
Behavioral Modeling	1 2 3 4 5		1 2 3 4 5		1 2 3 4 5	
Computer-Assisted Instruction (CAI)	1 2 3 4 5		1 2 3 4 5		1 2 3 4 5	
Business Games	1 2 3 4 5		1 2 3 4 5		1 2 3 4 5	
Business Games (computer assisted)	1 2 3 4 5		1 2 3 4 5		1 2 3 4 5	
Sensitivity Training (t groups)	1 2 3 4 5		1 2 3 4 5		1 2 3 4 5	
Home Study	1 2 3 4 5		1 2 3 4 5		1 2 3 4 5	
Reading Lists	1 2 3 4 5		1 2 3 4 5		1 2 3 4 5	
In-Basket Technique	1 2 3 4 5	B64	1 2 3 4 5	B80	1 2 3 4 5	B96

3. The effectiveness of a training program can be evaluated using several different approaches. For each approach, circle the number corresponding to its importance in assessing the effectiveness of your training programs. Also circle how frequently each approach is used.

	IMPORTANCE	FREQUENCY
	0 - Not at all important	0 - Never
	1 - Slightly important	1 - Seldom
	2 - Moderately important	2 - Sometimes
APPROACHES	3 - Very important	3 - Often
	4 - Extremely important	4 - Almost always

A. REACTIONS (i.e., How do people feel about the training program?)

Course evaluation/questionnaire	0 1 2 3 4	C1	0 1 2 3 4	C18
Training staff comments	0 1 2 3 4		0 1 2 3 4	
Trainee feedback	0 1 2 3 4		0 1 2 3 4	
Supervisors' feedback	0 1 2 3 4		0 1 2 3 4	
Other (Please specify)	0 1 2 3 4	C5	0 1 2 3 4	C22

_____

B. LEARNING (i.e., To what extent have the trainees' absorbed the knowledge and skills that they have been taught?)

Knowledge tests (paper & pencil tests)	0 1 2 3 4	C6	0 1 2 3 4	C23
Performance tests (mastery of a skill)	0 1 2 3 4		0 1 2 3 4	
Pretraining measurements compared with post-training measurements	0 1 2 3 4		0 1 2 3 4	
Training groups compared against control group	0 1 2 3 4		0 1 2 3 4	
Other (Please specify)	0 1 2 3 4	C10	0 1 2 3 4	C27

_____

C. BEHAVIOR ON THE JOB (i.e., To what extent did on-the job behavior of participants result of the training program?)

Appraisal of on-the-job behavior change from:

Supervisors	0 1 2 3 4	C11	0 1 2 3 4	C28
Co-workers	0 1 2 3 4		0 1 2 3 4	
Subordinates	0 1 2 3 4		0 1 2 3 4	
Customers	0 1 2 3 4		0 1 2 3 4	
Employee(themselves)	0 1 2 3 4		0 1 2 3 4	
Other (Please specify)	0 1 2 3 4	C16	0 1 2 3 4	C33

_____

D. RESULTS (What final results did the training produce?)

To what extent are programs evaluated using "bottom line: measurements (i.e., increased sales, reduction in customer complaints, etc.?)	0 1 2 3 4	C17	0 1 2 3 4	C34

Organizational Demographics

1. Please check the industry category that best describes your organization.   D1

    1 Retail, Wholesale, Services

    2 Consumer Goods Manufacturer

    3 Industrial Goods Manufacturer

    4 Finance, Insurance, Real Estate

2. What is the amount of your organization's annual sales? $ _____   D2

3. How many people are employed in your organization? _____   D3

4. How many sales people are employed in your organization? _____   D4

5. How many people are employed in the training department of your   D5
    organization? _____

6. Do you or other sales trainers in your department read trade journals   D6
    concerning training issues (such as Training and Development)?

        0 NO   1 YES

Control Cards

A data file and variable/value labels for the SPSS package are provided on the data diskette and in hard copy form in this section. Some suggested exercises for students using this database include: (1) running frequencies to check for missing values and wild code, (2) running regression to check for multivariate normality, outliers, etc., (3) performing transformations on variables that violate the multivariate assumptions, and (4) formulating research questions and applying the appropriate multivariate statistics for answering the questions.

```
TITLE 'SALES TRAINING DATABASE' .
DATA LIST RECORDS=3
  /1 SID 1-3 A1 4 A2 5 A3 6 A4 7 A5 8 A6 9 A7 10 A8 11 A9 12
     A10 13 A11 14 A12 15 A13 16 A14 17 A15 18 A16 19 A17 20
     A18 21 A19 22 A20 23 A21 24 A22 25 A23 26 A24 27 A25 28
     A26 29 A27 30 A28 31 A29 32 A30 33 A31 34 A32 35 A33 36
     A34 37 B1 35 B2 36 B3 37 B4 38 B5 39 B6 40 B7 41 B8 42
     B9 43 B10 44 B11 45 B12 46 B13 47 B14 48 B15 49 B16 50
     B17 51 B18 52 B19 53 B20 54 B21 52 B22 53 B23 54 B24 55
     B25 56 B26 57 B27 58 B28 59 B29 60 B30 61 B31 62 B32 63
     B33 64 B34 65 B35 66 B36 67 B37 68 B38 69 B39 70 B40 71
     B41 72
  /2 B42 1 B43 2 B44 3 B45 4 B46 5 B47 6 B48 7 B49 8 B50 9
     B51 10 B52 11 B53 12 B54 13 B55 14 B56 15 B57 16 B58 17
     B59 18 B60 19 B61 20 B62 21 B63 22 B64 23 B65 24 B66 25
     B67 26 B68 27 B69 28 B70 29 B71 30 B72 31 B73 32 B74 33
     B75 34 B76 35 B77 36 B78 37 B79 38 B80 39 B81 40 B82 41
     B83 42 B84 43 B85 44 B86 45 B87 46 B88 47 B89 48 B90 49
     B91 50 B92 51 B93 52 B94 53 B95 54 B96 55 C1 56 C2 57
     C3 58 C4 59 C5 60 C6 61 C7 62 C8 63 C9 64 C10 65
     C11 66 C12 67 C13 68 C14 69 C15 70 C16 71 C17 72
  /3 C18 1 C19 2 C20 3 C21 4 C22 5 C23 6 C24 7 C25 8
     C26 9 C27 10 C28 11 C29 12 C30 13 C31 14 C32 15
     C33 16 C34 17 D1 18-19 D2 20-29 D3 30-34 D4 35-39 D5 40-43
     D6 45 .


VARIABLE LABELS
 A1 'CONF/DISCUSSION-PRESENT'
/A2 'LECTURE METHOD-PRESENT'
/A3 'CASE STUDY-PRESENT'
/A4 'TV-LECTURE-PRESENT'
/A5 'FILM VIEWING-PRESENT'
/A6 'VIDEO TAPE/DISC-PRESENT'
/A7 'INTERACTIVE VIDEO-PRESENT'
/A8 'ROLE PLAY:NO RECORD-PRESENT'
/A9 'ROLE PLAY:VIDEO TAPE-PRESENT'
/A10 'BEHAVIORAL MODEL-PRESENT'
/A11 'CAI-PRESENT'
/A12 'BUSINESS GAMES-PRESENT'
/A13 'BUSINESS GAMES:CAI-PRESENT'
/A14 'SENSITIVITY TRAIN-PRESENT'
/A15 'HOME STUDY-PRESENT'
/A16 'READING LISTS-PRESENT'
/A17 'IN-BASKET-PRESENT'
/A18 'CONF/DISCUSSION-IN 5 YRS'
/A19 'LECTURE METHOD-IN 5 YRS'
/A20 'CASE STUDY-IN 5 YRS'
/A21 'TV-LECTURE-IN 5 YRS'
```

/A22 'FILM VIEWING-IN 5 YRS'
/A23 'VIDEO TAPE/DISC-IN 5 YRS'
/A24 'INTERACTIVE VIDEO-IN 5 YRS'
/A25 'ROLE PLAY:NO RECORD-IN 5 YRS'
/A26 'ROLE PLAY:VIDEO TAPE-IN 5 YRS'
/A27 'BEHAVIORAL MODEL-IN 5 YRS'
/A28 'CAI-IN 5 YRS'
/A29 'BUSINESS GAMES-IN 5 YRS'
/A30 'BUSINESS GAMES:CAI-IN 5 YRS'
/A31 'SENSITIVITY TRAIN-IN 5 YRS'
/A32 'HOME STUDY-IN 5 YRS'
/A33 'READING LISTS-IN 5 YRS'
/A34 'IN-BASKET-IN 5 YRS'
/B1 'CONF/DISCUSSION-AQUIRE KNOW'
/B2 'LECTURE METHOD-AQUIRE KNOW'
/B3 'CASE STUDY-AQUIRE KNOW'
/B4 'TV-LECTURE-AQUIRE KNOW'
/B5 'FILM VIEWING-AQUIRE KNOW'
/B6 'VIDEO TAPE/DISC-AQUIRE KNOW'
/B7 'ROLE PLAY:NO RECORD-AQUIRE KNOW'
/B8 'ROLE PLAY:VIDEO TAPE-AQUIRE KNOW'
/B9 'BEHAVIORAL MODEL-AQUIRE KNOW'
/B10 'CAI-AQUIRE KNOW'
/B11 'BUSINESS GAMES-AQUIRE KNOW'
/B12 'BUSINESS GAMES:CAI-AQUIRE KNOW'
/B13 'SENSITIVITY TRAIN-AQUIRE KNOW'
/B14 'HOME STUDY-AQUIRE KNOW'
/B15 'READING LISTS-AQUIRE KNOWLEDGE'
/B16 'IN-BASKET-AQUIRE KNOWLEDGE'
/B17 'CONF/DISCUSSION-RETENTION'
/B18 'LECTURE METHOD-RETENTION'
/B19 'CASE STUDY-RETENTION'
/B20 'TV-LECTURE-RETENTION'
/B21 'FILM VIEWING-RETENTION'
/B22 'VIDEO TAPE/DISC-RETENTION'
/B23 'ROLE PLAY:NO RECORD-RETENTION'
/B24 'ROLE PLAY:VIDEO TAPE-RETENTION'
/B25 'BEHAVIORAL MODEL-RETENTION'
/B26 'CAI-RETENTION'
/B27 'BUSINESS GAMES-RETENTION'
/B28 'BUSINESS GAMES:CAI-RETENTION'
/B29 'SENSITIVITY TRAIN-RETENTION'
/B30 'HOME STUDY-RETENTION'
/B31 'READING LISTS-RETENTION'
/B32 'IN-BASKET-RETENTION'
/B33 'CONF/DISCUSSION-ATTITUDE CHG'
/B34 'LECTURE METHOD-ATTITUDE CHG'
/B35 'CASE STUDY-ATTITUDE CHG'
/B36 'TV-LECTURE-ATTITUDE CHG'
/B37 'FILM VIEWING-ATTITUDE CHG'
/B38 'VIDEO TAPE/DISC-ATTITUDE CHG'
/B39 'ROLE PLAY:NO RECORD-ATTITUDE CHG'
/B40 'ROLE PLAY:VIDEO TAPE-ATTITUDE CHG'
/B41 'BEHAVIORAL MODEL-ATTITUDE CHG'
/B42 'CAI-ATTITUDE CHG'
/B43 'BUSINESS GAMES-ATTITUDE CHG'

/B44 'BUSINESS GAMES:CAI-ATTITUDE CHG'
/B45 'SENSITIVITY TRAIN-ATTITUDE CHG'
/B46 'HOME STUDY-ATTITUDE CHG'
/B47 'READING LISTS-ATTITUDE CHG'
/B48 'IN-BASKET-ATTITUDE CHG'
/B49 'CONF/DISCUSSION-INTER SKILLS'
/B50 'LECTURE METHOD-INTER SKILLS'
/B51 'CASE STUDY-INTER SKILLS'
/B52 'TV-LECTURE-INTER SKILLS'
/B53 'FILM VIEWING-INTER SKILLS'
/B54 'VIDEO TAPE/DISC-INTER SKILLS'
/B55 'ROLE PLAY:NO RECORD-INTER SKILLS'
/B56 'ROLE PLAY:VIDEO TAPE-INTER SKILLS'
/B57 'BEHAVIORAL MODEL-INTER SKILLS'
/B58 'CAI-INTER SKILLS'
/B59 'BUSINESS GAMES-INTER SKILLS'
/B60 'BUSINESS GAMES:CAI-INTER SKILLS'
/B61 'SENSITIVITY TRAIN-INTER SKILLS'
/B62 'HOME STUDY-INTER SKILLS'
/B63 'READING LISTS-INTER SKILLS'
/B64 'IN-BASKET-INTER SKILLS'
/B65 'CONF/DISCUSSION-PSOLVE SKILLS'
/B66 'LECTURE METHOD-PSOLVE SKILLS'
/B67 'CASE STUDY-PSOLVE SKILLS'
/B68 'TV-LECTURE-PSOLVE SKILLS'
/B69 'FILM VIEWING-PSOLVE SKILLS'
/B70 'VIDEO TAPE/DISC-PSOLVE SKILLS'
/B71 'ROLE PLAY:NO RECORD-PSOLVE SKILLS'
/B72 'ROLE PLAY:VIDEO TAPE-PSOLVE SKILLS'
/B73 'BEHAVIORAL MODEL-PSOLVE SKILLS'
/B74 'CAI-PSOLVE SKILLS'
/B75 'BUSINESS GAMES-PSOLVE SKILLS'
/B76 'BUSINESS GAMES:CAI-PSOLVE SKILLS'
/B77 'SENSITIVITY TRAIN-PSOLVE SKILLS'
/B78 'HOME STUDY-PSOLVE SKILLS'
/B79 'READING LISTS-PSOLVE SKILLS'
/B80 'IN-BASKET-PSOLVE SKILLS'
/B81 'CONF/DISCUSSION-PART ACCPT'
/B82 'LECTURE METHOD-PART ACCPT'
/B83 'CASE STUDY-PART ACCPT'
/B84 'TV-LECTURE-PART ACCPT'
/B85 'FILM VIEWING-PART ACCPT'
/B86 'VIDEO TAPE/DISC-PART ACCPT'
/B87 'ROLE PLAY:NO RECORD-PART ACCPT'
/B88 'ROLE PLAY:VIDEO TAPE-PART ACCPT'
/B89 'BEHAVIORAL MODEL-PART ACCPT'
/B90 'CAI-PART ACCPT'
/B91 'BUSINESS GAMES-PART ACCPT'
/B92 'BUSINESS GAMES:CAI-PART ACCPT'
/B93 'SENSITIVITY TRAIN-PART ACCPT'
/B94 'HOME STUDY-PART ACCPT'
/B95 'READING LISTS-PART ACCPT'
/B96 'IN-BASKET-PART ACCPT'
/C1 'REACTION:COURSE EVALUATION-IMP'
/C2 'REACTION:TRAIN STAFF COMMENTS-IMP'
/C3 'REACTION:TRAINEE FEEDBACK-IMP'

/C4 'REACTION:SUPERVISOR FEEDBACK-IMP'
/C5 'REACTION:OTHER-IMP'
/C6 'LEARNING:KNOWLEDGE TESTS-IMP'
/C7 'LEARNING:PERFORMANCE TESTS-IMP'
/C8 'LEARNING:PRE/POST MEASURES-IMP'
/C9 'LEARNING:TRAINING/CONTROL-IMP'
/C10 'LEARNING:OTHER-IMP'
/C11 'OTJ BEHAVIOR:SUPERVISORS-IMP'
/C12 'OTJ BEHAVIOR:CO-WORKERS-IMP'
/C13 'OTJ BEHAVIOR:SUBORDINATES-IMP'
/C14 'OTJ BEHAVIOR:CUSTOMERS-IMP'
/C15 'OTJ BEHAVIOR:EMPLOYEE-IMP'
/C16 'OTJ BEHAVIOR:OTHER-IMP'
/C17 'RESULTS:BOTTOM LINE-IMP'
/C18 'REACTION:COURSE EVALUATION-FREQ'
/C19 'REACTION:TRAIN STAFF COMMENTS-FREQ'
/C20 'REACTION:TRAINEE FEEDBACK-FREQ'
/C21 'REACTION:SUPERVISOR FEEDBACK-FREQ'
/C22 'REACTION:OTHER-FREQ'
/C23 'LEARNING:KNOWLEDGE TESTS-FREQ'
/C24 'LEARNING:PERFORMANCE TESTS-FREQ'
/C25 'LEARNING:PRE/POST MEASURES-FREQ'
/C26 'LEARNING:TRAINING/CONTROL-FREQ'
/C27 'LEARNING:OTHER-FREQ'
/C28 'OTJ BEHAVIOR:SUPERVISORS-FREQ'
/C29 'OTJ BEHAVIOR:CO-WORKERS-FREQ'
/C30 'OTJ BEHAVIOR:SUBORDINATES-FREQ'
/C31 'OTJ BEHAVIOR:CUSTOMERS-FREQ'
/C32 'OTJ BEHAVIOR:EMPLOYEE-FREQ'
/C33 'OTJ BEHAVIOR:OTHER-FREQ'
/C34 'RESULTS:BOTTOM LINE-FREQ'
/D1 'INDUSTRY CATEGORY'
/D2 'ANNUAL SALES'
/D3 'TOTAL NUMBER OF EMPLOYEES'
/D4 'NUMBER OF SALES PERSONS'
/D5 'NUMBER OF TRAINING DEPT EMPLOYEES'
/D6 'READ TRADE JOURNAL' .

VALUE LABELS A1 TO A34 0 'NEVER' 1 'SELDOM' 2 'SOMETIMES'
        3 'OFTEN' 4 'ALMOST ALWAYS'/
        B1 TO B96 1 'NOT EFFECTIVE' 2 'LIMITED EFFECTIVENESS'
        3 'MODERATELY EFFECTIVE' 4 'QUITE EFFECTIVE'
        5 'HIGHLY EFFECTIVE'/
        C1 TO C17 0 'NOT IMP AT ALL' 1 'SLIGHTLY IMP'
        2 'MODERATELY IMP' 3 'VERY IMP' 4 'EXTREMELY IMP'/
        C18 TO C34 0 'NEVER' 1 'SELDOM' 2 'SOMETIMES'
        3 'OFTEN' 4 'ALMOST ALWAYS'/
        D1 01 'RETAIL/WHOLESALE SERIVICES'
        02 'CONSUMER GOODS MFG' 03 'INDUSTRIAL GOODS MFG'
        04 'FINANCE/INS/REAL ESTATE'/
        D6 0 'NO' 1 'YES'.

RECODE A1 TO A34 (MISSING=0) .
RECODE C5 C10 C16 C22 C27 C33 (MISSING=0) .

1312 32 441101222212 33 44332132 22235543222223223554323222231 122344

2323111212111354222211131211135422221113121113542222111144444 2431 44444 4
4444 3410 1111113 4 250000000 700 283 12 1
23232222122222122132331231223221324322332434422232223233332222212222234
2223112213111344222412333332222333323232223322223332223222322332 2333 32223 3
4223 2233 22233 3 3 315500000 1300 60 8 1
3444122223200000004441122233111055554343555333133453334522222224333333345
      3322223552225222225222344354222254432245 5   3331043400   1
4441022400   1 2300000000010000 150 30 1
4420344433400001314204444344200054244445511111111544453111111111532444453
111111 5525555551111111552555555511111111552555555511111111133333 4433 33344 4
4444 4433 44444 2 1 93000000 440   7 1 0
54121 304020200111122 42433121032422244534433233224453442333213222455
34433233113222455333343233243334444552333342443344544432233344 2432 32443 4
3433 4211 11211 1 1 350000000 1700 350 2 0
632322233131 1022232322233242 11324222234333333333223443333333324333445
3333333324222344333333333242223443333333324222345333333333344 23 1 33344 3
4333 13 0 33333 3 2 26400000 200 35 1 0
74434144420023001044341444232330334224445 4442324223444 444332522321344
344222443511154514441152452234454543325234223555454433513233 3433 43344 3
4240 4420 00000 2 1 750000000 3500 2000 18 1
84331420433000104243 4 432444210253545555554 21254555554 3125514355334
1 411142435555551 41215152333351 41155254554342 3124444444421 42424 3
444444421 42404 3 2 283670000 1700 400   4 0
9322101000000000202203142030 20000325213344333243241334433325425142123 33
33333313241123441224211324112344332222241511334433334423433 1321 43234 4
3332 0300 41103 2 4 200000000 400 35 3 0
10323222202221211222121331332323231324323454344331332345434442312314213444
244321231221355324443211413112554344331124243244442542312334343343 3144433
334344333 3244433 49999999999 2200 6500 526 1
11131113031111101112222114132222035544423333221312322453322231242311 1333
2223212312111443131311142211113332222111544333433131211114244 3344 33334 2
4121 1100 00000 0 1 250000000 2300 150 15 1
122 314030040002103 212020010002 3243324232211223332423 22112 223333
42322114332223331234212433222432323332224332234324233222 4443 1320 0000000
4443 1320 0010000 3 40000000 675 28 60 1
13322223331200001204232233332222113243333443333222333444333322222 5222444
3333222324222 4443333222324333444333322242533344433332224444 41421 44444 4
434420410 33333 3 1 88750000 200 35 1 0
1432112221320222010032122313202220432233331323122132333142313212212 23441
323122132233443142312213323333314331231442444321424133122232 1222 32233 1
2231 1112 21222 1 3 900000000 2500 50 1 0
15441341020204001304234444430400443444553333333243344434443343323333443
444333333322255344443433342 3553333333334443335534333434344 3342 33344 4
4344 3340 33333 4 1 471763000 525 380 1 0
16433013441201001224330233 4240434433444444343343333544543333424333354
44423333343333444232332233433444444434333334334444444233343 44 2311 43334 3
4433 2210 23333 2 1 450000000 450 175 3 0
17433113032302012134232133332233314524342224332422333553333132522333444
23341132222224542223112224222223444322532211133343331123344 1332 32424 4
4443 1321 31324 3 4 326125000 1300 500 4 0
18333033213301003123332333303333324443332433233333322244333333333224222343

333333333322222333223333332222234322333344222223432233333333 3332 33133 3
4444 3331 43133 3 1 100000000 600 100 5 0
193300120333000030133001203330000544422454422442442245432243233 222454
322531242222235522241142222223552223214222222235422232131222 3300   2
2322 4400   1 3 673500000 1500 700 24 1
2032322213121200321113333323232302233223232333323333223243343333323333234
2334222422132343233512332322233424332235232344533434123223342232 33342 4
334102212 10002 0 4200000000042000 5000 70 1
2121322313331110100113203313432204344233444341332222345434222221 2211224
22322222232114552333111224222455445122221423345445522223243013 2004112304
43420242004112401 31000000000 7000 300 2 0
2232301110420110111414103304224404244232433452322313244355122231 4413154
3551222213332424444211112153241554441211215324155444111112333 3320 42243 3
4444 2210 30343 3 1 20000000 460 300 6 0
2322203303020000013333234242322213343344442333233335554233323 33334334554
23342333344345542222222233443455422222224444345542222333344 4 2333 44344 4
4444 2332 33233 3 2 38623000 400 40 3 0
24332223333212331331332224333123313443334433332343333443333234334 4333443
333334343422244333342225253225433332333444333332234244223 33 3311 42233 2
4433 3311 41233 2 2275000000018000 1100 60 1
25322123124203001322221232342233022422334232222332233533222222 3234224342
23222231142234422222222324224342322222232233224452232223333 34 2321 33322 2
4444 2321 43422 2 2 700000000 1200 150 3 0
26000000000000000000003212333321000045344423333332222443444433 2222425443555
333322244444444442224222233333333334552222335433555555522223344 2344 33344 2
3344 2344 33344 1 2 633000000 1000 60 1 0
27302220041 210000 313223341 33404353333334343332444554445323452 4244433
345433431313333323342224151224534442224525233524344223423 33 2333 33333 3
4444 3430 41003 4 1 30000000 250 50 0 0
2804000000400000000040202244000003443232333343333232224333433 322344322243
3343322433111442122421142211144212242113221114421224211424 2 2410 33342 3
4242 2410 33342 3 2 400000 4 1 4 0
293 2003242221012433 32033432322233422244232222343224524222345 323222452
32242332231115541114224324111554333322542422233 2 3234233332222 42233 4
444443333 44444 4 44000000000 3500 3000 20 1
3041112203011001112412133131110015332444444334434444444433333 343324444
33343332224455432242222323244444443344424442554433344443334 3432243344 3
3334 2431143343 2 2 5000000 95 64 0 0
31313102323313302122031024133334032422245335523333222443355 2223213122343
24421124141114422552111315222441344211342533434245513343332 2333 33343 3
4221 1220 11111 1 4 4518000 8000 500 5 0
32432223033222 111132232423324 04323123525441223322353445222 3322223454
244311422222245222242223333322234512253233235533443223122 3 3340 33342 4
4432 2220 31012 1 3200000000015000 400 20 1
33422022222 1110220312213313 31204323344434333433325342333233 3433434342
332233234333345 323223243323333 333223224223434 34422223232 012332233213
43331012231212223 4 150000000 1100 180 2 0
3444323303123002200443334233342023425341135235 32 422553533342 423311553
255532 223111442123511 423222333344432 534333442334332 3433 332041344 3
4422 2320 30334 1 4 150000000 800 100 3 0
35444222043 0000000444223043 0000323222454 2 322454 3 323222454
3 113111443 1 222222353 4 335333555 3 4434 44
4434 44   3 274000000 2400 500 2 0
364 4 4 444 02111144 4 4 444 22214242333434332113322243444211 3323222243
42221124 22224 23332233 22223 34423224 22224 33321133444 3403 32343 4
3444 4400 33342 0 1 200000000 4500 450 21 1

209

372300022034100000103220222333100042322334343313235233443221322412112244
2221321413111344232121241311113342321213523223354232132223 43 2322 33323 3
4442 2322 22103 3 2 500000000 5000 2300 14 1
383220330321110000 413113133232221523223455323312142344333 3121 423223443
233121 412234444222322 413222333233111 523234443233222 3233 2331   4
3333 2320   2 22000000000 5000 250 3 0
39331 3 2030000233332 322233120433334554433232343455443323234 33334444
33323233242234442424113324333454333422343344432442313234344 4433 42244 3
4444 4411 41244 1 1 90000000 1600 1400   4 0
4023333303230110022333333303 20110334323444232312332344423221233343 23344
22221223333334442333112222333444233211233333334442332113333 3 1331 44404 3
2334 1321 33303 3 3 225000000 2000 120   2 0
41432022040002102204310110300011053412355312213225234531221443543123554
22212225231125555111322243411333344413335251225232441333434 3 3421 44234 4
4443 2410 44234 4 1 250000000 1000 300   1 0
42432133031102000004322331312132244333333324332222233433344221222312 2432
122311113252224341324111225111445244311133423343444332123443 3332 34443 4
4443 4420 22134 3 41600000000 750 350   8 1
4333102203330000100332123144311004332233 221222 42343 321222 42433343
321222 424222443222322 434322443222332 424333443222332 3323 3410 33 3 1
3332 4400 33 3 0 1 340000000 1800 156   1 0
4444131404100201312 3 111104100201334223543242522422344334232324434444553
24252244231115531111522343522244322243252232224332222432423234 3344 43323 4
144444410 43313 4 2 75000000 1200 330 60 1
4523101212020000000022 013220221102231123443441122322244445555222223222233
2324211212222344 4221213222232444221242322223344432113 42
4 30 00000   0 1 62955000 350 300   1 0
46312004423 000000031400 44 4 11005344444534433 3224534433 535444453
3534 4251113534445 4452224 34444 5451114534444 3030 1122 33444 4
4   2000 33404 2 2 319750000 1200 100 30 1
47242123012200000003232230 221000424223233 2 12233223 1 12323222333
 4 12211111344 111132 111222 1113415123222 1112234444422 32342 4
334434400 20122 1 1 600000000 7000 4000 22 1
48333124020221111113331240202211154434434343333224444444332222335444333
333222233522255551124422233433355552334222445444555222322223443 2343 1112223
4343 1233 1112223 3 80000000 300 120 15 1
4922101333130000012222213332322213332225542442222211554244222222 23111554
2442111212111255535551122131125553555222213112434354411244 44 3423 42234 4
3344 2412 42234 4 2 24000000 400   20   1 0
50411134031010001044111330300000044234 44   3 44444   4 44322444
 2 34333344   3 34334444   3 35445554   3 42334 3321 43343 3
3433 3310 43233 3 2 5000000   75   40   2 0
51341000011000003003410000330000044111242311134413114231113231241322343
1111233132411144311142224 34 4441114331322 3331114421424002 42 000 3
42400342 000 0 31200000000 8000 300   1 0
524410131411010143233221344424221545322342422144352234232213324333 22453
2331222335111453121321443511134344424354453333232321333334 4 3342 42214 3
4443 0030 20004 2 4 400000000 2600 150   5 0
533322123332211031233221233322110342443341121131233334112113124224433 41
121313232133344111111312421333441111131242133333 1111113124444 3331 33314 2
4444 3331 333142 430000000000 19000 3000 100 1
54432023 1020000000432023 2 311105443344443333333534444333433343323 3444
33332223232122444222511232323355533342225332334443333112323 3 2233 44443 4
4123 2220 22222 2 1 124901000 800 650   3 0
552222222213321103212122223313331203343333255423333443315542432244343332 55
424433334333245333432443533334442323344343222444242324343 3 4411 43323 4

```
4343 4411 21113 2 3 700000000  800  735  9 1
 56330033032300000003300332323000033333333333333322333333333333322222233442
32222222222222333322211111222333444222322222244411133322223333 3343 33343 3
4344 4443 33333 3 3 278000000 2000 1500  10 1
 5732322203222110321323222223233220524222445444232452245544442324
        5252114553224113525111445355111 4            233443444 44443 3
443313420     0 4 125000000 1200  150   4 0
 582421222321111011033332333221210333333334333323322333333333333233322 2344
33333222332224542223222233222343333322323422244423342222232 3323 31033 3
4243 3331 10011 1 3600000000085000 4000  200 1
 59         322013131311024332333334322333 422334322332 322222334
222322 433222445222422 433223344422433 533133223322333 1243 1341 42233 2
4444 1340 42124 2 3 40000000  300  71   1 0
  60 2101201011000200  113233333313221231332    2232333    323223144
2    212       222       322      2234 233  31344 4
23321200 20002  2 46000000000 6000  200  20 1
 6132121213211103111321212132111034434444332422342333344342232232232333 3443
42232223342123432224122234222344232332232232322333232231223332 2331 33344 3
4322 1310 22012 2 4 736195000 8000 1650 300 1
 62332232 13211 0120323332 13233 232422233 344233222244 344233232222244
344233331211133 133313131422233 344232442322234 44533333333 2343 32344 3
4444 1223 31114 2 22700000000 7400  147  48 1
 6333233322212000211332334333120003343334 4 32233 232244 32233 233332234
32232 23232 344    2 23333 344    2 23232 344   2 23322 3213
3222 3333       3 993000000 2000 1500  24 1
 64444 44043404204224444 44043404205354444554442222433455433221232333 3455
43322124344444542224111434444444454211354544433545521134343 4443 42443 4
4444 2232 42433 4 4 100000000  800   80   4 0
 65313213222222321122132133132333232432323343322132232333333213224223243
33342132131222331224112314222232332222234242233223332223243 2322 32233 3
3233 2321 32233 3 3 69800000 1300  60   6 1
 663321220301000022132433433133441314333433344232432244335523232132222333
344232333141113332333112215222443455232431433333333441334223 3 2233332334 3
3333 2231431334 3 3 700000000  900  150   1 0
 67232333020200001332323330202000033433334 344233243334 344232252322234
23333224232224542335532342322245423353234232224542335323233442433 43343 4
444442220 20003 0 1 40000000 1500    0  2 0
 6833201333230000001323213423302023232334542444222233454344422122213 3454
244411122313 554255411121313 444455422221313 53435542223344 0422 42144 3
4444 0411 43134 3 2 23000000  400   19   1 0
  69 31002030 2  2 0 320120031 2  23333334 4  3 233344 4  3 333422244
3  2 333322255 1  1 133422233 4  2 452422244 3  2 43333 2333 31223 3
4322 2200 00000 0 32000000000 5000  500  28 1
 7033100304121101211332113141212114343234443443223423444344322 3344223444
22242234232224432334222334222444333322343422334442333223 3444 1431 43134 2
4444 0431 33134 2 1300000000035000  150  12 1
 71332223133212211324222322333222232512333 22 332233232431 33223323123343
1 341243131123331333123314322443333312441432234323432243343 3322 42244 3
4343 2212 43213 3 3 76000000013000 1000  60 1
 724420330233020023233223331423130433244254544233534435454543344232 33254
4452223312122455322411221212233555232545535543345435551244 2443 43443 4
3444 2440 42234 4 115000000003400026000  371 1
 73313033223310004323231223344300042322234431122224222355211211124232 22455
322222242222245521131114132224554333211422333334555343322432333 3113233
313334222 4004333 4 600000000 6000 4000  80 1
 74330003234230023013301221332110234223333342224324233333333433432223333
```

2224323322222245422232222432233334332423443223433533342343333 1202440003 4
4333 1202440003 4 4 250000000 1100 535 5 0
    75320012202200000004100144034100043 4543 12133 4542 121342 555
1 12133322334552123212332333455333221252333435533322124341 22433   4
4140 22200   2 3650000000025000 957 15 1
  763100321300020222 3100332300021233224445424343334345542323233432223453
222323234222334322241124343224433334222443223323223322244434 03 3441333 3
4434 02 1441212 1 21000000000 1200 700   2 0
  7722212103121200221313113221222203444333333333332222453344322423433453
34432241232224432334222125222453444322531411155344442252243 2332 43442 4
4342 2222 2 223 2 4 3000000 60 10 3 0
   78233134222211100002331342233211033422244422223113224442222311223222444
22223112222222444222231122322224442222311223222444222231122233 2231 33322 4
2233 1230 33322 4 4 42000000 1700 600   6 1
  793100321300020222 3100332300021233224445424343334345542323233432223453
222323234222334322241124343224433334222443223323223322244434 03 3441333 3
4434 02 1441212 1 21000000000 1200 700   2 0
  8044131404100201312 111110410020133422354324252242234433423324434444553
24252244231115531115223435222443222432522322244332224324232443344 43323 4
144444410 43313 4 2 75000000 1200 330 60 1

Introduction to the Disk Files

The instructor's disk contains the output and control cards for each technique discussed in the text. The following table describes the file types contained on the disk:

File Type	Description
.dat	Tab-delimited ASCII text file
.ls8	LISREL 8 syntax file
.out	LISREL 8 output file
.sas	SAS syntax file
.sav	SPSS data file
.spo	SPSS output file
.sps	SPSS syntax file

For example, the "CHAP03" subdirectory contains:

Filename	Contents
COMMON.SAS	Common factor analysis SAS control card
COMMON.SPO	Common factor analysis SPSS output
COMMON.SPS	Common factor analysis SPSS control card
OBLIQUE.SAS	Components w/oblique rotation SAS control card
OBLIQUE.SPO	Components w/oblique rotation SPSS output
OBLIQUE.SPS	Components w/oblique rotation SPSS control card
PC_Valid.SPO	Validation of principal components SPSS output
PC_Valid.SPS	Validation of principal components SPSS control card
VARIMAX.SAS	Components w/VARIMAX rotation SAS control card
VARIMAX.SPO	Components w/VARIMAX rotation SAS output
VARIMAX.SPS	Components w/VARIMAX rotation SPSS control card

while the "DATA" subdirectory contains:

Filename	Contents
HATCO.DAT	HATCO data tab-delimited ASCII text file
HATCO.SAV	HATCO data SPSS data file
HATSPSS.SPS	HATCO data SPSS control cards
HATSAS.SAS	HATCO data SAS control cards
HATMISS.DAT	HATCO missing data tab-delimited ASCII text file
HATMISS.SAV	HATCO missing data SPSS data file
SALES.DAT	Sales training raw data tab-delimited ASCII text file
SALESPSS.SPS	Sales training raw data SPSS control cards

SECTION THREE:

ANNOTATED COMPUTER OUTPUTS

CHAPTER 2:

EXAMINING YOUR DATA: TESTING THE ASSUMPTIONS

This section of the instructor's manual contains copies of the actual printouts from the SPSS statistical analysis program. The printouts contain examples of the analyses discussed in the text using the HATCO database.

Each of the printouts is annotated with comments to aid in the interpretation of the results. These suggestions are typed in the margins next to the appropriate data. If you wish to provide students with their own copies of the output without these comments, the output are provided on the computer diskette accompanying the instructor's manual.

An example of how to test the assumptions which are necessary to use multivariate analyses is included in this section. In addition, a missing data analysis is also provided. A brief description follows:

Examining Your Data: To test the assumptions, a SPSS procedure (EXAMINE) is illustrated for one of the predictor variables (X_1). The missing data analysis is performed using the SPSS procedure, MVA, on variables X_1 to X_{10}.

217

Examining Your Data: Descriptive Statistics

*Descriptive Statistics.
EXAMINE VARIABLES=X1 X2 X3 X4 X5 X6 X7 X9 X10
/PLOT NONE
/STATISTICS DESCRIPTIVES
/CINTERVAL 95
/MISSING LISTWISE
/NOTOTAL.

Case Processing Summary

	Cases					
	Valid		Missing		Total	
	N	Percent	N	Percent	N	Percent
Delivery Speed	100	100.0%	0	.0%	100	100.0%
Price Level	100	100.0%	0	.0%	100	100.0%
Price Flexibility	100	100.0%	0	.0%	100	100.0%
Manufacturer Image	100	100.0%	0	.0%	100	100.0%
Service	100	100.0%	0	.0%	100	100.0%
Salesforce Image	100	100.0%	0	.0%	100	100.0%
Product Quality	100	100.0%	0	.0%	100	100.0%
Usage Level	100	100.0%	0	.0%	100	100.0%
Satisfaction Level	100	100.0%	0	.0%	100	100.0%

Descriptives

			Statistic	Std. Error
Delivery Speed	Mean		3.515	.132
	95% Confidence Interval for Mean	Lower Bound	3.253	
		Upper Bound	3.777	
	5% Trimmed Mean		3.534	
	Median		3.400	
	Variance		1.744	
	Std. Deviation		1.321	
	Minimum		.0	
	Maximum		6.1	
	Range		6.1	
	Interquartile Range		2.100	
	Skewness		-.085	.241
	Kurtosis		-.511	.478

Descriptive statistics
for *delivery speed* (X_1).

219

Examining Your Data: Testing For Homoscedasticity.

```
*Testing For Homoscedasticity.
EXAMINE  VARIABLES=X1 X2 X3 X4 X5 X6 X7 X9 X10 BY X8 X11 X12 X13 X14
  /ID= ID
  /PLOT  SPREADLEVEL(1)
  /STATISTICS DESCRIPTIVES
  /CINTERVAL 95
  /MISSING LISTWISE
  /NOTOTAL.
```

Firm Size

Case Processing Summary

		Cases					
		Valid		Missing		Total	
	Firm Size	N	Percent	N	Percent	N	Percent
Delivery Speed	SMALL	60	100.0%	0	.0%	60	100.0%
	LARGE	40	100.0%	0	.0%	40	100.0%
Price Level	SMALL	60	100.0%	0	.0%	60	100.0%
	LARGE	40	100.0%	0	.0%	40	100.0%
Price Flexibility	SMALL	60	100.0%	0	.0%	60	100.0%
	LARGE	40	100.0%	0	.0%	40	100.0%
Manufacturer Image	SMALL	60	100.0%	0	.0%	60	100.0%
	LARGE	40	100.0%	0	.0%	40	100.0%
Service	SMALL	60	100.0%	0	.0%	60	100.0%
	LARGE	40	100.0%	0	.0%	40	100.0%
Salesforce Image	SMALL	60	100.0%	0	.0%	60	100.0%
	LARGE	40	100.0%	0	.0%	40	100.0%
Product Quality	SMALL	60	100.0%	0	.0%	60	100.0%
	LARGE	40	100.0%	0	.0%	40	100.0%
Usage Level	SMALL	60	100.0%	0	.0%	60	100.0%
	LARGE	40	100.0%	0	.0%	40	100.0%
Satisfaction Level	SMALL	60	100.0%	0	.0%	60	100.0%
	LARGE	40	100.0%	0	.0%	40	100.0%

220

Descriptives

	Firm			Statistic	Std. Error
Delivery Speed	SMALL	Mean		4.192	.134
		95% Confidence Interval for Mean	Lower Bound	3.924	
			Upper Bound	4.460	
		5% Trimmed Mean		4.198	
		Median		4.150	
		Variance		1.076	
		Std. Deviation		1.037	
		Minimum		2.1	
		Maximum		6.1	
		Range		4.0	
		Interquartile Range		1.775	
		Skewness		-.043	.309
		Kurtosis		-.994	.608
	LARGE	Mean		2.500	.161
		95% Confidence Interval for Mean	Lower Bound	2.174	
			Upper Bound	2.826	
		5% Trimmed Mean		2.500	
		Median		2.400	
		Variance		1.038	
		Std. Deviation		1.019	
		Minimum		.0	
		Maximum		4.9	
		Range		4.9	
		Interquartile Range		1.175	
		Skewness		.034	.374
		Kurtosis		.398	.733

Test of Homogeneity of Variance

	Levene Statistic	df1	df2	Sig.
Delivery Speed	.934	1	98	.336
Price Level	1.582	1	98	.211
Price Flexibility	1.194	1	98	.277
Manufacturer Image	6.549	1	98	.012
Service	7.819	1	98	.006
Salesforce Image	5.279	1	98	.024
Product Quality	8.748	1	98	.004
Usage Level	1.377	1	98	.243
Satisfaction Level	.323	1	98	.571

The Levene test is used to assess whether the variances of a single metric variable are equal across any number of groups. In this case, we are testing whether the variances are equal across two groups, small and large firm size. For *delivery speed*, the Levene test indicates that the variances are equal (significance = .336) so that the homoscedasticity assumption is met.

Delivery Speed

Spread vs. Level Plot of X1 By X8

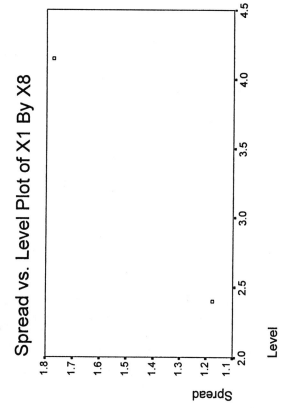

Level

* Data transformed using P =

Slope = .343

Examining Your Data: Missing Data Analysis

```
*Missing Data Analysis.
MVA
  x1 x2 x3 x4 x5 x6 x7 x9 x10
  /ID = id
  /TTEST PROB PERCENT=5
  /CROSSTAB PERCENT=5
  /MISMATCH PERCENT=5
  /DPATTERN DESCRIBE=x1 x2 x3 x4 x5 x6 x7 x9 x10
  /MPATTERN DESCRIBE=x1 x2 x3 x4 x5 x6 x7 x9 x10
  /TPATTERN PERCENT=1 DESCRIBE=x1 x2 x3 x4 x5 x6 x7 x9 x10
  /LISTWISE
  /PAIRWISE
  /EM ( TOLERANCE=0.001 CONVERGENCE=0.0001 ITERATIONS=200 )
  /REGRESSION ( TOLERANCE=0.001 FLIMIT=4.0 ADDTYPE=RESIDUAL ) .
```

Warnings

> There are no categorical variables.
> CROSSTAB is not produced.
>
> Less than half of the cases are complete. The
> /REGRESSION ADDTYPE is changed to
> NORMAL.

Univariate Statistics

	N	Mean	Std. Deviation	Missing Count	Missing Percent	No. of Extremes[a] Low	No. of Extremes[a] High
X1	45	4.0133	.9664	19	29.7	0	0
X2	54	1.8963	.8589	10	15.6	0	0
X3	50	8.1300	1.3194	14	21.9	0	0
X4	60	5.1467	1.1877	4	6.3	0	0
X5	59	2.8390	.7541	5	7.8	0	0
X6	63	2.6016	.7192	1	1.6	0	0
X7	60	6.7900	1.6751	4	6.3	0	0
X9	60	45.9667	9.4204	4	6.3	0	0
X10	60	4.7983	.8194	4	6.3	0	0

a. Number of cases outside the range (Q1 -
1.5*IQR, Q3 + 1.5*IQR).

> Unadjusted univariate summary
> statistics and the percentage of
> missing or out of range values for
> each variable. Note that the sample
> size changes for each variable.

224

Summary of Estimated Means

	X1	X2	X3	X4	X5	X6	X7	X9	X10
Listwise	4.0192	1.9500	8.3538	5.2692	2.9808	2.6000	6.7538	48.3077	4.8962
All Values	4.0133	1.8963	8.1300	5.1467	2.8390	2.6016	6.7900	45.9667	4.7983
EM	3.7108	2.0344	8.1097	5.1491	2.8226	2.6015	6.8439	45.8485	4.7665
Regression	3.9218	1.9376	8.0305	5.1565	2.8222	2.5858	6.8227	45.7345	4.7572

Summary of Estimated Standard Deviations

	X1	X2	X3	X4	X5	X6	X7	X9	X10
Listwise	.9583	.8860	1.1697	1.1030	.4875	.7440	1.3848	8.0487	.8022
All Values	.9664	.8589	1.3194	1.1877	.7541	.7192	1.6751	9.4204	.8194
EM	1.1463	1.0011	1.2724	1.1585	.7458	.7148	1.6804	9.2896	.8156
Regression	.9546	.8634	1.2789	1.1604	.7415	.7246	1.7302	9.2370	.8281

Summary results for the complete case (listwise), all-available (pairwise), regression and EM imputation methods.

225

Separate Variance t Tests[a]

		X1	X2	X3	X4	X5	X6	X7	X9	X10
X1	t	.	-.3	1.3	2.2	2.6	1.9	-1.1	2.6	2.1
	df	.	30.3	16.3	41.9	21.4	38.8	25.9	24.8	23.5
	P(2-tail)	.	.763	.223	.033	.017	.065	.273	.017	.049
	# Present	45	38	38	42	42	44	42	42	43
	# Missing	0	16	12	18	17	19	18	18	17
	Mean(Present)	4.0133	1.8737	8.2737	5.3405	3.0214	2.7068	6.6143	48.1667	4.9488
	Mean(Missing)		1.9500	7.6750	4.6944	2.3882	2.3579	7.2000	40.8333	4.4176
X2	t	-.5	.	.7	-2.2	-4.2	-2.4	-1.2	-1.1	-1.2
	df	7.0	.	10.3	12.1	17.8	12.0	11.0	9.3	18.6
	P(2-tail)	.646	.	.528	.044	.001	.034	.260	.318	.233
	# Present	38	54	42	50	49	53	51	52	50
	# Missing	7	0	8	10	10	10	9	8	10
	Mean(Present)	3.9737	1.8963	8.1810	4.9880	2.7041	2.5057	6.6824	45.4615	4.7540
	Mean(Missing)	4.2286		7.8625	5.9400	3.5000	3.1100	7.4000	49.2500	5.0200
X3	t	.4	1.4	.	1.1	2.0	.2	.0	1.9	.9
	df	10.3	18.3	.	16.0	14.9	23.2	16.5	28.7	18.2
	P(2-tail)	.693	.180	.	.286	.066	.818	.965	.073	.399
	# Present	38	42	50	48	47	49	47	46	48
	# Missing	7	12	0	12	12	14	13	14	12
	Mean(Present)	4.0342	1.9810	8.1300	5.2354	2.9468	2.6122	6.7957	47.0217	4.8417
	Mean(Missing)	3.9000	1.6000		4.7917	2.4167	2.5643	6.7692	42.5000	4.6250
X4	t	-.2	2.6	-.3	.	.2	1.4	1.5	.2	-2.4
	df	3.0	5.5	1.2	.	4.0	3.8	5.8	4.1	4.5
	P(2-tail)	.882	.046	.785	.	.888	.249	.197	.830	.064
	# Present	42	50	48	60	55	59	56	56	56
	# Missing	3	4	2	0	4	4	4	4	4
	Mean(Present)	4.0095	1.9420	8.1208	5.1467	2.8418	2.6254	6.8321	46.0179	4.7571
	Mean(Missing)	4.0667	1.3250	8.3500		2.8000	2.2500	6.2000	45.2500	5.3750

For each quantitative variable, pairs of groups are formed by indicator variables (present, missing).

a. Indicator variables with less than 5% missing are not displayed.

226

Assessing the randomness of missing data through group comparisons of observations with missing versus valid data.

Separate Variance t Tests[a]

		X1	X2	X3	X4	X5	X6	X7	X9	X10
X5	t	-.1	-.3	.8	.4	.	-.9	-.4	.5	.6
	df	2.2	6.4	2.1	7.1	.	4.8	4.5	4.4	4.5
	P(2-tail)	.900	.749	.502	.734	.	.423	.696	.669	.605
	# Present	42	49	47	55	59	58	55	55	55
	# Missing	3	5	3	5	0	5	5	5	5
	Mean(Present)	4.0071	1.8878	8.1957	5.1564	2.8390	2.5793	6.7582	46.1818	4.8200
	Mean(Missing)	4.1000	1.9800	7.1000	5.0400	.	2.8600	7.1400	43.6000	4.5600
X7	t	3.0	.9	.2	-2.1	.9	-1.5	.	.5	.4
	df	4.3	2.3	2.3	3.6	3.6	4.8	.	2.1	4.5
	P(2-tail)	.036	.440	.864	.118	.441	.193	.	.658	.704
	# Present	42	51	47	56	55	59	60	57	56
	# Missing	3	3	3	4	4	4	0	3	4
	Mean(Present)	4.0667	1.9196	8.1383	5.0732	2.8600	2.5814	6.7900	46.1404	4.8054
	Mean(Missing)	3.2667	1.5000	8.0000	6.1750	2.5500	2.9000	.	42.6667	4.7000
X9	t	6.1	-1.4	2.2	-1.1	-.9	-1.8	1.7	.	1.6
	df	37.2	1.0	3.4	3.9	4.1	4.0	9.1	.	5.7
	P(2-tail)	.000	.384	.101	.326	.401	.149	.128	.	.155
	# Present	42	52	46	56	55	59	57	60	56
	# Missing	3	2	4	4	4	4	3	0	4
	Mean(Present)	4.0786	1.8538	8.2609	5.1125	2.8218	2.5729	6.8158	45.9667	4.8214
	Mean(Missing)	3.1000	3.0000	6.6250	5.6250	3.0750	3.0250	6.3000	.	4.4750
X10	t	1.7	.8	-2.1	2.5	2.7	1.3	.9	2.4	.
	df	1.8	3.7	1.3	3.6	3.8	2.3	4.2	4.6	.
	P(2-tail)	.249	.463	.235	.076	.056	.302	.409	.066	.
	# Present	43	50	48	56	55	60	56	56	60
	# Missing	2	4	2	4	4	3	4	4	0
	Mean(Present)	4.0349	1.9200	8.0854	5.2321	2.8945	2.6233	6.8250	46.4286	4.7983
	Mean(Missing)	3.5500	1.6000	9.2000	3.9500	2.0750	2.1667	6.3000	39.5000	.

For each quantitative variable, pairs of groups are formed by indicator variables (present, missing).

a. Indicator variables with less than 5% missing are not displayed.

Percent Mismatch of Indicator Variables.[a,b]

	X4	X7	X9	X10	X5	X2	X3	X1
X4	6.25							
X7	12.50	6.25						
X9	12.50	9.38	6.25					
X10	12.50	12.50	12.50	6.25				
X5	14.06	14.06	14.06	14.06	7.81			
X2	21.88	18.75	15.63	21.88	23.44	15.63		
X3	21.88	25.00	28.13	21.88	23.44	31.25	21.88	
X1	32.81	32.81	32.81	29.69	31.25	35.94	29.69	29.69

The diagonal elements are the percentages missing, and the off-diagonal elements are the mismatch percentages of indicator variables.

a. Variables are sorted on missing patterns.

b. Indicator variables with less than 5% missing values are not displayed.

The percentage of missing data for each pair of combination. Based on the sample sizes for each pair of variables.

228

Missing Patterns (cases with missing values)

Case	# Missing	% Missing	Missing and Extreme Value Patterns[a]									Variable Values								
			X1	X3	X2	X5	X9	X7	X4	X10	X6	X1	X2	X3	X4	X5	X6	X7	X9	X10
205	1	11.1		S								5.10	1.40		4.80	3.30	2.60	3.80	49.00	4.90
202	2	22.2	S	S									.40		2.50	1.20	1.70	5.20	35.00	3.30
250	2	22.2	S	S									3.70		5.20	3.00	2.30	9.10	49.00	4.80
255	2	22.2	S	S									1.00		3.40	1.70	1.10	6.20	35.00	4.10
269	2	22.2	S	S									1.90		4.50	1.50	3.10	9.90	39.00	3.30
238	1	11.1	S										2.50	9.60	5.50	4.00	3.00	7.70	65.00	6.00
240	1	11.1	S										1.50	9.90	2.70	1.30	1.20	1.70	50.00	5.00
253	1	11.1	S										2.00	9.30	5.90	3.70	2.40	4.60	60.00	6.10
256	1	11.1	S										3.30	7.50	4.50	2.50	2.40	7.60	39.00	3.60
259	1	11.1	S										2.10	6.90	5.40	1.10	2.60	8.90	29.00	3.90
260	1	11.1	S										2.00	6.40	4.50	2.10	2.20	8.80	28.00	3.30
228	2	22.2	S						S				1.80	7.70		3.40	1.50	5.90	40.00	5.60
246	1	11.1							S			3.70	1.40	9.00		2.60	2.30	6.80	45.00	4.90
225	2	22.2		S					S			4.70	1.30			3.00	2.60	6.80	54.00	5.90
267	2	22.2		S					S			3.80	.80			2.20	2.60	5.30	42.00	5.10
222	2	22.2		S		S						3.90	2.20		4.60		2.50	8.30	47.00	5.00
241	2	22.2		S		S						3.10	1.90		4.50		3.10	3.80	54.00	4.80
229	1	11.1				S						5.30	1.40	9.70	6.10		3.90	6.80	54.00	5.90

- indicates an extreme low value, while + indicates an extreme high value. The range used is (Q1 - 1.5*IQR, Q3 + 1.5*IQR).

a. Cases and variables are sorted on missing patterns.

Missing Patterns (cases with missing values)

Case	# Missing	% Missing	Missing and Extreme Value Patterns[a] X1	X3	X2	X5	X6	X7	X4	X10	X9	Variable Values X1	X2	X3	X4	X5	X6	X7	X9	X10
216	2	22.2	S			S						.	1.60	6.40	5.00	.	2.10	8.40	25.00	3.40
218	2	22.2	S			S						.	2.80	5.20	5.00	.	2.70	8.40	38.00	3.70
232	2	22.2	S		S							.	.	8.20	5.00	3.60	2.50	9.00	53.00	5.20
248	2	22.2	S		S							.	.	6.40	5.30	3.00	2.50	7.10	46.00	4.50
237	1	11.1			S							4.90	.	7.40	6.90	4.60	4.00	9.60	62.00	6.20
249	1	11.1			S							5.30	.	8.50	3.70	3.50	1.90	4.80	58.00	4.30
220	1	11.1			S							6.50	.	9.00	7.00	3.20	3.70	8.00	33.00	5.40
213	2	22.2		S	S							3.10	.	.	7.80	3.60	4.00	5.90	43.00	5.20
257	2	22.2		S	S							3.60	.	.	5.80	3.70	2.50	9.30	44.00	4.80
203	2	22.2			S			S				3.00	.	9.10	7.10	3.50	3.40	.	55.00	5.20
231	1	11.1						S				3.70	.70	8.20	6.00	2.10	2.50	.	41.00	5.00
219	2	22.2						S			S	3.10	2.20	6.70	6.80	2.60	2.90	.	.	4.30
244	1	11.1									S	3.00	3.80	5.50	4.90	3.40	2.60	6.00	.	4.20
227	2	22.2			S						S	3.20	.	5.70	5.10	3.60	2.90	6.20	.	4.40
224	3	33.3	S		S						S	.	.	8.60	5.70	2.70	3.70	6.70	.	5.00
268	1	11.1								S		3.30	2.60	9.70	3.30	2.90	1.50	5.20	47.00	.
235	2	22.2					S			S		3.80	.80	8.70	2.90	1.60	.	5.60	39.00	.
204	3	33.3	S	S						S		.	1.50	.	4.80	1.90	2.50	7.20	36.00	4.80
207	3	33.3	S	S						S		.	1.50	.	4.80	1.90	2.50	7.20	36.00	4.80
221	3	33.3	S	S				S				.	1.60	.	4.80	2.00	2.80	.	32.00	4.30

– indicates an extreme low value, while + indicates an extreme high value. The range used is (Q1 – 1.5*IQR, Q3 + 1.5*IQR).

a. Cases and variables are sorted on missing patterns.

230

Tabulated Patterns

Number of Cases	_Missing Patterns[a]_ X1	X3	X2	X5	X9	X7	X4	X10	X6	Complete if...[b]	X1[c]	X2[c]	X3[c]	X4[c]	X5[c]	X6[c]	X7[c]	X9[c]	X10[c]
26										26	4.0192	1.9500	8.3538	5.2692	2.9808	2.6000	6.7538	48.3077	4.8962
1		X								27	5.1000	1.4000	.	4.8000	3.3000	2.6000	3.8000	49.0000	4.9000
4	X	X								37	.	1.7500	.	3.9000	1.8500	2.0500	7.6000	39.5000	3.8750
6	X									32	.	2.2333	8.2667	4.7500	2.4500	2.3000	6.5500	45.1667	4.6500
1							X			34	3.7000	1.8000	7.7000	.	3.4000	1.5000	5.9000	40.0000	5.6000
1							X			27	4.2500	1.4000	9.0000	.	2.6000	2.3000	6.8000	45.0000	4.9000
2		X								30	3.5000	1.0500	.	4.5500	2.6000	2.6000	6.0500	48.0000	5.5000
2				X						30	5.3000	2.0500	9.7000	6.1000	.	2.8000	6.0500	50.5000	4.9000
1	X			X						27	.	1.4000	5.8000	5.0000	.	3.9000	6.8000	54.0000	5.9000
2	X	X								35	.	2.2000	.	5.1500	3.3000	2.4000	8.4000	31.5000	3.5500
2			X							37	5.5667	.	7.3000	5.8667	3.7667	2.5000	8.0500	49.5000	4.8500
3			X							29	3.3500	.	8.3000	6.8000	3.6500	3.2000	7.4667	51.0000	5.3000
2		X								32	3.0000	.7000	.	7.1000	3.5000	3.2500	7.6000	43.5000	5.0000
1						X				31	3.7000	2.2000	9.1000	6.0000	2.1000	3.4000	.	55.0000	5.2000
1						X				27	3.1000	3.8000	8.2000	6.8000	2.6000	2.5000	.	41.0000	5.0000
1			X		X					29	3.0000	.	6.7000	4.9000	3.4000	2.9000	6.0000	.	4.3000
1			X		X					27	3.2000	.	5.5000	5.1000	3.6000	2.6000	6.2000	.	4.2000
1	X	X	X		X					31	.	.	.	5.7000	2.7000	2.9000	6.7000	.	4.4000
1					X					40	3.3000	2.6000	5.7000	3.3000	2.9000	3.7000	5.2000	.	5.0000
1								X		27	3.8000	.8000	8.6000	2.9000	1.6000	1.5000	5.6000	47.0000	.
1	X		X			X	X	X		28	.	.	9.7000	.	1.9000	2.5000	.	39.0000	.
2	X							X		40	.	1.5000	8.7000	4.8000	2.0000	2.8000	7.2000	36.0000	.
1	X	X		X		X			X	39	.	1.6000	.	4.8000	.	.	.	32.0000	4.3000

Patterns with less than 1% cases (0 or fewer) are not displayed.

a. Variables are sorted on missing patterns.

b. Number of complete cases if variables missing in that pattern (marked with X) are not used.

c. Means at each unique pattern

231

Listwise Statistics

Listwise Means

	X1	X2	X3	X4	X5	X6	X7	X9	X10
Number of cases	26								
	4.0192	1.9500	8.3538	5.2692	2.9808	2.6000	6.7538	48.3077	4.8962

Listwise Covariances

	X1	X2	X3	X4	X5	X6	X7	X9	X10
X1	.918								
X2	-.427	.785							
X3	.481	-.305	1.368						
X4	-.259	.313	-.079	1.217					
X5	.264	.182	.089	.025	.238				
X6	-.067	.234	-.057	.660	.077	.554			
X7	-.552	.434	-.373	.584	-.101	.545	1.918		
X9	4.622	.344	6.099	1.694	2.678	1.804	-1.101	64.782	
X10	.422	-.198	.680	.151	.119	.038	-.450	3.657	.644

Listwise Correlations

	X1	X2	X3	X4	X5	X6	X7	X9	X10
X1	1.000								
X2	-.502	1.000							
X3	.429	-.294	1.000						
X4	-.245	.320	-.061	1.000					
X5	.566	.421	.157	.046	1.000				
X6	-.094	.356	-.066	.804	.213	1.000			
X7	-.416	.354	-.230	.382	-.150	.529	1.000		
X9	.599	.048	.648	.191	.683	.301	-.099	1.000	
X10	.549	-.278	.725	.170	.304	.064	-.405	.566	1.000

The correlation obtained with a listwise or complete information approach.

232

Pairwise Statistics

Pairwise Frequencies

	X1	X2	X3	X4	X5	X6	X7	X9	X10
X1	45								
X2	38	54							
X3	38	42	50						
X4	42	50	48	60					
X5	42	49	47	55	59				
X6	44	53	49	59	58	63			
X7	42	51	47	56	55	59	60		
X9	42	52	46	56	55	59	57	60	
X10	43	50	48	56	55	60	56	56	60

Denotes sample sizes for complete pairs of variable values. The sample sizes on the diagonal are the univariate sample sizes.

Pairwise Means

	X1	X2	X3	X4	X5	X6	X7	X9	X10
X1	4.0133	1.8737	8.2737	5.3405	3.0214	2.7068	6.6143	48.1667	4.9488
X2	3.9737	1.8963	8.1810	4.9880	2.7041	2.5057	6.6824	45.4615	4.7540
X3	4.0342	1.9810	8.1300	5.2354	2.9468	2.6122	6.7957	47.0217	4.8417
X4	4.0095	1.9420	8.1208	5.1467	2.8418	2.6254	6.8321	46.0179	4.7571
X5	4.0071	1.8878	8.1957	5.1564	2.8390	2.5793	6.7582	46.1818	4.8200
X6	4.0182	1.9170	8.1184	5.1847	2.8603	2.6016	6.8102	46.0847	4.7983
X7	4.0667	1.9196	8.1383	5.0732	2.8600	2.5814	6.7900	46.1404	4.8054
X9	4.0786	1.8538	8.2609	5.1125	2.8218	2.5729	6.8158	45.9667	4.8214
X10	4.0349	1.9200	8.0854	5.2321	2.8945	2.6233	6.8250	46.4286	4.7983

Mean of quantitative variable when other variable is present.

233

Pairwise Standard Deviations

	X1	X2	X3	X4	X5	X6	X7	X9	X10
X1	.9664	.8840	1.2517	1.2380	.5891	.7321	1.5173	7.8365	.7179
X2	.8961	.8589	1.3408	1.1224	.7283	.6795	1.6686	9.4027	.8591
X3	1.0071	.8583	1.3194	1.1643	.6947	.7412	1.6007	9.8036	.8351
X4	.9936	.8711	1.3397	1.1877	.7719	.7279	1.7186	9.6474	.8264
X5	.9701	.8880	1.2429	1.2289	.7541	.7235	1.6616	9.2298	.8070
X6	.9770	.8534	1.3305	1.1604	.7424	.7192	1.6821	9.4564	.8194
X7	.9755	.8656	1.3377	1.1719	.7603	.7343	1.6751	9.3855	.8411
X9	.9677	.8318	1.2421	1.2065	.7697	.7268	1.7141	9.4204	.8396
X10	.9822	.8697	1.3242	1.1609	.7392	.7226	1.7120	9.5114	.8194

Standard deviation of quantitative variable when other variable is present.

Pairwise Covariances

	X1	X2	X3	X4	X5	X6	X7	X9	X10
X1	.934								
X2	-.379	.738							
X3	.524	-.411	1.741						
X4	-.122	.292	-.102	1.411					
X5	.209	.284	.041	.409	.569				
X6	.022	.151	-.035	.684	.185	.517			
X7	-.204	.502	-.767	.801	.084	.496	2.806		
X9	2.850	1.167	7.323	2.591	5.055	1.840	-3.247	88.745	
X10	.363	-.138	.776	.363	.318	.138	-.368	5.343	.671

Pairwise Correlations

	X1	X2	X3	X4	X5	X6	X7	X9	X10
X1	1.000								
X2	-.479	1.000							
X3	.416	-.357	1.000						
X4	-.099	.299	-.065	1.000					
X5	.366	.440	.047	.432	1.000				
X6	.031	.260	-.035	.810	.344	1.000			
X7	-.138	.348	-.358	.398	.066	.402	1.000		
X9	.376	.149	.601	.223	.712	.268	-.202	1.000	
X10	.514	-.184	.702	.378	.533	.233	-.256	.669	1.000

The correlation obtained with a pairwise or all-available information approach.

EM Estimated Statistics

EM Means[a]

X1	X2	X3	X4	X5	X6	X7	X9	X10
3.7108	2.0344	8.1097	5.1491	2.8226	2.6015	6.8439	45.8485	4.7665

a. Little's MCAR test: Chisquare = 174.464, df = 159, Prob = .190

EM Covariances[a]

	X1	X2	X3	X4	X5	X6	X7	X9	X10
X1	1.3141								
X2	-.3774	1.0022							
X3	.5990	-.4938	1.6189						
X4	-.1769	.3760	-.1574	1.3421					
X5	.5516	.3674	4.888E-02	.3606	.5562				
X6	.1254	.2068	-6.2660E-02	.6365	.1796	.5109			
X7	-.4129	.5630	-.6680	.7846	8.557E-02	.4876	2.8238		
X9	5.9698	1.9970	6.3336	2.0967	4.6892	1.7108	-2.9728	86.2970	
X10	.5954	-3.8588E-02	.6216	.3461	.3400	.1289	-.3239	5.0838	.6653

a. Little's MCAR test: Chisquare = 174.464, df = 159, Prob = .190

EM Correlations[a]

	X1	X2	X3	X4	X5	X6	X7	X9	X10
X1	1.000								
X2	-.329	1.000							
X3	.411	-.388	1.000						
X4	.133	.324	-.107	1.000					
X5	.645	.492	.052	.417	1.000				
X6	.153	.289	-.069	.769	.337	1.000			
X7	-.214	-.335	-.312	.403	.068	.406	1.000		
X9	.561	.215	.536	.195	.677	.258	-.190	1.000	
X10	.637	-.047	.599	.366	.559	.221	-.236	.671	1.000

a. Little's MCAR test: Chisquare = 174.464, df = 159, Prob = .190

Regression Estimated Statistics

Regression Means[a]

X1	X2	X3	X4	X5	X6	X7	X9	X10
3.9218	1.9376	8.0305	5.1565	2.8222	2.5858	6.8227	45.7345	4.7572

a. Random normal variate is added to each estimate.

Regression Covariances[a]

	X1	X2	X3	X4	X5	X6	X7	X9	X10
X1	.9112								
X2	-.4090	.7455							
X3	.4371	-.3445	1.6357						
X4	-5.7039E-02	.2690	-8.9155E-02	1.3466					
X5	.2393	.2860	.1105	.3576	.5498				
X6	6.324E-02	.1561	-6.0298E-02	.6726	.2019	.5251			
X7	-.2477	.5465	-.6566	.8634	.1229	.5183	2.9934		
X9	2.8026	1.0817	7.0139	2.2045	4.6389	1.7569	-2.0887	85.3224	
X10	.3081	-6.5374E-02	.7072	.3399	.3521	.1372	-.3255	5.2509	.6858

a. Random normal variate is added to each estimate.

Regression Correlations[a]

	X1	X2	X3	X4	X5	X6	X7	X9	X10
X1	1.000								
X2	-.496	1.000							
X3	.358	-.312	1.000						
X4	-.051	.269	-.060	1.000					
X5	.338	.447	.116	.416	1.000				
X6	.091	.250	-.065	.800	.376	1.000			
X7	-.150	.366	-.297	.430	.096	.413	1.000		
X9	.318	.136	.594	.206	.677	.262	-.131	1.000	
X10	.390	-.091	.668	.354	.573	.229	-.227	.686	1.000

a. Random normal variate is added to each estimate.

CHAPTER 3:

FACTOR ANALYSIS

This section of the instructor's manual contains copies of the actual printouts from the SPSS statistical analysis program. The printouts contain examples of the analyses discussed in the text using the HATCO database.

Each of the printouts is annotated with comments to aid in the interpretation of the results. These suggestions are typed in the margins next to the appropriate data. If you wish to provide students with their own copies of the output without these comments, the output are provided on the computer diskette accompanying the instructor's manual.

Two examples of principal components factor analysis and one example of common factor analysis are included in this section. A brief description follows:

Principal Components Factor Analysis with VARIMAX Rotation: Principal components factor analysis with an orthogonal (VARIMAX) rotation is performed on the seven attributes (X_1 to X_7).

Principal Components Factor Analysis with Oblique Rotation: Principal components factor analysis with an oblique rotation is performed on the seven attributes (X_1 to X_7).

Common Factor Analysis: Common factor analysis is performed on the seven attributes (X_1 to X_7).

Validation of Principal Components Factor Analysis: Validation of the components factor analysis with VARIMAX rotation results using a split-sample approach.

Principal Components Factor Analysis with VARIMAX Rotation

*Principal Components Analysis with Varimax Rotation (without X5).
FACTOR
/VARIABLES X1 X2 X3 X4 X6 X7
/CRITERIA ITERATE(50)
/FORMAT BLANK(0)
/PRINT ALL
/PLOT EIGEN ROTAT(1,2)
/EXTRACTION PC
/ROTATION VARIMAX.

Descriptive Statistics

	Mean	Std. Deviation	Analysis N
Delivery Speed	3.515	1.321	100
Price Level	2.364	1.196	100
Price Flexibility	7.894	1.387	100
Manufacturer Image	5.248	1.131	100
Salesforce Image	2.665	.771	100
Product Quality	6.971	1.585	100

Correlation Matrix[a]

		Delivery Speed	Price Level	Price Flexibility	Manufacturer Image	Salesforce Image	Product Quality
Correlation	Delivery Speed	1.000	-.349	.509	.050	.077	-.483
	Price Level	-.349	1.000	-.487	.272	.186	.470
	Price Flexibility	.509	-.487	1.000	-.116	-.034	-.448
	Manufacturer Image	.050	.272	-.116	1.000	.788	.200
	Salesforce Image	.077	.186	-.034	.788	1.000	.177
	Product Quality	-.483	.470	-.448	.200	.177	1.000
Sig. (1-tailed)	Delivery Speed		.000	.000	.309	.223	.000
	Price Level	.000		.000	.003	.032	.000
	Price Flexibility	.000	.000		.125	.367	.000
	Manufacturer Image	.309	.003	.125		.000	.023
	Salesforce Image	.223	.032	.367	.000		.039
	Product Quality	.000	.000	.000	.023	.039	

a. Determinant = .117

241

Inverse of Correlation Matrix

	Delivery Speed	Price Level	Price Flexibility	Manufacturer Image	Salesforce Image	Product Quality
Delivery Speed	1.589	.116	-.544	-.207	-.093	.527
Price Level	.116	1.539	.476	-.331	.052	-.397
Price Flexibility	-.544	.476	1.631	.173	-.170	.240
Manufacturer Image	-.207	-.331	.173	2.793	-2.109	-.051
Salesforce Image	-.093	.052	-.170	-2.109	2.690	-.201
Product Quality	.527	-.397	.240	-.051	-.201	1.594

KMO and Bartlett's Test

Kaiser-Meyer-Olkin Measure of Sampling Adequacy.		.665
Bartlett's Test of Sphericity	Approx. Chi-Square	205.965
	df	15
	Sig.	.000

Overall test for appropriateness of factor analysis. Assesses the degree to which the correlation matrix is an identity matrix (i.e., no intercorrelations). As shown here, the correlation matrix is significant (appropriate) and the analysis can proceed.

Anti-image Matrices

		Delivery Speed	Price Level	Price Flexibility	Manufacturer Image	Salesforce Image	Product Quality
Anti-image Covariance	Delivery Speed	.629	4.75E-02	-.210	-4.655E-02	-2.184E-02	.208
	Price Level	4.75E-02	.650	.190	-7.706E-02	1.260E-02	-.162
	Price Flexibility	-.210	.190	.613	3.791E-02	-3.864E-02	9.23E-02
	Manufacturer Image	-4.7E-02	-7.7E-02	3.79E-02	.358	-.281	-1.2E-02
	Salesforce Image	-2.2E-02	1.26E-02	-3.9E-02	-.281	.372	-4.7E-02
	Product Quality	.208	-.162	9.23E-02	-1.154E-02	-4.680E-02	.627
Anti-image Correlation	Delivery Speed	.721[a]	7.43E-02	-.338	-9.808E-02	-4.515E-02	.331
	Price Level	7.43E-02	.787[a]	.301	-.160	2.565E-02	-.253
	Price Flexibility	-.338	.301	.748[a]	8.092E-02	-8.093E-02	.149
	Manufacturer Image	-9.8E-02	-.160	8.09E-02	.542[a]	-.769	-2.4E-02
	Salesforce Image	-4.5E-02	2.56E-02	-8.1E-02	-.769	.532[a]	-9.7E-02
	Product Quality	.331	-.253	.149	-2.434E-02	-9.689E-02	.779[a]

a. Measures of Sampling Adequacy(MSA)

Communalities

	Initial	Extraction
Delivery Speed	1.000	.658
Price Level	1.000	.580
Price Flexibility	1.000	.646
Manufacturer Image	1.000	.882
Salesforce Image	1.000	.872
Product Quality	1.000	.616

Extraction Method: Principal Component Analysis.

> Principal components will extract two factors since there are two variables with eigenvalues at or exceeding 1.0. The two factor solution explains 70.9 percent of the total variance observed.

Total Variance Explained

Component	Initial Eigenvalues			Extraction Sums of Squared Loadings			Rotation Sums of Squared Loadings		
	Total	% of Variance	Cumulative %	Total	% of Variance	Cumulative %	Total	% of Variance	Cumulative %
1	2.513	41.892	41.892	2.513	41.892	41.892	2.370	39.497	39.497
2	1.740	28.992	70.883	1.740	28.992	70.883	1.883	31.386	70.883
3	.597	9.958	80.842						
4	.530	8.826	89.668						
5	.416	6.929	96.596						
6	.204	3.404	100.000						

Extraction Method: Principal Component Analysis.

Although only two factors have eigenvalues exceeding 1.0, the scree test indicates that a three factor solution may be appropriate.

Scree Plot

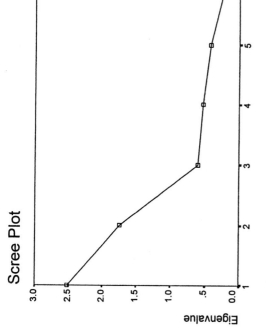

Component Number

Component Matrix[a]

	Component	
	1	2
Delivery Speed	-.627	.514
Price Level	.759	-6.8E-02
Price Flexibility	-.730	.337
Manufacturer Image	.494	.798
Salesforce Image	.425	.832
Product Quality	.767	-.168

Extraction Method: Principal Component Analysis.

a. 2 components extracted.

Reproduced Correlations

		Delivery Speed	Price Level	Price Flexibility	Manufacturer Image	Salesforce Image	Product Quality
Reproduced Correlation	Delivery Speed	.658[b]	-.511	.631	.101	.161	-.567
	Price Level	-.511	.580[b]	-.576	.321	.266	.593
	Price Flexibility	.631	-.576	.646[b]	-9.188E-02	-3.026E-02	-.616
	Manufacturer Image	.101	.321	-9.2E-02	.882[b]	.874	.245
	Salesforce Image	.161	.266	-3.0E-02	.874	.872[b]	.187
	Product Quality	-.567	.593	-.616	.245	.187	.616[b]
Residual[a]	Delivery Speed		.161	-.121	-5.042E-02	-8.417E-02	8.41E-02
	Price Level	.161		8.92E-02	-4.854E-02	-7.982E-02	-.123
	Price Flexibility	-.121	8.92E-02		-2.422E-02	-4.058E-03	.168
	Manufacturer Image	-5.0E-02	-4.9E-02	-2.4E-02		-8.577E-02	-4.5E-02
	Salesforce Image	-8.4E-02	-8.0E-02	-4.1E-03	-8.577E-02		-9.2E-03
	Product Quality	8.41E-02	-.123	.168	-4.506E-02	-9.210E-03	

Extraction Method: Principal Component Analysis.

a. Residuals are computed between observed and reproduced correlations. There are 10 (66.0%) nonredundant residuals with absolute values > 0.05.

b. Reproduced communalities

246

Rotated Component Matrix[a]

	Component	
	1	2
Delivery Speed	-.787	.194
Price Level	.714	.266
Price Flexibility	-.804	-1.1E-02
Manufacturer Image	.102	.933
Salesforce Image	2.54E-02	.934
Product Quality	.764	.179

Extraction Method: Principal
Component Analysis.
Rotation Method: Varimax with Kaiser
Normalization.

a. Rotation converged in 3
iterations.

Component Transformation Matrix

Component	1	2
1	.902	.431
2	-.431	.902

Extraction Method: Principal
Component Analysis.
Rotation Method: Varimax with
Kaiser Normalization.

Component Plot in Rotated Space

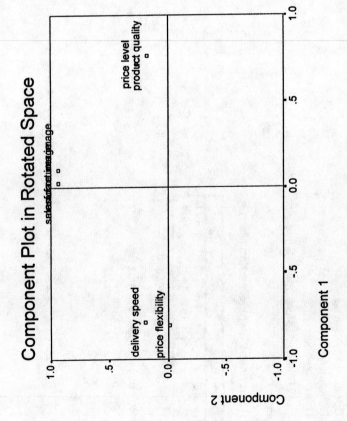

Component 1

Component 2

price level
product quality

sales force image
service time

delivery speed
price flexibility

248

Component Score Coefficient Matrix

	Component	
	1	2
Delivery Speed	-.352	.159
Price Level	.289	.095
Price Flexibility	-.345	.050
Manufacturer Image	-.020	.499
Salesforce Image	-.053	.504
Product Quality	.317	.044

Extraction Method: Principal Component Analysis.
Rotation Method: Varimax with Kaiser Normalization.

Factor score coefficients used to calculate the regression method factor scores for each case.

Component Score Covariance Matrix

Component	1	2
1	1.000	.000
2	.000	1.000

Extraction Method: Principal Component Analysis.
Rotation Method: Varimax with Kaiser Normalization.

Principal Components Factor Analysis with Oblique Rotation

*Principal Components Analysis with Oblique Rotation (without X5).
FACTOR
/VARIABLES X1 X2 X3 X4 X6 X7
/CRITERIA ITERATE(50)
/FORMAT BLANK(0)
/PRINT ALL
/PLOT EIGEN ROTAT(1,2)
/EXTRACTION PC
/ROTATION OBLIMIN .

The initial solution is omitted from this section since it is the same for both the orthogonal and oblique rotations.

The pattern and structure matrices have quite comparable loadings, due to the low correlation (.12) between the factors.

Pattern Matrix[a]

	Component	
	1	2
Delivery Speed	-.803	.248
Price Level	.704	.219
Price Flexibility	-.808	4.34E-02
Manufacturer Image	5.15E-02	.931
Salesforce Image	-2.6E-02	.937
Product Quality	.759	.129

Extraction Method: Principal Component Analysis.
Rotation Method: Oblimin with Kaiser Normalization.

a. Rotation converged in 5 iterations.

250

Structure Matrix

	Component	
	1	2
Delivery Speed	-.773	.151
Price Level	.730	.304
Price Flexibility	-.802	-5.4E-02
Manufacturer Image	.164	.938
Salesforce Image	8.76E-02	.934
Product Quality	.774	.220

Extraction Method: Principal Component Analysis.
Rotation Method: Oblimin with Kaiser Normalization.

Component Correlation Matrix

Component	1	2
1	1.000	.121
2	.121	1.000

Extraction Method: Principal Component Analysis.
Rotation Method: Oblimin with Kaiser Normalization.

An examination of the variable loadings indicates an identical interpretation as the VARIMAX rotation.

251

Component Score Coefficient Matrix

	Component	
	1	2
Delivery Speed	-.341	.140
Price Level	.295	.110
Price Flexibility	-.341	.031
Manufacturer Image	.013	.497
Salesforce Image	-.020	.501
Product Quality	.319	.062

Extraction Method: Principal
Component Analysis.
Rotation Method: Oblimin with Kaiser
Normalization.

Component Score Covariance Matrix

Component	1	2
1	1.015	.242
2	.242	1.015

Extraction Method: Principal
Component Analysis.
Rotation Method: Oblimin with Kaiser
Normalization.

Common Factor Analysis

*Common Factor Analysis.
FACTOR
/VARIABLES X1 X2 X3 X4 X6 X7
/PRINT INITIAL EXTRACTION ROTATION FSCORE
/CRITERIA MINEIGEN(1) ITERATE(150)
/PLOT EIGEN ROTAT(1,2)
/EXTRACTION PAF
/CRITERIA ITERATE(150)
/ROTATION VARIMAX .

The output used for testing assumptions in factor analysis have been removed from this section since these assumptions are addressed in the principal components analyses above.

Communalities

	Initial	Extraction
Delivery Speed	.371	.497
Price Level	.350	.430
Price Flexibility	.387	.522
Manufacturer Image	.642	.867
Salesforce Image	.628	.717
Product Quality	.373	.483

Extraction Method: Principal Axis Factoring.

Common factor analysis extracts 2 factors since a minimum eigenvalue of 1.0 was specified (see scree test). The two factor solution explains 58.6 percent of the total variance observed.

253

Total Variance Explained

Factor	Initial Eigenvalues			Extraction Sums of Squared Loadings			Rotation Sums of Squared Loadings		
	Total	% of Variance	Cumulative %	Total	% of Variance	Cumulative %	Total	% of Variance	Cumulative %
1	2.513	41.892	41.892	2.071	34.522	34.522	1.858	30.963	30.963
2	1.740	28.992	70.883	1.446	24.102	58.625	1.660	27.662	58.625
3	.597	9.958	80.842						
4	.530	8.826	89.668						
5	.416	6.929	96.596						
6	.204	3.404	100.000						

Extraction Method: Principal Axis Factoring.

Although only two factors have eigenvalues exceeding 1.0, the scree test indicates that a three factor solution may be appropriate.

Scree Plot

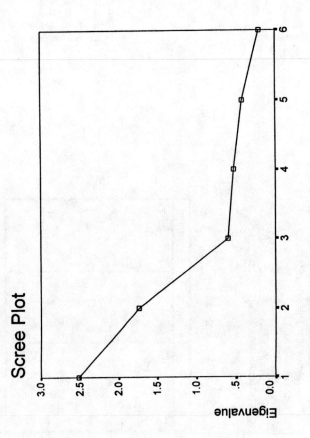

Factor Matrix[a]

	Factor	
	1	2
Delivery Speed	-.485	.512
Price Level	.629	-.188
Price Flexibility	-.601	.401
Manufacturer Image	.629	.687
Salesforce Image	.524	.665
Product Quality	.640	-.270

Extraction Method: Principal Axis Factoring.

a. 2 factors extracted. 33 iterations required.

Rotated Factor Matrix[a]

	Factor	
	1	2
Delivery Speed	-.693	.133
Price Level	.620	.215
Price Flexibility	-.722	-2.6E-02
Manufacturer Image	.109	.925
Salesforce Image	3.65E-02	.846
Product Quality	.677	.155

Extraction Method: Principal Axis Factoring.
Rotation Method: Varimax with Kaiser Normalization.

a. Rotation converged in 3 iterations.

Factor Transformation Matrix

Factor	1	2
1	.811	.584
2	-.584	.811

Extraction Method: Principal Axis Factoring.
Rotation Method: Varimax with Kaiser Normalization.

Factor Plot in Rotated Factor Space

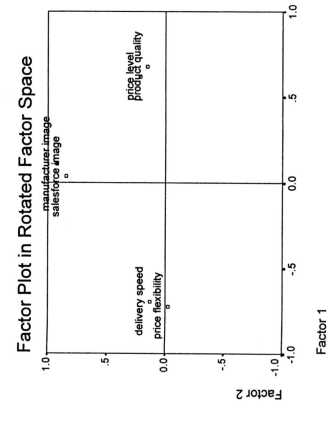

Factor Score Coefficient Matrix

	Factor	
	1	2
Delivery Speed	-.305	.061
Price Level	.227	.011
Price Flexibility	-.331	.042
Manufacturer Image	.005	.687
Salesforce Image	-.047	.298
Product Quality	.283	.008

Extraction Method: Principal Axis Factoring.
Rotation Method: Varimax with Kaiser Normalization.

Factor Score Covariance Matrix

Factor	1	2
1	.781	2.49E-02
2	2.49E-02	.898

Extraction Method: Principal Axis Factoring.
Rotation Method: Varimax with Kaiser Normalization.

Factor score coefficients are used to calculate regression method factor scores for each case.

Validation of Principal Components Factor Analysis

*Validation of Components Factor Analysis by Split-Sample Estimation with VARIMAX Rotation.

```
SET SEED=34567.
COMPUTE SPLIT=UNIFORM(1)>.52.
EXECUTE.
SORT CASES BY SPLIT .
SPLIT FILE
LAYERED BY SPLIT .
FACTOR
/VARIABLES X1 X2 X3 X4 X6 X7
/CRITERIA ITERATE(50)
/FORMAT BLANK(0)
/PRINT ALL
/PLOT EIGEN ROTAT(1,2)
/EXTRACTION PC
/ROTATION VARIMAX.
```

For validation purposes, only the communalities, total variance explained output, and VARIMAX-rotated loadings are included in this section.

SPLIT = .00

Communalities[a]

	Initial	Extraction
Delivery Speed	1.000	.640
Price Level	1.000	.616
Price Flexibility	1.000	.686
Manufacturer Image	1.000	.894
Salesforce Image	1.000	.841
Product Quality	1.000	.659

Extraction Method: Principal Component Analysis.

a. SPLIT = .00

Total Variance Explained[a]

Component	Initial Eigenvalues			Extraction Sums of Squared Loadings			Rotation Sums of Squared Loadings		
	Total	% of Variance	Cumulative %	Total	% of Variance	Cumulative %	Total	% of Variance	Cumulative %
1	2.421	40.350	40.350	2.421	40.350	40.350	2.417	40.289	40.289
2	1.915	31.922	72.272	1.915	31.922	72.272	1.919	31.983	72.272
3	.633	10.553	82.825						
4	.512	8.536	91.360						
5	.324	5.400	96.760						
6	.194	3.240	100.000						

Extraction Method: Principal Component Analysis.

a. SPLIT = .00

Rotated Component Matrix[a,b]

	Component	
	1	2
Delivery Speed	-.695	.397
Price Level	.772	.142
Price Flexibility	-.822	-9.8E-02
Manufacturer Image	4.53E-02	.944
Salesforce Image	5.56E-02	.916
Product Quality	.811	4.27E-02

Extraction Method: Principal Component Analysis.
Rotation Method: Varimax with Kaiser Normalization.

a. Rotation converged in 3 iterations.

b. SPLIT = .00

SPLIT = 1.00

Communalities[a]

	Initial	Extraction
Delivery Speed	1.000	.709
Price Level	1.000	.547
Price Flexibility	1.000	.698
Manufacturer Image	1.000	.865
Salesforce Image	1.000	.894
Product Quality	1.000	.563

Extraction Method: Principal Component Analysis.

a. SPLIT = 1.00

The sample is split into two equal samples of 50 respondents each. Both samples are comparable in terms of both loadings and communalities. Each is a two factor solution which explains over 70 percent of the total variance observed.

Total Variance Explained[a]

Component	Initial Eigenvalues			Extraction Sums of Squared Loadings			Rotation Sums of Squared Loadings		
	Total	% of Variance	Cumulative %	Total	% of Variance	Cumulative %	Total	% of Variance	Cumulative %
1	2.676	44.597	44.597	2.676	44.597	44.597	2.278	37.964	37.964
2	1.600	26.670	71.267	1.600	26.670	71.267	1.998	33.304	71.267
3	.642	10.695	81.962						
4	.470	7.837	89.799						
5	.427	7.113	96.911						
6	.185	3.089	100.000						

Extraction Method: Principal Component Analysis.

a. SPLIT = 1.00

Rotated Component Matrix[a,b]

	Component	
	1	2
Delivery Speed	.842	-1.6E-03
Price Level	-.625	.396
Price Flexibility	.829	.107
Manufacturer Image	-.167	.915
Salesforce Image	8.12E-03	.945
Product Quality	-.681	.315

Extraction Method: Principal Component Analysis.
Rotation Method: Varimax with Kaiser Normalization.

a. Rotation converged in 3 iterations.

b. SPLIT = 1.00

CHAPTER 4:

MULTIPLE REGRESSION

This section of the instructor's manual contains copies of the actual printouts from the SPSS statistical analysis program. The printouts contain examples of the analyses discussed in the text using the HATCO database.

Each of the printouts is annotated with comments to aid in the interpretation of the results. These suggestions are typed in the margins next to the appropriate data. If you wish to provide students with their own copies of the output without these comments, the output are provided on the computer diskette accompanying the instructor's manual.

An example of stepwise multiple regression is included in this section. A brief description follows:

Multiple Regression: A stepwise multiple regression in which the dependent variable is X_9 (level of product usage) which is predicted by the seven attribute ratings (X_1 to X_7).

Validation of Multiple Regression Results: Validation of the multiple regression results using a split-sample approach.

265

Multiple Regression

REGRESSION
  /DESCRIPTIVES ALL
  /STATISTICS ALL
  /CRITERIA=PIN(.05) POUT(.10)
  /DEPENDENT X9
  /METHOD=STEPWISE X1 X2 X3 X4 X5 X6 X7
  /PARTIALPLOT ALL
  /SCATTERPLOT=(*ZRESID,X9)
  /RESIDUALS HIST(ZRESID) NORM(ZRESID) ID(ID)
  /CASEWISE ALL SRE MAH SDR COOK LEVER
  /SAVE PRED ZPRED MAHAL COOK LEVER RESID ZRESID SRESID DRESID SDRESID DFBETA SDBETA DFFIT SDFIT COVRATIO.

Warnings

STATISTICS keywords LINE, END, and HISTORY are no longer supported.

Descriptive Statistics

	Mean	Std. Deviation	Variance	N
Usage Level	46.100	8.989	80.798	100
Delivery Speed	3.515	1.321	1.744	100
Price Level	2.364	1.196	1.430	100
Price Flexibility	7.894	1.387	1.922	100
Manufacturer Image	5.248	1.131	1.280	100
Service	2.916	.751	.564	100
Salesforce Image	2.665	.771	.594	100
Product Quality	6.971	1.585	2.513	100

266

Correlations

		Usage Level	Delivery Speed	Price Level	Price Flexibility	Manufacturer Image	Service	Salesforce Image	Product Quality
Pearson Correlation	Usage Level	1.000	.676	.082	.559	.224	.701	.256	-.192
	Delivery Speed	.676	1.000	-.349	.509	.050	.612	.077	-.483
	Price Level	.082	-.349	1.000	-.487	.272	.513	.186	.470
	Price Flexibility	.559	.509	-.487	1.000	-.116	.067	-.034	-.448
	Manufacturer Image	.224	.050	.272	-.116	1.000	.299	.788	.200
	Service	.701	.612	.513	.067	.299	1.000	.241	-.055
	Salesforce Image	.256	.077	.186	-.034	.788	.241	1.000	.177
	Product Quality	-.192	-.483	.470	-.448	.200	-.055	.177	1.000
Covariance	Usage Level	80.798	8.031	.880	6.967	2.280	4.732	1.774	-2.743
	Delivery Speed	8.031	1.744	-.551	.933	7.533E-02	.607	7.851E-02	-1.010
	Price Level	.880	-.551	1.430	-.808	.368	.461	.172	.890
	Price Flexibility	6.967	.933	-.808	1.922	-.182	6.939E-02	-3.668E-02	-.985
	Manufacturer Image	2.280	7.533E-02	.368	-.182	1.280	.254	.687	.359
	Service	4.732	.607	.461	6.939E-02	.254	.564	.139	-6.569E-02
	Salesforce Image	1.774	7.851E-02	.172	-3.668E-02	.687	.139	.594	.217
	Product Quality	-2.743	-1.010	.890	-.985	.359	-6.569E-02	.217	2.513
Sig. (1-tailed)	Usage Level	.	.000	.209	.000	.012	.000	.005	.028
	Delivery Speed	.000	.	.000	.000	.309	.000	.223	.000
	Price Level	.209	.000	.	.000	.003	.000	.032	.000
	Price Flexibility	.000	.000	.000	.	.125	.255	.367	.000
	Manufacturer Image	.012	.309	.003	.125	.	.001	.000	.023
	Service	.000	.000	.000	.255	.001	.	.008	.293
	Salesforce Image	.005	.223	.032	.367	.000	.008	.	.039
	Product Quality	.028	.000	.000	.000	.023	.293	.039	.

Correlations

		Usage Level	Delivery Speed	Price Level	Price Flexibility	Manufacturer Image	Service	Salesforce Image	Product Quality
Sum of Squares and Cross-products	Usage Level	7999.000	795.050	87.160	689.760	225.720	468.440	175.650	-271.510
	Delivery Speed	795.050	172.688	-54.596	92.329	7.458	60.106	7.772	-100.037
	Price Level	87.160	-54.596	141.530	-79.962	36.453	45.618	16.994	88.146
	Price Flexibility	689.760	92.329	-79.962	190.316	-18.031	6.870	-3.631	-97.507
	Manufacturer Image	225.720	7.458	36.453	-18.031	126.730	25.133	68.058	35.509
	Service	468.440	60.106	45.618	6.870	25.133	55.874	13.806	-6.504
	Salesforce Image	175.650	7.772	16.994	-3.631	68.058	13.806	58.828	21.449
	Product Quality	-271.510	-100.037	88.146	-97.507	35.509	-6.504	21.449	248.786
N	Usage Level	100	100	100	100	100	100	100	100
	Delivery Speed	100	100	100	100	100	100	100	100
	Price Level	100	100	100	100	100	100	100	100
	Price Flexibility	100	100	100	100	100	100	100	100
	Manufacturer Image	100	100	100	100	100	100	100	100
	Service	100	100	100	100	100	100	100	100
	Salesforce Image	100	100	100	100	100	100	100	100
	Product Quality	100	100	100	100	100	100	100	100

Variables Entered/Removed[a]

Model	Variables Entered	Variables Removed	Method
1	Service	.	Stepwise (Criteria: Probability-of-F-to-enter <= .050, Probability-of-F-to-remove >= .100).
2	Price Flexibility	.	Stepwise (Criteria: Probability-of-F-to-enter <= .050, Probability-of-F-to-remove >= .100).
3	Salesforce Image	.	Stepwise (Criteria: Probability-of-F-to-enter <= .050, Probability-of-F-to-remove >= .100).

a. Dependent Variable: Usage Level

Three variables enter the equation in the following order: *service, price flexibility,* and *salesforce image.* As each enters the predictive equation, the value of R^2 increases.

Model Summary[d]

Model	R	R Square	Adjusted R Square	Std. Error of the Estimate	Change Statistics					Selection Criteria			
					R Square Change	F Change	df1	df2	Sig. F Change	Akaike Information Criterion	Amemiya Prediction Criterion	Mallows' Prediction Criterion	Schwarz Bayesian Criterion
1	.701[a]	.491	.486	6.446	.491	94.525	1	98	.000	374.664	.530	112.071	379.875
2	.869[b]	.755	.750	4.498	.264	104.252	1	97	.000	303.680	.261	6.287	311.495
3	.877[c]	.768	.761	4.394	.014	5.656	1	96	.019	299.955	.251	2.707	310.376

a. Predictors: (Constant), Service

b. Predictors: (Constant), Service, Price Flexibility

c. Predictors: (Constant), Service, Price Flexibility, Salesforce Image

d. Dependent Variable: Usage Level

At each step, both the regression model and its coefficients are significant. A significant F ratio indicates that the amount of variation explained by the regression model is more than the variation explained by the average. The partial *t* values indicate that the beta coefficients are significant predictors of the dependent variable. The final model includes *service, price flexibility, and salesforce image.*

ANOVA[a]

Model		Sum of Squares	df	Mean Square	F	Sig.
1	Regression	3927.309	1	3927.309	94.525	.000[a]
	Residual	4071.691	98	41.548		
	Total	7999.000	99			
2	Regression	6036.513	2	3018.256	149.184	.000[b]
	Residual	1962.487	97	20.232		
	Total	7999.000	99			
3	Regression	6145.700	3	2048.567	106.115	.000[c]
	Residual	1853.300	96	19.305		
	Total	7999.000	99			

a. Predictors: (Constant), Service

b. Predictors: (Constant), Service, Price Flexibility

c. Predictors: (Constant), Service, Price Flexibility, Salesforce Image

d. Dependent Variable: Usage Level

Coefficients[a]

Model		Unstandardized Coefficients B	Std. Error	Standardized Coefficients Beta	t	Sig.	95% Confidence Interval for B Lower Bound	Upper Bound	Correlations Zero-order	Partial	Part	Collinearity Statistics Tolerance	VIF
1	(Constant)	21.653	2.596		8.341	.000	16.502	26.804					
	Service	8.384	.862	.701	9.722	.000	6.673	10.095	.701	.701	.701	1.000	1.000
2	(Constant)	-3.489	3.057		-1.141	.257	-9.556	2.578					
	Service	7.974	.603	.666	13.221	.000	6.777	9.171	.701	.802	.665	.996	1.004
	Price Flexibility	3.336	.327	.515	10.210	.000	2.688	3.985	.559	.720	.514	.996	1.004
3	(Constant)	-6.520	3.247		-2.008	.047	-12.965	-.075					
	Service	7.621	.607	.637	12.547	.000	6.416	8.827	.701	.788	.616	.936	1.068
	Price Flexibility	3.376	.320	.521	10.562	.000	2.742	4.010	.559	.733	.519	.993	1.007
	Salesforce Image	1.406	.591	.121	2.378	.019	.232	2.579	.256	.236	.117	.939	1.064

a. Dependent Variable: Usage Level

270

The largest, significant t-value enters the regression equation next. This criteria is specified in the syntax as the probability of F-to-enter (PIN = .05). So, the next variable to enter is *price flexibility* (t = 10.210, p = .000) followed by *salesforce image* (t = 2.378, p = .019). After *salesforce image* enters the equation, the probability of F-to-enter criteria is no longer met.

Excluded Variables[a]

Model		Beta In	t	Sig.	Partial Correlation	Collinearity Statistics		
						Tolerance	VIF	Minimum Tolerance
1	Delivery Speed	.396[a]	4.812	.000	.439	.626	1.599	.626
	Price Level	-.377[a]	-5.007	.000	-.453	.737	1.357	.737
	Price Flexibility	.515[a]	10.210	.000	.720	.996	1.004	.996
	Manufacturer Image	.016[a]	.216	.830	.022	.911	1.098	.911
	Salesforce Image	.093[a]	1.252	.214	.126	.942	1.062	.942
	Product Quality	-.154[a]	-2.178	.032	-.216	.997	1.003	.997
2	Delivery Speed	.016[b]	.205	.838	.021	.405	2.469	.405
	Price Level	-.020[b]	-.267	.790	-.027	.464	2.156	.464
	Manufacturer Image	.095[b]	1.808	.074	.181	.892	1.121	.892
	Salesforce Image	.121[b]	2.378	.019	.236	.939	1.064	.936
	Product Quality	.094[b]	1.683	.096	.169	.799	1.252	.797
3	Delivery Speed	.030[c]	.389	.698	.040	.403	2.483	.403
	Price Level	-.029[c]	-.405	.687	-.041	.462	2.163	.462
	Manufacturer Image	-.002[c]	-.021	.983	-.002	.357	2.805	.357
	Product Quality	.071[c]	1.273	.206	.130	.768	1.301	.768

a. Predictors in the Model: (Constant), Service

b. Predictors in the Model: (Constant), Service, Price Flexibility

c. Predictors in the Model: (Constant), Service, Price Flexibility, Salesforce Image

d. Dependent Variable: Usage Level

Coefficient Correlations[a]

Model			Service	Price Flexibility	Salesforce Image
1	Correlations	Service	1.000		
	Covariances	Service	.744		
2	Correlations	Service	1.000	-.067	
		Price Flexibility	-.067	1.000	
	Covariances	Service	.364	-1.313E-02	
		Price Flexibility	-1.313E-02	.107	
3	Correlations	Service	1.000	-.077	-.244
		Price Flexibility	-.077	1.000	.052
		Salesforce Image	-.244	.052	1.000
	Covariances	Service	.369	-1.499E-02	-8.752E-02
		Price Flexibility	-1.499E-02	.102	9.824E-03
		Salesforce Image	-8.752E-02	9.824E-03	.349

a. Dependent Variable: Usage Level

272

Swept Correlation Matrix[a]

Model	Rows	Service	Usage Level	Delivery Speed	Price Level	Price Flexibility	Manufacturer Image	Salesforce Image	Product Quality
1	Service	1.000^x	-.701^x	-.612^x	-.513^x	-.067^x	-.299^x	-.241^x	.055^x
	Usage Level	.701^yy	.509^yy	.248^y	-.278^y	.512^y	.015^y	.087^y	-.154^y
	Delivery Speed	.612~	.248~	.626~	-.663	.469	-.132	-.070	-.449
	Price Level	.513~	-.278~	-.663	.737~	-.521	.119	.063	.498
	Price Flexibility	.067~	.512~	.469	-.521	.996~	-.136	-.050	-.444
	Manufacturer Image	.299~	.015~	-.132	.119	-.136	.911~	.716	.216
	Salesforce Image	.241~	.087~	-.070	.063	-.050	.716	.942~	.191
	Product Quality	-.055~	-.154~	-.449	.498	-.444	.216	.191	.997~
2	Service	1.004^xx	-.666^xy	-.581^x	-.548^x	-.067	-.308^x	-.244^x	.025^x
	Usage Level	.666^yx	.245^yy	.007^y	-.009^y	.515^yx	.085^y	.113^y	.075^y
	Delivery Speed	.581~	.007~	.405~	-.418	.471~	-.068	-.047	-.240
	Price Level	.548~	-.009~	-.418	.464~	-.524~	.048	.036	.265
	Price Flexibility	-.067	-.515^xy	-.471^x	.524^x	1.004^xx	.137^x	.051^x	.446^x
	Manufacturer Image	.308~	.085~	-.068	.048	-.137~	.892~	.709	.156
	Salesforce Image	.244~	.113~	-.047	.036	-.051~	.709	.939~	.168
	Product Quality	-.025~	.075~	-.240	.265	-.446~	.156	.168	.799~
3	Service	1.068^xx	-.637^xy	-.593^x	-.538^x	-.080	-.123^x	-.260	.069^x
	Usage Level	.637^yx	.232^yy	.012^y	-.014^y	.521^yx	-.001^y	.121^yx	.055^y
	Delivery Speed	.593~	.012~	.403~	-.416	.468~	-.033	-.050~	-.231
	Price Level	.538~	-.014~	-.416	.462~	-.522~	.020	.039~	.259
	Price Flexibility	-.080	-.521^xy	-.468^x	.522^x	1.007^xx	.098^x	.054	.437^x
	Manufacturer Image	.123~	-.001~	-.033	.020	-.098~	.357~	.755~	.029
	Salesforce Image	-.260	-.121^xy	.050^x	-.039^x	.054	-.755^x	1.064^xx	-.179^x
	Product Quality	-.069~	.055~	-.231	.259	-.437~	.029	.179~	.768~

xx. This variable is an independent variable.

xy. Row variable is an independent variable, column variable is the dependent variable.

x~. Row variable is an independent variable, column variable is an excluded independent variable.

yx. Row variable is the independent variable, column variable is an independent variable.

yy. This variable is the dependent variable.

y~. Row variable is the dependent variable, column variable is an excluded independent variable.

~x. Row variable is an excluded independent variable, column variable is an independent variable.

~y. Row variable is an excluded independent variable, column variable is the dependent variable.

~~. This variable is an excluded predictor.

a. Dependent Variable: Usage Level

Collinearity diagnostics for each step in the procedure. The condition index and loadings do not indicate support for the existence of multicollinearity.

Collinearity Diagnostics[a]

Model	Dimension	Eigenvalue	Condition Index	Variance Proportions			
				(Constant)	Service	Price Flexibility	Salesforce Image
1	1	1.969	1.000	.02	.02		
	2	3.132E-02	7.928	.98	.98		
2	1	2.941	1.000	.00	.01	.00	
	2	4.595E-02	8.000	.03	.85	.19	
	3	1.347E-02	14.778	.97	.14	.80	
3	1	3.882	1.000	.00	.00	.00	.00
	2	5.997E-02	8.046	.01	.02	.11	.85
	3	4.541E-02	9.246	.02	.91	.14	.04
	4	1.237E-02	17.719	.97	.07	.75	.10

a. Dependent Variable: Usage Level

274

Casewise Diagnostics[a]

Case Number	ID	Std. Residual	Usage Level	Stud. Residual	Stud. Deleted Residual	Centered Leverage Value	Mahal. Distance	Cook's Distance
1	1.0	-1.434	32.0	-1.449	-1.457	.011	1.049	.011
2	2.0	.814	43.0	.840	.838	.051	5.033	.011
3	3.0	-.294	48.0	-.306	-.304	.066	6.564	.002
4	4.0	-.546	32.0	-.556	-.554	.025	2.453	.003
5	5.0	-.061	58.0	-.064	-.064	.081	8.040	.000
6	6.0	.538	45.0	.543	.541	.010	1.020	.002
7	7.0	-2.857	46.0	-2.983	-3.115	.073	7.219	.201
8	8.0	1.174	44.0	1.191	1.194	.019	1.917	.011
9	9.0	1.569	63.0	1.591	1.604	.018	1.775	.018
10	10	1.338	54.0	1.362	1.368	.024	2.410	.016
11	11	-2.360	32.0	-2.400	-2.462	.023	2.301	.050
12	12	-.815	47.0	-.822	-.821	.008	.801	.003
13	13	.046	39.0	.047	.047	.033	3.222	.000
14	14	-2.342	38.0	-2.386	-2.447	.026	2.566	.053
15	15	.132	54.0	.134	.133	.021	2.095	.000
16	16	-.044	49.0	-.045	-.045	.032	3.163	.000
17	17	-1.419	38.0	-1.453	-1.462	.036	3.541	.025
18	18	-1.706	40.0	-1.746	-1.765	.035	3.438	.036
19	19	-.651	54.0	-.669	-.667	.045	4.412	.006
20	20	.359	55.0	.365	.363	.021	2.095	.001
21	21	-.011	41.0	-.011	-.011	.023	2.255	.000
22	22	.447	35.0	.463	.462	.060	5.908	.004
23	23	-.149	55.0	-.151	-.151	.020	1.971	.000
24	24	.434	36.0	.442	.440	.025	2.432	.002
25	25	-.605	49.0	-.609	-.607	.006	.596	.002
26	26	-.227	49.0	-.229	-.228	.004	.417	.000
27	27	.511	36.0	.520	.518	.026	2.548	.003
28	28	-.477	54.0	-.491	-.489	.045	4.425	.003
29	29	-.892	49.0	-.914	-.913	.038	3.748	.010
30	30	-.305	46.0	-.313	-.311	.041	4.055	.001
31	31	.323	43.0	.329	.327	.021	2.079	.001
32	32	-.040	53.0	-.040	-.040	.011	1.132	.000
33	33	.808	60.0	.822	.820	.023	2.304	.006
34	34	.105	47.0	.106	.106	.024	2.421	.000
35	35	.233	35.0	.241	.240	.055	5.491	.001
36	36	-.507	39.0	-.510	-.508	.004	.421	.001
37	37	-.176	44.0	-.181	-.180	.040	3.912	.000
38	38	-.034	46.0	-.034	-.034	.013	1.331	.000
39	39	.043	29.0	.044	.044	.065	6.388	.000
40	40	-1.407	28.0	-1.432	-1.440	.024	2.359	.018
41	41	-.562	40.0	-.565	-.563	.002	.227	.001
42	42	-.061	58.0	-.064	-.064	.081	8.040	.000
43	43	-.260	53.0	-.269	-.268	.058	5.755	.001
44	44	-.376	48.0	-.379	-.377	.004	.370	.001
45	45	.431	38.0	.440	.438	.028	2.768	.002
46	46	-.314	54.0	-.326	-.324	.058	5.735	.002
47	47	.784	55.0	.802	.801	.034	3.393	.007
48	48	-.013	43.0	-.013	-.013	.045	4.431	.000
49	49	1.724	57.0	1.737	1.756	.006	.553	.012
50	50	.360	53.0	.372	.371	.054	5.327	.002

a. Dependent Variable: Usage Level

Listing of selected diagnostic measures for each observation. All of the measure discussed in Chapter Four and the Addendum to Chapter Four can be obtained.

Casewise Diagnostics[a]

Case Number	ID	Std. Residual	Usage Level	Stud. Residual	Stud. Deleted Residual	Centered Leverage Value	Mahal. Distance	Cook's Distance
51	51	.072	41.0	.073	.073	.013	1.270	.000
52	52	.202	53.0	.204	.203	.011	1.047	.000
53	53	-.523	50.0	-.541	-.539	.053	5.231	.005
54	54	-1.549	32.0	-1.565	-1.577	.010	.989	.012
55	55	.228	39.0	.234	.233	.037	3.639	.001
56	56	.256	47.0	.260	.258	.017	1.687	.000
57	57	.650	62.0	.677	.675	.068	6.730	.010
58	58	1.003	65.0	1.026	1.027	.034	3.397	.012
59	59	-.063	46.0	-.064	-.063	.002	.199	.000
60	60	.289	50.0	.292	.290	.008	.821	.000
61	61	.666	54.0	.679	.677	.030	2.945	.005
62	62	1.090	60.0	1.108	1.109	.021	2.056	.010
63	63	-.165	47.0	-.167	-.166	.015	1.473	.000
64	64	-1.278	36.0	-1.309	-1.314	.037	3.676	.021
65	65	1.256	40.0	1.293	1.297	.045	4.496	.025
66	66	-.435	45.0	-.440	-.438	.010	.978	.001
67	67	.871	59.0	.892	.891	.036	3.565	.010
68	68	1.032	46.0	1.044	1.045	.013	1.288	.006
69	69	1.474	58.0	1.499	1.509	.022	2.186	.019
70	70	.319	49.0	.321	.320	.003	.346	.000
71	71	-.403	50.0	-.420	-.419	.071	7.034	.004
72	72	.251	55.0	.259	.258	.053	5.257	.001
73	73	-.154	51.0	-.157	-.156	.030	2.996	.000
74	74	1.560	60.0	1.575	1.588	.010	.964	.012
75	75	.717	41.0	.726	.724	.013	1.292	.003
76	76	-1.001	49.0	-1.013	-1.013	.013	1.274	.006
77	77	.018	42.0	.018	.018	.011	1.064	.000
78	78	-.782	47.0	-.803	-.801	.040	3.916	.008
79	79	1.311	39.0	1.351	1.357	.049	4.808	.028
80	80	1.495	56.0	1.511	1.521	.010	1.001	.012
81	81	1.311	59.0	1.331	1.337	.020	2.014	.014
82	82	-.391	47.0	-.412	-.410	.090	8.911	.005
83	83	.923	41.0	.952	.952	.050	4.964	.015
84	84	-1.938	37.0	-1.949	-1.979	.001	.129	.011
85	85	1.263	53.0	1.271	1.275	.003	.284	.005
86	86	.331	43.0	.334	.333	.008	.809	.001
87	87	1.090	51.0	1.097	1.098	.003	.250	.004
88	88	-1.601	36.0	-1.612	-1.626	.004	.363	.009
89	89	-.656	34.0	-.665	-.663	.016	1.612	.003
90	90	.817	60.0	.839	.838	.042	4.176	.010
91	91	.223	49.0	.227	.226	.023	2.230	.000
92	92	-1.651	39.0	-1.692	-1.709	.037	3.682	.035
93	93	-.172	43.0	-.180	-.179	.073	7.266	.001
94	94	1.220	36.0	1.259	1.262	.051	5.030	.026
95	95	-1.097	31.0	-1.113	-1.114	.019	1.862	.009
96	96	.370	25.0	.392	.390	.096	9.485	.005
97	97	1.451	60.0	1.466	1.475	.011	1.099	.012
98	98	1.110	38.0	1.140	1.142	.041	4.101	.018
99	99	.457	42.0	.462	.460	.010	1.015	.001
100	100	-2.696	33.0	-2.741	-2.840	.022	2.186	.062

a. Dependent Variable: Usage Level

Residuals Statistics[a]

	Minimum	Maximum	Mean	Std. Deviation	N
Predicted Value	23.373	60.592	46.100	7.879	100
Std. Predicted Value	-2.885	1.839	.000	1.000	100
Standard Error of Predicted Value	.467	1.429	.847	.236	100
Adjusted Predicted Value	23.180	60.388	46.104	7.915	100
Residual	-12.552	7.574	3.055E-15	4.327	100
Std. Residual	-2.857	1.724	.000	.985	100
Stud. Residual	-2.983	1.737	.000	1.004	100
Deleted Residual	-13.687	7.694	-4.294E-03	4.497	100
Stud. Deleted Residual	-3.115	1.756	-.004	1.017	100
Mahal. Distance	.129	9.485	2.970	2.185	100
Cook's Distance	.000	.201	.010	.022	100
Centered Leverage Value	.001	.096	.030	.022	100

a. Dependent Variable: Usage Level

Charts

Histogram

Dependent Variable: Usage Level

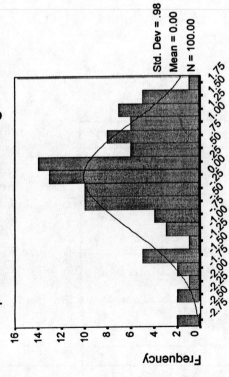

Std. Dev = .98
Mean = 0.00
N = 100.00

Regression Standardized Residual

This histogram of standardized residuals is based on the temporary variable ZRESID. The graph indicates that the errors are normally distributed.

Normal P-P Plot

Dependent Variable: Usage Level

Observed Cum Prob

Expected Cum Prob

The normal probability plot of the standardized residuals indicates that the residuals are from a normal distribution as the plotted values fall along the line.

278

Scatterplot

Dependent Variable: Usage Level

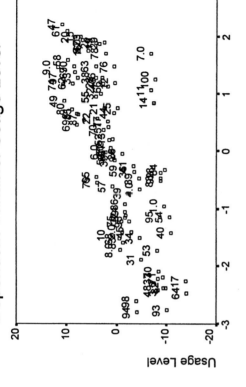

Usage Level

Partial Regression Plot

Dependent Variable: Usage Level

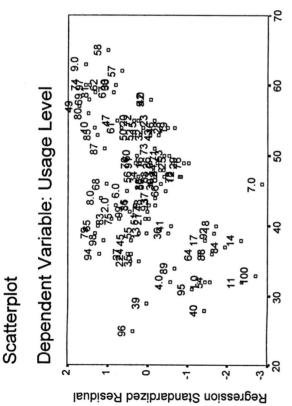

Price Flexibility

The partial regression plot depicts the studentized residuals versus the predicted values. The residuals fall within a generally random pattern indicating linearity and homoscedasticity in the overall equation.

In the following three illustrations, the standardized partial regression plots indicate a linear relationship. The *service* and *price flexibility* plots are well-defined indicating a strong relationship with the dependent variable.

279

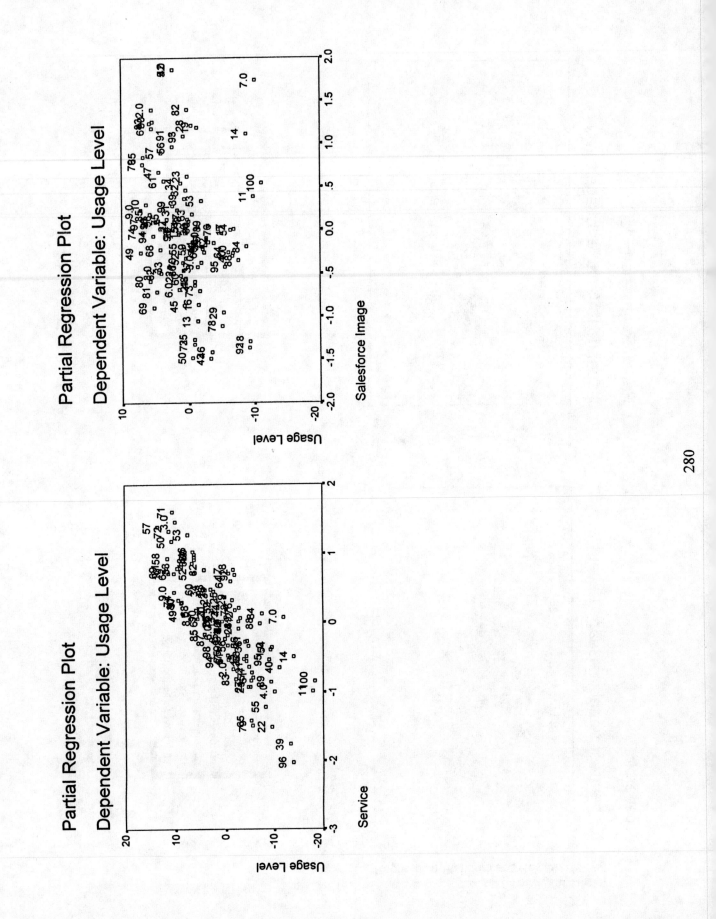

Partial Regression Plot

Dependent Variable: Usage Level

Salesforce Image

Partial Regression Plot

Dependent Variable: Usage Level

Service

Validation of Multiple Regression Results

```
*Split-Sample Validation of the Stepwise Estimation.
SET SEED=34567.
COMPUTE SPLIT=UNIFORM(1)>.52.
EXECUTE.
SORT CASES BY SPLIT .
SPLIT FILE
LAYERED BY SPLIT .
REGRESSION
  /DESCRIPTIVES ALL
  /STATISTICS ALL
  /CRITERIA=PIN(.05) POUT(.10)
  /DEPENDENT X9
  /METHOD=STEPWISE X1 X2 X3 X4 X5 X6 X7.
```

For validation purposes, only the Model Summary and Coefficients sections are included.

The data set is split into two equal samples of 50 respondents each. Comparison of the overall model to the step-wise results of the two subsamples demonstrates a high level of similarity. In comparing the coefficients, *salesforce image* does not enter one of the equations due to its weak predictive ability.

Model Summary

SPLIT	Model	R	R Square	Adjusted R Square	Std. Error of the Estimate	R Square Change	F Change	df1	df2	Sig. F Change	Akaike Information Criterion	Amemiya Prediction Criterion	Mallows' Prediction Criterion	Schwarz Bayesian Criterion
.00	1	.723a	.522	.512	6.398	.522	52.454	1	48	.000	187.561	.518	37.840	191.385
	2	.791b	.625	.609	5.725	.103	12.949	1	47	.001	177.394	.422	21.731	183.130
	3	.864c	.746	.729	4.766	.120	21.811	1	46	.000	159.990	.298	2.589	167.638
	4	.861d	.741	.730	4.764	-.005	.948	1	48	.335	159.010	.292	1.508	164.746
1.00	1	.716e	.512	.502	6.249	.512	50.411	1	48	.000	185.203	.528	89.314	189.027
	2	.888d	.788	.779	4.166	.276	61.010	1	47	.000	145.599	.239	14.881	151.335
	3	.909f	.826	.814	3.816	.038	10.026	1	46	.003	137.741	.205	6.344	145.389

(Change Statistics columns: R Square Change, F Change, df1, df2, Sig. F Change; Selection Criteria columns: Akaike Information Criterion, Amemiya Prediction Criterion, Mallows' Prediction Criterion, Schwarz Bayesian Criterion)

a. Predictors: (Constant), Delivery Speed

b. Predictors: (Constant), Delivery Speed, Service

c. Predictors: (Constant), Delivery Speed, Service, Price Flexibility

d. Predictors: (Constant), Service, Price Flexibility

e. Predictors: (Constant), Service

f. Predictors: (Constant), Service, Price Flexibility, Salesforce Image

Coefficients[a]

SPLIT	Model		Unstandardized Coefficients		Standardized Coefficients		t	Sig.	95% Confidence Interval for B		Correlations			Collinearity Statistics	
			B	Std. Error	Beta	Std. Error			Lower Bound	Upper Bound	Zero-order	Partial	Part	Tolerance	VIF
.00	1	(Constant)	28.203	2.546			11.077	.000	23.084	33.323					
		Delivery Speed	4.999	.690	.723	.100	7.242	.000	3.611	6.387	.723	.723	.723	1.000	1.000
	2	(Constant)	20.212	3.182			6.353	.000	13.811	26.612					
		Delivery Speed	3.277	.781	.474	.113	4.194	.000	1.705	4.849	.723	.522	.374	.625	1.601
		Service	4.738	1.317	.406	.113	3.598	.001	2.089	7.387	.697	.465	.321	.625	1.601
	3	(Constant)	-.808	5.222			-.155	.878	-11.320	9.704					
		Delivery Speed	.815	.837	.118	.121	.974	.335	-.870	2.500	.723	.142	.072	.377	2.651
		Service	7.418	1.237	.636	.106	5.995	.000	4.928	9.909	.697	.662	.446	.490	2.039
		Price Flexibility	2.747	.588	.447	.096	4.670	.000	1.563	3.932	.487	.567	.347	.603	1.658
	4	(Constant)	-3.363	4.512			-.745	.460	-12.441	5.715					
		Service	8.278	.866	.710	.074	9.555	.000	6.535	10.021	.697	.813	.710	.999	1.001
		Price Flexibility	3.108	.457	.506	.074	6.803	.000	2.189	4.027	.487	.704	.505	.999	1.001
1.00	1	(Constant)	21.378	3.683			5.805	.000	13.974	28.782					
		Service	8.777	1.236	.716	.101	7.100	.000	6.291	11.262	.716	.716	.716	1.000	1.000
	2	(Constant)	-4.156	4.088			-1.017	.315	-12.380	4.068					
		Service	7.563	.839	.617	.068	9.018	.000	5.876	9.250	.716	.796	.606	.966	1.036
		Price Flexibility	3.669	.470	.534	.068	7.811	.000	2.724	4.614	.648	.752	.525	.966	1.036
	3	(Constant)	-8.651	4.004			-2.160	.036	-16.712	-.590					
		Service	7.037	.786	.574	.064	8.954	.000	5.455	8.618	.716	.797	.551	.922	1.084
		Price Flexibility	3.632	.430	.529	.063	8.439	.000	2.766	4.499	.648	.779	.519	.965	1.036
		Salesforce Image	2.447	.773	.200	.063	3.166	.003	.891	4.003	.361	.423	.195	.951	1.051

a. Dependent Variable: Usage Level

282

CHAPTER 5:

DISCRIMINANT ANALYSIS AND LOGISTIC REGRESSION

This section of the instructor's manual contains copies of the actual printouts from the SPSS statistical analysis program. The printouts contain examples of the analyses discussed in the text using the HATCO database.

Each of the printouts is annotated with comments to aid in the interpretation of the results. These suggestions are typed in the margins next to the appropriate data. If you wish to provide students with their own copies of the output without these comments, the output are provided on the computer diskette accompanying the instructor's manual.

Two examples of discriminant analysis and one example of logistic regression are included in this section. A brief description follows:

Two-Group Analysis: A stepwise discriminant analysis in which the dependent variable, X_{11} (type of buying process), is distinguished in terms of seven attribute ratings (X_1 to X_7).

Three-Group Analysis: The same seven attributers act as independent variables, but this time the categorical dependent measure is X_{14} (type of buying situation) with three values: new task, modified rebuy, or straight rebuy.

Logistic Regression: A stepwise logistic regression in which the dependant variable is X_{11} (type of buying process) which is predicted by the seven attribute ratings (X_1 to X_7).

Two-Group Discriminant Analysis

*2-Group Discriminant Analysis.
SET SEED 54321.
COMPUTE RANDZ=UNIFORM(1) > .65 .
EXECUTE .
DISCRIMINANT
 /GROUPS X11(0 1)
 /VARIABLES X1 X2 X3 X4 X5 X6 X7
 /SELECT=RANDZ(0)
 /ANALYSIS ALL
 /METHOD MAHAL
 /PIN= .05
 /POUT= .10
 /PRIORS SIZE
 /HISTORY STEP END
 /STATISTICS ALL
 /PLOT=COMBINED SEPARATE MAP
 /CLASSIFY=NONMISSING SEPARATE.

Analysis Case Processing Summary

Unweighted Cases		N	Percent
Valid		60	60.0
Excluded	Missing or out-of-range group codes	0	.0
	At least one missing discriminating variable	0	.0
	Both missing or out-of-range group codes and at least one missing discriminating	0	.0
	Unselected	40	40.0
	Total	40	40.0
Total		100	100.0

Group Statistics

| Specification Buying | | Mean | Std. Deviation | Valid N (listwise) | |
				Unweighted	Weighted
Specification Buying	Delivery Speed	2.227	1.053	22	22.000
	Price Level	2.973	1.187	22	22.000
	Price Flexibility	6.873	.763	22	22.000
	Manufacturer Image	5.155	.815	22	22.000
	Service	2.577	.936	22	22.000
	Salesforce Image	2.555	.580	22	22.000
	Product Quality	8.464	.945	22	22.000
Total Value Analysis	Delivery Speed	4.258	1.099	38	38.000
	Price Level	2.082	1.119	38	38.000
	Price Flexibility	8.568	1.280	38	38.000
	Manufacturer Image	5.437	1.319	38	38.000
	Service	3.179	.501	38	38.000
	Salesforce Image	2.832	.919	38	38.000
	Product Quality	6.013	1.322	38	38.000
Total	Delivery Speed	3.513	1.458	60	60.000
	Price Level	2.408	1.214	60	60.000
	Price Flexibility	7.947	1.384	60	60.000
	Manufacturer Image	5.333	1.160	60	60.000
	Service	2.958	.745	60	60.000
	Salesforce Image	2.730	.817	60	60.000
	Product Quality	6.912	1.683	60	60.000

285

Tests of Equality of Group Means

	Wilks' Lambda	F	df1	df2	Sig.
Delivery Speed	.542	48.992	1	58	.000
Price Level	.873	8.453	1	58	.005
Price Flexibility	.645	31.881	1	58	.000
Manufacturer Image	.986	.822	1	58	.368
Service	.846	10.576	1	58	.002
Salesforce Image	.973	1.620	1	58	.208
Product Quality	.499	58.176	1	58	.000

Significance tests for the equality of group means for each variable. *Delivery speed, price level, price flexibility, service,* and *product quality* have extreme significance and therefore the group means are not equal. *Manufacturer image* and *salesforce image* have no significance and therefore the group means are considered equal.

Pooled Within-Groups Matrices[a]

		Delivery Speed	Price Level	Price Flexibility	Manufacturer Image	Service	Salesforce Image	Product Quality
Covariance	Delivery Speed	1.173	-.315	.236	4.304E-02	.434	1.686E-03	-.212
	Price Level	-.315	1.309	-.431	.309	.500	.145	.356
	Price Flexibility	.236	-.431	1.257	-.156	-9.102E-02	-3.361E-02	7.645E-02
	Manufacturer Image	4.304E-02	.309	-.156	1.350	.163	.744	.268
	Service	.434	.500	-9.102E-02	.163	.477	7.315E-02	6.176E-02
	Salesforce Image	1.686E-03	.145	-3.361E-02	.744	7.315E-02	.660	.190
	Product Quality	-.212	.356	7.645E-02	.268	6.176E-02	.190	1.438
Correlation	Delivery Speed	1.000	-.254	.195	.034	.581	.002	-.164
	Price Level	-.254	1.000	-.336	.233	.633	.156	.259
	Price Flexibility	.195	-.336	1.000	-.120	-.118	-.037	.057
	Manufacturer Image	.034	.233	-.120	1.000	.203	.788	.192
	Service	.581	.633	-.118	.203	1.000	.130	.075
	Salesforce Image	.002	.156	-.037	.788	.130	1.000	.195
	Product Quality	-.164	.259	.057	.192	.075	.195	1.000

a. The covariance matrix has 58 degrees of freedom.

Covariance Matrices[a]

		Delivery Speed	Price Level	Price Flexibility	Manufacturer Image	Service	Salesforce Image	Product Quality
Specification Buying	Delivery Speed	1.110	.424	-.131	.268	.773	6.606E-02	-8.801E-02
	Price Level	.424	1.410	-.187	.231	.934	9.394E-02	1.134E-02
	Price Flexibility	-.131	-.187	.582	-.245	-.158	-.158	9.944E-02
	Manufacturer Image	.268	.231	-.245	.664	.247	.308	2.017E-02
	Service	.773	.934	-.158	.247	.875	9.416E-02	-3.087E-02
	Salesforce Image	6.606E-02	9.394E-02	-.158	.308	9.416E-02	.337	.163
	Product Quality	-8.801E-02	1.134E-02	9.944E-02	2.017E-02	-3.087E-02	.163	.893
Total Value Analysis	Delivery Speed	1.208	-.735	.445	-8.462E-02	.242	-3.485E-02	-.283
	Price Level	-.735	1.252	-.570	.354	.254	.175	.551
	Price Flexibility	.445	-.570	1.640	-.105	-5.312E-02	3.724E-02	6.340E-02
	Manufacturer Image	-8.462E-02	.354	-.105	1.740	.116	.991	.409
	Service	.242	.254	-5.312E-02	.116	.251	6.122E-02	.114
	Salesforce Image	-3.485E-02	.175	3.724E-02	.991	6.122E-02	.844	.206
	Product Quality	-.283	.551	6.340E-02	.409	.114	.206	1.748
Total	Delivery Speed	2.127	-.737	1.045	.178	.715	.135	-1.384
	Price Level	-.737	1.474	-.781	.245	.365	8.466E-02	.865
	Price Flexibility	1.045	-.781	1.914	-4.006E-02	.151	7.790E-02	-.906
	Manufacturer Image	.178	.245	-4.006E-02	1.346	.201	.749	.100
	Service	.715	.365	.151	.201	.554	.111	-.287
	Salesforce Image	.135	8.466E-02	7.790E-02	.749	.111	.667	2.693E-02
	Product Quality	-1.384	.865	-.906	.100	-.287	2.693E-02	2.832

a. The total covariance matrix has 59 degrees of freedom.

288

Analysis 1
Box's Test of Equality of Covariance Matrices

Log Determinants

Specification Buying	Rank	Log Determinant
Specification Buying	3	-.601
Total Value Analysis	3	1.087
Pooled within-groups	3	.677

The ranks and natural logarithms of determinants printed are those of the group covariance matrices.

Test Results

Box's M		11.675
F	Approx.	1.824
	df1	6
	df2	12620.653
	Sig.	.090

Tests null hypothesis of equal population covariance matrices.

The test for equality of covariance matrices is critical for discriminant analysis. In this case, there is some evidence that there are differences (prob. = .09). The researcher may consider use of logistic regression, which is less affected by this condition.

289

Stepwise Statistics

Variables Entered/Removed[a,b,c,d]

		Min. D Squared					
					Exact F		
Step	Entered	Statistic	Between Groups	Statistic	df1	df2	Sig.
1	Product Quality	4.175	Specification Buying and Total Value Analysis	58.176	1	58.000	9.488E-11
2	Price Flexibility	6.837	Specification Buying and Total Value Analysis	46.810	2	57.000	.000
3	Delivery Speed	8.403	Specification Buying and Total Value Analysis	37.683	3	56.000	1.785E-13

At each step, the variable that maximizes the Mahalanobis distance between the two closest groups is entered.

a. Maximum number of steps is 14.

b. Maximum significance of F to enter is .05.

c. Minimum significance of F to remove is .10.

d. F level, tolerance, or VIN insufficient for further computation.

Three variables enter the equation in the following order: *product quality, price flexibility,* and *delivery speed.* At each step, the overall model is significant (F statistic) indicating a significant difference in group means.

Specification of the selection method to be used for the analysis and the statistical criteria.

Variables in the Analysis

Step		Tolerance	Sig. of F to Remove	Min. D Squared	Between Groups
1	Product Quality	1.000	.000		
2	Product Quality	.997	.000	2.288	Specification Buying and Total Value Analysis
	Price Flexibility	.997	.000	4.175	Specification Buying and Total Value Analysis
3	Product Quality	.965	.000	4.886	Specification Buying and Total Value Analysis
	Price Flexibility	.954	.004	6.615	Specification Buying and Total Value Analysis
	Delivery Speed	.932	.007	6.837	Specification Buying and Total Value Analysis

To enter the equation, each variable must meet the criteria specified in the syntax, probability of F-to-enter (PIN = .05). At each step, the variable with the largest D Squared will enter the equation. So, the first variable to enter is *product quality* (4.175) followed by *price flexibility* (6.873) and *delivery speed* (8.403). After *delivery speed* enters the equation, the probability of F-to-enter criteria is no longer met.

Variables Not in the Analysis

Step		Tolerance	Min. Tolerance	Sig. of F to Enter	Min. D Squared	Between Groups
0	Delivery Speed	1.000	1.000	.000	3.516	Specification Buying and Total Value Analysis
	Price Level	1.000	1.000	.005	.607	Specification Buying and Total Value Analysis
	Price Flexibility	1.000	1.000	.000	2.288	Specification Buying and Total Value Analysis
	Manufacturer Image	1.000	1.000	.368	.059	Specification Buying and Total Value Analysis
	Service	1.000	1.000	.002	.759	Specification Buying and Total Value Analysis
	Salesforce Image	1.000	1.000	.208	.116	Specification Buying and Total Value Analysis
	Product Quality	1.000	1.000	.000	4.175	Specification Buying and Total Value Analysis
1	Delivery Speed	.973	.973	.000	6.615	Specification Buying and Total Value Analysis
	Price Level	.933	.933	.503	4.242	Specification Buying and Total Value Analysis
	Price Flexibility	.997	.997	.000	6.837	Specification Buying and Total Value Analysis
	Manufacturer Image	.963	.963	.095	4.596	Specification Buying and Total Value Analysis
	Service	.994	.994	.010	5.229	Specification Buying and Total Value Analysis
	Salesforce Image	.962	.962	.053	4.745	Specification Buying and Total Value Analysis
2	Delivery Speed	.932	.932	.007	8.403	Specification Buying and Total Value Analysis
	Price Level	.809	.809	.419	6.967	Specification Buying and Total Value Analysis
	Manufacturer Image	.946	.946	.054	7.600	Specification Buying and Total Value Analysis
	Service	.980	.980	.007	8.363	Specification Buying and Total Value Analysis
	Salesforce Image	.959	.958	.064	7.536	Specification Buying and Total Value Analysis
3	Price Level	.788	.788	.238	8.728	Specification Buying and Total Value Analysis
	Manufacturer Image	.937	.920	.120	8.972	Specification Buying and Total Value Analysis
	Service	.570	.542	.248	8.716	Specification Buying and Total Value Analysis
	Salesforce Image	.957	.925	.109	9.010	Specification Buying and Total Value Analysis

Wilks' Lambda

Step	Number of Variables	Lambda	df1	df2	df3	Exact F Statistic	df1	df2	Sig.
1	1	.499	1	1	58	58.176	1	58.000	9.488E-11
2	2	.378	2	1	58	46.810	2	57.000	.000
3	3	.331	3	1	58	37.683	3	56.000	1.785E-13

Pairwise Group Comparisons[a,b,c]

Step			Specification Buying	Total Value Analysis
1	Specification Buying	F		58.176
		Sig.		.000
	Total Value Analysis	F	58.176	
		Sig.	.000	
2	Specification Buying	F		46.810
		Sig.		.000
	Total Value Analysis	F	46.810	
		Sig.	.000	
3	Specification Buying	F		37.683
		Sig.		.000
	Total Value Analysis	F	37.683	
		Sig.	.000	

a. 1, 58 degrees of freedom for step 1.

b. 2, 57 degrees of freedom for step 2.

c. 3, 56 degrees of freedom for step 3.

Summary of Canonical Discriminant Functions

Eigenvalues

Function	Eigenvalue	% of Variance	Cumulative %	Canonical Correlation
1	2.019a	100.0	100.0	.818

a. First 1 canonical discriminant functions were used in the analysis.

Wilks' Lambda

Test of Function(s)	Wilks' Lambda	Chi-square	df	Sig.
1	.331	62.424	3	.000

Standardized Canonical Discriminant Function Coefficients

	Function
	1
Delivery Speed	.447
Price Flexibility	.472
Product Quality	-.659

Canonical correlation is the degree of association between the discriminant scores and the groups. In a two-group discriminant analysis, this is the same as the Pearson correlation coefficient between the discriminant score and the group variable. By squaring the canonical correlation, the research may interpret the amount of variation explained by the model. In this case, the model accounts for 66.91 percent of the variation in the dependant variable.

The standardized coefficients may be used to compare each variable's relative influence in the discriminant equation. In this case, the discriminating power of *product quality* (-.659) is strongest. Signs do not affect rankings.

294

Structure Matrix

	Function
	1
Product Quality	-.705
Delivery Speed	.647
Price Flexibility	.522
Price Level[a]	-.443
Manufacturer Image[a]	-.168
Service[a]	.155
Salesforce Image[a]	-.145

Pooled within-groups correlations between discriminating variables and standardized canonical discriminant functions
Variables ordered by absolute size of correlation within function.

a. This variable not used in the analysis.

Canonical Discriminant Function Coefficients

	Function
	1
Delivery Speed	.413
Price Flexibility	.421
Product Quality	-.549
(Constant)	-1.003

Unstandardized coefficients

This set of coefficients is used for classification of subjects. The unstandardized coefficients are used since the subjects' response on each variable will be in the original units. Group classification is determined by comparison of the discriminant score with the cutting score.

Functions at Group Centroids

	Function
	1
Specification Buying	-1.836
Total Value Analysis	1.063

Unstandardized canonical discriminant functions evaluated at group means

The mean discriminant function scores for each group.

Classification Statistics

Classification Processing Summary

Processed		100
Excluded	Missing or out-of-range group codes	0
	At least one missing discriminating variable	0
Used in Output		100

Prior Probabilities for Groups

Specification Buying	Prior	Cases Used in Analysis	
		Unweighted	Weighted
Specification Buying	.367	22	22.000
Total Value Analysis	.633	38	38.000
Total	1.000	60	60.000

Classification Function Coefficients

	Specification Buying	
	Specification Buying	Total Value Analysis
Delivery Speed	2.021	3.219
Price Flexibility	4.728	5.950
Product Quality	5.932	4.340
(Constant)	-44.606	-45.848

Fisher's linear discriminant functions

Discriminant coefficients are used in the classification equations. Each subject will have two equations, one for each group. The equation with the largest discriminant score is the group into which the subject is classified.

Separate-Groups Graphs

Canonical Discriminant Function 1

Specification Buying = Specification Buying

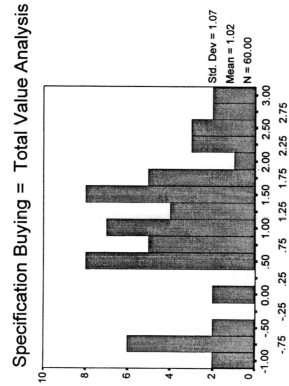

Canonical Discriminant Function 1

Specification Buying = Total Value Analysis

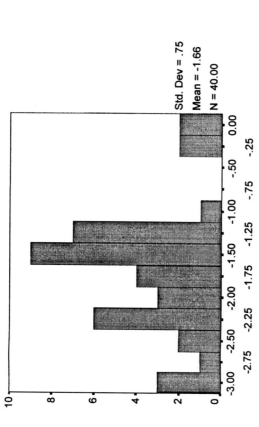

297

Classification Results [a,b]

			Predicted Group Membership		
			SPECIFICATION BUYING	TOTAL VALUE ANALYSIS	Total
Cases Selected	Original	Count	Specification Buying		
			SPECIFICATION BUYING	21	1	22
			TOTAL VALUE ANALYSIS	4	34	38
		%	SPECIFICATION BUYING	95.5	4.5	100.0
			TOTAL VALUE ANALYSIS	10.5	89.5	100.0
Cases Not Selected	Original	Count	SPECIFICATION BUYING	15	3	18
			TOTAL VALUE ANALYSIS	3	19	22
		%	SPECIFICATION BUYING	83.3	16.7	100.0
			TOTAL VALUE ANALYSIS	13.6	86.4	100.0

a. 91.7% of selected original grouped cases correctly classified.

b. 85.0% of unselected original grouped cases correctly classified.

298

Three-Group Discriminant Analysis

```
*3-Group Discriminant Analysis.
SET SEED 54321.
COMPUTE RANDZ=UNIFORM(1) > .65 .
EXECUTE.
DISCRIMINANT
  /GROUPS=X14(1,3)
  /VARIABLES X1 X2 X3 X4 X5 X6 X7
  /SELECT=RANDZ(0)
  /ANALYSIS ALL
  /METHOD MAHAL
  /PIN= .05
  /POUT= .10
  /PRIORS  SIZE
  /HISTORY STEP END
  /STATISTICS ALL
  /PLOT=COMBINED SEPARATE MAP
  /CLASSIFY=NONMISSING POOLED .
```

Analysis Case Processing Summary

Unweighted Cases		N	Percent
Valid		60	60.0
Excluded	Missing or out-of-range group codes	0	.0
	At least one missing discriminating variable	0	.0
	Both missing or out-of-range group codes and at least one missing discriminating	0	.0
	Unselected	40	40.0
	Total	40	40.0
Total		100	100.0

Group Statistics

Type of Buying Situation		Mean	Std. Deviation	Valid N (listwise)	
				Unweighted	Weighted
New Task	Delivery Speed	2.429	1.162	21	21.000
	Price Level	2.157	.915	21	21.000
	Price Flexibility	7.233	.881	21	21.000
	Manufacturer Image	5.067	.867	21	21.000
	Service	2.281	.670	21	21.000
	Salesforce Image	2.686	.731	21	21.000
	Product Quality	7.762	1.373	21	21.000
Modified Rebuy	Delivery Speed	3.227	1.130	15	15.000
	Price Level	3.520	1.379	15	15.000
	Price Flexibility	6.980	1.343	15	15.000
	Manufacturer Image	5.587	1.120	15	15.000
	Service	3.353	.638	15	15.000
	Salesforce Image	2.687	.766	15	15.000
	Product Quality	7.307	1.750	15	15.000
Straight Rebuy	Delivery Speed	4.642	1.023	24	24.000
	Price Level	1.933	.893	24	24.000
	Price Flexibility	9.175	.700	24	24.000
	Manufacturer Image	5.408	1.387	24	24.000
	Service	3.304	.372	24	24.000
	Salesforce Image	2.796	.939	24	24.000
	Product Quality	5.921	1.406	24	24.000
Total	Delivery Speed	3.513	1.458	60	60.000
	Price Level	2.408	1.214	60	60.000
	Price Flexibility	7.947	1.384	60	60.000
	Manufacturer Image	5.333	1.160	60	60.000
	Service	2.958	.745	60	60.000
	Salesforce Image	2.730	.817	60	60.000
	Product Quality	6.912	1.683	60	60.000

300

Tests of Equality of Group Means

	Wilks' Lambda	F	df1	df2	Sig.
Delivery Speed	.550	23.346	2	57	.000
Price Level	.709	11.674	2	57	.000
Price Flexibility	.461	33.362	2	57	.000
Manufacturer Image	.967	.961	2	57	.389
Service	.546	23.692	2	57	.000
Salesforce Image	.996	.126	2	57	.882
Product Quality	.754	9.293	2	57	.000

Significance tests for the equality of group means for each variable. *Delivery speed, price level, price flexibility, service,* and *product quality* have extreme significance and therefore the group means are not equal. *Manufacturer image* and *salesforce image* have no significance and therefore the group means are considered equal.

Pooled Within-Groups Matrices[a]

		Delivery Speed	Price Level	Price Flexibility	Manufacturer Image	Service	Salesforce Image	Product Quality
Covariance	Delivery Speed	1.210	-.554	.140	6.082E-02	.335	8.698E-02	-.592
	Price Level	-.554	1.083	-.346	.170	.269	.109	.661
	Price Flexibility	.140	-.346	.913	-8.589E-02	-9.962E-02	2.392E-02	-.102
	Manufacturer Image	6.082E-02	.170	-8.589E-02	1.348	.104	.772	.192
	Service	.335	.269	-9.962E-02	.104	.313	9.904E-02	1.785E-02
	Salesforce Image	8.698E-02	.109	2.392E-02	.772	9.904E-02	.688	7.372E-02
	Product Quality	-.592	.661	-.102	.192	1.785E-02	7.372E-02	2.210
Correlation	Delivery Speed	1.000	-.484	.134	.048	.544	.095	-.362
	Price Level	-.484	1.000	-.348	.140	.462	.127	.427
	Price Flexibility	.134	-.348	1.000	-.077	-.186	.030	-.071
	Manufacturer Image	.048	.140	-.077	1.000	.160	.802	.111
	Service	.544	.462	-.186	.160	1.000	.213	.021
	Salesforce Image	.095	.127	.030	.802	.213	1.000	.060
	Product Quality	-.362	.427	-.071	.111	.021	.060	1.000

a. The covariance matrix has 57 degrees of freedom.

302

Covariance Matrices[a]

Type of Buying		Delivery Speed	Price Level	Price Flexibility	Manufacturer Image	Service	Salesforce Image	Product Quality
New Task	Delivery Speed	1.351	-.289	.375	.226	.553	.164	-.986
	Price Level	-.289	.837	-6.700E-02	5.100E-02	.287	.105	.559
	Price Flexibility	.375	-6.700E-02	.775	9.617E-02	.173	.224	-.381
	Manufacturer Image	.226	5.100E-02	9.617E-02	.752	.139	.473	.118
	Service	.553	.287	.173	.139	.449	.157	-.218
	Salesforce Image	.164	.105	.224	.473	.157	.534	.203
	Product Quality	-.986	.559	-.381	.118	-.218	.203	1.884
Modified Rebuy	Delivery Speed	1.276	-.789	.282	-9.619E-03	.253	.100	-.814
	Price Level	-.789	1.902	-1.220	.604	.551	.442	1.229
	Price Flexibility	.282	-1.220	1.803	-.965	-.470	-.572	3.729E-02
	Manufacturer Image	-9.619E-03	.604	-.965	1.254	.287	.768	-.311
	Service	.253	.551	-.470	.287	.407	.264	.191
	Salesforce Image	.100	.442	-.572	.768	.264	.587	-.243
	Product Quality	-.814	1.229	3.729E-02	-.311	.191	-.243	3.062
Straight Rebuy	Delivery Speed	1.047	-.641	-.150	-3.993E-02	.195	1.149E-02	-.114
	Price Level	-.641	.798	-5.522E-02	8.406E-03	8.116E-02	-8.899E-02	.404
	Price Flexibility	-.150	-5.522E-02	.491	.291	-.111	.213	5.707E-02
	Manufacturer Image	-3.993E-02	8.406E-03	.291	1.923	-3.830E-02	1.035	.563
	Service	.195	8.116E-02	-.111	-3.830E-02	.139	-5.216E-02	.118
	Salesforce Image	1.149E-02	-8.899E-02	.213	1.035	-5.216E-02	.882	.154
	Product Quality	-.114	.404	5.707E-02	.563	.118	.154	1.976
Total	Delivery Speed	2.127	-.737	1.045	.178	.715	.135	-1.384
	Price Level	-.737	1.474	-.781	.245	.365	8.466E-02	.865
	Price Flexibility	1.045	-.781	1.914	-4.006E-02	.151	7.790E-02	-.906
	Manufacturer Image	.178	.245	-4.006E-02	1.346	.201	.749	.100
	Service	.715	.365	.151	.201	.554	.111	-.287
	Salesforce Image	.135	8.466E-02	7.790E-02	.749	.111	.667	2.693E-02
	Product Quality	-1.384	.865	-.906	.100	-.287	2.693E-02	2.832

a. The total covariance matrix has 59 degrees of freedom.

303

Analysis 1
Box's Test of Equality of Covariance Matrices

Log Determinants

Type of Buying	Rank	Log Determinant
New Task	3	-.353
Modified Rebuy	3	.557
Straight Rebuy	3	-1.736
Pooled within-groups	3	-.219

The ranks and natural logarithms of determinants printed are those of the group covariance matrices.

Test Results

Box's M		26.753
F	Approx.	2.049
	df1	12
	df2	10917.416
	Sig.	.017

Tests null hypothesis of equal population covariance matrices.

Tests for equivalence of covariance matrices of each group. In this case, there is a rather high significance level (.017). Possible remedy is to assess normality of variables, which can affect the test statistic. This is less of problem with smaller sample sizes.

Stepwise Statistics

Variables Entered/Removed[a,b,c,d]

		Min. D Squared			Exact F		
Step	Entered	Statistic	Between Groups	Statistic	df1	df2	Sig.
1	Delivery Speed	.526	New Task and Modified Rebuy	4.606	1	57.000	3.613E-02
2	Price Level	2.718	Modified Rebuy and Straight Rebuy	12.325	2	56.000	3.668E-05
3	Price Flexibility	4.201	New Task and Modified Rebuy	11.824	3	55.000	4.384E-06

At each step, the variable that maximizes the Mahalanobis distance
between the two closest groups is entered.

a. Maximum number of steps is 14.

b. Maximum significance of F to enter is .05.

c. Minimum significance of F to remove is .10.

d. F level, tolerance, or VIN insufficient for further computation.

Three variables enter the equation in the following order: *delivery speed, price level,* and *price flexibility.* At step 3, the overall model is significant (F statistic) indicating all three groups are significantly different from one another. The greatest difference is between groups 1 and 3.

Specification of the selection method to be used for the analysis and the statistical criteria.

Variables in the Analysis

Step		Tolerance	Sig. of F to Remove	Min. D Squared	Between Groups
1	Delivery Speed	1.000	.000		
2	Delivery Speed	.766	.000	.046	New Task and Straight Rebuy
	Price Level	.766	.000	.526	New Task and Modified Rebuy
3	Delivery Speed	.764	.000	1.757	New Task and Modified Rebuy
	Price Level	.684	.000	.660	New Task and Modified Rebuy
	Price Flexibility	.878	.000	2.718	Modified Rebuy and Straight Rebuy

Variables Not in the Analysis

Step		Tolerance	Min. Tolerance	Sig. of F to Enter	Min. D Squared	Between Groups
0	Delivery Speed	1.000	1.000	.000	.526	New Task and Modified Rebuy
	Price Level	1.000	1.000	.000	.046	New Task and Straight Rebuy
	Price Flexibility	1.000	1.000	.000	.070	New Task and Modified Rebuy
	Manufacturer Image	1.000	1.000	.389	.024	Modified Rebuy and Straight Rebuy
	Service	1.000	1.000	.000	.008	Modified Rebuy and Straight Rebuy
	Salesforce Image	1.000	1.000	.882	.000	New Task and Modified Rebuy
	Product Quality	1.000	1.000	.000	.094	New Task and Modified Rebuy
1	Price Level	.766	.766	.000	2.718	Modified Rebuy and Straight Rebuy
	Price Flexibility	.982	.982	.000	.660	New Task and Modified Rebuy
	Manufacturer Image	.998	.998	.506	.698	New Task and Modified Rebuy
	Service	.704	.704	.000	2.537	Modified Rebuy and Straight Rebuy
	Salesforce Image	.991	.991	.980	.531	New Task and Modified Rebuy
	Product Quality	.869	.869	.326	.529	New Task and Modified Rebuy
2	Price Flexibility	.878	.684	.000	4.201	New Task and Modified Rebuy
	Manufacturer Image	.963	.739	.991	2.719	Modified Rebuy and Straight Rebuy
	Service	.017	.017	.435	2.975	Modified Rebuy and Straight Rebuy
	Salesforce Image	.952	.736	.589	2.766	Modified Rebuy and Straight Rebuy
	Product Quality	.786	.693	.127	2.755	Modified Rebuy and Straight Rebuy
3	Manufacturer Image	.962	.665	.982	4.206	New Task and Modified Rebuy
	Service	.017	.017	.585	4.376	New Task and Modified Rebuy
	Salesforce Image	.944	.652	.535	4.432	New Task and Modified Rebuy
	Product Quality	.780	.615	.121	4.678	New Task and Modified Rebuy

Wilks' Lambda

Step	Number of Variables	Lambda	df1	df2	df3	Exact F			
						Statistic	df1	df2	Sig.
1	1	.550	1	2	57	23.346	2	57.000	3.921E-08
2	2	.361	2	2	57	18.587	4	112.000	.000
3	3	.222	3	2	57	20.540	6	110.000	5.122E-16

307

Pairwise Group Comparisons[a,b,c]

Step	Type of Buying		New Task	Modified Rebuy	Straight Rebuy
1	New Task	F		4.606	45.335
		Sig.		.036	.000
	Modified Rebuy	F	4.606		15.274
		Sig.	.036		.000
	Straight Rebuy	F	45.335	15.274	
		Sig.	.000	.000	
2	New Task	F		17.749	26.405
		Sig.		.000	.000
	Modified Rebuy	F	17.749		12.325
		Sig.	.000		.000
	Straight Rebuy	F	26.405	12.325	
		Sig.	.000	.000	
3	New Task	F		11.824	34.432
		Sig.		.000	.000
	Modified Rebuy	F	11.824		18.934
		Sig.	.000		.000
	Straight Rebuy	F	34.432	18.934	
		Sig.	.000	.000	

a. 1, 57 degrees of freedom for step 1.

b. 2, 56 degrees of freedom for step 2.

c. 3, 55 degrees of freedom for step 3.

Summary of Canonical Discriminant Functions

Eigenvalues

Function	Eigenvalue	% of Variance	Cumulative %	Canonical Correlation
1	1.935[a]	78.4	78.4	.812
2	.532[a]	21.6	100.0	.589

a. First 2 canonical discriminant functions were used in the analysis.

Wilks' Lambda

Test of Function(s)	Wilks' Lambda	Chi-square	df	Sig.
1 through 2	.222	84.177	6	.000
2	.653	23.879	2	.000

Standardized Canonical Discriminant Function Coefficients

	Function	
	1	2
Delivery Speed	.785	.559
Price Level	.495	.995
Price Flexibility	.788	-.285

> Similar to the two-group discriminant analysis, except there are two functions due to the use of three groups.

> As interpreted in the two-group discriminant analysis, the standardized coefficients may be used to compare each variable's relative influence in the discriminant equation.

309

Structure Matrix

	Function	
	1	2
Price Flexibility	.721*	-.556
Delivery Speed	.650*	.039
Price Level	-.159	.824*
Service^a	.509	.817*
Product Quality^a	-.129	.243*
Manufacturer Image ^a	.046	.188*
Salesforce Image ^a	.161	.171*

Pooled within-groups correlations between
discriminating variables and standardized
canonical discriminant functions
Variables ordered by absolute size of correlation
within function.

*. Largest absolute correlation between
each variable and any discriminant
function

a. This variable not used in the analysis.

Canonical Discriminant Function Coefficients

	Function	
	1	2
Delivery Speed	.713	.508
Price Level	.476	.957
Price Flexibility	.825	-.298
(Constant)	-10.207	-1.720

Unstandardized coefficients

Functions at Group Centroids

Type of Buying Situation	Function	
	1	2
New Task	-1.482	-.579
Modified Rebuy	-.473	1.206
Straight Rebuy	1.592	-.247

Unstandardized canonical discriminant
functions evaluated at group means

Classification Statistics

Classification Processing Summary

Processed		100
Excluded	Missing or out-of-range group codes	0
	At least one missing discriminating variable	0
Used in Output		100

Prior Probabilities for Groups

Type of Buying Situation	Prior	Cases Used in Analysis	
		Unweighted	Weighted
New Task	.350	21	21.000
Modified Rebuy	.250	15	15.000
Straight Rebuy	.400	24	24.000
Total	1.000	60	60.000

Classification Function Coefficients

	Type of Buying Situation		
	New Task	Modified Rebuy	Straight Rebuy
Delivery Speed	4.207	5.833	6.568
Price Level	7.356	9.543	9.135
Price Flexibility	10.060	10.360	12.498
(Constant)	-50.478	-63.750	-82.323

Fisher's linear discriminant functions

Interpreted the same as in the two-group discriminant analysis. Since this is a three-group discriminant analysis, there are three equations - one for each group.

```
                          Territorial Map
Canonical Discriminant
Function 2
         -6.0       -4.0       -2.0         .0        2.0        4.0        6.0
          +---------+---------+---------+---------+---------+---------+---------+
     6.0 +                                                        223        +
         I                                                        233          I
         I                                                         23          I
         I                                                         23          I
         I                                                        23          I
         I                                                        23          I
     4.0 +         +         +         +         +    223        +          +
         I                                              233                  I
         I222                                           23                   I
         I11122                                         23                   I
         I     11222                                    23                   I
         I       111222                                 23                   I
     2.0 +        111222        +         +         223+         +          +
         I           111222                        233                      I
         I             111222            *        23                        I
         I               111222                  23                         I
         I                 111222              23                           I
         I                   111222    23                                   I
      .0 +         +         + 1112223         +         +          +
         I                      113            *                            I
         I                *      13                                         I
         I                       13                                         I
         I                       13                                         I
         I                       13                                         I
    -2.0 +         +         +   +13        +         +          +
         I                       13                                         I
         I                       13                                         I
         I                       13                                         I
         I                       13                                         I
         I                       13                                         I
    -4.0 +         +         +   + 13       +         +          +
         I                       13                                         I
         I                       13                                         I
         I                       13                                         I
         I                      13                                          I
         I                      13                                          I
    -6.0 +                      13                                          +
          +---------+---------+---------+---------+---------+---------+---------+
         -6.0       -4.0       -2.0         .0        2.0        4.0        6.0
                     Canonical Discriminant Function 1
```

—

Symbols used in territorial map

Symbol   Group   Label
------   -----   --------------------

  1   1   New Task
  2   2   Modified Rebuy
  3   3   Straight Rebuy
  *   Indicates a group centroid

Separate-Groups Graphs

Canonical Discriminant Functions

Type of Buying Situation = New Task

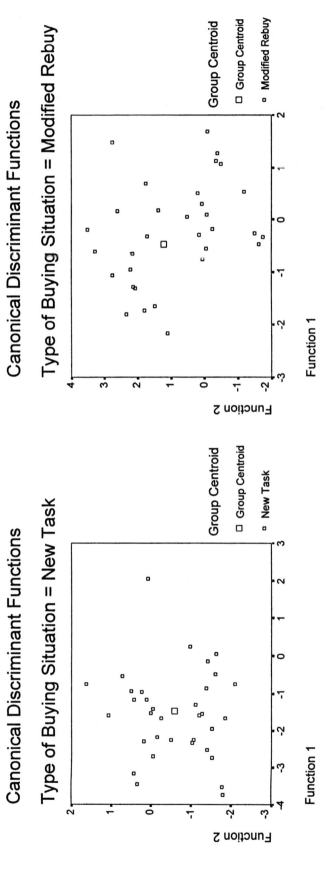

Group Centroid

□ Group Centroid

▫ New Task

Canonical Discriminant Functions

Type of Buying Situation = Modified Rebuy

Group Centroid

□ Group Centroid

▫ Modified Rebuy

Canonical Discriminant Functions

Type of Buying Situation = Straight Rebuy

Group Centroid
□ Group Centroid
▫ Straight Rebuy

Function 1

Function 2

Canonical Discriminant Functions

Type of Buying Situa

Type of Buying Situa
□ Group Centroids
▫ Straight Rebuy
▫ Modified Rebuy
▪ New Task

Function 1

Function 2

314

Classification Results[b,c,d]

			Type of Buying Situation	Predicted Group Membership			Total
				New Task	Modified Rebuy	Straight Rebuy	
Cases Selected	Original	Count	New Task	16	3	2	21
			Modified Rebuy	3	9	3	15
			Straight Rebuy	0	0	24	24
		%	New Task	76.2	14.3	9.5	100.0
			Modified Rebuy	20.0	60.0	20.0	100.0
			Straight Rebuy	.0	.0	100.0	100.0
	Cross-validated	Count	New Task	16	3	2	21
			Modified Rebuy	3	9	3	15
			Straight Rebuy	1	0	23	24
		%	New Task	76.2	14.3	9.5	100.0
			Modified Rebuy	20.0	60.0	20.0	100.0
			Straight Rebuy	4.2	.0	95.8	100.0
Cases Not Selected	Original	Count	New Task	12	1	0	13
			Modified Rebuy	4	8	5	17
			Straight Rebuy	0	0	10	10
		%	New Task	92.3	7.7	.0	100.0
			Modified Rebuy	23.5	47.1	29.4	100.0
			Straight Rebuy	.0	.0	100.0	100.0

a. Cross validation is done only for those cases in the analysis. In cross validation, each case is classified by the functions derived from all cases other than that case.

b. 81.7% of selected original grouped cases correctly classified.

c. 75.0% of unselected original grouped cases correctly classified.

d. 80.0% of selected cross-validated grouped cases correctly classified.

Stepwise Logistic Regression

```
*Logistic Regression Analysis.
SET SEED=123456.
COMPUTE RANDZ=UNIFORM(1)>.60.
LOGISTIC REGRESSION X11 WITH X1, X2, X3, X4, X5, X6, X7
/METHOD=FSTEP
/SELECT=RANDZ EQ 0
/PRINT=ALL
/CRITERIA=ITERATE(50)
/CASEWISE=PRED PGROUP RESID SRESID ZRESID LEVER COOK DFBETA .
```

```
Total number of cases:      100 (Unweighted)
Number of selected cases:    64
Number of unselected cases:  36

Number of selected cases:                     64
Number rejected because of missing data:       0
Number of cases included in the analysis:     64
```

Dependent Variable Encoding:

```
Original    Internal
Value       Value
0           0
1           1
```

Dependent Variable.. X11   Specification Buying

Beginning Block Number 0. Initial Log Likelihood Function

-2 Log Likelihood 86.459467

* Constant is included in the model.

Estimation terminated at iteration number 2 because
Log Likelihood decreased by less than .01 percent.

        Iteration History:

Iteration Log Likelihood   Constant
    1   -43.229889   .37500000
    2   -43.229733   .37948775

Classification Table for X11
The Cut Value is .50
Selected cases RANDZ EQ .00

                              Predicted
                     Specification BuTotal Value Anal   Percent Correct
                          S   I   T
                     +------+--------+
Observed
  Specification Bu S I 0   I   26   I   .00%
                     +------+--------+
  Total Value Anal T I 0   I   38   I   100.00%
                     +------+--------+
                                        Overall   59.38%

Classification Table for X11
The Cut Value is .50
Unselected cases RANDZ NE .00

                              Predicted
                     Specification BuTotal Value Anal   Percent Correct
                          S   I   T
                     +------+--------+
Observed
  Specification Bu S I 0   I   14   I   .00%
                     +------+--------+
  Total Value Anal T I 0   I   22   I   100.00%
                     +------+--------+
                                        Overall   61.11%

Group prediction for the analysis sample and then the hold out sample, based only on the constant in the equation.

317

------------- Variables in the Equation -------------

Variable	B	S.E.	Wald	df	Sig	R
Constant	.3795	.2545	2.2232	1	.1360	

Variable	Exp(B)	95% CI for Exp(B) Lower Upper

Beginning Block Number 1.   Method: Forward Stepwise (COND)

------------- Variables not in the Equation -------------
Residual Chi Square   43.433 with   7 df   Sig = .0000

Variable	Score	df	Sig	R
X1	20.2065	1	.0000	.4589
X2	11.4393	1	.0007	.3304
X3	28.5378	1	.0000	.5540
X4	.0046	1	.9457	.0000
X5	1.4815	1	.2235	.0000
X6	.4770	1	.4898	.0000
X7	33.3445	1	.0000	.6021

Variable(s) Entered on Step Number
1..   X7   Product Quality

Estimation terminated at iteration number 6 because
Log Likelihood decreased by less than .01 percent.

Iteration History:

Iteration	Log Likelihood	Constant	X7
1	-24.402625	6.567924	-.8745524
2	-20.169186	11.192305	-1.4698765
3	-18.964376	15.141049	-1.9745694
4	-18.819049	17.102281	-2.2248186
5	-18.816185	17.428836	-2.2664594
6	-18.816184	17.436171	-2.2673943

> The variable with the highest score will be entered into the equation. This would be X_7, with a score of 33.3445.

Now that a variable has been entered into the equation, we have a model Chi-square. At this point, the model Chi-square and the improvement are the same amount.

```
-2 Log Likelihood        37.632
Goodness of Fit          60.277
Cox & Snell - R^2          .534
Nagelkerke - R^2           .720
```

	Chi-Square	df	Significance
Model	48.827	1	.0000
Block	48.827	1	.0000
Step	48.827	1	.0000

--------- Hosmer and Lemeshow Goodness-of-Fit Test ------------

X11 = Specification Bu X11 = Total Value Anal

Group	Observed	Expected	Observed	Expected	Total
1	7.000	6.836	.000	.164	7.000
2	6.000	5.512	.000	.488	6.000
3	5.000	4.167	.000	.833	5.000
4	4.000	4.328	2.000	1.672	6.000
5	1.000	2.813	5.000	3.187	6.000
6	1.000	1.268	4.000	3.732	5.000
7	1.000	.853	7.000	7.147	8.000
8	1.000	.182	5.000	5.818	6.000
9	.000	.034	6.000	5.966	6.000
10	.000	.007	9.000	8.993	9.000

	Chi-Square	df	Significance
Goodness-of-fit test	7.9136	8	.4420

Classification Table for X11
The Cut Value is .50
Selected cases RANDZ EQ .00

```
                               Predicted
                    Specification BuTotal Value Anal
                         S  I    T
                    +-------I-------+
Observed
  Specification Bu S I  23  I    3  I      88.46%
                    +-------I-------+
  Total Value Anal T I   4  I   34  I      89.47%
                    +-------I-------+
                                      Overall    89.06%
```

Classification Table for X11
The Cut Value is .50
Unselected cases RANDZ NE .00

```
                               Predicted
                    Specification BuTotal Value Anal
                         S  I    T
                    +-------I-------+
Observed
  Specification Bu S I   8  I    6  I      57.14%
                    +-------I-------+
  Total Value Anal T I   3  I   19  I      86.36%
                    +-------I-------+
                                      Overall    75.00%
```

----------- Variables in the Equation ------------

Variable	B	S.E.	Wald	df	Sig	R
X7	-2.2674	.5763	15.4791	1	.0001	-.3948
Constant	17.4362	4.4621	15.2693	1	.0001	

Variable	Exp(B)	95% CI for Exp(B)	
		Lower	Upper
X7	.1036	.0335	.3205

Correlation Matrix:

	Constant	X7
Constant	1.00000	-.99570
X7	-.99570	1.00000

```
------------- Model if Term Removed -------------
         Based on Conditional Parameter Estimates

Term       Log                            Significance
Removed    Likelihood    -2 Log LR    df  of Log LR

X7         -44.641       51.649       1     .0000

------------- Variables not in the Equation -------------
Residual Chi Square    16.601 with    6 df    Sig =  .0109

Variable    Score     df    Sig      R

X1          8.8633    1    .0029    .2817
X2           .1257    1    .7230    .0000
X3         12.1831    1    .0005    .3432
X4          3.1200    1    .0773    .1138
X5          5.8323    1    .0157    .2105
X6          7.6037    1    .0058    .2546

Variable(s) Entered on Step Number
2..    X3      Price Flexibility

Estimation terminated at iteration number 6 because
Log Likelihood decreased by less than .01 percent.

        Iteration History:

Iteration  Log Likelihood   Constant        X3           X7
   1        -20.078021      .4620140     .5564472     -.6248465
   2        -14.946175     2.5405896     .8144124    -1.1429693
   3        -13.305457     4.7503335    1.0282612    -1.6328561
   4        -13.014280     5.9500713    1.1802725    -1.9357135
   5        -12.999139     6.2346929    1.2304988    -2.0221591
   6        -12.999076     6.2519172    1.2341824    -2.0280630

-2 Log Likelihood      25.998
Goodness of Fit        53.222
Cox & Snell - R^2        .611
Nagelkerke - R^2         .825

            Chi-Square    df   Significance
Model         60.461       2       .0000
Block         60.461       2       .0000
Step          11.634       1       .0006
```

The next variable to enter the equation is X_3, with a score of 12.1831.

The model Chi-square is now 60.461 with an improvement of 11.634. This is found by subtracting the previous model Chi-square from the present model Chi-square: 60.461 − 48.827 = 11.634.

321

-------- Hosmer and Lemeshow Goodness-of-Fit Test--------

X11 = Specification Bu X11 = Total Value Anal

Group	Observed	Expected	Observed	Expected	Total
1	6.000	5.942	.000	.058	6.000
2	6.000	5.854	.000	.146	6.000
3	6.000	5.748	.000	.252	6.000
4	5.000	4.675	1.000	1.325	6.000
5	1.000	2.453	5.000	3.547	6.000
6	.000	.966	7.000	6.034	7.000
7	2.000	.247	4.000	5.753	6.000
8	.000	.091	6.000	5.909	6.000
9	.000	.021	6.000	5.979	6.000
10	.000	.002	9.000	8.998	9.000

Chi-Square   df   Significance

Goodness-of-fit test   16.2179   8   .0394

Classification Table for X11
The Cut Value is .50
Selected cases RANDZ EQ .00

Predicted
Specification BuTotal Value Anal
S I I T

		S	I	I	T	Percent Correct
Observed		+	-	-	+	
Specification Bu	S	I	24	I	2 I	92.31%
		+	-	-	+	
Total Value Anal	T	I	1	I	37 I	97.37%
		+	-	-	+	
				Overall		95.31%

Group predictions with the constant, X₇, and X₃ in the equation

322

```
Classification Table for X11
The Cut Value is .50
Unselected cases  RANDZ NE  .00

                                      Predicted
                          Specification BuTotal Value Anal  Percent Correct
                                   S     I     T
Observed                      +-----+-----+
    Specification Bu   S    I  I  10 I   4 I              71.43%
                              +-----+-----+
    Total Value Anal   T    I  I   0 I  22 I             100.00%
                              +-----+-----+
                                               Overall    88.89%

------------ Variables in the Equation ------------

Variable       B        S.E.     Wald    df     Sig       R

X3          1.2342    .4362    8.0047    1    .0047    .2635
X7         -2.0281    .6093   11.0777    1    .0009   -.3240
Constant    6.2519   4.6114    1.8380    1    .1752


                      95% CI for Exp(B)
Variable    Exp(B)    Lower    Upper

X3          3.4356   1.4611   8.0781
X7           .1316    .0399    .4344


Correlation Matrix:

            Constant      X3        X7
Constant    1.00000   -.35676   -.75286
X3          -.35676   1.00000   -.33746
X7          -.75286   -.33746   1.00000


------------ Model if Term Removed ------------
        Based on Conditional Parameter Estimates

Term       Log                                     Significance
Removed    Likelihood   -2 Log LR    df            of Log LR

X3         -20.408      14.819       1              .0001
X7         -29.065      32.132       1              .0000
```

```
--------- Variables not in the Equation ---------    Sig = .0872
Residual Chi Square     9.606 with     5 df

Variable        Score       df      Sig       R

X1             3.1914        1      .0740     .1174
X2             2.7486        1      .0973     .0931
X4             3.3479        1      .0673     .1249
X5             6.9853        1      .0082     .2401
X6             7.1422        1      .0075     .2439
```

```
Variable(s) Entered on Step Number
3..      X6      Salesforce Image

Estimation terminated at iteration number 7 because
Log Likelihood decreased by less than .01 percent.

          Iteration History:

Iteration  Log Likelihood    Constant        X3         X6         X7
    1        -19.188335      -.0617904     .5341691   .3236561   -.6531142
    2        -12.655345      1.0572351     .8066292   .8487164   -1.2545807
    3         -9.865573      2.0830012    1.1108914  1.4854462   -1.9192439
    4         -8.849317      3.0744281    1.4026119  2.1838401   -2.5972008
    5         -8.625821      3.9676523    1.5990086  2.6989831   -3.1039529
    6         -8.611239      4.3202683    1.6632512  2.8682428   -3.2786681
    7         -8.611159      4.3517672    1.6683506  2.8815287   -3.2929696
```

```
-2 Log Likelihood           17.222
Goodness of Fit             65.245
Cox & Snell - R^2            .661
Nagelkerke - R^2             .892

                Chi-Square    df    Significance

Model              69.237      3       .0000
Block              69.237      3       .0000
Step                8.776      1       .0031
```

The next variable to enter is X6, with a score of 7.1422.

New model Chi-square is 69.237, with an improvement of 8.776. This is found as mentioned before: 69.237 – 60.461 = 8.776.

```
---------- Hosmer and Lemeshow Goodness-of-Fit Test----------

    X11   = Specification Bu X11   = Total Value Anal

Group  Observed  Expected   Observed  Expected   Total

  1      6.000    5.998       .000      .002     6.000
  2      6.000    5.988       .000      .012     6.000
  3      6.000    5.905       .000      .095     6.000
  4      6.000    5.268       .000      .732     6.000
  5      1.000    2.197      5.000     3.803     6.000
  6       .000     .474      6.000     5.526     6.000
  7      1.000     .150      5.000     5.850     6.000
  8       .000     .017      6.000     5.983     6.000
  9       .000     .002      6.000     5.998     6.000
 10       .000     .000     10.000    10.000    10.000

                     Chi-Square    df  Significance

Goodness-of-fit test    7.4423      8     .4897
```

```
Classification Table for X11
The Cut Value is .50
Selected cases RANDZ EQ .00

                                   Predicted
                         Specification BuTotal Value Anal   Percent Correct
                            S    I       T
                         +-------I-------+
Observed
   Specification Bu   S   I  25  I   1   I        96.15%
                         +-------I-------+
   Total Value Anal   T   I   2  I  36   I        94.74%
                         +-------I-------+
                                         Overall  95.31%
```

Group predictions with the constant, X_7, X_3, and X_6 in the equation.

Classification Table for X11
The Cut Value is .50
Unselected cases RANDZ NE .00

Predicted

		Specification Bu	Total Value Anal	Percent Correct
		S	T	
Observed				
Specification Bu	S	I 12 I	2 I	85.71%
Total Value Anal	T	I 2 I	20 I	90.91%
		Overall		88.89%

------------ Variables in the Equation ------------

Variable	B	S.E.	Wald	df	Sig	R
X3	1.6684	.6561	6.4655	1	.0110	.2273
X6	2.8815	1.2877	5.0072	1	.0252	.1865
X7	-3.2930	1.1743	7.8641	1	.0050	-.2604
Constant	4.3518	6.4967	.4487	1	.5030	

Variable	Exp(B)	95% CI for Exp(B) Lower	Upper
X3	5.3034	1.4658	19.1889
X6	17.8415	1.4299	222.6131
X7	.0371	.0037	.3710

Correlation Matrix:

	Constant	X3	X6	X7
Constant	1.00000	-.43596	-.17838	-.58225
X3	-.43596	1.00000	.47500	-.41875
X6	-.17838	.47500	1.00000	-.80235
X7	-.58225	-.41875	-.80235	1.00000

---------- Model if Term Removed ----------

Based on Conditional Parameter Estimates

Term Removed	Log Likelihood	-2 Log LR	df	Significance of Log LR
X3	-16.106	14.990	1	.0001
X6	-14.435	11.647	1	.0006
X7	-28.086	38.950	1	.0000

---------- Variables not in the Equation ----------

Residual Chi Square   3.221 with   4 df   Sig = .5215

Variable	Score	df	Sig	R
X1	1.0393	1	.3080	.0000
X2	1.0539	1	.3046	.0000
X4	.6305	1	.4272	.0000
X5	2.4717	1	.1159	.0739

No more variables can be deleted or added.

> No variables may enter the equation and no variables may be removed for the equation due to the values set by PIN and POUT.

> A casewise listing of the temporary variables created by the casewise subcommand. Diagnostic measures similar to those for multiple regression are available.

CASE Observed X11	Pred	PGroup	Resid	SResid	ZResid	Lever	Cook	DFB0	DFB1	DFB2	DFB3
1 U T	.9954	T	.0046	.	.0683	.0201	.0001	.0461	.0017	.0084	-.0108
2 S S	.2188	T	-.2188	-.8215	-.5293	.2681	.1026	.2521	.0750	-.1382	-.0763
3 U S	.0047	S	-.0047	.	-.0685	.0163	.0001	.0037	.0046	.0080	-.0083
4 S S	.0541	S	-.0541	-.3482	-.2392	.0817	.0051	.1298	.0233	.0771	-.0726
5 S T	1.0000	T	-.0000	.0001	.0001	.0000	.0000	.0000	.0000	.0000	.0000
6 S S	.0001	S	-.0000	-.0162	-.0115	.0017	.0000	-.0017	.0001	.0005	-.0005
7 S T	.9997	T	-.0003	-.0242	-.0171	.0028	.0000	-.0007	.0005	.0010	-.0007
8 S S	.1562	S	-.1562	-.6335	-.4303	.1535	.0336	-.6126	.0983	.1371	-.0744
9 S T	.9747	T	-.0253	-.2337	-.1610	.0623	.0017	-.1225	.0253	.0275	-.0171
10 S S	.0143	S	-.0143	-.1729	-.1205	.0353	.0005	.0555	.0086	.0170	-.0234
11 U T	.9997	T	.0003	.	.0183	.0022	.0000	.0014	.0004	.0009	-.0009
12 U T **	.3557	S	.6443	.	1.3459	.4685	1.5967	-9.5051	.4664	-.9455	1.2532
13 U S **	.5414	S	-.5414	.	-1.0865	.3184	.5514	-.0578	-.0486	.7489	-.2755
14 S T	.9993	T	-.0007	.0369	-.0260	.0043	.0000	.0013	.0008	.0020	-.0017
15 S T	.9974	T	.0026	.0719	-.0506	.0108	.0000	-.0065	.0032	.0039	-.0036
16 S T	.9999	T	.0001	.0115	.0081	.0006	.0001	-.0004	.0001	.0002	-.0002
17 S T	.8583	T	.1417	.6552	.4063	.2883	.0669	1.6728	-.0480	.2123	-.2489
18 U T	.8901	T	.1099	.	.3514	.1339	.0191	.4986	.0197	-.0112	-.0775
19 S T	.9999	T	.0001	.0130	.0092	.0009	.0000	.0000	.0001	.0003	-.0002
20 U T	.9974	T	.0026	.	-.0506	.0108	.0000	-.0065	.0032	.0039	-.0036
21 U T	.9585	T	.0415	.	.2080	.0609	.0028	.0410	.0236	.0126	-.0315

#	Lbl		P										
22	S	T	.9975	T	.0025		.0504	.0101	.0000	.0159	.0018	.0034	.0052
23	U	T	.8416	T	.1584	.0716	.4339	.2862	.0755	-1.5407	.1584	.1312	.0177
24	U	S	.2737	S	-.2737	.	-.6139	.1192	.0510	-.4678	.0912	.1270	-.0905
25	T	T	1.0000	T	.0000	.0014	.0010	.0000	.0000	.0000	.0000	.0000	.0000
26	U	S	1.0000	T	.0000		-.0063	.0005	.0000	.0004	.0000	.0001	-.0002
27	U	T	.2418	S	-.2418	.0110	-.5648	.1214	.0441	-.4655	.0927	.1235	-.0890
28	S	T	.9999	T	.0001	.0261	.0078	.0007	.0000	.0000	.0001	.0002	-.0002
29	S	T	.9997	T	.0003		.0185	.0022	.0000	.0008	.0005	.0006	-.0008
30	S	S	.0080	S	-.0080	-.1282	-.0898	.0229	.0002	-.0130	.0067	.0111	-.0131
31	U	S	.0343	S	-.0343		-.1885	.0562	.0021	.0000	.0237	.0302	-.0369
32	S	T	.8051	T	.1949	.7710	.4920	.2708	.0899	-1.5982	.1635	.1127	.0297
33	U	T	1.0000	T	.0000		.0030	.0001	.0000	.0001	.0000	.0000	.0000
34	S	S	.0555	S	-.0555	-.3522	-.2424	.0795	.0051	.1160	.0270	.0297	-.0573
35	S	S	.4878	S	-.4878	-1.5497	-.9760	.4428	.7570	-1.7508	.0896	.9767	-.2524
36	U	S	.2233	S	-.2233		-.5362	.1352	.0449	.4925	.0306	.1907	-.1823
37	S	S	.0001	T	-.0001	-.0129	-.0091	.0008	.0000	.0005	.0001	.0003	-.0003
38	S	T	.9520	S	-.0480	.3267	.2246	.0779	.0043	-.1692	.0389	.0312	-.0243
39	S	S	.0026	S	-.0026	-.0725	-.0510	.0124	.0000	.0165	.0019	.0058	-.0064
40	S	S	.0005	S	-.0005	-.0315	-.0223	.0036	.0000	.0027	.0005	.0015	-.0015
41	U	S	.2459	T	-.2459		-.5710	.1408	.0534	.6834	.0193	.1871	-.1976
42	S	T	1.0000	T	.0000	.0001	.0001	.0000	.0000	.0000	.0000	.0000	.0000
43	S	T	.9607	T	.0393	.2970	.2022	.0915	.0041	-.0292	.0288	-.0061	-.0203
44	S	T	1.0000	T	.0000	-.0015	.0010	.0000	.0000	.0000	.0000	.0000	.0000
45	U	S	.0004	S	-.0004		-.0193	.0031	.0000	.0019	.0004	.0013	-.0012
46	U	T	.9652	T	-.0348	-.0273	.1899	.0820	.0032	-.0438	.0272	.0022	-.0184
47	U	T	.0001	T	.0000		.0001	.0000	.0000	.0000	.0000	.0002	.0000
48	S	S	.0001	T	-.0001	-.0114	-.0081	.0007	.0000	.0003	.0001	.0002	-.0002
49	S	T	.9799	T	.0201	.2053	.1433	.0358	.0008	-.0068	.0153	.0183	-.0199
50	U	T	.9901	T	.0099		.0998	.0295	.0003	.0643	.0048	.0073	-.0158
51	S	T	.9997	T	-.0003	.0245	.0173	.0021	.0000	.0023	.0003	.0008	-.0009
52	S	S	.0121	S	-.0121		-.1108	.0536	.0007	.1188	.0029	.0255	-.0293
53	S	S	.0131	S	-.0131	-.1655	-.1154	.0340	.0005	.0478	.0084	.0138	-.0209
54	U	S	.0007	S	-.0007	-.0373	-.0263	.0047	.0000	.0050	.0006	.0019	-.0020
55	S	T	.9985	T	.0015		-.0392	.0065	.0000	.0066	.0014	.0026	-.0032
56	S	T	.9017	T	.0983	.4869	.3303	.1265	.0158	-.1050	.0470	.1363	-.0762
57	S	S	.0326	S	-.0326	-.2721	-.1837	.1037	.0039	.2993	.0060	.0201	-.0566
58	S	S	.9748	S	.0252	-.2340	-.1607	.0686	.0019	-.1448	.0269	.0264	-.0152
59	S	S	.9999	S	.0001	.0108	.0077	.0007	.0000	.0007	.0001	.0002	-.0002
60	U	S	.0098	S	-.0098		-.0997	.0436	.0005	.0826	.0035	.0227	-.0237
61	S	T	1.0000	T	.0000	.0002	.0002	.0000	.0000	.0000	.0000	.0000	.0000
62	S	T	1.0000	T	.0000	.0045	.0032	.0001	.0000	.0001	.0000	.0000	.0000
63	U	T	.9637	T	.0363	.9249	.1940	.0717	.0029	-.1531	.0329	.0283	-.0201
64	S	S	.7793	S	.2207	-.0360	.5321	.4171	.2026	3.4885	-.1450	.2769	-.4155
65	S	T	.0006	S	-.0006	-.2375	-.0254	.0050	.0013	-.0070	.0005	.0016	-.0020
66	T	S	.9735	T	-.0265		-.1651	.0462	.0013	-.0359	.0207	.0186	-.0211
67	S	T	.9990	T	.0010	.0450	.0317	.0064	.0000	-.0015	.0013	.0028	-.0021
68	U	S	.2410	S	-.2410		-.5635	.1365	.0502	-.6998	.1090	.1138	-.0698

Case	Sel	Obs	Flag										
69	U	T		.9997	-.0003		.0166	.0019	.0000	.0022	.0003	.0006	-.0008
70	S	S		.0058	-.0058	-.1100	-.0766	.0336	.0002	.0615	.0018	.0145	-.0159
71	S	S		.0060	-.0060	-.1108	-.0777	-.0190	.0001	-.0107	-.0053	.0093	-.0105
72	U	T		.9945	-.0055		-.0746	-.0179	-.0001	-.0328	-.0034	-.0057	-.0097
73	U	T		1.0000	.0000		.0061	-.0004	.0000	-.0002	.0001	.0001	-.0001
74	S	T		.9636	-.0364	.2817	-.1944	-.0646	-.0026	-.1208	-.0307	-.0298	-.0229
75	S	S		.0206	-.0206	-.2088	-.1452	-.0426	-.0009	-.0529	-.0125	-.0287	-.0315
76	U	T	**	.4562	.5438		1.0919	.5735	1.6031	-11.4611	.6753	-.7275	1.2370
77	S	T		.9997	-.0003	.0230	-.0163	.0019	.0000	.0019	.0003	.0007	-.0008
78	S	T		.9996	-.0004	.0296	-.0209	.0027	.0000	-.0015	-.0005	-.0007	-.0010
79	U	S		.0006	-.0006		-.0239	-.0044	.0000	-.0059	-.0004	.0014	-.0018
80	S	T		.9259	.0741	.4100	.2829	-.0842	.0074	-.0835	-.0434	-.0175	-.0340
81	U	T		.9998	.0002		.0124	.0012	.0000	-.0011	-.0002	-.0004	-.0005
82	S	T		.9958	.0042	-.0938	.0652	.0362	.0002	-.0464	-.0011	-.0147	-.0126
83	S	S		.1789	-.1789	-.7064	-.4668	.2100	.0579	-.0268	-.0799	-.0664	-.0649
84	S	T	**	.4668	.5332	1.3173	1.0687	.1219	.1586	-.6409	-.0178	-.1761	.1680
85	U	S	**	.9854	-.9854		-8.2023	.0293	2.0325	-.3906	-.7418	-1.3162	1.2232
86	S	S		.0007	-.0007	-.0375	-.0264	-.0051	.0000	-.0053	-.0006	.0021	-.0021
87	S	S	**	.9834	-.9834	-2.9084	-7.7027	-.0306	1.8760	-.8782	-.6897	-1.2296	1.2065
88	S	S	**	.4051	-.5949	1.4397	1.2119	.1280	.2157	-.0641	-.0495	-.3134	-.2102
89	S	S		.0685	-.0685	-.3957	-.2713	.0929	.0075	-.2390	.0222	-.0860	-.0907
90	U	T		.9991	-.0009		-.0298	-.0060	.0000	-.0018	.0012	-.0026	-.0019
91	S	T		.9089	.0911	.4728	.3166	.1454	.0170	-.1821	.0507	.1428	-.0720
92	S	T		.8772	.1228	.5594	.3742	.1625	.0272	.6466	.0153	-.0254	-.0872
93	U	T		.9930	-.0070		-.0838	-.0568	.0004	-.0924	-.0003	-.0223	-.0208
94	S	S		.0008	-.0008	-.0406	-.0287	.0048	.0000	-.0002	-.0011	.0019	-.0018
95	S	T		.9940	-.0060	.1109	.0775	.0265	.0002	.0654	.0016	.0098	-.0138
96	U	S		.0014	-.0014		-.0372	-.0077	.0000	-.0054	-.0014	.0037	-.0035
97	U	T		.9877	.0123		.1114	.0307	-.0004	-.0284	.0118	.0154	-.0129
98	S	S		.0011	-.0011	-.0461	-.0325	.0057	.0000	-.0008	.0013	.0023	-.0023
99	U	S		.0224	-.0224		-.1515	.0454	.0011	.0758	.0122	.0282	-.0343
100	S	T		.9997	.0003	.0228	.0161	.0018	.0000	.0009	.0003	.0007	-.0007

S=Selected U=Unselected cases
** = Misclassified cases
The Cut Value is .50

CHAPTER 6:

MULTIVARIATE ANALYSIS OF VARIANCE (MANOVA)

This section of the instructor's manual contains copies of the actual printouts from the SPSS statistical analysis program. The printouts contain examples of the analyses discussed in the text using the HATCO database.

Each of the printouts is annotated with comments to aid in the interpretation of the results. These suggestions are typed in the margins next to the appropriate data. If you wish to provide students with their own copies of the output without these comments, the output are provided on the computer diskette accompanying the instructor's manual.

Three examples of MANOVA are included in this section. A brief description follows:

Two-Group MANOVA: A MANOVA analysis is preformed where the dependent variables are X_9 (level of product usage) and X_{10} (level of satisfaction) and the predictor variable is X_{11} (type of buying process).

Three-Group MANOVA: A MANOVA analysis is preformed where the dependent variables are again X_9 (level of product usage) and X_{10} (level of satisfaction), but now the predictor variable is X_{14} (type of buying situation).

Two-Factor MANOVA: A MANOVA analysis is preformed where the dependent variables are X_9 (level of product usage) and X_{10} (level of satisfaction), but now the predictor variables are X_{11} (type of buying process) and X_{14} (type of buying situation).

Two-Group Multivariate Analysis of Variance

```
*Multivariate Analysis of Variance (2 Group).
MANOVA X9 X10 BY X11(0 1)
/PRINT CELLINFO (MEANS CORR COV)
 DESIGN (COLLINEARITY)
 HOMOGENITY(BARTLETT COCHRAN BOXM)
 SIGNIF(MULT UNIV STEPDOWN)
 SIGNIF(EFSIZE)
 PARAMETERS (ESTIM)
 ERROR(CORR)
/PLOT= ALL
/POWER T(.05) F(.05)
/METHOD=UNIQUE
/ERROR WITHIN+RESIDUAL
/DESIGN.
```

* * * * * * A n a l y s i s   o f   v a r i a n c e * * * * * * *

```
   100 cases accepted.
     0 cases rejected because of out-of-range factor values.
     0 cases rejected because of missing data.
     2 non-empty cells.

     1 design will be processed.
```

```
          CELL NUMBER
            1   2

Variable
  X11       1   2
```

Cell Means and Standard Deviations

Variable .. X9   Usage Level

FACTOR	CODE	Mean	Std. Dev.	N
X11	SPECIFIC	42.100	7.788	40
X11	TOTAL VA	48.767	8.798	60
For entire sample		46.100	8.989	100

Variable .. X10   Satisfaction Level

FACTOR	CODE	Mean	Std. Dev.	N
X11	SPECIFIC	4.295	.782	40
X11	TOTAL VA	5.088	.754	60
For entire sample		4.771	.856	100

Univariate Homogeneity of Variance Tests

332

Variable .. X9   Usage Level

Cochrans C(49,2) =   .56065, P = .396 (approx.)
Bartlett-Box F(1,25742) = .67741, P = .411

Variable .. X10   Satisfaction Level

Cochrans C(49,2) =   .51791, P = .803 (approx.)
Bartlett-Box F(1,25742) = .05993, P = .807

These two tests provide information as to the equality of variances for each variable. The significance levels indicate that the variances in the two groups are equal.

333

****** A n a l y s i s   o f   V a r i a n c e -- design 1 ******

Cell Number .. 1
Variance-Covariance matrix

	X9	X10
X9	60.656	
X10	5.011	.611

Correlation matrix with Standard Deviations on Diagonal

	X9	X10
X9	7.788	
X10	.823	.782

Determinant of Covariance matrix of dependent variables = 11.93771
LOG(Determinant) =   2.47970

- - - - - - -

Cell Number .. 2
Variance-Covariance matrix

	X9	X10
X9	77.402	
X10	3.707	.569

Correlation matrix with Standard Deviations on Diagonal

	X9	X10
X9	8.798	
X10	.559	.754

Determinant of Covariance matrix of dependent variables = 30.25880
LOG(Determinant) =   3.40979

- - - - - - -

Pooled within-cells Variance-Covariance matrix

	X9	X10
X9	70.738	
X10	4.226	.585

Determinant of pooled Covariance matrix of dependent vars. = 23.54422
LOG(Determinant) =   3.15888

Information for respondents with
$X_{11} = 0$, *specifcation buying.*

Information for respondents with
$X_{11} = 1$, *total value analysis.*

334

```
* * * * * * A n a l y s i s   o f   V a r i a n c e  --  design   1 * * * * * * *

Multivariate test for Homogeneity of Dispersion matrices

Boxs M =                 11.68446
F WITH (3,375423) DF =    3.80369, P =    .010 (Approx.)
Chi-Square with 3 DF =   11.41116, P =    .010 (Approx.)
```

Box's M test the equality of the variance/covariance matrices. Significant levels indicate unequal variance/covariance matrices.

```
- - - - - - - - - - - - - - - - - - - - - - - - - - - - - - - - - -

Correspondence between Effects and Columns of BETWEEN-Subjects DESIGN 1

Starting  Ending
Column    Column     Effect Name

   1         1       CONSTANT
   2         2       X11

- - - - - - - - - - - - - - - - - - - - - - - - - - - - - - - - - -

Collinearity Diagnostics using Singular Value Decomposition
                                            VARIANCE PROPORTIONS

ROOT NO.   SING VALS COND INDEX        1            2

   1        1.095      1.000          .400         .400
   2         .894      1.225          .600         .600

- - - - - - - - - - - - - - - - - - - - - - - - - - - - - - - - - -

WITHIN+RESIDUAL Correlations with Std. Devs. on Diagonal

             X9        X10

X9         8.411
X10         .657      .765

- - - - - - - - - - - - - - - - - - - - - - - - - - - - - - - - - -

Statistics for WITHIN+RESIDUAL correlations

Log(Determinant) =           -.56450
Bartlett test of sphericity =    54.47408 with 1 D. F.
Significance =                      .000

F(max) criterion =          120.85482 with (2,98) D. F.
```

336

> Test for the difference between groups based on X_{11}.

> The significance levels for all statistics indicate that there is a significant difference between the groups of X_{11}. Note: For two-group MANOVA, Hotelling's T^2 = Hotelling's $* (n-2)$ or $T^2 = .26870 * 98 = 26.3326$.

> The univariate tests indicate which variables contain the difference between the two groups. It must be cautioned that this test does not adjust the significance level for four tests rather than one.

> Stepdown tests for difference between the two groups on one variable, while controlling for the effects of other variables. Provides a purer measure of the effect of each variable. Remember, order is important since this is a sequential test. Variables are entered in the order they are entered in the original MANOVA syntax

```
* * * * * A n a l y s i s   o f   v a r i a n c e -- design   1 * * * * * * *

EFFECT .. X11
Multivariate Tests of Significance (S = 1, M = 0, N = 47 1/2)

Test Name      Value     Exact F  Hypoth. DF  Error DF  Sig. of F

Pillais        .21179   13.03186      2.00      97.00    .000
Hotellings     .26870   13.03186      2.00      97.00    .000
Wilks          .78821   13.03186      2.00      97.00    .000
Roys           .21179
Note.. F statistics are exact.

- - - - - - - - - - - - - - - - - - - - - - - - - - - - - - - - - - - - - -
Multivariate Effect Size and Observed Power at .0500 Level

TEST NAME    Effect Size   Noncent.    Power

(All)            .212       26.064      1.00

- - - - - - - - - - - - - - - - - - - - - - - - - - - - - - - - - - - - - -
EFFECT .. X11 (Cont.)
Univariate F-tests with (1,98) D. F.

Variable  Hypoth. SS    Error SS  Hypoth. MS  Error MS        F  Sig. of F

X9      1066.66667  6932.33333  1066.66667  70.73810  15.07910    .000
X10       15.10507    57.36083    15.10507    .58531  25.80675    .000

Variable  ETA Square   Noncent.    Power

X9          .13335      15.07910   .96985
X10         .20844      25.80675   .99904

- - - - - - - - - - - - - - - - - - - - - - - - - - - - - - - - - - - - - -
Roy-Bargman Stepdown F - tests

Variable  Hypoth. MS    Error MS  StepDown F  Hypoth. DF  Error DF  Sig. of F

X9      1066.66667    70.73810    15.07910        1          98      .000
X10        3.24605      .33627     9.65317        1          97      .002

- - - - - - - - - - - - - - - - - - - - - - - - - - - - - - - - - - - - - -
```

> T-values can be calculated as the square root of the F-value. Note that these F-values are calculated on a pooled variance estimate and differ from the examples in the text.

Used to estimate values for each group.

****** A n a l y s i s   o f   V a r i a n c e -- design   1 ******

Estimates for X9
--- Individual univariate .9500 confidence intervals
--- two-tailed observed power taken at .0500 level

X11

Parameter	Coeff.	Std. Err.	t-Value	Sig. t	Lower -95%	CL- Upper
2	-3.3333333	.85840	-3.88318	.00019	-5.03681	-1.62986

Parameter	Noncent.	Power
2	15.07910	.970

Estimates for X10
--- Individual univariate .9500 confidence intervals
--- two-tailed observed power taken at .0500 level

X11

Parameter	Coeff.	Std. Err.	t-Value	Sig. t	Lower -95%	CL- Upper
2	-.3966667	.07808	-5.08003	.00000	-.55162	-.24171

Parameter	Noncent.	Power
2	25.80675	.999

Adjusted and Estimated Means
Variable .. X9

CELL	Obs. Mean	Usage Level Adj. Mean	Est. Mean	Raw Resid.	Std. Resid.
1	42.100	42.100	42.100	.000	.000
2	48.767	48.767	48.767	.000	.000

Saturated design specified, PMEANS plot skipped.

Adjusted and Estimated Means (Cont.)
Variable .. X10

CELL	Obs. Mean	Satisfaction Level Adj. Mean	Est. Mean	Raw Resid.	Std. Resid.
1	4.295	4.295	4.295	.000	.000
2	5.088	5.088	5.088	.000	.000

Saturated design specified, PMEANS plot skipped.

337

Mean vs. variance for Usage Level

Mean vs. std. dev. for Usage Level

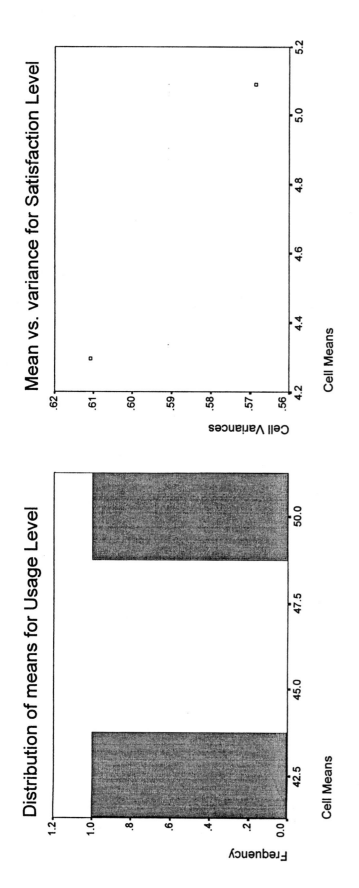

Mean vs. variance for Satisfaction Level

Cell Variances

Cell Means

Distribution of means for Usage Level

Frequency

Cell Means

Distribution of means for Satisfaction Level

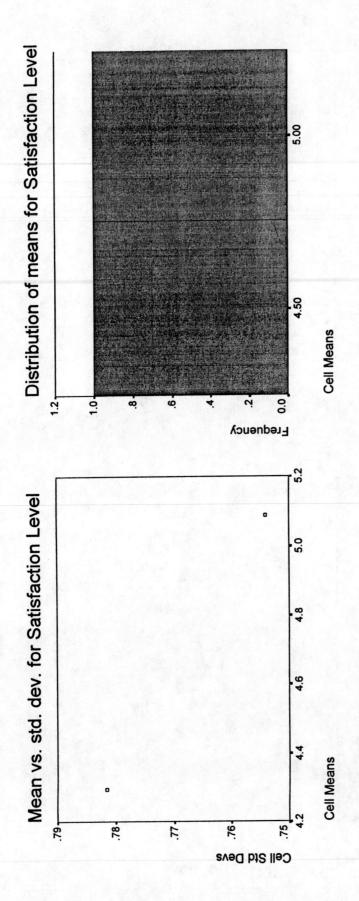

Cell Means

Mean vs. std. dev. for Satisfaction Level

Cell Means

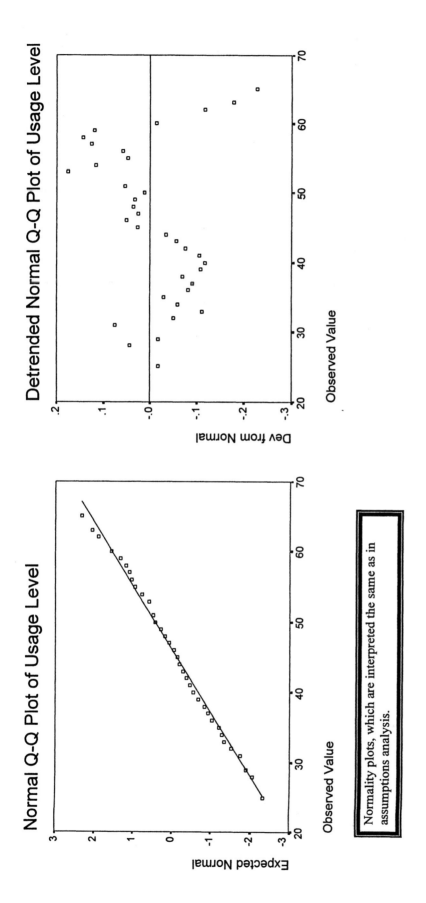

Detrended Normal Q-Q Plot of Usage Level

Normal Q-Q Plot of Usage Level

Normality plots, which are interpreted the same as in assumptions analysis.

341

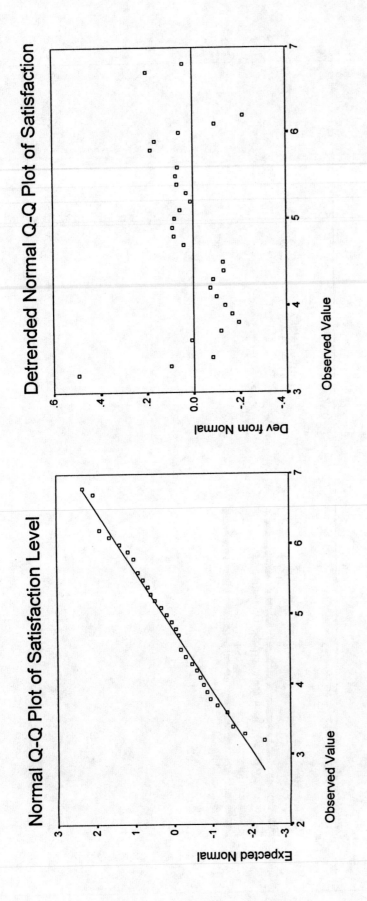

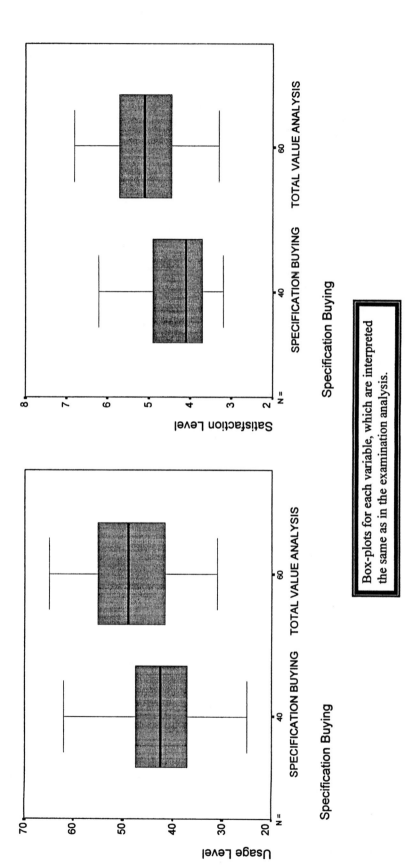

Box-plots for each variable, which are interpreted the same as in the examination analysis.

Dependent variable: X9

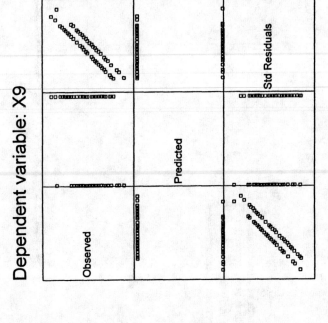

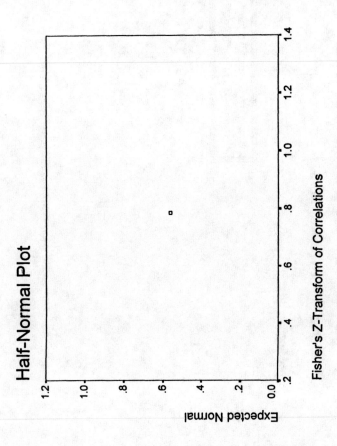

Half-Normal Plot

Fisher's Z-Transform of Correlations

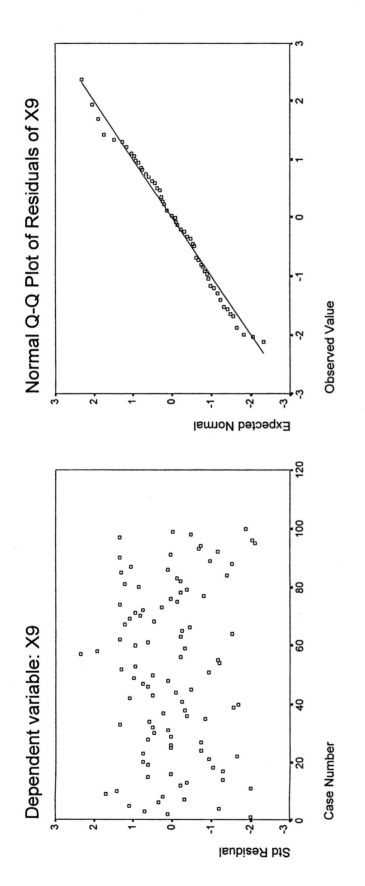

Normal Q-Q Plot of Residuals of X9

Dependent variable: X9

345

Detrended Normal Q-Q Plot of Residuals of

Dependent variable: X10

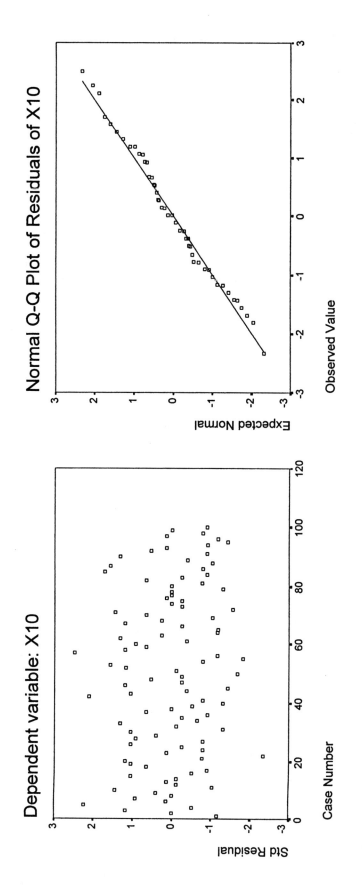

Normal Q-Q Plot of Residuals of X10

Dependent variable: X10

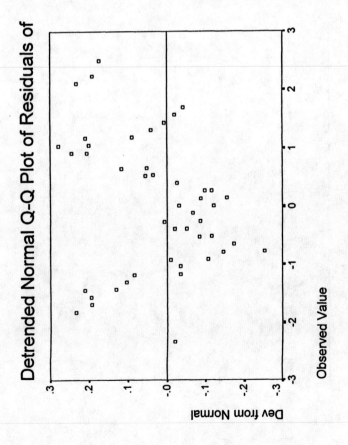

Detrended Normal Q-Q Plot of Residuals of

Three-Group Multivariate Analysis of Variance

```
*Multivariate Analysis of Variance (3 groups).
MANOVA X9 X10 BY X14(1,3)
/PRINT CELLINFO (MEANS CORR COV)
    DESIGN (COLLINEARITY)
    HOMOGENITY(BARTLETT COCHRAN BOXM)
    SIGNIF(MULT UNIV STEPDOWN)
    SIGNIF(EFSIZE)
    PARAMETERS (ESTIM)
    ERROR(CORR)
/PLOT= ALL
/POWER T(.05) F(.05)
/METHOD=UNIQUE
/ERROR WITHIN+RESIDUAL
/DESIGN.
```

* * * * * * A n a l y s i s   o f   V a r i a n c e * * * * * * *

```
   100 cases accepted.
     0 cases rejected because of out-of-range factor values.
     0 cases rejected because of missing data.
     3 non-empty cells.

     1 design will be processed.
```

- -

```
              CELL NUMBER
               1   2   3
Variable
  X14          1   2   3
```

Cell Means and Standard Deviations

Variable .. X9		Usage Level		
FACTOR	CODE	Mean	Std. Dev.	N
X14	NEW TASK	36.912	5.059	34
X14	MODIFIED	46.531	5.304	32
X14	STRAIGHT	54.882	4.873	34
For entire sample		46.100	8.989	100

- -

Variable .. X10   CODE   Satisfaction Level
          FACTOR   Mean   Std. Dev.   N

X14   NEW TASK   3.929   .531   34
X14   MODIFIED   5.003   .487   32
X14   STRAIGHT   5.394   .713   34
For entire sample   4.771   .856   100

- -

Univariate Homogeneity of Variance Tests

Variable .. X9   Usage Level

     Cochrans C(32,3) =   .36309, P =   .965 (approx.)
     Bartlett-Box F(2,21129) =   .11385, P =   .892

Variable .. X10   Satisfaction Level

     Cochrans C(32,3) =   .49505, P =   .033 (approx.)
     Bartlett-Box F(2,21129) =   2.66967, P =   .070

******* A n a l y s i s   o f   V a r i a n c e -- design   1 *******

Cell Number .. 1
Variance-Covariance matrix

```
              X9         X10

X9        25.598
X10         .648       .282
Correlation matrix with Standard Deviations on Diagonal

              X9         X10

X9         5.059
X10         .241       .531
```

Determinant of Covariance matrix of dependent variables =   6.80214
LOG(Determinant) =   1.91724

- - - - - - -

Cell Number .. 2
Variance-Covariance matrix

```
              X9         X10

X9        28.128
X10        1.366       .237
Correlation matrix with Standard Deviations on Diagonal

              X9         X10

X9         5.304
X10         .529       .487
```

Determinant of Covariance matrix of dependent variables =   4.80275
LOG(Determinant) =   1.56919

- - - - - - -

Information for respondents with
$X_{14} = 1$, *new task.*

Information for respondents with
$X_{14} = 2$, *modified rebuy.*

351

* * * * * A n a l y s i s   o f   V a r i a n c e -- design   1 * * * * * * *

Cell Number .. 3
Variance-Covariance matrix

```
            X9          X10

X9       23.743
X10        .763         .509
```

Correlation matrix with Standard Deviations on Diagonal

```
            X9          X10

X9        4.873
X10        .219         .713
```

Determinant of Covariance matrix of dependent variables =   11.50461
LOG(Determinant) =   2.44275

- -

Pooled within-cells Variance-Covariance matrix

```
            X9          X10

X9       25.776
X10        .917         .345
```

Determinant of pooled Covariance matrix of dependent vars. =   8.05083
LOG(Determinant) =   2.08578

- -

Multivariate test for Homogeneity of Dispersion matrices

Boxs M =   9.79592
F WITH (6,229276) DF =   1.58394, P =   .147 (Approx.)
Chi-Square with 6 DF =   9.50389, P =   .147 (Approx.)

- -

Correspondence between Effects and Columns of BETWEEN-Subjects DESIGN 1

```
Starting  Ending
Column    Column    Effect Name

  1         1       CONSTANT
  2         3       X14
```

```
* * * * * A n a l y s i s   o f   V a r i a n c e  -- design   1 * * * * * * *

Collinearity Diagnostics using Singular Value Decomposition
                                  VARIANCE PROPORTIONS

ROOT NO.    SING VALS  COND INDEX        1          2          3

   1          1.228      1.000          .001       .246       .246
   2          1.000      1.228          .997       .002       .000
   3           .701      1.751          .002       .753       .754

- - - - - - - - - - - - - - - - - - - - - - - - - - - - - - - - - - - - -

WITHIN+RESIDUAL Correlations with Std. Devs. on Diagonal

                X9        X10

X9            5.077
X10            .307       .587

- - - - - - - - - - - - - - - - - - - - - - - - - - - - - - - - - - - - -

Statistics for WITHIN+RESIDUAL correlations

Log(Determinant) =            -.09927
Bartlett test of sphericity =  9.47987 with 1 D. F.
Significance =                   .002

F(max) criterion =            74.72507 with (2, 97) D. F.

- - - - - - - - - - - - - - - - - - - - - - - - - - - - - - - - - - - - -
```

```
* * * * * * A n a l y s i s   o f   V a r i a n c e -- design   1 * * * * * * *

EFFECT .. X14
Multivariate Tests of Significance (S = 2, M = -1/2, N = 47 )

Test Name        Value      Approx. F   Hypoth. DF   Error DF   Sig. of F

Pillais          .77089     30.41887      4.00       194.00      .000
Hotellings      2.65480     63.05157      4.00       190.00      .000
Wilks            .26405     45.41066      4.00       192.00      .000
Roys             .72253
Note.. F statistic for WILKS' Lambda is exact.

- - - - - - - - - - - - - - - - - - - - - - - - - - - - - - - - - - - - - - -

Multivariate Effect Size and Observed Power at .0500 Level

TEST NAME     Effect Size     Noncent.      Power

Pillais          .385         121.675        1.00
Hotellings       .570         252.206        1.00
Wilks            .486         181.643        1.00

- - - - - - - - - - - - - - - - - - - - - - - - - - - - - - - - - - - - - - -

EFFECT .. X14 (Cont.)
Univariate F-tests with (2,97) D. F.

Variable   Hypoth. SS   Error SS   Hypoth. MS   Error MS      F       Sig. of F

X9        5498.76654  2500.23346  2749.38327   25.77560  106.66611     .000
X10          39.00680    33.45910    19.50340     .34494   56.54156     .000

Variable   ETA Square   Noncent.    Power

X9          .68743     213.33222   1.00000
X10         .53828     113.08313   1.00000

- - - - - - - - - - - - - - - - - - - - - - - - - - - - - - - - - - - - - - -

Roy-Bargman Stepdown F - tests

Variable   Hypoth. MS   Error MS   StepDown F   Hypoth. DF   Error DF   Sig. of F

X9        2749.38327   25.77560   106.66611         2          97         .000
X10          2.78337     .31560     8.81939         2          96         .000
```

Test for the difference between groups based on X_{14}.

The significance levels for all statistics indicate that there is a significant difference between the groups of X_{14}.

Interpreted the same as in two-group MANOVA.

Interpreted the same as in two-group MANOVA.

354

```
* * * * * * A n a l y s i s   o f   V a r i a n c e  -- design  1 * * * * * * *

Estimates for X9
--- Individual univariate .9500 confidence intervals
--- two-tailed observed power taken at .0500 level

X14

Parameter    Coeff.    Std. Err.    t-Value    Sig. t    Lower -95%    CL- Upper

    2     -9.1966912    .71461    -12.86951    .00000    -10.61500    -7.77839
    3      .42279418    .72558      .58270     .5145     -1.01728     1.86286


Parameter    Noncent.    Power

    2     165.62430     1.000
    3        .33954      .046

-- -- -- -- -- -- -- -- -- -- -- -- -- -- -- -- -- -- -- -- -- -- --

Estimates for X10
--- Individual univariate .9500 confidence intervals
--- two-tailed observed power taken at .0500 level

X14

Parameter    Coeff.    Std. Err.    t-Value    Sig. t    Lower -95%    CL- Upper

    2     -.84613971    .08267    -10.23542    .00000    -1.01021     -.68207
    3     .227573529    .08394      2.71126    .00793      .06098      .39416


Parameter    Noncent.    Power

    2     104.76382     1.000
    3       7.35093      .763

-- -- -- -- -- -- -- -- -- -- -- -- -- -- -- -- -- -- -- -- -- -- --

Adjusted and Estimated Means
Variable .. X9                    Usage Level
CELL    Obs. Mean    Adj. Mean    Est. Mean    Raw Resid.    Std. Resid.

  1      36.912       36.912       36.912        .000          .000
  2      46.531       46.531       46.531        .000          .000
  3      54.882       54.882       54.882        .000          .000

Saturated design specified, PMEANS plot skipped.
```

355

* * * * * * A n a l y s i s   o f   V a r i a n c e -- design 1 * * * * * *

Adjusted and Estimated Means (Cont.)
Variable .. X10   Satisfaction Level
CELL   Obs. Mean   Adj. Mean   Est. Mean   Raw Resid.   Std. Resid.

1   3.929   3.929   3.929   .000   .000
2   5.003   5.003   5.003   .000   .000
3   5.394   5.394   5.394   .000   .000

Saturated design specified, PMEANS plot skipped.

- -

Mean vs. variance for Usage Level

Mean vs. std. dev. for Usage Level

Mean vs. variance for Satisfaction Level

Cell Variances

Cell Means

Distribution of means for Usage Level

Frequency

Cell Means

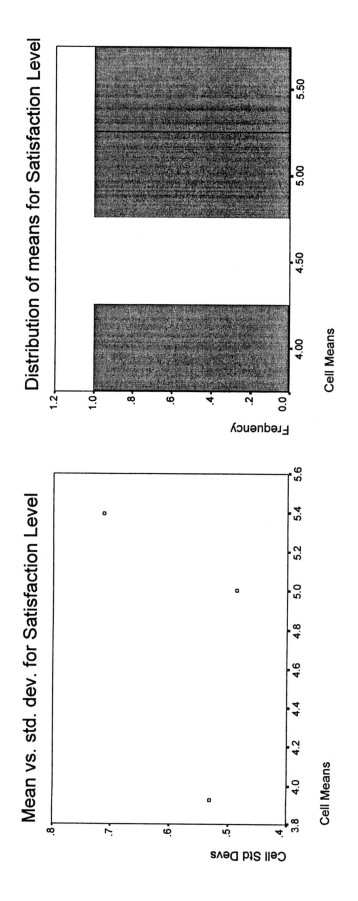

359

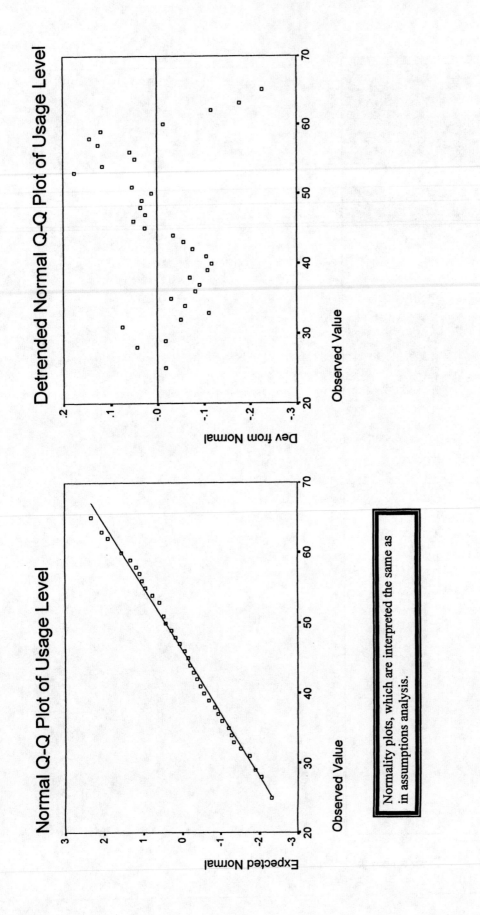

Normality plots, which are interpreted the same as in assumptions analysis.

Normal Q-Q Plot of Satisfaction Level

Detrended Normal Q-Q Plot of Satisfaction

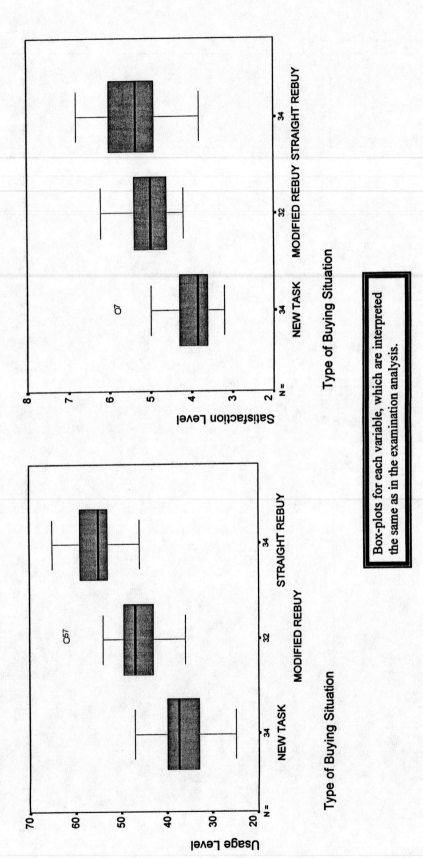

Box-plots for each variable, which are interpreted the same as in the examination analysis.

Dependent variable: X9

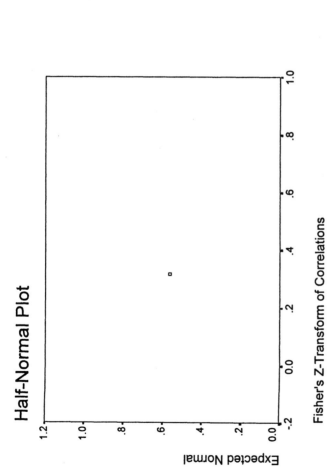

Half-Normal Plot

363

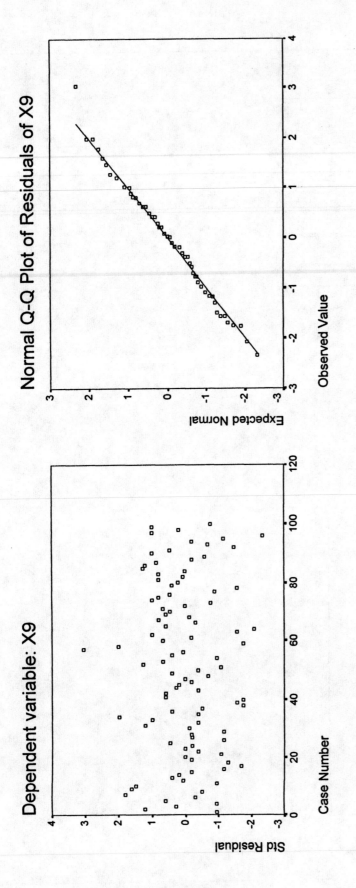

Detrended Normal Q-Q Plot of Residuals of

Dependent variable: X10

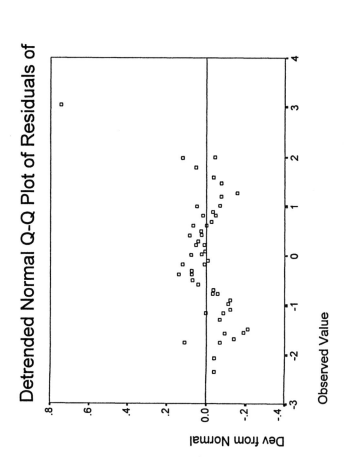

Normal Q-Q Plot of Residuals of X10

Dependent variable: X10

Detrended Normal Q-Q Plot of Residuals of

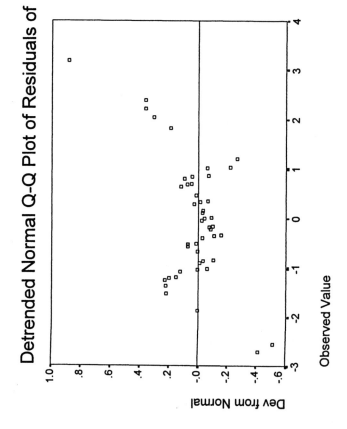

Observed Value

Two-Factor Multivariate Analysis of Variance

*Multivariate Analysis of Variance (2 Factor).
MANOVA X9 X10 BY X13 (0,1) X14(1,3)
/PRINT CELLINFO (MEANS CORR COV)
DESIGN (COLLINEARITY)
HOMOGENITY(BARTLETT COCHRAN BOXM)
SIGNIF(MULT UNIV STEPDOWN)
SIGNIF(EFSIZE)
PARAMETERS (ESTIM)
ERROR(CORR)
/PLOT=ALL
/POWER T(.05) F(.05)
/METHOD=UNIQUE
/ERROR WITHIN+RESIDUAL
/DESIGN.

* * * * * * A n a l y s i s   o f   V a r i a n c e * * * * * *

```
     100 cases accepted.
       0 cases rejected because of out-of-range factor values.
       0 cases rejected because of missing data.
       6 non-empty cells.

       1 design will be processed.
```

```
                 CELL NUMBER
                 1   2   3   4   5   6
Variable
  X13            1   1   1   2   2   2
  X14            1   2   3   1   2   3
```

```
Cell Means and Standard Deviations
Variable .. X9                  Usage Level
  FACTOR          CODE          Mean    Std. Dev.     N

X13        FIRM TYP
  X14        NEW TASK          38.278     3.923       18
  X14        MODIFIED          46.937     6.137       16
  X14        STRAIGHT          56.313     4.094       16
X13        FIRM TYP
  X14        NEW TASK          35.375     5.841       16
  X14        MODIFIED          46.125     4.485       16
  X14        STRAIGHT          53.611     5.260       18
For entire sample               46.100     8.989      100
```

```
Variable .. X10                 Satisfaction Level
```

Identifies cell membership. For example, cell 1 is made up of the first value for X_{13} and the first value for X_{14}.

368

FACTOR	CODE	Mean	Std. Dev.	N
X13	FIRM TYP			
X14	NEW TASK	3.972	.375	18
X14	MODIFIED	5.150	.502	16
X14	STRAIGHT	5.488	.650	16
X13	FIRM TYP			
X14	NEW TASK	3.881	.675	16
X14	MODIFIED	4.856	.438	16
X14	STRAIGHT	5.311	.775	18
For entire sample		4.771	.856	100

Univariate Homogeneity of Variance Tests

Variable .. X9   Usage Level

    Cochrans C(16,6) =   .24825, P = .447 (approx.)
    Bartlett-Box F(5,11280) =   1.06212, P = .380

Variable .. X10   Satisfaction Level

    Cochrans C(16,6) =   .29070, P = .115 (approx.)
    Bartlett-Box F(5,11280) =   2.36279, P = .038

These two tests provide information as to the equality of variances for each variable.

369

* * * * * * A n a l y s i s   o f   V a r i a n c e -- design   1 * * * * * * *

Cell Number .. 1
Variance-Covariance matrix

	X9	X10
X9	15.389	
X10	-.162	.141

Correlation matrix with Standard Deviations on Diagonal

	X9	X10
X9	3.923	
X10	-.110	.375

Determinant of Covariance matrix of dependent variables =   2.14265
LOG(Determinant) =   .76204

- - - - - - - -

Cell Number .. 2
Variance-Covariance matrix

	X9	X10
X9	37.662	
X10	1.643	.252

Correlation matrix with Standard Deviations on Diagonal

	X9	X10
X9	6.137	
X10	.533	.502

370

****** A n a l y s i s   o f   V a r i a n c e -- design   1 ******

Cell Number .. 2 (Cont.)

Determinant of Covariance matrix of dependent variables =   6.79041
LOG(Determinant) =   1.91551

- - - - - - - - -

Cell Number .. 3
Variance-Covariance matrix

	X9	X10
X9	16.762	
X10	.984	.423

Correlation matrix with Standard Deviations on Diagonal

	X9	X10
X9	4.094	
X10	.370	.650

Determinant of Covariance matrix of dependent variables =   6.11357
LOG(Determinant) =   1.81051

- - - - - - - - -

Cell Number .. 4
Variance-Covariance matrix

	X9	X10
X9	34.117	
X10	1.461	.456

Correlation matrix with Standard Deviations on Diagonal

	X9	X10
X9	5.841	
X10	.370	.675

Cell Number .. 4 (Cont.)

Determinant of Covariance matrix of dependent variables =   13.43312
LOG(Determinant) =   2.59772

- - - - - -

Cell Number .. 5
Variance-Covariance matrix

	X9	X10
X9	20.117	
X10	1.053	.192

Correlation matrix with Standard Deviations on Diagonal

	X9	X10
X9	4.485	
X10	.536	.438

Determinant of Covariance matrix of dependent variables =   2.75381
LOG(Determinant) =   1.01298

- - - - - -

Cell Number .. 6
Variance-Covariance matrix

	X9	X10
X9	27.663	
X10	.375	.600

Correlation matrix with Standard Deviations on Diagonal

	X9	X10
X9	5.260	
X10	.092	.775

```
* * * * * A n a l y s i s   o f   V a r i a n c e  -- design   1 * * * * * * *

Cell Number .. 6 (Cont.)

Determinant of Covariance matrix of dependent variables =        16.45368
LOG(Determinant) =                                               2.80055
- - - - - - - -

Pooled within-cells Variance-Covariance matrix

                 X9        X10

X9            25.125
X10             .859      .345

Determinant of pooled Covariance matrix of dependent vars. =      7.93198
LOG(Determinant) =                                               2.07090
- - - - - - - - - - - - - - - - - - - - - - - - - - - - - - - - - - - - - -

Multivariate test for Homogeneity of Dispersion matrices

Boxs M =                  24.04982
F WITH (15,46618) DF =     1.51627,  P =   .090  (Approx.)
Chi-Square with 15 DF =   22.75172,  P =   .090  (Approx.)

- - - - - - - - - - - - - - - - - - - - - - - - - - - - - - - - - - - - - -

Correspondence between Effects and Columns of BETWEEN-Subjects DESIGN 1

Starting  Ending
Column    Column    Effect Name

   1         1      CONSTANT
   2         2      X13
   3         4      X14
   5         6      X13 BY X14

- - - - - - - - - - - - - - - - - - - - - - - - - - - - - - - - - - - - - -

Collinearity Diagnostics using Singular Value Decomposition
                                    VARIANCE PROPORTIONS
ROOT NO.   SING VALS COND INDEX       1      2      3      4

   1         1.249     1.000        .005   .005   .113   .120
   2         1.211     1.032        .002   .002   .130   .121
   3         1.000     1.250        .494   .494   .000   .004
   4          .996     1.255        .495   .495   .003   .003
   5          .710     1.759        .005   .005   .355   .375
   6          .691     1.808        .000   .000   .398   .377
```

Box's M tests the equality of the variance/covariance matrices. Significant levels indicate unequal variance/covariance matrices.

373

```
* * * * * A n a l y s i s   o f   V a r i a n c e -- design  1 * * * * * * *

Collinearity Diagnostics using Singular Value Decomposition  (Cont.)
                                    VARIANCE PROPORTIONS
ROOT NO.          5       6

    1          .113    .120
    2          .130    .121
    3          .000    .004
    4          .003    .003
    5          .355    .375
    6          .398    .377

- - - - - - - - - - - - - - - - - - - - - - - - - - - - - - - - - - - - - -
WITHIN+RESIDUAL Correlations with Std. Devs. on Diagonal

              X9      X10

X9          5.012
X10          .292    .587

- - - - - - - - - - - - - - - - - - - - - - - - - - - - - - - - - - - - - -

Statistics for WITHIN+RESIDUAL correlations

Log(Determinant) =              -.08891
Bartlett test of sphericity =   8.22460 with 1 D. F.
Significance =                   .004

F(max) criterion =              72.81498 with (2,94) D. F.

- - - - - - - - - - - - - - - - - - - - - - - - - - - - - - - - - - - - - -
```

Test whether there is an interaction effect.

All four multivariate tests indicate that the interaction effect is not significant.

The univariate tests confirm that there is no interaction effect for either dependent variable.

****** A n a l y s i s   o f   V a r i a n c e -- design 1 ******

EFFECT .. X13 BY X14
Multivariate Tests of Significance (S = 2, M = -1/2, N = 45 1/2)

Test Name	Value	Approx. F	Hypoth. DF	Error DF	Sig. of F
Pillais	.01954	.46383	4.00	188.00	.762
Hotellings	.01992	.45819	4.00	184.00	.766
Wilks	.98046	.46103	4.00	186.00	.764
Roys	.01923				

Note.. F statistic for WILKS' Lambda is exact.

- -

Multivariate Effect Size and Observed Power at .0500 Level

TEST NAME	Effect Size	Noncent.	Power
Pillais	.010	1.855	.16
Hotellings	.010	1.833	.16
Wilks	.010	1.844	.16

- -

EFFECT .. X13 BY X14 (Cont.)
Univariate F-tests with (2,94) D. F.

Variable	Hypoth. SS	Error SS	Hypoth. MS	Error MS	F	Sig. of F
X9	21.68180	2361.76389	10.84090	25.12515	.43148	.651
X10	.17013	32.43514	.08507	.34505	.24653	.782

Variable	ETA Square	Noncent.	Power
X9	.00910	.86295	.12181
X10	.00522	.49306	.09096

- -

Roy-Bargman Stepdown F - tests

Variable	Hypoth. MS	Error MS	StepDown F	Hypoth. DF	Error DF	Sig. of F
X9	10.84090	25.12515	.43148	2	94	.651
X10	.15802	.31909	.49521	2	93	.611

Test for the difference between groups based on X_{14}.

The significance levels for all statistics indicate that there is a significant difference between the groups of X_{14}.

* * * * * * A n a l y s i s   o f   V a r i a n c e -- design   1 * * * * * * *

EFFECT .. X14
Multivariate Tests of Significance (S = 2, M = -1/2, N = 45 1/2)

Test Name	Value	Approx. F	Hypoth. DF	Error DF	Sig. of F
Pillais	.78570	30.41103	4.00	188.00	.000
Hotellings	2.85220	65.60050	4.00	184.00	.000
Wilks	.25026	46.45218	4.00	186.00	.000
Roys	.73690				

Note.. F statistic for WILKS' Lambda is exact.

Multivariate Effect Size and Observed Power at .0500 Level

TEST NAME	Effect Size	Noncent.	Power
Pillais	.393	121.644	1.00
Hotellings	.588	262.402	1.00
Wilks	.500	185.809	1.00

EFFECT .. X14 (Cont.)
Univariate F-tests with (2,94) D. F.

Variable	Hypoth. SS	Error SS	Hypoth. MS	Error MS	F	Sig. of F
X9	5580.66404	2361.76389	2790.33202	25.12515	111.05734	.000
X10	39.25048	32.43514	19.62524	.34505	56.87574	.000

Variable	ETA Square	Noncent.	Power
X9	.70264	222.11468	1.00000
X10	.54754	113.75148	1.00000

Roy-Bargman Stepdown F - tests

Variable	Hypoth. MS	Error MS	StepDown F	Hypoth. DF	Error DF	Sig. of F
X9	2790.33202	25.12515	111.05734	2	94	.000
X10	2.79276	.31909	8.75218	2	93	.000

****** A n a l y s i s   o f   V a r i a n c e -- design 1 ******

EFFECT .. X13
Multivariate Tests of Significance (S = 1, M = 0, N = 45 1/2)

Test Name	Value	Exact F	Hypoth. DF	Error DF	Sig. of F
Pillais	.05587	2.75176	2.00	93.00	.069
Hotellings	.05918	2.75176	2.00	93.00	.069
Wilks	.94413	2.75176	2.00	93.00	.069
Roys	.05587				

Note.. F statistics are exact.

> Test for the difference between groups based on X_{13}.

> The significance levels for all statistics indicate that there is not a significant difference between the groups of X_{13}.

- - - - - - - - - - - - - - - - - - - -

Multivariate Effect Size and Observed Power at .0500 Level

TEST NAME	Effect Size	Noncent.	Power
(All)	.056	5.504	.53

> Due to the low power (power = .53), the researcher might consider raising the required α level. The low power is a result of the small sample sizes per group.

- - - - - - - - - - - - - - - - - - - -

EFFECT .. X13 (Cont.)
Univariate F-tests with (1,94) D. F.

Variable	Hypoth. SS	Error SS	Hypoth. MS	Error MS	F	Sig. of F
X9	114.01923	2361.76389	114.01923	25.12515	4.53805	.036
X10	.87188	32.43514	.87188	.34505	2.52679	.115

Variable	ETA Square	Noncent.	Power
X9	.04605	4.53805	.55657
X10	.02618	2.52679	.34953

> The univariate tests indicate a significant difference for X_9 but not X_{10}. Because of this, the set of dependent variables is found to be nonsignificant (sig. of F = .069)

- - - - - - - - - - - - - - - - - - - -

Roy-Bargman Stepdown F - tests

Variable	Hypoth. MS	Error MS	StepDown F	Hypoth. DF	Error DF	Sig. of F
X9	114.01923	25.12515	4.53805	1	94	.036
X10	.30858	.31909	.96706	1	93	.328

- - - - - - - - - - - - - - - - - - - -

* * * * * A n a l y s i s o f V a r i a n c e -- design 1 * * * * * *

Estimates for X9
--- Individual univariate .9500 confidence intervals
--- two-tailed observed power taken at .0500 level

X13

Parameter	Coeff.	Std. Err.	t-Value	Sig. t	Lower -95%	CL- Upper
2	1.0694444	.50202	2.13027	.03576	.07267	2.06622

Parameter	Noncent.	Power
2	4.53805	.556

X14

Parameter	Coeff.	Std. Err.	t-Value	Sig. t	Lower -95%	CL- Upper
3	-9.2800926	.70655	-13.13445	.00000	-10.68296	-7.87723
4	.42476519	.71676	.59262	.55486	-.99838	1.84792

Parameter	Noncent.	Power
3	172.51377	1.000
4	.35120	.049

X13 BY X14

Parameter	Coeff.	Std. Err.	t-Value	Sig. t	Lower -95%	CL- Upper
5	.381944444	.70655	.54058	.59008	-1.02092	1.78481
6	-.66319444	.71676	-.92526	.35720	-2.08634	.75995

Parameter	Noncent.	Power
5	.29223	.043
6	.85612	.171

- - - - - - - - - - - - - - - - -

Estimates for X10
--- Individual univariate .9500 confidence intervals
--- two-tailed observed power taken at .0500 level

X13

Parameter	Coeff.	Std. Err.	t-Value	Sig. t	Lower -95%	CL- Upper
2	.09351819	.05883	1.58959	.11529	-.02329	.21033

Parameter	Noncent.	Power
2	2.52679	.349

* * * * * * A n a l y s i s   o f   V a r i a n c e -- design 1 * * * * * * *

Estimates for X10 (Cont.)

X14

Parameter	Coeff.	Std. Err.	t-Value	Sig. t	Lower -95%	CL- Upper
3	-.84965278	.08280	-10.26151	.00000	-1.01405	-.68525
4	.226736111	.08400	2.69933	.00824	.05996	.39351

Parameter	Noncent.	Power
3	105.29865	1.000
4	7.28639	.759

X13 BY X14

Parameter	Coeff.	Std. Err.	t-Value	Sig. t	Lower -95%	CL- Upper
5	-.04803241	.08280	-.58010	.56323	-.21243	.11637
6	.053356481	.08400	.63522	.52683	-.11342	.22013

Parameter	Noncent.	Power
5	.33652	.046
6	.40350	.066

Adjusted and Estimated Means
Variable .. X9

CELL	Obs. Mean	Adj. Mean	Usage Level Est. Mean	Raw Resid.	Std. Resid.
1	38.278	38.278	38.278	.000	.000
2	46.937	46.937	46.937	.000	.000
3	56.313	56.313	56.313	.000	.000
4	35.375	35.375	35.375	.000	.000
5	46.125	46.125	46.125	.000	.000
6	53.611	53.611	53.611	.000	.000

Adjusted and Estimated Means (Cont.)
Variable .. X10

CELL	Obs. Mean	Adj. Mean	Satisfaction Level Est. Mean	Raw Resid.	Std. Resid.
1	3.972	3.972	3.972	.000	.000
2	5.150	5.150	5.150	.000	.000
3	5.488	5.488	5.488	.000	.000

****** A n a l y s i s   o f   V a r i a n c e -- design 1 ******

Adjusted and Estimated Means (Cont.)
Variable .. X10   Satisfaction Level
CELL   Obs. Mean   Adj. Mean   Est. Mean   Raw Resid.   Std. Resid.

4   3.881   3.881   3.881   .000   .000
5   4.856   4.856   4.856   .000   .000
6   5.311   5.311   5.311   .000   .000

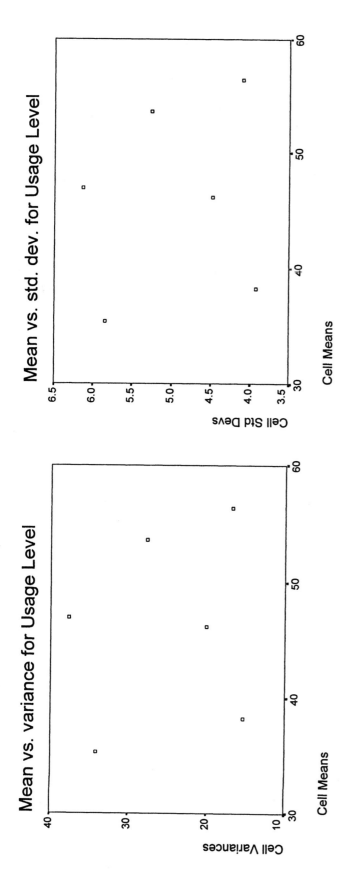

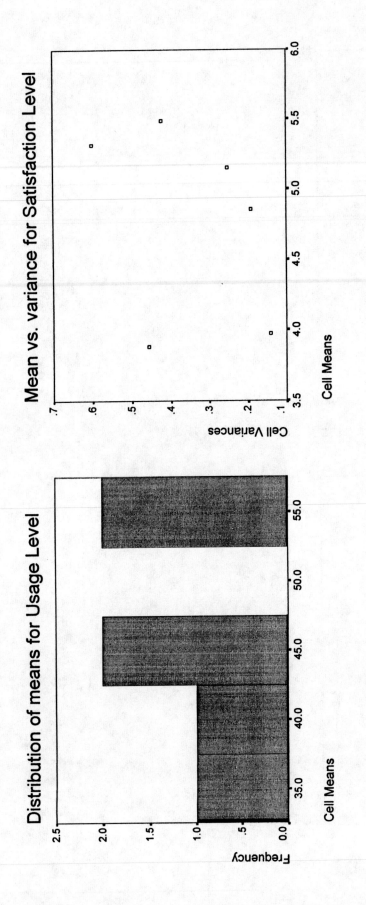

Mean vs. variance for Satisfaction Level

Distribution of means for Usage Level

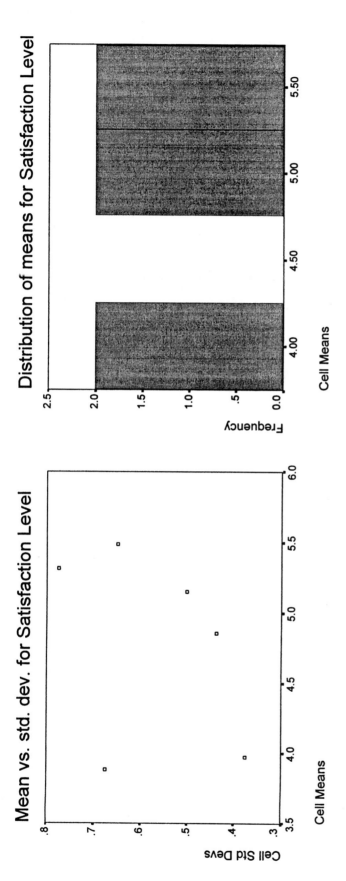

Distribution of means for Satisfaction Level

Mean vs. std. dev. for Satisfaction Level

Normal Q-Q Plot of Usage Level

Detrended Normal Q-Q Plot of Usage Level

Normality plots, which are interpreted the same as in assumptions analysis.

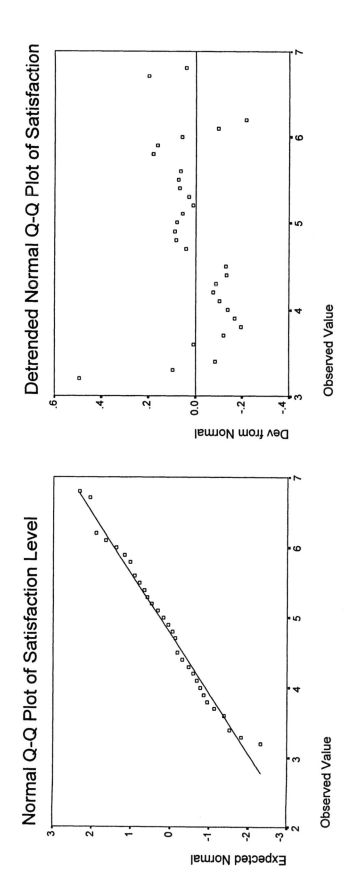

Normal Q-Q Plot of Satisfaction Level

Detrended Normal Q-Q Plot of Satisfaction

385

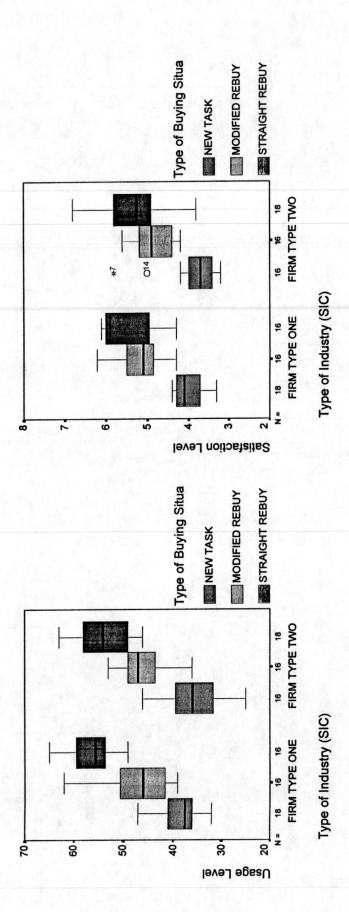

Box-plots for each variable, which are interpreted the same as in the examination analysis.

Dependent: X9

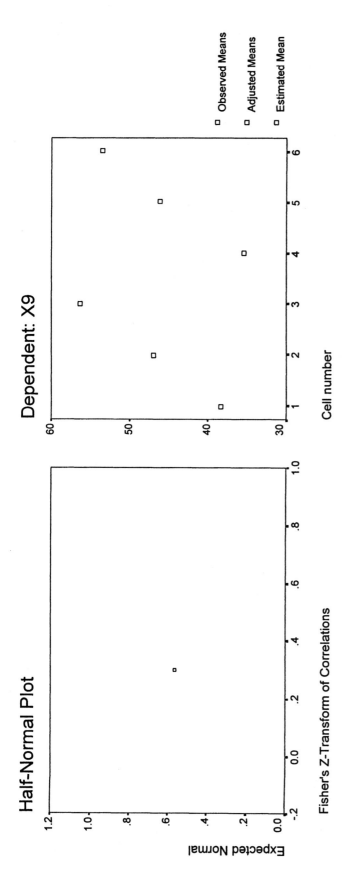

Half-Normal Plot

Expected Normal

Fisher's Z-Transform of Correlations

Cell number

□ Observed Means

□ Adjusted Means

□ Estimated Mean

Dependent variable: X9

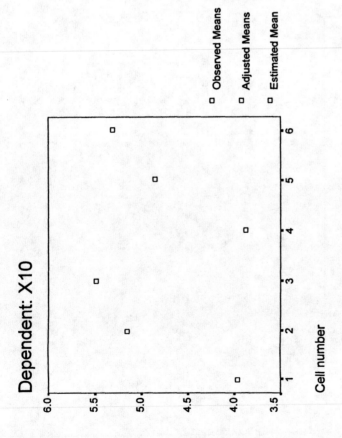

	Observed	Predicted	Std Residuals
Observed			
Predicted			
Std Residuals			

Dependent: X10

□ Observed Means

□ Adjusted Means

□ Estimated Mean

Cell number

388

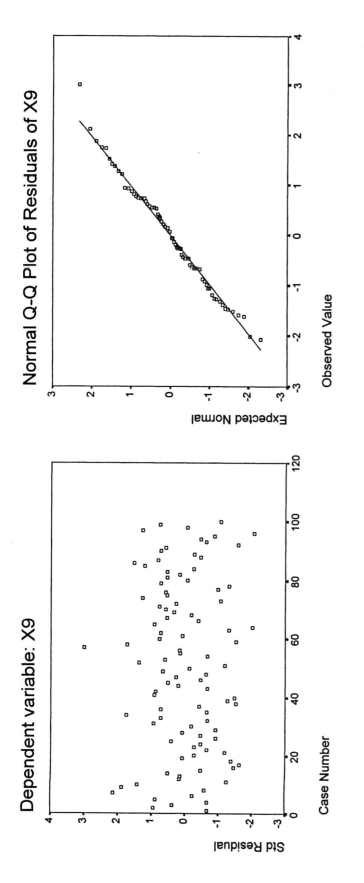

389

Dependent variable: X10

Detrended Normal Q-Q Plot of Residuals of

Normal Q-Q Plot of Residuals of X10

Dependent variable: X10

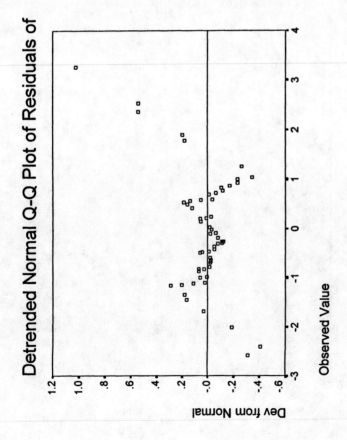

Detrended Normal Q-Q Plot of Residuals of

Observed Value

Dev from Normal

CHAPTER 7:

CONJOINT ANALYSIS

This section of the instructor's manual contains copies of the actual printouts from the SPSS statistical analysis program. The printouts contain examples of the analyses discussed in the text using an additional HATCO database (for a complete description of this database, see Chapter Seven of the text).

Each of the printouts is annotated with comments to aid in the interpretation of the results. These suggestions are typed in the margins next to the appropriate data. If you wish to provide students with their own copies of the output without these comments, the output are provided on the computer diskette accompanying the instructor's manual.

An example of conjoint analysis is included in this section. A brief description follows:

Conjoint Analysis: A set of five product attributes at two and three levels are combined in a set of eighteen (full profile presentation method), which are then rated and the part-worth estimates derived. Also, three hypothetical products are evaluated to assess consumer acceptance. Market share estimates among the three products are obtained through three methods.

Conjoint Analysis: Estimating Part-Worth Estimates

```
CONJOINT PLAN='CPLAN1.SAV'
/FACTORS=
 MIXTURE 'Product Form' ('Premixed' 'Concentrate' 'Powder')
 NUMAPP 'Number of Applications' ('50' '100' '200')
 GERMFREE 'Disinfectant' ('Yes' 'No')
 BIOPROT 'Biodegradable' ('No' 'Yes')
 PRICE 'Price per Application' ('35 cents' '49 cents' '79 cents')
/SUBJECT=QN
/SCORE=PROD1 PROD2 PROD3 PROD4 PROD5 PROD6 PROD7 PROD8 PROD9
       PROD10 PROD11 PROD12 PROD13 PROD14 PROD15 PROD16
       PROD17 PROD18 PROD19 PROD20 PROD21 PROD22
/UTILITY='UTIL.SAV'.
```

Factor	Model	Levels	Label
MIXTURE	d	3	Product Form
NUMAPP	d	3	Number of Applications
GERMFREE	d	2	Disinfectant
BIOPROT	d	2	Biodegradable
PRICE	d	3	Price per Application

(Models: d=discrete, l=linear, i=ideal, ai=antiideal, <=less, >=more)

All the factors are orthogonal.

> Five factors, of 2 or 3 levels, are evaluated.

> Each of the factors is defined as discrete, which means that separate part-worth estimates are calculated for each level and there is no hypothesized relationship on the levels.

394

SUBJECT NAME: 104.00

```
Importance  Utility(s.e.)  Factor

                            MIXTURE       Product Form
            +--+
10.00  I I  -.0556( .2696)   -I            Premixed
            +--+  .1111( .2696)   I--        Concentrate
       I I  -.0556( .2696)   -I            Powder
       I

                            NUMAPP        Number of Applications
+---------+
I30.00 I I  -.2222( .2696)   ---I          50
       +---------+ -.0556( .2696)   -I     100
       I I  .2778( .2696)   I----          200
       I

                            GERMFREE      Disinfectant
       +-+
5.00   I I  .0417( .2022)   I-             Yes
       +-+ -.0417( .2022)   -I             No
       I

                            BIOPROT       Biodegradable
+--------+
I25.00 I I  -.2083( .2022)   ---I          No
       +--------+ .2083( .2022)   I---     Yes
       I

                            PRICE         Price per Application
+---------+
I30.00 I I  .2778( .2696)   I----          35 cents
       +---------+ -.2222( .2696)   ---I   49 cents
       I I  -.0556( .2696)   -I            79 cents
       I

       4.4444( .2132) CONSTANT
```

Pearson's R   = .537   Significance = .0108

Kendall's tau = .410   Significance = .0222
Kendall's tau = .671 for 4 holdouts   Significance = .1103

Simulation results:
```
Card:   23   24   25
Score:  4.4  4.9  5.2
```

SUBJECT NAME: 107.00

Conjoint Analysis Results for Subject 107:

Compare both individual part-worth estimates and factor importance scores with other subjects to highlight differences.

Much higher and statistically significant predictive accuracy for this subject.

Card 24 is the preferred product with the highest utility score.

Importance   Utility(s.e.)   Factor

```
        +--+
14.29  I  I   -.0556( .3750)   MIXTURE    Product Form
       +--+    .6111( .3750)      I         Premixed
       +--+   -.5556( .3750)      I-        Concentrate
          I                       -I        Powder
          I

        +---+
20.41  I   I   .4444( .3750)   NUMAPP     Number of Applications
       +---+   .6111( .3750)      I-        50
          I  -1.0556( .3750)      I-        100
          I                       --I       200

         ++
 5.10  II      -.2083( .2812)   GERMFREE   Disinfectant
       ++       .2083( .2812)      I        Yes
        I                          I        No

        +--+
13.27  I  I    .5417( .2812)   BIOPROT    Biodegradable
       +--+   -.5417( .2812)      I-        No
          I                       -I        Yes

        +--------+
46.94  I        I  1.4444( .3750)  PRICE    Price per Application
       +--------+   .9444( .3750)    I--      35 cents
          I       -2.3889( .3750)    I--      49 cents
          I                          ----I    79 cents

          I        4.1111( .2964)  CONSTANT
```

Pearson's R   = .929   Significance = .0000

Kendall's tau = .784   Significance = .0000
Kendall's tau = .707 for 4 holdouts   Significance = .0899

Simulation results:
```
Card:   23   24   25
Score:  1.4  3.9  3.2
```

SUBJECT NAME: 109.00

Importance   Utility(s.e.)   Factor

```
         +---+                  MIXTURE
10.20 I  I       -.4444( .2696)    -I        Product Form
         +---+    .3889( .2696)    I-          Premixed
         I        .0556( .2696)    I           Concentrate
         I                                     Powder
```

```
+--------+                      NUMAPP      Number of Applications
I26.53 I  I     -.9444( .2696)   ---I          50
+---------+     -.2778( .2696)     -I          100
         I      1.2222( .2696)   I----         200
         I
```

```
+--------+                      GERMFREE    Disinfectant
I26.53 I  I     1.0833( .2022)   I---          Yes
+---------+    -1.0833( .2022)     --I          No
         I
```

```
         +---+                  BIOPROT     Biodegradable
10.20 I  I      -.4167( .2022)    -I          No
         +---+    .4167( .2022)    I-          Yes
         I
```

```
+--------+                      PRICE       Price per Application
I26.53 I  I      .3889( .2696)   I-            35 cents
+---------+      .8889( .2696)   I---          49 cents
         I     -1.2778( .2696)   ----I         79 cents
         I

          3.8889( .2132) CONSTANT
```

Pearson's R   = .949   Significance = .0000

Kendall's tau = .720   Significance = .0001
Kendall's tau = .707 for 4 holdouts   Significance = .0899

Simulation results:
    Card: 23   24   25
    Score: 2.7 7.9 7.1

397

Results for the remaining 97 respondents are
deleted from this listing due to space limitations.

Conjoint Analysis Results for Total Sample:

Aggregate results for all subjects.

Choice Simulator Results for the Three-product Formulations:
Maximum Utility Criterion
Bradley-Terry-Luce Model
Logit Model
The third-product formulation (card 25) is the most preferred.

SUBFILE SUMMARY

Averaged Importance	Utility	Factor	
		MIXTURE	Product Form
16.78I	I -.3311	-I	Premixed
	I .1922	I-	Concentrate
	I .1389	I-	Powder
	I		
		NUMAPP	Number of Applications
I19.55I	I -.4161	--I	50
	I .0206	I	100
	I .3956	I--	200
	I		
		GERMFREE	Disinfectant
I19.03I	I .4858	I--	Yes
	I -.4858	--I	No
	I		
		BIOPROT	Biodegradable
10.47	I I -.0767	I--	No
	I I .0767	I	Yes
	I		
		PRICE	Price per Application
I34.17	I .9622	I----	35 cents
	I .0689	I	49 cents
	I -1.0311	----I	79 cents
	I		
	3.5931	CONSTANT	

Pearson's R   = .988   Significance = .0000

Kendall's tau = .895   Significance = .0000
Kendall's tau = .667 for 4 holdouts   Significance = .0871

Simulation results:
Card: 23   24   25
Score: 2.4 4.8 5.7

SUBFILE SUMMARY

No reversals occured in this split file group.

Simulation Summary (100 subjects/ 90 subjects with non-negative scores)

Card	Max Utility*	BTL	Logit
23	5.00%	20.07%	9.52%
24	25.50	36.83	32.56
25	69.50	43.10	57.92

* Includes tied simulation

CHAPTER 8:

CANONICAL CORRELATION ANALYSIS

This section of the instructor's manual contains copies of the actual printouts from the SPSS statistical analysis program. The printouts contain examples of the analyses discussed in the text using the HATCO database.

Each of the printouts is annotated with comments to aid in the interpretation of the results. These suggestions are typed in the margins next to the appropriate data. If you wish to provide students with their own copies of the output without these comments, the output are provided on the computer diskette accompanying the instructor's manual.

An example of canonical correlation analysis is included in this section. A brief description follows:

Canonical Correlation Analysis: Canonical correlation analysis with the seven attribute ratings (X_1 to X_7) as the independent variables predicting multiple dependent variables, X_9 (level of product usage) and X_{10} (level of satisfaction).

399

Canonical Correlation Analysis

```
*Canonical Correlation Analysis.
MANOVA X9 X10 WITH X1 TO X7
/PRINT = ERROR (SSCP COV COR) SIGNIF (HYPOTH EIGEN DIMENR)
/DISCRIM =RAW STAN ESTIM COR ALPHA(1.0)
/RESIDUALS=CASEWISE PLOT
/DESIGN.
```

SPSS performs canonical correlation within the MANOVA procedure.

```
    100 cases accepted.
      0 cases rejected because of out-of-range factor values.
      0 cases rejected because of missing data.
      1 non-empty cell.

        1 design will be processed.
```

- -

Adjusted WITHIN CELLS Correlations with Std. Devs. on Diagonal

```
                 X9        X10

X9             4.424
X10            -.009      .396
```

- -

Statistics for ADJUSTED WITHIN CELLS correlations

```
Log(Determinant) =              -.00008
Bartlett test of sphericity =    .00762 with 1 D. F.
Significance =                   .930

F(max) criterion =          124.95658 with (2,92) D. F.
```

- -

Adjusted WITHIN CELLS Variances and Covariances

```
                 X9        X10

X9             19.569
X10            -.016      .157
```

- -

Adjusted WITHIN CELLS Sum-of-Squares and Cross-Products

```
                 X9        X10

X9           1800.323
```

400

X10   -1.478   14.408

* * * * * * A n a l y s i s   o f   V a r i a n c e -- design   1 * * * * * * *

EFFECT .. WITHIN CELLS Regression
Adjusted Hypothesis Sum-of-Squares and Cross-Products

```
              X9        X10
X9        6198.677
X10        542.568    58.058
```

Multivariate Tests of Significance (S = 2 , M = 2 , N = 44 1/2)

Test Name	Value	Approx. F	Hypoth. DF	Error DF	Sig. of F
Pillais	1.13793	17.34849	14.00	184.00	.000
Hotellings	7.53526	48.44098	14.00	180.00	.000
Wilks	.09041	30.23526	14.00	182.00	.000
Roys	.87781				

Note.. F statistic for WILKS' Lambda is exact.

Multivariate test statistics indicate significant relationships.

Eigenvalues and Canonical Correlations

Root No.	Eigenvalue	Pct.	Cum. Pct.	Canon Cor.	Sq. Cor
1	7.184	95.334	95.334	.937	.878
2	.352	4.666	100.000	.510	.260

Canonical correlations for first and second canonical function/roots.

Dimension Reduction Analysis

Roots	Wilks L.	F	Hypoth. DF	Error DF	Sig. of F
1 TO 2	.09041	30.23526	14.00	182.00	.000
2 TO 2	.73988	5.39083	6.00	92.00	.000

EFFECT .. WITHIN CELLS Regression (Cont.)
Univariate F-tests with (7,92) D. F.

Variable	Sq. Mul. R	Adj. R-sq.	Hypoth. MS	Error MS	F
X9	.77493	.75781	885.52526	19.56873	45.25206
X10	.80118	.78605	8.29404	.15660	52.96181

Variable	Sig. of F
X9	.000

X10

****** A n a l y s i s   o f   V a r i a n c e -- design 1 ******

Raw canonical coefficients for DEPENDENT variables
      Function No.

Variable   1   2

X9   .056   -.148
X10   .678   1.517

- -

Standardized canonical coefficients for DEPENDENT variables
      Function No.

Variable   1   2

X9   .501   -1.330
X10   .580   1.298

- -

Correlations between DEPENDENT and canonical variables
      Function No.

Variable   1   2

X9   .913   -.408
X10   .936   .352

- -

Variance in dependent variables explained by canonical variables

CAN. VAR.   Pct Var DE Cum Pct DE Pct Var CO Cum Pct CO

   1   85.470   85.470   75.026   75.026
   2   14.530   100.000   3.780   78.806

- -

Raw canonical coefficients for COVARIATES
      Function No.

COVARIATE   1   2

X1   .170   .730
X2   .086   .726
X3   .410   -.115
X4   .308   1.287
X5   .593   -2.037
X6   -.066   -.955
X7   .000   -.301

***** A n a l y s i s   o f   V a r i a n c e -- design   1 *******

Standardized canonical coefficients for COVARIATES
CAN. VAR.

COVARIATE	1	2
X1	.225	.965
X2	.103	.868
X3	.569	-.160
X4	.348	1.456
X5	.445	-1.530
X6	-.051	-.736
X7	-.001	-.478

> Standardized canonical coefficient present on variable (treated as a covariate).

Correlations between COVARIATES and canonical variables
CAN. VAR.

Covariate	1	2
X1	.764	-.109
X2	.061	-.141
X3	.624	-.123
X4	.414	.626
X5	.765	-.222
X6	.348	.199
X7	-.278	-.219

> Canonical loadings for independent variable.

Variance in covariates explained by canonical variables

CAN. VAR.	Pct Var DE	Cum Pct DE	Pct Var CO	Cum Pct CO
1	24.238	24.238	27.612	27.612
2	2.140	26.378	8.228	35.840

> Standardized variance of the independent variable (own).

Regression analysis for WITHIN CELLS error term
-- Individual Univariate .9500 confidence intervals
Dependent variable .. X9   Usage Level

COVARIATE	B	Beta	Std. Err.	t-Value	Sig. of t
X1	-.05758	-.00846	2.013	-.029	.977
X2	-.69691	-.09270	2.090	-.333	.740
X3	3.36822	.51954	.411	8.191	.000
X4	-.04220	-.00531	.667	-.063	.950
X5	8.36914	.69947	3.918	2.136	.035
X6	1.28067	.10983	.947	1.352	.180

X7   .56693   .09998   .355   1.595   .114

* * * * * A n a l y s i s   o f   V a r i a n c e -- design   1 * * * * * * *

Regression analysis for WITHIN CELLS error term   (Cont.)

Dependent variable .. X9   Usage Level

COVARIATE	Lower -95%	CL- Upper
X1	-4.055	3.940
X2	-4.848	3.454
X3	2.551	4.185
X4	-1.367	1.282
X5	.587	16.151
X6	-.600	3.162
X7	-.139	1.273

Dependent variable .. X10   Satisfaction Level

COVARIATE	B	Beta	Std. Err.	t-Value	Sig. of t
X1	.24000	.37049	.180	1.333	.186
X2	.17611	.24612	.187	.942	.349
X3	.28995	.46989	.037	7.882	.000
X4	.42850	.56666	.060	7.183	.000
X5	.13164	.11559	.351	.376	.708
X6	-.19619	-.17676	.085	-2.315	.023
X7	-.04598	-.08519	.032	-1.446	.152

COVARIATE	Lower -95%	CL- Upper
X1	-.118	.598
X2	-.195	.547
X3	.217	.363
X4	.310	.547
X5	-.565	.828
X6	-.364	-.028
X7	-.109	.017

(Cont.)

```
* * * * * * A n a l y s i s   o f   V a r i a n c e  --  design   1 * * * * * *

EFFECT .. CONSTANT
Adjusted Hypothesis Sum-of-Squares and Cross-Products

                 X9        X10

X9            81.987
X10            4.564      .254

 - - - - - - - - - - - - - - - - - - - - - - - - - - - - - - - - - - - - - - - - - -
Multivariate Tests of Significance (S = 1, M = 0, N = 44 1/2)

Test Name      Value    Exact F  Hypoth. DF  Error DF  Sig. of F

Pillais       .05989    2.89845    2.00       91.00     .060
Hotellings    .06370    2.89845    2.00       91.00     .060
Wilks         .94011    2.89845    2.00       91.00     .060
Roys          .05989
Note.. F statistics are exact.

 - - - - - - - - - - - - - - - - - - - - - - - - - - - - - - - - - - - - - - - - - -
Eigenvalues and Canonical Correlations

Root No.   Eigenvalue    Pct.    Cum. Pct.   Canon Cor.

   1          .064     100.000   100.000       .245

 - - - - - - - - - - - - - - - - - - - - - - - - - - - - - - - - - - - - - - - - - -
EFFECT .. CONSTANT (Cont.)
Univariate F-tests with (1,92) D. F.

Variable  Hypoth. SS  Error SS   Hypoth. MS  Error MS      F      Sig. of F

X9        81.98728  1800.32318   81.98728   19.56873   4.18971     .044
X10         .25410    14.40759     .25410     .15660   1.62254     .206

 - - - - - - - - - - - - - - - - - - - - - - - - - - - - - - - - - - - - - - - - - -
EFFECT .. CONSTANT (Cont.)
Raw discriminant function coefficients
             Function No.

Variable        1

X9            .192
X10          1.349
```

405

```
* * * * * A n a l y s i s   o f   V a r i a n c e -- design   1 * * * * * * *

EFFECT .. CONSTANT (Cont.)
Standardized discriminant function coefficients
     Function No.

Variable          1

X9              .850
X10             .534

- - - - - - - - - - - - - - - - - - - - - - - - - - - - -

Estimates of effects for canonical variables
     Canonical Variable

Parameter         1

1             -2.724

- - - - - - - - - - - - - - - - - - - - - - - - - - - - -

Correlations between DEPENDENT and canonical variables
     Canonical Variable

Variable          1

X9              .846
X10             .526

- - - - - - - - - - - - - - - - - - - - - - - - - - - - -

Observed and Predicted Values for Each Case
Dependent Variable.. X9                Usage Level

Case No.    Observed   Predicted  Raw Resid.  Std Resid.

    1        32.000      38.181     -6.181      -1.397
    2        43.000      39.368      3.632        .821
    3        48.000      49.033     -1.033       -.234
    4        32.000      35.058     -3.058       -.691
    5        58.000      57.744      .256         .058
    6        45.000      43.503     1.497         .338
    7        46.000      58.959    -12.959      -2.929
    8        44.000      37.642      6.358       1.437
    9        63.000      57.287      5.713       1.291
   10        54.000      48.780      5.220       1.180
   11        32.000      41.610     -9.610      -2.172
   12        47.000      51.527     -4.527      -1.023
   13        39.000      38.908      .092        -.021
   14        38.000      48.414    -10.414      -2.354
   15        54.000      53.991      .009         .002
```

16	49.000	48.192	-.808	-.183
17	38.000	43.113	-5.113	-1.156
18	40.000	47.751	-7.751	-1.752
19	54.000	57.415	-3.415	-.772
20	55.000	53.991	1.009	.228
21	41.000	41.246	-.246	-.056
22	35.000	32.357	2.643	.597
23	55.000	55.612	-.612	-.138
24	36.000	34.179	1.821	.412
25	49.000	50.747	-1.747	-.395
26	49.000	49.154	-.154	-.035
27	36.000	33.842	2.158	.488
28	54.000	56.596	-2.596	-.587
29	49.000	52.041	-3.041	-.687
30	46.000	47.883	-1.883	-.426
31	43.000	41.718	1.282	.290
32	53.000	53.055	-.055	-.012
33	60.000	55.843	4.157	.940
34	47.000	46.763	.237	.053
35	35.000	33.921	1.079	.244
36	39.000	40.787	-1.787	-.404
37	44.000	45.549	-1.549	-.350
38	46.000	46.933	-.933	-.211
39	29.000	28.944	.056	.013
40	28.000	35.030	-7.030	-1.589
41	40.000	42.065	-2.065	-.467
42	58.000	57.749	.251	.057
43	53.000	54.371	-1.371	-.310
44	48.000	48.631	-.631	-.143
45	38.000	36.705	1.295	.293
46	54.000	55.581	-1.581	-.357
47	55.000	49.815	5.185	1.172
48	43.000	43.759	-.759	-.172
49	57.000	50.770	6.230	1.408
50	53.000	51.402	1.598	.361
51	41.000	40.203	.797	.180
52	53.000	52.160	.840	.190
53	50.000	52.998	-2.998	-.678
54	32.000	39.808	-7.808	-1.765
55	39.000	37.473	1.527	.345
56	47.000	45.883	1.117	.252
57	62.000	60.162	1.838	.416
58	65.000	61.547	3.453	.781
59	46.000	45.322	.678	.153
60	50.000	48.660	1.340	.303
61	54.000	49.350	4.650	1.051
62	60.000	54.564	5.436	1.229
63	47.000	48.479	-1.479	-.334
64	36.000	40.497	-4.497	-1.017
65	40.000	35.567	4.433	1.002
66	45.000	47.309	-2.309	-.522

Case No.	Observed	Predicted	Raw Resid.	Std Resid.
67	59.000	55.306	3.694	.835
68	46.000	40.252	5.748	1.299
69	58.000	51.243	6.757	1.527
70	49.000	48.051	.949	.215
71	50.000	51.591	-1.591	-.360
72	55.000	53.976	1.024	.231
73	51.000	50.697	.303	.068
74	60.000	54.283	5.717	1.292
75	41.000	38.391	2.609	.590
76	49.000	54.411	-5.411	-1.223
77	42.000	41.482	.518	.117
78	47.000	49.483	-2.483	-.561
79	39.000	34.292	4.708	1.064
80	56.000	50.037	5.963	1.348
81	59.000	52.981	6.019	1.361
82	47.000	47.274	-.274	-.062
83	41.000	36.810	4.190	.947
84	37.000	44.994	-7.994	-1.807
85	53.000	46.824	6.176	1.396
86	43.000	42.263	.737	.167
87	51.000	45.551	5.449	1.232
88	36.000	42.436	-6.436	-1.455
89	34.000	37.616	-3.616	-.817
90	60.000	56.655	3.345	.756
91	49.000	48.114	.886	.200
92	39.000	46.473	-7.473	-1.689
93	43.000	42.153	.847	.191
94	36.000	30.719	5.281	1.194
95	31.000	35.548	-4.548	-1.028
96	25.000	23.319	1.681	.380
97	60.000	55.128	4.872	1.101
98	38.000	33.356	4.644	1.050
99	42.000	40.618	1.382	.313
100	33.000	44.173	-11.173	-2.526

* * * * * A n a l y s i s o f V a r i a n c e -- design 1 * * * * * *

Observed and Predicted Values for Each Case
Dependent Variable.. X10   Satisfaction Level

Case No.	Observed	Predicted	Raw Resid.	Std Resid.
1	4.200	4.163	.037	.094
2	4.300	4.206	.094	.237
3	5.200	5.048	.152	.385
4	3.900	4.271	-.371	-.937
5	6.800	6.495	.305	.770

6	4.400	4.341	.059	.149
7	5.800	5.771	.029	.074
8	4.300	4.087	.213	.537
9	5.400	5.297	.103	.260
10	5.400	4.924	.476	1.202
11	4.300	4.346	-.046	-.117
12	5.000	4.889	.111	.281
13	4.400	4.027	.373	.943
14	5.000	4.843	.157	.398
15	5.900	6.104	-.204	-.514
16	4.700	5.229	-.529	-1.336
17	4.400	4.381	.019	.048
18	5.600	4.883	.717	1.812
19	5.900	5.734	.166	.418
20	6.000	6.104	-.104	-.262
21	4.500	4.225	.275	.696
22	3.300	3.383	-.083	-.209
23	5.200	5.946	-.746	-1.885
24	3.700	3.701	-.001	-.003
25	4.900	5.232	-.332	-.840
26	5.900	5.365	.535	1.352
27	3.700	3.672	.028	.070
28	5.800	5.684	.116	.292
29	5.400	4.963	.437	1.105
30	5.100	4.675	.425	1.075
31	3.300	4.179	-.879	-2.221
32	5.000	5.741	-.741	-1.872
33	6.100	6.063	.037	.095
34	3.800	4.606	-.806	-2.037
35	4.100	3.597	.503	1.270
36	3.600	4.058	-.458	-1.157
37	4.800	4.737	.063	.158
38	5.100	4.974	.126	.318
39	3.900	3.343	.557	1.408
40	3.300	3.585	-.285	-.721
41	3.700	4.160	-.460	-1.163
42	6.700	6.471	.229	.577
43	5.900	5.573	.327	.827
44	4.800	5.117	-.317	-.801
45	3.200	3.433	-.233	-.588
46	6.000	5.693	.307	.777
47	4.900	4.879	.021	.053
48	4.700	4.563	.137	.345
49	4.900	4.956	-.056	-.141
50	3.800	4.690	-.890	-2.250
51	5.000	4.940	.060	.152
52	5.200	4.992	.208	.526
53	5.500	5.084	.416	1.051
54	3.700	3.966	-.266	-.672
55	3.700	3.792	-.092	-.233
56	4.200	5.127	-.927	-2.343

57	6.200	5.866	.334	.845
58	6.000	5.893	.107	.269
59	5.600	5.015	.585	1.479
60	5.000	4.714	.286	.723
61	4.800	4.870	-.070	-.176
62	6.100	5.960	.140	.353
63	5.300	5.123	.177	.447
64	4.200	4.178	.022	.055
65	3.400	3.274	.126	.319
66	4.900	4.684	.216	.547
67	6.000	5.539	.461	1.165
68	4.500	4.314	.186	.470
69	4.300	4.922	-.622	-1.571
70	4.800	4.797	.003	.009
71	5.400	5.253	.147	.373
72	3.900	4.839	-.939	-2.374
73	4.900	5.395	-.495	-1.252
74	5.100	5.046	.054	.137
75	4.100	4.656	-.556	-1.405
76	5.200	5.190	.010	.027
77	5.100	5.042	.058	.146
78	5.100	4.758	.342	.865
79	3.300	3.129	.171	.433
80	5.100	4.972	.128	.324
81	4.500	5.057	-.557	-1.409
82	5.600	5.541	.059	.149
83	4.100	4.001	.099	.249
84	4.400	4.547	-.147	-.371
85	5.600	5.127	.473	1.194
86	3.700	3.931	-.231	-.585
87	5.500	5.001	.499	1.261
88	4.300	4.342	-.042	-.106
89	4.000	4.476	-.476	-1.202
90	6.100	5.624	.476	1.203
91	4.400	5.236	-.836	-2.113
92	5.500	4.781	.719	1.818
93	5.200	5.156	.044	.112
94	3.600	3.336	.264	.667
95	4.000	4.000	.000	.001
96	3.000	3.151	-.249	-.630
97	5.200	5.268	-.068	-.172
98	3.700	3.456	.244	.616
99	4.300	4.808	-.508	-1.284
100	4.400	4.527	-.127	-.321

Dependent variable: X9

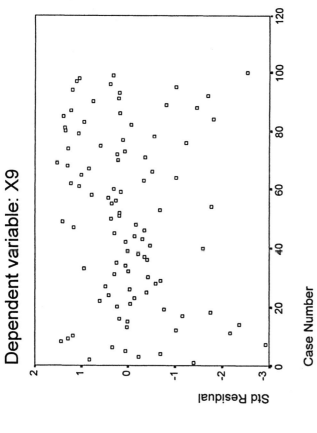

Dependent variable: X9

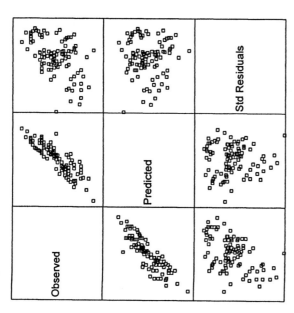

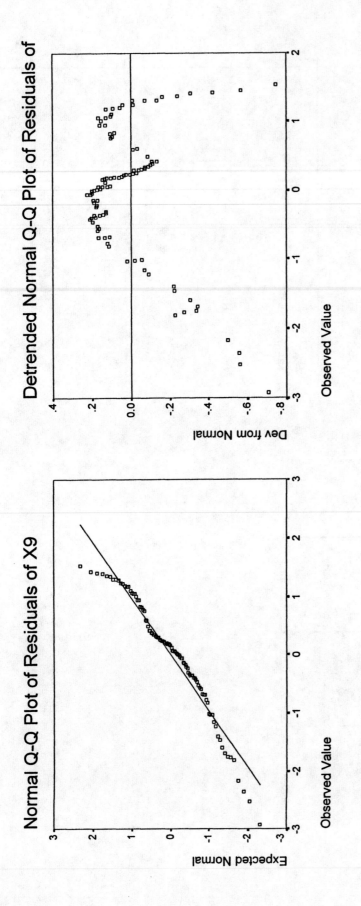

Normal Q-Q Plot of Residuals of X9

Detrended Normal Q-Q Plot of Residuals of

412

Dependent variable: X10

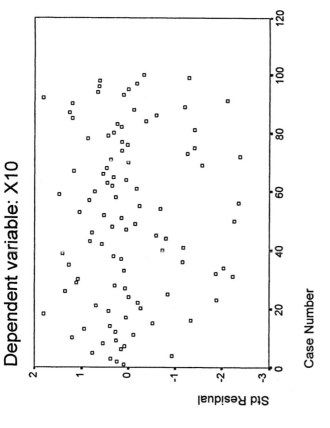

Dependent variable: X10

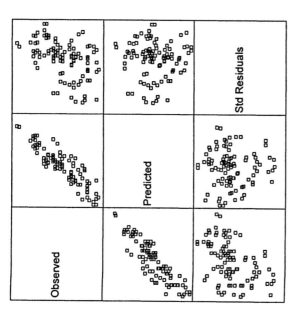

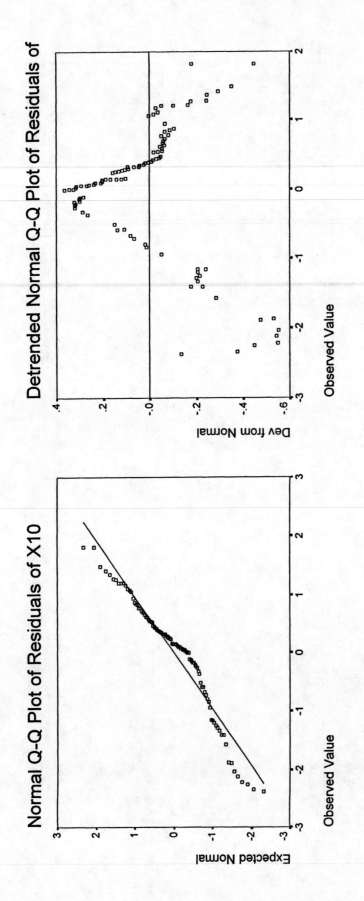

Normal Q-Q Plot of Residuals of X10

Detrended Normal Q-Q Plot of Residuals of

CHAPTER 9:

CLUSTER ANALYSIS

This section of the instructor's manual contains copies of the actual printouts from the SPSS statistical analysis program. The printouts contain examples of the analyses discussed in the text using the HATCO database.

Each of the printouts is annotated with comments to aid in the interpretation of the results. These suggestions are typed in the margins next to the appropriate data. If you wish to provide students with their own copies of the output without these comments, the output are provided on the computer diskette accompanying the instructor's manual.

Three examples of cluster analysis are included in this section. A brief description follows:

Hierarchical Cluster Analysis: An agglomerative hierarchical analysis is performed on the observations. Similarity is derived from the seven attribute ratings (X_1 to X_7).

Nonhierarchical Cluster Analysis – Specified Seed Points: A nonhierarchical cluster procedure is used to "fine-tune" the results from the hierarchical analysis. Once the cluster centers are established, they are input as the stating points (also referred to as seed points).

Nonhierarchical Cluster Analysis – Random Seed Points: The same nonhierarchical cluster procedure is used, but this time to assess the stability of the solution when the seed points are not specified.

Hierarchical Cluster Analysis

```
*Hierarchical Cluster Analysis.
PROXIMITIES
  X1 X2 X3 X4 X5 X6 X7
/MATRIX OUT ('C:\WINDOWS\TEMP\SPSSCLUS.TMP')
/VIEW=CASE
/MEASURE=SEUCLID
/PRINT=NONE
/STANDARDIZE=NONE.
CLUSTER
/MATRIX IN ('C:\WINDOWS\TEMP\SPSSCLUS.TMP')
/METHOD=WARD(WCLUS)
/PRINT=SCHEDUAL DISTANCE CLUSTER(2,5)
/PLOT=DENDROGRAM VICICLE
/SAVE=CLUSTER(2,5).
ERASE FILE=
'C:\WINDOWS\TEMP\SPSSCLUS.TMP'.
```

The computer program searches for the smallest value indicating the least (or most similar) objects and forms clusters. The dissimilarity matrix is then updated and the program continues until one cluster is left. Note: The remainder of the dissimilarity matrix has been deleted from the printed output. The complete listing can be obtained by running the analysis.

Proximity Matrix

Case	Squared Euclidean Distance									
	1:Case 1	2:Case 2	3:Case 3	4:Case 4	5:Case 5	6:Case 6	7:Case 7	8:Case 8	9:Case 9	10:Case 10
1:Case 1		28.160	37.550	10.720	27.380	33.590	25.670	24.510	16.670	25.020
2:Case 2	28.160		13.090	9.680	50.760	12.010	20.330	9.530	31.510	7.660
3:Case 3	37.550	13.090		26.670	61.810	17.920	28.320	10.660	33.840	4.750
4:Case 4	10.720	9.680	26.670		39.500	12.190	19.590	15.470	18.350	13.540
5:Case 5	27.380	50.760	61.810	39.500		69.430	15.290	63.710	22.570	43.300
6:Case 6	33.590	12.010	17.920	12.190	69.430		25.880	12.120	24.540	11.750
7:Case 7	25.670	20.330	28.320	19.590	15.290	25.880		33.540	7.320	13.870
8:Case 8	24.510	9.530	10.660	15.470	63.710	12.120	33.540		36.420	13.730
9:Case 9	16.670	31.510	33.840	18.350	22.570	24.540	7.320	36.420		17.250
10:Case 10	25.020	7.660	4.750	13.540	43.300	11.750	13.870	13.730	17.250	
11:Case 11	8.280	20.260	36.070	8.840	29.980	20.330	17.590	17.030	15.510	24.360
12:Case 12	17.460	19.400	24.510	10.300	35.600	9.170	9.430	21.510	4.010	11.560
13:Case 13	7.440	24.800	34.490	7.920	45.080	15.570	26.610	16.610	15.350	23.460
14:Case 14	9.160	14.980	28.090	7.520	17.200	20.030	5.330	21.470	6.830	13.840
15:Case 15	16.860	29.040	38.690	15.100	12.600	28.510	5.890	36.430	6.030	21.840
16:Case 16	10.900	37.020	43.050	19.860	26.580	31.250	21.570	26.330	14.830	33.000

This is a dissimilarity matrix

Ward Linkage

Agglomeration Schedule

Stage	Cluster Combined Cluster 1	Cluster Combined Cluster 2	Coefficients	Stage Cluster First Appears Cluster 1	Stage Cluster First Appears Cluster 2	Next Stage
1	15	20	.000	0	0	60
2	5	42	5.000E-03	0	0	94
3	24	27	1.000E-02	0	0	74
4	47	61	2.000E-02	0	0	78
5	19	28	4.000E-02	0	0	60
6	67	90	7.000E-02	0	0	39
7	18	92	.105	0	0	65
8	51	77	.140	0	0	72
9	33	62	.175	0	0	63
10	36	41	.210	0	0	45
11	85	87	.260	0	0	69
12	65	79	.310	0	0	68
13	43	46	.360	0	0	76
14	25	44	.410	0	0	63
15	38	63	.475	0	0	54
16	69	81	.555	0	0	52
17	94	98	.650	0	0	73
18	56	91	.745	0	0	66
19	50	72	.840	0	0	52
20	75	99	.950	0	0	62
21	1	95	1.060	0	0	72
22	16	73	1.170	0	0	61
23	37	48	1.280	0	0	58
24	11	100	1.405	0	0	69
25	4	89	1.545	0	0	62
26	84	88	1.685	0	0	45
27	2	83	1.825	0	0	82
28	29	78	1.965	0	0	61
29	3	71	2.105	0	0	75
30	23	32	2.245	0	0	66
31	17	64	2.435	0	0	83
32	12	76	2.650	0	0	67
33	8	68	2.865	0	0	70
34	9	74	3.130	0	0	55
35	52	60	3.420	0	0	57
36	10	34	3.755	0	0	43
37	26	59	4.105	0	0	64
38	49	97	4.525	0	0	81
39	7	67	4.995	0	6	77
40	13	21	5.515	0	0	51
41	82	93	6.040	0	0	91
42	40	54	6.565	0	0	53
43	10	30	7.097	36	0	50
44	66	80	7.632	0	0	59
45	36	84	8.189	10	26	70
46	22	55	8.749	0	0	71
47	6	70	9.409	0	0	57
48	45	86	10.239	0	0	53
49	39	96	11.079	0	0	68

Stage 1: Clusters 15 and 20 are combined. This new cluster is next combined at stage 60.

Stage 45: Clusters 36 and 84 combined. The new cluster is combined at stage 70. Cluster 36 was formed at stage 10 and cluster 84 was formed at stage 26.

Agglomeration Schedule

Stage	Cluster Combined		Coefficients	Stage Cluster First Appears		Next Stage
	Cluster 1	Cluster 2		Cluster 1	Cluster 2	
50	10	53	11.965	43	0	56
51	13	35	13.025	40	0	71
52	50	69	14.468	19	16	65
53	40	45	15.970	42	48	73
54	14	38	17.558	0	15	59
55	9	58	19.213	34	0	67
56	10	31	21.261	50	0	58
57	6	52	23.516	47	35	88
58	10	37	25.869	56	23	75
59	14	66	28.244	54	44	80
60	15	19	30.704	1	5	77
61	16	29	33.179	22	28	78
62	4	75	35.714	25	20	74
63	25	33	38.537	14	9	64
64	25	26	41.568	63	37	84
65	18	50	44.879	7	52	76
66	23	56	48.546	30	18	87
67	9	12	52.279	55	32	80
68	39	65	56.214	49	12	89
69	11	85	60.252	24	11	87
70	8	36	64.364	33	45	83
71	13	22	68.580	51	46	90
72	1	51	73.083	21	8	84
73	40	94	77.887	53	17	85
74	4	24	82.785	62	3	82
75	3	10	88.133	29	58	79
76	18	43	93.522	65	13	92
77	7	15	98.977	39	60	86
78	16	47	104.835	61	4	90
79	3	57	111.625	75	0	91
80	9	14	118.530	67	59	81
81	9	49	126.007	80	38	86
82	2	4	134.773	27	74	85
83	8	17	143.875	70	31	88
84	1	25	156.719	72	64	92
85	2	40	170.259	82	73	89
86	7	9	185.590	77	81	94
87	11	23	201.110	69	66	93
88	6	8	218.441	57	83	93
89	2	39	236.111	85	68	96
90	13	16	258.731	71	78	95
91	3	82	281.428	79	41	97
92	1	18	305.027	84	76	95
93	6	11	333.081	88	87	96
94	5	7	364.898	2	86	98
95	1	13	398.082	92	90	98
96	2	6	446.283	89	93	97
97	2	3	522.981	96	91	99
98	1	5	614.954	95	94	99
99	1	2	994.752	98	97	0

See text for analysis of clustering coefficient for clusters 10 to 1 (stage 90 to 99)

418

Cluster Membership

Case	5 Clusters	4 Clusters	3 Clusters	2 Clusters
1:Case 1	1	1	1	1
2:Case 2	2	2	2	2
3:Case 3	3	3	2	2
4:Case 4	2	2	2	2
5:Case 5	4	4	3	1
6:Case 6	5	2	2	2
7:Case 7	4	4	3	1
8:Case 8	5	2	2	2
9:Case 9	4	4	3	1
10:Case 10	3	3	2	2
11:Case 11	5	2	2	2
12:Case 12	4	4	3	1
13:Case 13	1	1	1	1
14:Case 14	4	4	3	1
15:Case 15	4	4	3	1
16:Case 16	1	1	1	1
17:Case 17	5	2	2	2
18:Case 18	1	1	1	1
19:Case 19	4	4	3	1
20:Case 20	4	4	3	1
21:Case 21	1	1	1	1
22:Case 22	1	1	1	1
23:Case 23	5	2	2	2
24:Case 24	2	2	2	2
25:Case 25	1	1	1	1
26:Case 26	1	1	1	1
27:Case 27	2	2	2	2
28:Case 28	4	4	3	1
29:Case 29	1	1	1	1
30:Case 30	3	3	2	2
31:Case 31	3	3	2	2
32:Case 32	5	2	2	2
33:Case 33	1	1	1	1
34:Case 34	3	3	2	2
35:Case 35	1	1	1	1
36:Case 36	5	2	2	2
37:Case 37	3	3	2	2
38:Case 38	4	4	3	1
39:Case 39	2	2	2	2
40:Case 40	2	2	2	2
41:Case 41	5	2	2	2
42:Case 42	4	4	3	1
43:Case 43	1	1	1	1
44:Case 44	1	1	1	1
45:Case 45	2	2	2	2
46:Case 46	1	1	1	1
47:Case 47	1	1	1	1
48:Case 48	3	3	2	2
49:Case 49	4	4	3	1
50:Case 50	1	1	1	1

Shows group membership of each case for the 5, 4, 3, and 2 cluster solution.

419

Cluster Membership

Case	5 Clusters	4 Clusters	3 Clusters	2 Clusters
51:Case 51	1	1	1	1
52:Case 52	5	2	2	2
53:Case 53	3	3	2	2
54:Case 54	2	2	2	2
55:Case 55	1	1	1	1
56:Case 56	5	2	2	2
57:Case 57	3	3	2	2
58:Case 58	4	4	3	1
59:Case 59	1	1	1	1
60:Case 60	5	2	2	2
61:Case 61	1	1	1	1
62:Case 62	1	1	1	1
63:Case 63	4	4	3	1
64:Case 64	5	2	2	2
65:Case 65	2	2	2	2
66:Case 66	4	4	3	1
67:Case 67	4	4	3	1
68:Case 68	5	2	2	2
69:Case 69	1	1	1	1
70:Case 70	5	2	2	2
71:Case 71	3	3	2	2
72:Case 72	1	1	1	1
73:Case 73	1	1	1	1
74:Case 74	4	4	3	1
75:Case 75	2	2	2	2
76:Case 76	4	4	3	1
77:Case 77	1	1	1	1
78:Case 78	1	1	1	1
79:Case 79	2	2	2	2
80:Case 80	4	4	3	1
81:Case 81	1	1	1	1
82:Case 82	3	3	2	2
83:Case 83	2	2	2	2
84:Case 84	5	2	2	2
85:Case 85	5	2	2	2
86:Case 86	2	2	2	2
87:Case 87	5	2	2	2
88:Case 88	5	2	2	2
89:Case 89	2	2	2	2
90:Case 90	4	4	3	1
91:Case 91	5	2	2	2
92:Case 92	1	1	1	1
93:Case 93	3	3	2	2
94:Case 94	2	2	2	2
95:Case 95	1	1	1	1
96:Case 96	2	2	2	2
97:Case 97	4	4	3	1
98:Case 98	2	2	2	2
99:Case 99	2	2	2	2
100:Case 100	5	2	2	2

Dendrogram

Dendrogram using Ward Method

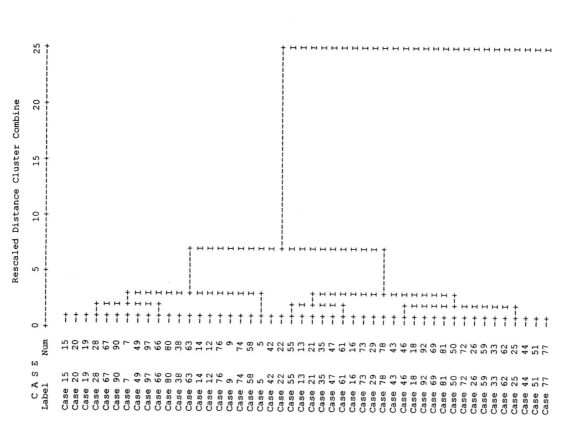

See text for analysis of dendrogram.

421

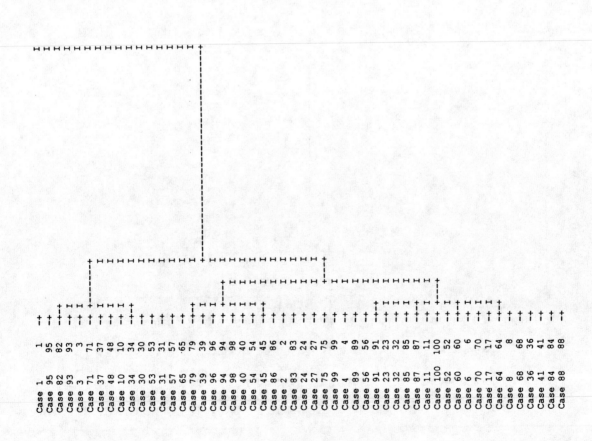

Nonhierarchical Cluster Analysis: Specified Seed Points

*Non-hierarchical Cluster Analysis (Prespecified Cluster Seed Points).
QUICK CLUSTER X1 X2 X3 X4 X5 X6 X7
/INITIAL= (4.46 1.576 8.9   4.926 2.992 2.51 5.904
          2.57 3.152 6.888 5.57   2.84   2.82 8.038)
/CRITERIA=CLUSTERS (2)
/PRINT=CLUSTER ANOVA
/SAVE=CLUSTER(NHCLUS).

Initial cluster seeds specified by the researcher.

Initial Cluster Centers

	Cluster	
	1	2
Delivery Speed	4.46	2.57
Price Level	1.576	3.152
Price Flexibility	8.9	6.888
Manufacturer Image	4.926	5.57
Service	2.992	2.84
Salesforce Image	2.51	2.82
Product Quality	5.904	8.038

Input from INITIAL Subcommand

Iteration History[a]

	Change in Cluster Centers	
Iteration	1	2
1	.086	.143
2	.000	.000

a. Convergence achieved due to no or small distance change. The maximum distance by which any center has changed is .000. The current iteration is 2. The minimum distance between initial centers is 3.898.

Cluster Membership

Case	Cluster	Distance
1	1	2.439
2	2	1.875
3	2	2.841
4	2	2.571
5	1	4.279
6	2	2.385
7	1	3.310
8	2	2.259
9	1	2.224
10	2	1.879
11	1	2.227
12	1	2.551
13	1	2.632
14	1	1.801
15	1	2.267
16	1	1.949
17	2	2.626
18	1	1.842
19	1	2.389
20	1	2.267
21	1	2.000
22	1	3.587
23	2	3.023
24	2	2.348
25	1	2.270
26	1	1.950
27	2	2.355
28	1	2.313
29	1	2.500
30	2	2.135
31	2	1.009
32	2	2.612
33	1	2.055
34	2	1.379
35	1	3.426
36	2	1.699
37	2	2.210
38	1	1.772
39	2	3.420
40	2	2.073
41	2	1.574
42	1	4.242
43	1	1.768
44	1	2.341
45	2	2.451
46	1	1.886
47	1	2.854
48	2	2.085
49	1	2.181
50	1	2.879

Cluster Membership

Case	Cluster	Distance
51	1	2.030
52	2	2.494
53	2	2.770
54	2	1.595
55	1	2.684
56	2	2.013
57	2	3.928
58	1	2.690
59	1	2.062
60	2	2.205
61	1	2.795
62	1	1.976
63	1	1.811
64	2	2.750
65	2	3.143
66	1	1.293
67	1	2.559
68	2	2.008
69	1	2.102
70	2	1.985
71	2	3.123
72	1	2.827
73	1	1.848
74	1	1.751
75	2	1.714
76	1	2.790
77	1	1.906
78	1	2.653
79	2	3.256
80	1	1.079
81	1	2.050
82	2	4.266
83	2	1.886
84	2	1.396
85	2	2.202
86	2	1.777
87	2	2.201
88	2	1.559
89	2	2.351
90	1	2.741
91	2	2.153
92	1	1.949
93	2	3.987
94	2	2.240
95	1	2.812
96	2	3.510
97	1	2.418
98	2	1.934
99	2	1.706
100	1	2.102

Final Cluster Centers

	Cluster	
	1	2
Delivery Speed	4.4	2.6
Price Level	1.6	3.2
Price Flexibility	8.9	6.8
Manufacturer Image	4.9	5.6
Service	3.0	2.9
Salesforce Image	2.5	2.8
Product Quality	5.9	8.1

Final cluster centers as determined by the procedure. A close match between centers and the specified centers indicates a relatively stable cluster solution.

ANOVA

	Cluster		Error		F	Sig.
	Mean Square	df	Mean Square	df		
Delivery Speed	81.563	1	.930	98	87.717	.000
Price Level	66.457	1	.766	98	86.753	.000
Price Flexibility	109.637	1	.823	98	133.175	.000
Manufacturer Image	11.302	1	1.178	98	9.596	.003
Service	.188	1	.568	98	.331	.566
Salesforce Image	2.123	1	.579	98	3.670	.058
Product Quality	123.372	1	1.280	98	96.404	.000

The F tests should be used only for descriptive purposes because the clusters have been chosen to maximize the differences among cases in different clusters. The observed significance levels are not corrected for this and thus cannot be interpreted as tests of the hypothesis that the cluster means are equal.

Delivery speed, price level, price flexibility, manufacturer image, and product quality have significant difference between cluster centers. Service and salesforce image do not have any significant differences, although salesforce image is close.

Number of Cases in each Cluster

Cluster	1	52.000
	2	48.000
Valid		100.000
Missing		.000

Nonhierarchical Cluster Analysis: Random Seed Points

*Non-hierarchical Cluster Analysis (Random Selection of Cluster Seed Points).
SET SEED 345678.
QUICK CLUSTER   X1 X2 X3 X4 X5 X6 X7
   /CRITERIA=CLUSTERS (2) NOINITIAL
   /PRINT=CLUSTER ANOVA INITIAL
   /SAVE=CLUSTER(NHRCLUS).

Initial Cluster Centers

	Cluster	
	1	2
Delivery Speed	4.1	1.8
Price Level	.6	3.0
Price Flexibility	6.9	6.3
Manufacturer Image	4.7	6.6
Service	2.4	2.5
Salesforce Image	2.3	4.0
Product Quality	5.2	8.4

Initial cluster seeds chosen randomly by the computer.

Iteration History[a]

	Change in Cluster Centers	
Iteration	1	2
1	2.241	1.939
2	.243	.289
3	.000	.000

a. Convergence achieved due to no or small distance change. The maximum distance by which any center has changed is .000. The current iteration is 3. The minimum distance between initial centers is 5.307.

427

Cluster Membership

Case	Cluster	Distance
1	1	2.439
2	2	1.875
3	2	2.841
4	2	2.571
5	1	4.279
6	2	2.385
7	1	3.310
8	2	2.259
9	1	2.224
10	2	1.879
11	1	2.227
12	1	2.551
13	1	2.632
14	1	1.801
15	1	2.267
16	1	1.949
17	2	2.626
18	1	1.842
19	1	2.389
20	1	2.267
21	1	2.000
22	1	3.587
23	2	3.023
24	2	2.348
25	1	2.270
26	1	1.950
27	2	2.355
28	1	2.313
29	1	2.500
30	2	2.135
31	2	1.009
32	2	2.612
33	1	2.055
34	2	1.379
35	1	3.426
36	2	1.699
37	2	2.210
38	1	1.772
39	2	3.420
40	2	2.073
41	2	1.574
42	1	4.242
43	1	1.768
44	1	2.341
45	2	2.451
46	1	1.886
47	1	2.854
48	2	2.085
49	1	2.181
50	1	2.879

Cluster Membership

Case	Cluster	Distance
51	1	2.030
52	2	2.494
53	2	2.770
54	2	1.595
55	1	2.684
56	2	2.013
57	2	3.928
58	1	2.690
59	1	2.062
60	2	2.205
61	1	2.795
62	1	1.976
63	1	1.811
64	2	2.750
65	2	3.143
66	1	1.293
67	1	2.559
68	2	2.008
69	1	2.102
70	2	1.985
71	2	3.123
72	1	2.827
73	1	1.848
74	1	1.751
75	2	1.714
76	1	2.790
77	1	1.906
78	1	2.653
79	2	3.256
80	1	1.079
81	1	2.050
82	2	4.266
83	2	1.886
84	2	1.396
85	2	2.202
86	2	1.777
87	2	2.201
88	2	1.559
89	2	2.351
90	1	2.741
91	2	2.153
92	1	1.949
93	2	3.987
94	2	2.240
95	1	2.812
96	2	3.510
97	1	2.418
98	2	1.934
99	2	1.706
100	1	2.102

Final Cluster Centers

	Cluster	
	1	2
Delivery Speed	4.4	2.6
Price Level	1.6	3.2
Price Flexibility	8.9	6.8
Manufacturer Image	4.9	5.6
Service	3.0	2.9
Salesforce Image	2.5	2.8
Product Quality	5.9	8.1

ANOVA

	Cluster		Error			
	Mean Square	df	Mean Square	df	F	Sig.
Delivery Speed	81.563	1	.930	98	87.717	.000
Price Level	66.457	1	.766	98	86.753	.000
Price Flexibility	109.637	1	.823	98	133.175	.000
Manufacturer Image	11.302	1	1.178	98	9.596	.003
Service	.188	1	.568	98	.331	.566
Salesforce Image	2.123	1	.579	98	3.670	.058
Product Quality	123.372	1	1.280	98	96.404	.000

The F tests should be used only for descriptive purposes because the clusters have been chosen to maximize the differences among cases in different clusters. The observed significance levels are not corrected for this and thus cannot be interpreted as tests of the hypothesis that the cluster means are equal.

Number of Cases in each Cluster

Cluster	1	52.000
	2	48.000
Valid		100.000
Missing		.000

Similar results as the nonhierarchical results above, offering further evidence as to the validity of the cluster solution.

CHAPTER 10:

MULTIDIMENSIONAL SCALING (MDS)

This section of the instructor's manual contains copies of the actual printouts from the SPSS statistical analysis program. The printouts contain examples of the analyses discussed in the text using an additional database for the multidimensional scaling procedure (for a complete description of the database see Chapter Ten of the text).

Each of the printouts is annotated with comments to aid in the interpretation of the results. These suggestions are typed in the margins next to the appropriate data. If you wish to provide students with their own copies of the output without these comments, the output are provided on the computer diskette accompanying the instructor's manual.

An example of multidimensional scaling and correspondence analysis is included in this section. A brief description follows:

Multidimensional Scaling: Multidimensional scaling is performed on the perceptions of respondents concerning the similarity/dissimilarity of HATCO and nine competing firms in the market.

Correspondence Analysis: Correspondence analysis is performed on eight binary (yes/no) attribute ratings of ten firms.

Multidimensional Scaling: Alscal Procedure

```
ALSCAL
  VARIABLES= var1 var2 var3 var4 var5 var6 var7 var8 var9 var10
  /SHAPE=symmetric /INPUT ROWS(10)
  /LEVEL=ratio (1)
  /CONDITION=MATRIX
  /MODEL=INDSCAL
  /CRITERIA= CONVERGE(.001) STRESSMIN(.001) ITER(50) CUTOFF(0)
  DIMENS(1,5)
  /PLOT=DEFAULT ALL
  /PRINT=HEADER .
```

Alscal Procedure Options

Data Options-

```
Number of Rows (Observations/Matrix).    10
Number of Columns (Variables)  .  .  .   10
Number of Matrices  .  .  .  .  .  .  .  18
Measurement Level  .  .  .  .  .  .  .   Ratio
Data Matrix Shape  .  .  .  .  .  .  .   Symmetric
Type .  .  .  .  .  .  .  .  .  .  .  .  Dissimilarity
Approach to Ties  .  .  .  .  .  .  .  . Leave Tied
Conditionality  .  .  .  .  .  .  .  .   Matrix
Data Cutoff at .  .  .  .  .  .  .  .  .  .000000
```

Model Options-

```
Model .  .  .  .  .  .  .  .  .  .  .  . Indscal
>Note # 14697
>You have requested a solution with one dimension in a weighted model.
>Subject weights are undefined in a one dimensional model.  ALSCAL continues
>the analysis with a minimum of two dimensions in the solution.

Maximum Dimensionality  .  .  .  .  .  . 5
Minimum Dimensionality  .  .  .  .  .  . 2
Negative Weights  .  .  .  .  .  .  .  . Not Permitted
```

> Denotes that the input matrix contains 10 objects for 18 subjects. Since the matrix is defined as symmetric, only the lower portion is read by the program.

> The analyses will define results for two to five dimensions.

432

Output Options-

Job Option Header . . . . . .   Printed
Data Matrices . . . .   Not Printed
Configurations and Transformations .   Plotted
Output Dataset . . . . . .   Not Created
Initial Stimulus Coordinates . . .   Computed
Initial Subject Weights . . . .   Computed

Algorithmic Options-

Maximum Iterations   50
Convergence Criterion 00100
Minimum S-stress 00100
Missing Data Estimated by . . .   Ulbounds
Iteration history for the 5 dimensional solution (in squared distances)

Young's S-stress formula 1 is used.

Iteration	S-stress	Improvement
0	.28986	
1	.28986	
2	.28010	.00976
3	.27967	.00043

Iterations stopped because
S-stress improvement is less than   .001000

433

Stress and squared correlation (RSQ) in distances

RSQ values are the proportion of variance of the scaled data (disparities) in the partition (row, matrix, or entire data) which is accounted for by their corresponding distances.
Stress values are Kruskal's stress formula 1.

Matrix	Stress	RSQ	Matrix	Stress	RSQ
1	.272	.531	2	.182	.493
3	.213	.609	4	.138	.754
5	.160	.620	6	.184	.780
7	.130	.760	8	.154	.589
9	.179	.568	10	.262	.653
11	.147	.661	12	.180	.581
13	.251	.597	14	.133	.687
15	.181	.457	16	.194	.618
17	.096	.792	18	.371	.595

Averaged (rms) over matrices
Stress = .20068   RSQ = .63034

Configuration derived in 5 dimensions

Stimulus Coordinates

Stimulus Number	Stimulus Name	Dimension 1	2	3	4	5
1	VAR1	-1.3139	-.4158	.0686	.2934	-1.5844
2	VAR2	-1.4977	-.5954	.2087	.0142	.0737
3	VAR3	-.2241	-1.3106	.8732	-.4454	1.0045
4	VAR4	.9367	-.3319	-1.9322	1.2380	-.0245
5	VAR5	1.0591	-.8439	-1.4602	.5274	.8825
6	VAR6	-.9114	.6003	.1087	-1.3124	-1.8285
7	VAR7	-.3540	1.5602	.3399	-1.3229	1.4072
8	VAR8	.8879	.7910	1.7578	1.7202	-.4131
9	VAR9	.8352	-1.3828	.2478	-1.1080	-.4488
10	VAR10	-1.2407	1.2650	-.2122	-.4953	-.0151

Subject weights measure the importance of each dimension to each subject. Squared weights sum to RSQ.

A subject with weights proportional to the average weights has a weirdness of zero, the minimum value.
A subject with one large weight and many low weights has a weirdness near one.
A subject with exactly one positive weight has a weirdness of one, the maximum value for nonnegative weights.

Subject Weights

Subject Number	Weirdness	Dimension 1	2	3	4	5
1	.3663	.3570	.4525	.2060	.3854	.0899
2	.0574	.4356	.3502	.2649	.2428	.2270
3	.2548	.5335	.1805	.3112	.2975	.3263
4	.1328	.6568	.3521	.2938	.2273	.2457
5	.1504	.4043	.4370	.2996	.3535	.2264
6	.0450	.5523	.3927	.3639	.3389	.2714
7	.1037	.6141	.3545	.3556	.2435	.2668
8	.1738	.3671	.4711	.3328	.2759	.2127
9	.1577	.5134	.2497	.2830	.2869	.2826
10	.3380	.5602	.4852	.2631	.1603	.0960
11	.1922	.5460	.3043	.3536	.2089	.3183
12	.4862	.4928	.3990	.1031	.4085	.0405
13	.1507	.5958	.2659	.2864	.2100	.2119
14	.1346	.4964	.3460	.3572	.2962	.3255
15	.0852	.4067	.3307	.3027	.2424	.1773
16	.0973	.5047	.3234	.2984	.3411	.2319
17	.2787	.5341	.3666	.4120	.1853	.4097
18	.1898	.5588	.3232	.3278	.2329	.1302

Overall importance of each dimension: .2639 .1316 .0949 .0798 .0600

Flattened Subject Weights

Subject Number	Plot Symbol	Variable 1	2	3	4
1	1	-1.4453	1.7095	-1.2866	1.9435
2	2	-.4107	.2979	-.1628	-.1473
3	3	-.4031	-2.0330	-.2899	.2913
4	4	1.4225	-.3202	-.4359	-.8168
5	5	-1.5455	.7538	-.1653	-.8206
6	6	-.3833	-.1981	.3186	.2104
7	7	.6500	-.4175	.4504	-.7171
8	8	-1.8471	1.3307	.6589	-.0087
9	9	.2761	-1.1633	-.1322	-.2315
10	A	1.1617	1.8361	-.3518	-1.3579
11	B	.2255	-.7545	.7761	-.9730
12	C	.7943	1.1853	-3.3705	2.4590
13	D	1.6340	-.8777	.0935	-.6957
14	E	-.7174	-.4802	.5204	-.0850
15	F	-.5844	.2253	.8719	-.0128
16	G	-.1800	-.4746	-.1203	-.7204
17	H	-.5549	-.4380	1.1405	-1.4703
18	I	1.1012	-.1815	.9052	-.3922

Iteration history for the 4 dimensional solution (in squared distances)

Young's S-stress formula 1 is used.

Iteration	S-stress	Improvement
0	.32730	
1	.32730	.01611
2	.31119	.00084
3	.31036	

Iterations stopped because
S-stress improvement is less than .001000

Stress and squared correlation (RSQ) in distances

RSQ values are the proportion of variance of the scaled data (disparities) in the partition (row, matrix, or entire data) which is accounted for by their corresponding distances. Stress values are Kruskal's stress formula 1.

Matrix	Stress	RSQ	Matrix	Stress	RSQ
1	.287	.452	2	.194	.472
3	.206	.609	4	.147	.710
5	.191	.495	6	.195	.675
7	.151	.676	8	.179	.507
9	.205	.467	10	.259	.651
11	.186	.510	12	.176	.587
13	.228	.639	14	.186	.473
15	.195	.436	16	.221	.482
17	.158	.582	18	.368	.578

Averaged (rms) over matrices
Stress = .21363 RSQ = .55569

Configuration derived in 4 dimensions

Stimulus Coordinates

Stimulus Number	Stimulus Name	Dimension 1	2	3	4
1	VAR1	-1.2027	-.4739	-.4474	-1.2619
2	VAR2	-1.3506	-.2598	-.8501	-.3264
3	VAR3	-.7378	1.2734	-.6031	-.1043
4	VAR4	1.8028	-.2243	-.8486	-.4819
5	VAR5	1.3229	.7652	-1.2422	.3061
6	VAR6	.6931	-.1881	1.7522	.7395
7	VAR7	-.3812	-1.3370	.7343	1.5864
8	VAR8	.4104	-.7156	1.6801	-1.7806
9	VAR9	.0649	1.4579	-.1259	1.3152
10	VAR10	-.6216	-1.7291	-.0493	.0079

Subject weights measure the importance of each dimension to each subject.
Squared weights sum to RSQ.

A subject with weights proportional to the average weights has a weirdness of
zero, the minimum value.
A subject with one large weight and many low weights has a weirdness near one.
A subject with exactly one positive weight has a weirdness of one,
the maximum value for nonnegative weights.

Subject Weights

Subject Number	Weird- ness	1	2	3	4
1	.2054	.2858	.4212	.3647	.2449
2	.0691	.4094	.3321	.3259	.2960
3	.2917	.5726	.1923	.3215	.3756
4	.1043	.5417	.4640	.3674	.2574
5	.0798	.3911	.3933	.3193	.2915
6	.0478	.5002	.4085	.4071	.3042
7	.0962	.5407	.4123	.3877	.2524
8	.0689	.4082	.4023	.3300	.2640
9	.1875	.4725	.2821	.2426	.3250
10	.1716	.4400	.4746	.4231	.2304
11	.0813	.4656	.3082	.3436	.2830
12	.3031	.3822	.4662	.2099	.4242
13	.2874	.6039	.3935	.3173	.1385
14	.0316	.4102	.3614	.3226	.2650
15	.0805	.3935	.3111	.3447	.2569
16	.0597	.4526	.3379	.2879	.2827
17	.0688	.5038	.3428	.3651	.2774
18	.0536	.4964	.3958	.3223	.2661

Overall importance of
each dimension: .2170   .1434   .1138   .0815

Flattened Subject Weights

Subject Number	Plot Symbol	Variable 1	2	3
1	1	-2.2254	1.4793	1.5071
2	2	-.3798	-.3219	.2703
3	3	1.6469	-2.9653	-.3552
4	4	-.3287	.6447	-.1775
5	5	-.8228	.5826	-.0620
6	6	-.1913	-.1198	.6698
7	7	.4876	.0377	-.4094
8	8	-.5940	.6892	.1377
9	9	.8859	-1.0353	-1.5428
10	A	-.8160	1.0722	1.2720
11	B	-.3346	-.8769	.4752
12	C	-1.3215	1.3504	-2.9086
13	D	2.1765	.3203	-.4062
14	E	-.3463	.2040	.2149
15	F	-.3581	-.4496	1.0802
16	G	.3355	-.2120	-.6274
17	H	.4639	-.6379	.4701
18	I	.3959	.2382	-.4271

Iteration history for the 3 dimensional solution (in squared distances)

Young's S-stress formula 1 is used.

Iteration	S-stress	Improvement
0	.38002	
1	.38002	
2	.36220	.01782
3	.36088	.00132
4	.36050	.00039

Iterations stopped because
S-stress improvement is less than   .001000

Stress and squared correlation (RSQ) in distances

RSQ values are the proportion of variance of the scaled data (disparities) in the partition (row, matrix, or entire data) which is accounted for by their corresponding distances. Stress values are Kruskal's stress formula 1.

Matrix	Stress	RSQ	Matrix	Stress	RSQ
1	.323	.320	2	.216	.464
3	.217	.571	4	.153	.731
5	.236	.391	6	.216	.585
7	.173	.654	8	.214	.456
9	.234	.419	10	.269	.558
11	.219	.453	12	.226	.454
13	.252	.543	14	.222	.433
15	.225	.413	16	.246	.429
17	.183	.599	18	.352	.540

Averaged (rms) over matrices
Stress = .23655   RSQ = .50073

Configuration derived in 3 dimensions

Stimulus Coordinates

Stimulus Number	Stimulus Name	Dimension 1	2	3
1	VAR1	-1.0479	.1705	-1.2750
2	VAR2	-1.2008	.7187	-.5288
3	VAR3	-.0462	1.2340	-.8558
4	VAR4	1.3042	-.0857	1.2987
5	VAR5	1.0699	1.0402	1.0439
6	VAR6	.6237	-1.6028	.1144
7	VAR7	-1.0335	-1.0526	1.1885
8	VAR8	1.0080	-1.0003	-1.7037
9	VAR9	.6385	1.2885	.3509
10	VAR10	-1.3158	-.7106	.3669

Subject weights measure the importance of each dimension to each subject.

Squared weights sum to RSQ.

A subject with weights proportional to the average weights has a weirdness of
zero, the minimum value.
A subject with one large weight and many low weights has a weirdness near one.
A subject with exactly one positive weight has a weirdness of one,
the maximum value for nonnegative weights.

Subject Weights

Subject Number	Weird- ness	Dimension 1	2	3
1	.2913	.3677	.3978	.1632
2	.0907	.4331	.4067	.3330
3	.1833	.4929	.3620	.4434
4	.0775	.6463	.4370	.3504
5	.0872	.4032	.3800	.2901
6	.0340	.5320	.4088	.3671
7	.0767	.6031	.4303	.3244
8	.1483	.3975	.4111	.3593
9	.1180	.4488	.3140	.3447
10	.0955	.5122	.4510	.3040
11	.0845	.4592	.3484	.3476
12	.0512	.4994	.3468	.2900
13	.3118	.6363	.3164	.1958
14	.0151	.4616	.3548	.3068
15	.0554	.4276	.3728	.3021
16	.0515	.4812	.3280	.2993
17	.0861	.5125	.4187	.4012
18	.1193	.5757	.3396	.3052

Overall importance of
each dimension: .2501   .1455   .1052

440

```
Flattened Subject Weights

                        Variable
Subject    Plot       1          2
Number     Symbol
  1          1       -.3888     2.9390
  2          2       -.9641      .7274
  3          3       -.7417    -1.1133
  4          4       -.7925     -.4090
  5          5       -.8283      .9262
  6          6       -.1570     -.1986
  7          7        .6501     -.0815
  8          8      -1.5885      .8704
  9          9       -.1887     -.9871
 10          A       -.2112      .9751
 11          B       -.3563     -.4966
 12          C        .5504     -.3990
 13          D       3.0190    -1.2052
 14          E       -.0662     -.1082
 15          F       -.5649      .4948
 16          G        .4331     -.6516
 17          H       -.6334     -.1529
 18          I       1.2441    -1.1299
```

Iteration history for the 2 dimensional solution (in squared distances)

        Young's S-stress formula 1 is used.

```
     Iteration    S-stress    Improvement

        0          .49012
        1          .49012
        2          .44321       .04691
        3          .44042       .00279
        4          .44033       .00010
```

        Iterations stopped because
        S-stress improvement is less than   .001000

        Stress and squared correlation (RSQ) in distances

RSQ values are the proportion of variance of the scaled data (disparities)
in the partition (row, matrix, or entire data) which
is accounted for by their corresponding distances.
    Stress values are Kruskal's stress formula 1.

The two-dimensional solution is presented.

441

Object coordinates in two-dimensional space.

Matrix	Stress	RSQ	Matrix	Stress	RSQ
1	.358	.274	2	.297	.353
3	.302	.378	4	.237	.588
5	.308	.308	6	.282	.450
7	.247	.547	8	.302	.332
9	.320	.271	10	.280	.535
11	.299	.341	12	.301	.343
13	.292	.455	14	.302	.328
15	.290	.371	16	.311	.327
17	.281	.433	18	.370	.443

Averaged (rms) over matrices
Stress = .30043   RSQ = .39323

Configuration derived in 2 dimensions

Stimulus Coordinates

Stimulus Number	Stimulus Name	Dimension 1	2
1	VAR1	.6077	1.2221
2	VAR2	.3501	1.3025
3	VAR3	-.6334	.9673
4	VAR4	-1.1740	-.9958
5	VAR5	-1.4989	-.1782
6	VAR6	.5022	-1.3253
7	VAR7	1.4608	-.1062
8	VAR8	.3209	-1.6578
9	VAR9	-1.1906	.2491
10	VAR10	1.2552	.5224

Subject weights measure the importance of each dimension to each subject. Squared weights sum to RSQ.

A subject with weights proportional to the average weights has a weirdness of zero, the minimum value.
A subject with one large weight and many low weights has a weirdness near one.
A subject with exactly one positive weight has a weirdness of one, the maximum value for nonnegative weights.

Subject Weights

Subject Number	Weird-ness	Dimension 1	2
1	.0163	.3864	.3534
2	.0034	.4322	.4077
3	.1527	.3946	.4717
4	.0322	.5724	.5106
5	.0138	.4089	.3755
6	.0052	.4876	.4612
7	.0169	.5458	.4988
8	.0801	.4438	.3671
9	.0899	.3537	.3824
10	.0249	.5235	.5108
11	.0902	.3966	.4290
12	.0678	.4476	.3776
13	.0142	.4969	.4560
14	.0325	.4273	.3810
15	.0263	.4356	.4260
16	.0037	.4183	.3902
17	.0204	.4724	.4578
18	.1187	.5253	.4086

Overall importance of each dimension: .2094 .1838

Subject weights for each respondent.

Flattened Subject Weights

Subject Number	Plot Symbol	Variable 1
1	1	.2788
2	2	-.0368
3	3	-2.4539
4	4	.5337
5	5	.2387
6	6	-.0662
7	7	.2872
8	8	1.3014
9	9	-1.4304
10	A	-.3836
11	B	-1.4357
12	C	1.1033
13	D	.2440
14	E	.5377
15	F	-.4048
16	G	.0767
17	H	-.3112
18	I	1.9210

Derived Stimulus Configuration

Individual differences (weighted) Euclidean distan

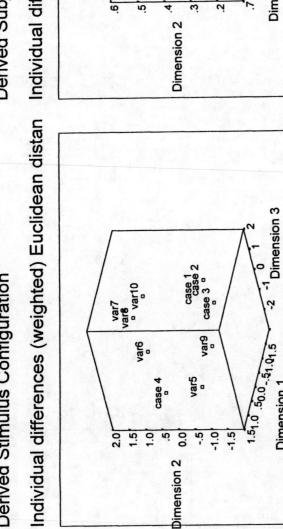

Derived Subject Weights

Individual differences (weighted) Euclidean distan

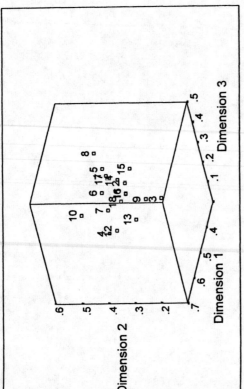

Three-dimensional results.

Scatterplot of Linear Fit

Individual differences (weighted) Euclidean

Flattened Subject Weights

Individual differences (weighted) Euclidean distan

Derived Subject Weights

Individual differences (weighted) Euclidean distan

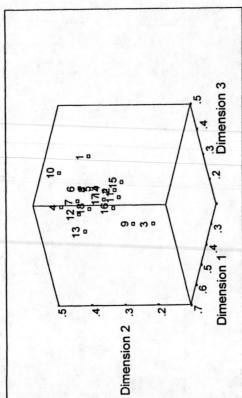

Derived Stimulus Configuration

Individual differences (weighted) Euclidean distan

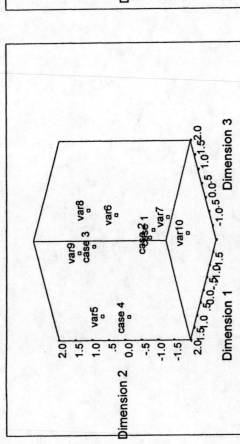

Scatterplot of Linear Fit

Individual differences (weighted) Euclidean

Flattened Subject Weights

Individual differences (weighted) Euclidean distan

447

Derived Stimulus Configuration

Individual differences (weighted) Euclidean distan

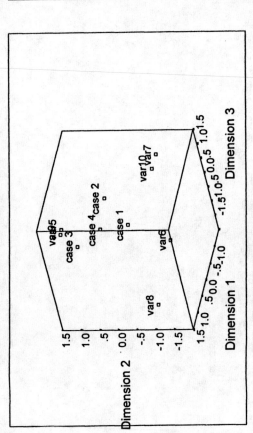

Derived Subject Weights

Individual differences (weighted) Euclidean distan

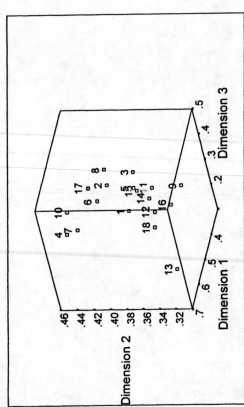

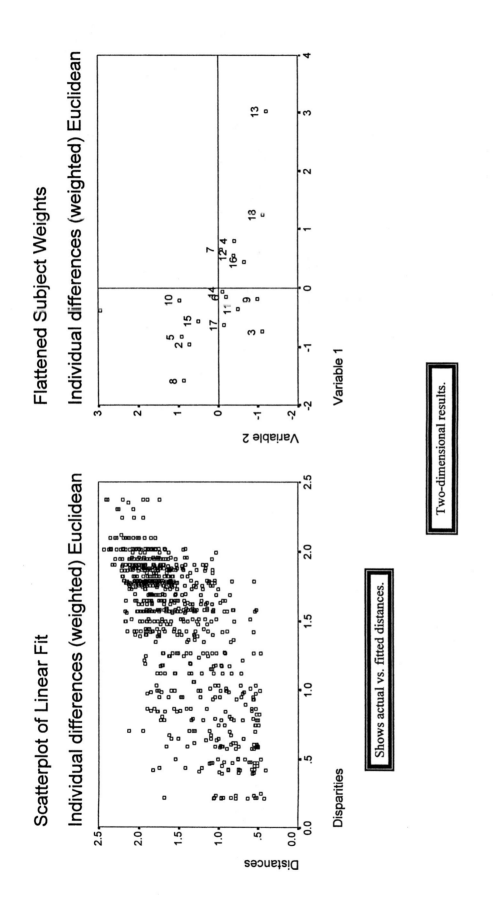

Scatterplot of Linear Fit

Individual differences (weighted) Euclidean

Flattened Subject Weights

Individual differences (weighted) Euclidean

Shows actual vs. fitted distances.

Two-dimensional results.

449

Derived Subject Weights

Individual differences (weighted) Euclidean

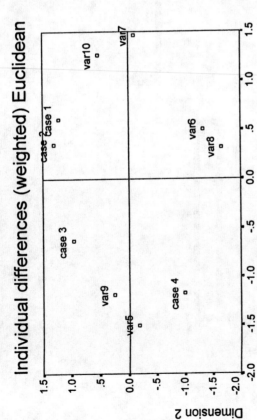

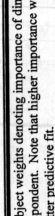

Subject weights denoting importance of dimensions to each respondent. Note that higher importance weights will give better predictive fit.

Derived Stimulus Configuration

Individual differences (weighted) Euclidean

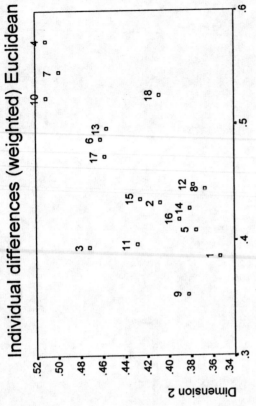

Graphical portrayal of stimuli map.

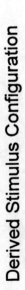

450

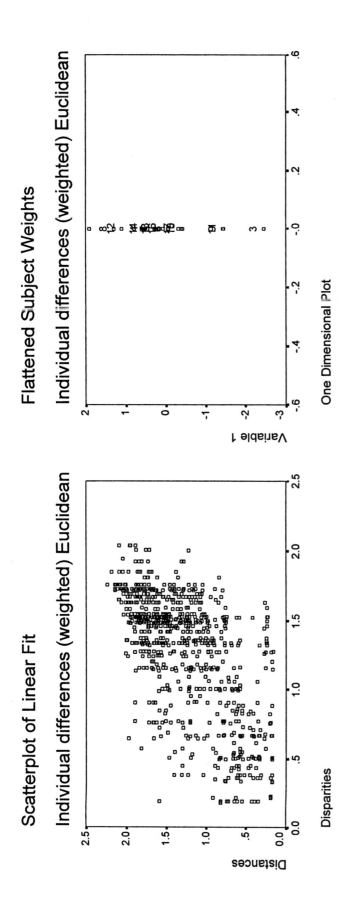

Scatterplot of Linear Fit

Individual differences (weighted) Euclidean

Flattened Subject Weights

Individual differences (weighted) Euclidean

Multidimensional Scaling: Correspondence Analysis

```
A N A C O R - VERSION 0.4
            BY
   DEPARTMENT OF DATA THEORY
UNIVERSITY OF LEIDEN, THE NETHERLANDS
```

The table to be analyzed:

	1 HATCO	2 Firm A	3 Firm B	4 Firm C	5 Firm D	6 Firm E	7 Firm F	8 Firm G	9 Firm H	10 Firm I	Margin
1	4	3	1	13	9	6	3	18	2	10	69
2	15	16	15	11	11	14	16	12	14	14	138
3	15	14	6	4	4	15	14	13	7	13	105
4	16	13	8	13	9	17	15	16	6	12	125
5	14	14	10	11	11	14	12	13	10	14	123
6	7	18	13	4	9	16	14	5	4	16	106
7	6	6	14	10	11	8	7	4	14	4	84
8	15	18	9	2	3	15	16	7	8	8	101
Margin	92	102	76	68	67	105	97	88	65	91	851

The Rowprofiles:

	1 HATCO	2 Firm A	3 Firm B	4 Firm C	5 Firm D	6 Firm E	7 Firm F	8 Firm G	9 Firm H	10 Firm I	Margin
1	.058	.043	.014	.188	.130	.087	.043	.261	.029	.145	1.000
2	.109	.116	.109	.080	.080	.101	.116	.087	.101	.101	1.000
3	.143	.133	.057	.038	.038	.143	.133	.124	.067	.124	1.000
4	.128	.104	.064	.104	.072	.136	.120	.128	.048	.096	1.000
5	.114	.114	.081	.089	.089	.114	.098	.106	.081	.114	1.000
6	.066	.170	.123	.038	.085	.151	.132	.047	.038	.151	1.000
7	.071	.071	.167	.119	.131	.095	.083	.048	.167	.048	1.000
8	.149	.178	.089	.020	.030	.149	.158	.069	.079	.079	1.000
Margin	.108	.120	.089	.080	.079	.123	.114	.103	.076	.107	

Frequency data of attribute descriptors for HATCO and competing firms.

The Columnprofiles:

	1 HATCO	2 Firm A	3 Firm B	4 Firm C	5 Firm D	6 Firm E	7 Firm F	8 Firm G	9 Firm H	10 Firm I	Margin
1	.043	.029	.013	.191	.134	.057	.031	.205	.031	.110	.081
2	.163	.157	.197	.162	.164	.133	.165	.136	.215	.154	.162
3	.163	.137	.079	.059	.060	.143	.144	.148	.108	.143	.123
4	.174	.127	.105	.191	.134	.162	.155	.182	.092	.132	.147
5	.152	.137	.132	.162	.164	.133	.124	.148	.154	.154	.145
6	.076	.176	.171	.059	.134	.152	.144	.057	.062	.176	.125
7	.065	.059	.184	.147	.164	.076	.072	.045	.215	.044	.099
8	.163	.176	.118	.029	.045	.143	.165	.080	.123	.088	.119
Margin	1.000	1.000	1.000	1.000	1.000	1.000	1.000	1.000	1.000	1.000	1.000

Dimension	Singular Value	Inertia	Proportion Explained	Cumulative Proportion
1	.27666	.07654	.531	.531
2	.21866	.04781	.332	.863
3	.12366	.01529	.106	.969
4	.05155	.00266	.018	.988
5	.02838	.00081	.006	.993
6	.02400	.00058	.004	.997
7	.01951	.00038	.003	1.000
Total		.14407	1.000	1.000

> Contains the eigenvalues (*inertia*) and cumulative percent of variation explained (*cumulative proportion*) for each dimension. A two-dimensional solution explains 86 percent of the variation; whereas, adding one more dimension only contributes an additional 10 percent.

Row Scores:

Row	Marginal Profile	Dim 1	Dim 2
1	.081	1.506	-.298
2	.162	-.081	.245
3	.123	-.202	-.502
4	.147	.204	-.245
5	.145	-.115	-.046
6	.125	-.440	-.099
7	.099	-.044	1.235
8	.119	-.676	-.285

Contribution of row points to the inertia of each dimension:

Row	Marginal Profile	Dim 1	2
1	.081	.665	.033
2	.162	.004	.045
3	.123	.018	.142
4	.147	.022	.040
5	.145	.007	.001
6	.125	.087	.006
7	.099	.001	.689
8	.119	.196	.044
		1.000	1.000

Contribution of dimensions to the inertia of each row point:

Row	Marginal Profile	Dim 1	2	Total
1	.081	.961	.030	.991
2	.162	.093	.678	.772
3	.123	.138	.677	.816
4	.147	.289	.330	.619
5	.145	.469	.058	.527
6	.125	.358	.014	.372
7	.099	.002	.989	.991
8	.119	.789	.111	.901

Column Scores:

Column	Marginal Profile	Dim 1	2
1 HATCO	.108	-.247	-.293
2 Firm A	.120	-.537	-.271
3 Firm B	.089	-.444	-.740
4 Firm C	.080	1.017	.371
5 Firm D	.079	.510	.556
6 Firm E	.123	-.237	-.235
7 Firm F	.114	-.441	-.209
8 Firm G	.103	.884	-.511
9 Firm H	.076	-.206	-.909
10 Firm I	.107	-.123	-.367

Contribution of column points to the inertia of each dimension:

Column	Marginal Profile	Dim 1	2
1 HATCO	.108	.024	.042
2 Firm A	.120	.125	.040
3 Firm B	.089	.063	.224
4 Firm C	.080	.299	.050
5 Firm D	.079	.074	.111
6 Firm E	.123	.025	.031
7 Firm F	.114	.080	.023
8 Firm G	.103	.292	.123
9 Firm H	.076	.012	.289
10 Firm I	.107	.006	.066
		1.000	1.000

Contribution of dimensions to the inertia of each column point:

Column	Marginal Profile	Dim 1	2	Total
1 HATCO	.108	.206	.228	.433
2 Firm A	.120	.772	.156	.928
3 Firm B	.089	.294	.648	.942
4 Firm C	.080	.882	.093	.975
5 Firm D	.079	.445	.418	.863
6 Firm E	.123	.456	.356	.812
7 Firm F	.114	.810	.144	.954
8 Firm G	.103	.762	.201	.963
9 Firm H	.076	.049	.748	.797
10 Firm I	.107	.055	.390	.446

Variances and Correlation Matrix of the singular values:

Dim	Variances	Correlations between dimensions	
1	.001	1.000	
2	.001	-.030	1.000

Variances and Correlation Matrix of scores of Row   1

Dim	Variances	Correlations between dimensions	
1	.039	1.000	
2	.287	.632	1.000

Variances and Correlation Matrix of scores of Row   2

```
Dim Variances        Correlations between dimensions
 1    .033            1.000
 2    .034             .079   1.000
```

Variances and Correlation Matrix of scores of Row   3

```
Dim Variances        Correlations between dimensions
 1    .072            1.000
 2    .041            -.329   1.000
```

Variances and Correlation Matrix of scores of Row   4

```
Dim Variances        Correlations between dimensions
 1    .042            1.000
 2    .037             .205   1.000
```

Variances and Correlation Matrix of scores of Row   5

```
Dim Variances        Correlations between dimensions
 1    .029            1.000
 2    .036            -.023   1.000
```

Variances and Correlation Matrix of scores of Row   6

```
Dim Variances        Correlations between dimensions
 1    .041            1.000
 2    .108            -.061   1.000
```

Variances and Correlation Matrix of scores of Row   7

```
Dim Variances        Correlations between dimensions
 1    .309            1.000
 2    .026            -.081   1.000
```

Variances and Correlation Matrix of scores of Row   8

```
Dim Variances        Correlations between dimensions
 1    .036            1.000
 2    .089            -.501   1.000
```

Variances and Correlation Matrix of scores of Column   1   HATCO

Dim Variances   Correlations between dimensions
 1   .043   1.000
 2   .067   -.135   1.000

Variances and Correlation Matrix of scores of Column   2   Firm A

Dim Variances   Correlations between dimensions
 1   .031   1.000
 2   .063   -.371   1.000

Variances and Correlation Matrix of scores of Column   3   Firm B

Dim Variances   Correlations between dimensions
 1   .107   1.000
 2   .048   .673   1.000

Variances and Correlation Matrix of scores of Column   4   Firm C

Dim Variances   Correlations between dimensions
 1   .060   1.000
 2   .142   -.725   1.000

Variances and Correlation Matrix of scores of Column   5   Firm D

Dim Variances   Correlations between dimensions
 1   .093   1.000
 2   .064   -.607   1.000

Variances and Correlation Matrix of scores of Column   6   Firm E

Dim Variances   Correlations between dimensions
 1   .034   1.000
 2   .038   -.149   1.000

Variances and Correlation Matrix of scores of Column   7   Firm F

Dim Variances   Correlations between dimensions
 1   .023   1.000
 2   .043   -.445   1.000

Variances and Correlation Matrix of scores of Column 8 Firm G

Dim	Variances	Correlations between dimensions	
1	.096	1.000	
2	.119	.721	1.000

Variances and Correlation Matrix of scores of Column 9 Firm H

Dim	Variances	Correlations between dimensions	
1	.162	1.000	
2	.097	.206	1.000

Variances and Correlation Matrix of scores of Column 10 Firm I

Dim	Variances	Correlations between dimensions	
1	.073	1.000	
2	.049	.087	1.000

The data-matrix permuted according to the scores in dimension: 1

	2 Firm A	3 Firm B	7 Firm F	1 HATCO	6 Firm E	9 Firm H	10 Firm I	5 Firm D	8 Firm G	4 Firm C	Margin
8	18	9	16	15	15	8	8	3	7	2	101
6	18	13	14	7	16	4	16	9	5	4	106
3	14	6	14	15	15	7	13	4	13	4	105
2	16	15	16	15	14	14	14	11	12	11	138
7	6	14	7	6	8	14	4	11	4	10	84
5	14	10	12	14	14	10	14	11	13	11	123
4	13	8	15	16	17	6	12	9	16	13	125
1	3	1	3	4	6	2	10	9	18	13	69
Margin	102	76	97	92	105	65	91	67	88	68	851

The data-matrix permuted according to the scores in dimension: 2

	8 Firm G	10 Firm I	1 HATCO	2 Firm A	6 Firm E	7 Firm F	4 Firm C	5 Firm D	3 Firm B	9 Firm H	Margin
3	13	13	15	14	15	14	4	4	6	7	105
1	18	10	4	3	6	3	13	9	1	2	69
8	7	8	15	18	15	16	2	3	9	8	101
4	16	12	16	13	17	15	13	9	8	6	125
6	5	16	7	18	16	14	4	9	13	4	106
5	13	14	14	14	14	12	11	11	10	10	123
2	12	14	15	16	14	16	11	11	15	14	138
7	4	4	6	6	8	7	10	11	14	14	84
Margin	88	91	92	102	105	97	68	67	76	65	851

458

Firm Scores

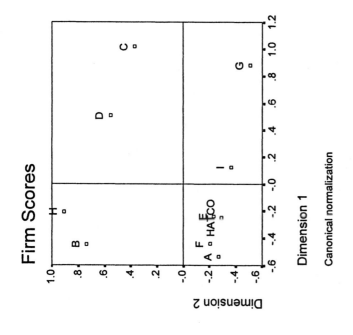

Attribute Scores

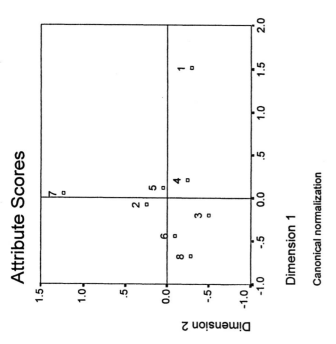

459

The graph illustrates the relative
proximities of both firms and attributes.

Attribute and Firm Scores

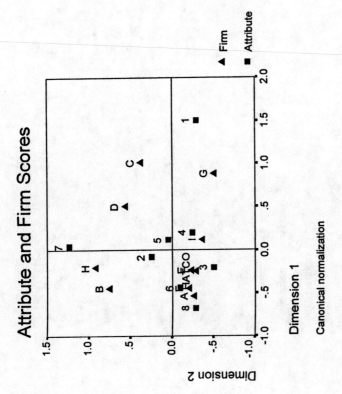

Dimension 1

Canonical normalization

▲ Firm

■ Attribute

CHAPTER 11:

STRUCTURAL EQUATION MODELING

This section of the instructor's manual contains copies of the actual printouts from the LISREL 8 statistical analysis program (see Chapter One of the text for a complete reference). The printouts contain examples of the analyses discussed in the text using the HATCO database (confirmatory factor analysis) and an additional database for estimation of the structural model (see Chapter Eleven for a complete description of this additional database).

Each of the printouts is annotated with comments to aid in the interpretation of the results. These suggestions are typed in the margins next to the appropriate data. If you wish to provide students with their own copies of the output without these comments, the output are provided on the computer diskette accompanying the instructor's manual.

An example of confirmatory factor analysis and structural model estimation is included in this section. A brief description follows:

Confirmatory Factor Analysis: A confirmatory factor analysis is performed on six of the attribute ratings (X_1 to X_7, X_5 is excluded) with two hypothesized dimensions.

Structural Model Estimation: A structural model is hypothesized using additional data gathered by HATCO. A number of determining factors, grouped in three basic areas (exogenous constructs) are hypothesized to affect usage levels, which in turn relates to satisfaction.

[NOTE: This is a completely different database form the HATCO data, even though several of the variables are similar.]

Structural Equation Modeling: Confirmatory Factor Analysis

```
        WINDOWS  L I S R E L  8.12a
                     BY
        KARL G JORESKOG AND DAG SORBOM


     This program is published exclusively by
        Scientific Software International, Inc.
        1525 East 53rd Street - Suite 530
        Chicago, Illinois 60615, U.S.A.
     Voice: (800)247-6113, (312)684-4920, Fax: (312)684-4979
    Copyright by Scientific Software International, Inc., 1981-94.
Partial copyright by WATCOM Group, Inc., 1993 and MicroHelp, Inc., 1993.
       Use of this program is subject to the terms specified in the
                 Universal Copyright Convention.


The following lines were read from file C:\5THEDI~1\CHAP11\HATCO2.LS8:

title 'CONFIRMATORY FACTOR ANALYSIS -- RESPECIFIED'
DA NI=7 NO=100 MA=KM
KM  FU FI=C:\5thedi~1\chap11\HATCOR.TXT FO=5
(7F9.0)
SELECT
1 2 3 4  6 7 /
MO NX=6 NK=2 PH=ST TD=SY,FI
LA
'DelvSpd' 'PriceLvl' 'PriceFlx' 'MfgImage'
'Service' 'SalesImg' 'Quality'
LK
'Strategy' 'Image'
PA LX
1 (1 0)
1 (1 0)
1 (1 0)
1 (0 1)
1 (0 1)
1 (1 0)
FR TD(1,1) TD (2,2) TD(3,3) TD(5,5) TD(6,6)
VA .005 TD(4,4)
OU  SS TV RS MI ND=3

'CONFIRMATORY FACTOR ANALYSIS -- RESPECIFIED'

           NUMBER OF INPUT VARIABLES    7
           NUMBER OF Y - VARIABLES      0
           NUMBER OF X - VARIABLES      6
           NUMBER OF ETA - VARIABLES    0
           NUMBER OF KSI - VARIABLES    2
           NUMBER OF OBSERVATIONS     100
```

Revised model which sets measurement error of variable X_4 to .005 to remedy offending estimate.

'CONFIRMATORY FACTOR ANALYSIS -- RESPECIFIED'

CORRELATION MATRIX TO BE ANALYZED

	DelvSpd	PriceLvl	PriceFlx	MfgImage	SalesImg	Quality
DelvSpd	1.000					
PriceLvl	-0.349	1.000				
PriceFlx	0.509	-0.487	1.000			
MfgImage	0.050	0.272	-0.116	1.000		
SalesImg	0.077	0.186	-0.034	0.788	1.000	
Quality	-0.483	0.470	-0.448	0.200	0.177	1.000

> **Input data matrix: Correlations**

'CONFIRMATORY FACTOR ANALYSIS -- RESPECIFIED'

PARAMETER SPECIFICATIONS

LAMBDA-X

	Strategy	Image
DelvSpd	1	0
PriceLvl	2	0
PriceFlx	3	0
MfgImage	0	4
SalesImg	0	5
Quality	6	0

PHI

	Strategy	Image
Strategy	0	
Image	7	0

THETA-DELTA

DelvSpd	PriceLvl	PriceFlx	MfgImage	SalesImg	Quality
8	9	10	0	11	12

> **Indicators of estimated parameters. Note that the error term (diagonal of theta delta) for *MfgImage* is not estimated, set to .005.**

'CONFIRMATORY FACTOR ANALYSIS -- RESPECIFIED'
Number of Iterations = 7

LISREL ESTIMATES (MAXIMUM LIKELIHOOD)

LAMBDA-X

	Strategy	Image
DelvSpd	0.643 (0.103) 6.263	- -
PriceLvl	-0.654 (0.102) -6.381	- -
PriceFlx	0.718 (0.101) 7.118	- -
MfgImage	- -	0.997 (0.071) 14.001
SalesImg	- -	0.790 (0.083) 9.467
Quality	-0.692 (0.101) -6.821	- -

> Estimated factor loadings followed by the standard error (in parentheses) and t-values on the two hypothesized factors. All factor loadings are statistically significant (prob. of .05 = 1.96)

PHI

	Strategy	Image
Strategy	1.000	
Image	-0.202 (0.110) -1.826	1.000

> Correlation among factors estimated to be -.202.

THETA-DELTA

DelvSpd	PriceLvl	PriceFlx	MfgImage	SalesImg	Quality
0.586 (0.106) 5.550	0.573 (0.105) 5.463	0.484 (0.101) 4.769	0.005	0.376 (0.054) 6.977	0.521 (0.102) 5.081

SQUARED MULTIPLE CORRELATIONS FOR X - VARIABLES

DelvSpd	PriceLvl	PriceFlx	MfgImage	SalesImg	Quality
0.414	0.427	0.516	0.995	0.624	0.479

GOODNESS OF FIT STATISTICS

CHI-SQUARE WITH 9 DEGREES OF FREEDOM = 15.745 (P = 0.0724)
ESTIMATED NON-CENTRALITY PARAMETER (NCP) = 6.745
90 PERCENT CONFIDENCE INTERVAL FOR NCP = (0.0 ; 21.878)

MINIMUM FIT FUNCTION VALUE = 0.159
POPULATION DISCREPANCY FUNCTION VALUE (F0) = 0.0681
90 PERCENT CONFIDENCE INTERVAL FOR F0 = (0.0 ; 0.221)
ROOT MEAN SQUARE ERROR OF APPROXIMATION (RMSEA) = 0.0870
90 PERCENT CONFIDENCE INTERVAL FOR RMSEA = (0.0 ; 0.157)
P-VALUE FOR TEST OF CLOSE FIT (RMSEA < 0.05) = 0.178

EXPECTED CROSS-VALIDATION INDEX (ECVI) = 0.401
90 PERCENT CONFIDENCE INTERVAL FOR ECVI = (0.333 ; 0.554)
ECVI FOR SATURATED MODEL = 0.424
ECVI FOR INDEPENDENCE MODEL = 2.263

CHI-SQUARE FOR INDEPENDENCE MODEL WITH 15 DEGREES OF FREEDOM = 212.033
INDEPENDENCE AIC = 224.033
MODEL AIC = 39.745
SATURATED AIC = 42.000
INDEPENDENCE CAIC = 245.664
MODEL CAIC = 83.007
SATURATED CAIC = 117.709

ROOT MEAN SQUARE RESIDUAL (RMR) = 0.0750
STANDARDIZED RMR = 0.0750
GOODNESS OF FIT INDEX (GFI) = 0.949
ADJUSTED GOODNESS OF FIT INDEX (AGFI) = 0.881
PARSIMONY GOODNESS OF FIT INDEX (PGFI) = 0.407

NORMED FIT INDEX (NFI) = 0.926
NON-NORMED FIT INDEX (NNFI) = 0.943
PARSIMONY NORMED FIT INDEX (PNFI) = 0.555
COMPARATIVE FIT INDEX (CFI) = 0.966
INCREMENTAL FIT INDEX (IFI) = 0.967
RELATIVE FIT INDEX (RFI) = 0.876

CRITICAL N (CN) = 137.232

Overall model fit statistics:

Nonsignificance of chi-square indicates that the observed and estimated correlation matrices are not significantly different (i.e., nonsignificance indicates good model fit).

The output also contains many other absolute, as well as, incremental and parsimonious fit measures. Throughout the fit indices, acceptable support is indicated.

465

'CONFIRMATORY FACTOR ANALYSIS -- RESPECIFIED'

FITTED COVARIANCE MATRIX

	DelvSpd	PriceLvl	PriceFlx	MfgImage	SalesImg	Quality
DelvSpd	1.000					
PriceLvl	-0.421	1.000				
PriceFlx	0.462	-0.470	1.000			
MfgImage	-0.129	0.132	-0.145	1.000		
SalesImg	-0.103	0.104	-0.115	0.788	1.000	
Quality	-0.445	0.453	-0.497	0.139	0.110	1.000

FITTED RESIDUALS

	DelvSpd	PriceLvl	PriceFlx	MfgImage	SalesImg	Quality
DelvSpd	0.000					
PriceLvl	0.071	0.000				
PriceFlx	0.047	-0.018	0.000			
MfgImage	0.180	0.141	0.028	0.000		
SalesImg	0.180	0.082	0.080	0.000	0.000	
Quality	-0.037	0.017	0.049	0.061	0.067	0.000

SUMMARY STATISTICS FOR FITTED RESIDUALS
SMALLEST FITTED RESIDUAL =   -0.037
  MEDIAN FITTED RESIDUAL =   0.028
 LARGEST FITTED RESIDUAL =   0.180

STEMLEAF PLOT
- 0|420000000000
  0|23
  0|5567788
  1|4
  1|88

STANDARDIZED RESIDUALS

	DelvSpd	PriceLvl	PriceFlx	MfgImage	SalesImg	Quality
DelvSpd	0.000					
PriceLvl	1.826	0.000				
PriceFlx	1.535	-0.595	0.000			
MfgImage	2.707	2.157	0.508	0.000		
SalesImg	2.234	1.028	1.067	0.000	0.000	
Quality	-1.091	0.523	1.959	1.011	0.868	0.000

SUMMARY STATISTICS FOR STANDARDIZED RESIDUALS
SMALLEST STANDARDIZED RESIDUAL =   -1.091
  MEDIAN STANDARDIZED RESIDUAL =   0.523
 LARGEST STANDARDIZED RESIDUAL =   2.707

Standardized residuals of the predicted correlation matrix. Values that exceed ±2.5 are considered significant. In this case, one standardized residual (between *MfgImage* and *DelvSpd*) exceeds this threshold value.

466

STEMLEAF PLOT
 - 1 | 1
 - 0 | 60000000000
   0 | 559
   1 | 00158
   2 | 0227
LARGEST POSITIVE STANDARDIZED RESIDUALS
RESIDUAL FOR MfgImage AND DelvSpd   2.707

467

'CONFIRMATORY FACTOR ANALYSIS -- RESPECIFIED'
QPLOT OF STANDARDIZED RESIDUALS

N O R M A L   Q U A N T I L E S

STANDARDIZED RESIDUALS

Plot of residuals similar to normal probability plot found in regression. Values should fall along the diagonal.

'CONFIRMATORY FACTOR ANALYSIS -- RESPECIFIED'
MODIFICATION INDICES AND EXPECTED CHANGE

MODIFICATION INDICES FOR LAMBDA-X

	Strategy	Image
DelvSpd	--	7.359
PriceLvl	--	4.634
PriceFlx	--	0.269
MfgImage	0.321	--
SalesImg	0.321	--
Quality	--	1.029

EXPECTED CHANGE FOR LAMBDA-X

	Strategy	Image
DelvSpd	--	0.242
PriceLvl	--	0.192
PriceFlx	--	0.045
MfgImage	-0.052	--
SalesImg	0.041	--
Quality	--	0.089

STANDARDIZED EXPECTED CHANGE FOR LAMBDA-X

	Strategy	Image
DelvSpd	--	0.242
PriceLvl	--	0.192
PriceFlx	--	0.045
MfgImage	-0.052	--
SalesImg	0.041	--
Quality	--	0.089

NO NON-ZERO MODIFICATION INDICES FOR PHI

MODIFICATION INDICES FOR THETA-DELTA

	DelvSpd	PriceLvl	PriceFlx	MfgImage	SalesImg	Quality
DelvSpd	--					
PriceLvl	3.333	--				
PriceFlx	2.357	0.355	--			
MfgImage	1.712	2.182	0.216	0.321		
SalesImg	0.182	0.046	0.927	0.321	--	
Quality	1.191	0.274	3.837	0.038	1.009	--

EXPECTED CHANGE FOR THETA-DELTA

	DelvSpd	PriceLvl	PriceFlx	MfgImage	SalesImg	Quality
DelvSpd	- -					
PriceLvl	0.158	- -				
PriceFlx	0.144	-0.057	- -			
MfgImage	0.068	0.076	-0.023	-0.245		
SalesImg	0.022	-0.011	0.047	0.194	- -	
Quality	-0.099	0.048	0.198	-0.010	0.050	- -

MAXIMUM MODIFICATION INDEX IS   7.36 FOR ELEMENT (1, 2) OF LAMBDA-X

'CONFIRMATORY FACTOR ANALYSIS -- RESPECIFIED'
STANDARDIZED SOLUTION

LAMBDA-X

	Strategy	Image
DelvSpd	0.643	- -
PriceLvl	-0.654	- -
PriceFlx	0.718	- -
MfgImage	- -	0.997
SalesImg	- -	0.790
Quality	-0.692	- -

PHI

	Strategy	Image
Strategy	1.000	
Image	-0.202	1.000

THE PROBLEM USED   5384 BYTES (= 0.5% OF AVAILABLE WORKSPACE)

          TIME USED: 0.3 SECONDS

Standardized parameter estimates
similar to standardized coefficients in
other multivariate methods (e.g.,
regression and discriminant analysis).

470

Structural Equation Modeling: Estimating a Structural Model

```
              WINDOWS  L I S R E L  8.12a
                          BY
              KARL G JORESKOG AND DAG SORBOM


           This program is published exclusively by
              Scientific Software International, Inc.
              1525 East 53rd Street - Suite 530
              Chicago, Illinois 60615, U.S.A.
    Voice: (800)247-6113, (312)684-4920, Fax: (312)684-4979
    Copyright by Scientific Software International, Inc., 1981-94.
Partial copyright by WATCOM Group, Inc., 1993 and MicroHelp, Inc., 1993.
    Use of this program is subject to the terms specified in the
                  Universal Copyright Convention.


The following lines were read from file C:\5THEDI~1\CHAP11\STRUC1.LS8:

title 'CAUSAL MODEL WITH MULTIPLE INDICATORS'
DA  NI=15 NO=136 MA=KM
KM  FU FI=C:\5thedi-1\chap11\STRUC1.TXT FO=5
(8F6.4/7F6.4)
MO NX=13 NK=3 NY=2 NE=2 GA=FU,FI PS=SY,FI C
BE=FU,FI TE=SY,FI PH=SY,FR
LA
'USAGE' 'SATISFAC' 'PRODQUAL' 'INVACCUR'
'TECHSUPT' 'NEWPROD' 'DELIVERY'
'MKTLEADR' 'PRDVALUE' 'LOWPRICE' 'NEGOTIAT'
'MUTUALTY' 'INTEGRTY' 'FLEXBLTY' 'PROBRES'
LK
'FIRMPROD' 'PRICEFAC' 'RELATFAC'
LE
'USAGE' 'SATISFAC'
PA LX
1 (0 0 0)
1 (1 0 0)
1 (1 0 0)
1 (1 0 0)
1 (1 0 0)
1 (1 0 0)
1 (0 1 0)
1 (0 1 0)
1 (0 0 0)
1 (0 0 1)
1 (0 0 1)
1 (0 0 1)
```

```
PA GA
1 (1 1 1)
1 (0 0 0)
PA BE
1 (0 0)
1 (1 0)
PA PHI
1
1 1
1 1 1
PA PS
1
0 1
VA 1 LX(1,1) LX(7,2) LX(10,3) LY(1,1) LY(2,2)
VA 0.00 TE(2,2) TE(1,1)
OU SE TV RS SS MI ND=3 AD=OFF
```

Sets values of 1.0 for:
Three exogenous indicators to ensure scale invariance for constructs and
Single indicators for two endogenous constructs

'CAUSAL MODEL WITH MULTIPLE INDICATORS'

```
                    NUMBER OF INPUT VARIABLES 15
                    NUMBER OF Y - VARIABLES    2
                    NUMBER OF X - VARIABLES   13
                    NUMBER OF ETA - VARIABLES  2
                    NUMBER OF KSI - VARIABLES  3
                    NUMBER OF OBSERVATIONS   136
```

'CAUSAL MODEL WITH MULTIPLE INDICATORS'

CORRELATION MATRIX TO BE ANALYZED

	USAGE	SATISFAC	PRODQUAL	INVACCUR	TECHSUPT	NEWPROD
USAGE	1.000					
SATISFAC	0.411	1.000				
PRODQUAL	0.288	0.168	1.000			
INVACCUR	0.359	0.158	0.784	1.000		
TECHSUPT	0.268	0.141	0.676	0.637	1.000	
NEWPROD	0.212	0.081	0.581	0.622	0.627	1.000
DELIVERY	0.250	0.060	0.632	0.644	0.538	0.699
MKTLEADR	0.305	0.127	0.690	0.667	0.551	0.625
PRDVALUE	0.328	0.133	0.293	0.263	0.336	0.290
LOWPRICE	0.268	0.046	0.184	0.124	0.230	0.260
NEGOTIAT	0.142	0.104	0.289	0.249	0.299	0.219
MUTUALTY	0.329	0.062	0.327	0.292	0.112	0.292
INTEGRTY	0.519	0.077	0.413	0.385	0.265	0.346
FLEXBLTY	0.510	0.090	0.330	0.272	0.192	0.151
PROBRES	0.341	0.173	0.154	0.173	0.182	0.153

CORRELATION MATRIX TO BE ANALYZED

	DELIVERY	MKTLEADR	PRDVALUE	LOWPRICE	NEGOTIAT	MUTUALTY
DELIVERY	1.000					
MKTLEADR	0.692	1.000				
PRDVALUE	0.206	0.174	1.000			
LOWPRICE	0.110	0.254	0.301	1.000		
NEGOTIAT	0.155	0.299	0.307	0.676	1.000	
MUTUALTY	0.326	0.253	0.179	0.114	0.173	1.000
INTEGRTY	0.259	0.262	0.347	0.225	0.205	0.410
FLEXBLTY	0.210	0.225	0.348	0.259	0.162	0.555
PROBRES	0.107	0.102	0.272	0.052	0.093	0.202

CORRELATION MATRIX TO BE ANALYZED

	INTEGRTY	FLEXBLTY	PROBRES
INTEGRTY	1.000		
FLEXBLTY	0.532	1.000	
PROBRES	0.411	0.425	1.000

'CAUSAL MODEL WITH MULTIPLE INDICATORS'

PARAMETER SPECIFICATIONS

LAMBDA-X

	FIRMPROD	PRICEFAC	RELATFAC
PRODQUAL	0	0	0
INVACCUR	1	0	0
TECHSUPT	2	0	0
NEWPROD	3	0	0
DELIVERY	4	0	0
MKTLEADR	5	0	0
PRDVALUE	0	0	0
LOWPRICE	0	6	0
NEGOTIAT	0	7	0
MUTUALTY	0	0	0
INTEGRTY	0	0	8
FLEXBLTY	0	0	9
PROBRES	0	0	10

BETA

	USAGE	SATISFAC
USAGE	0	0
SATISFAC	11	0

Measurement model for exogenous constructs. Note one indicator per construct (*PRODQUAL*, *PRDVALUE*, and *MUTUALITY*) is not estimated to ensure scale invariance.

Specifies structural relationship of *USAGE* predicting *SATISFAC*.

473

```
GAMMA

           FIRMPROD   PRICEFAC   RELATFAC
           --------   --------   --------
USAGE         12         13         14
SATISFAC       0          0          0
```

USAGE predicted by all three exogenous factors.

```
PHI

           FIRMPROD   PRICEFAC   RELATFAC
           --------   --------   --------
FIRMPROD      15
PRICEFAC      16         17
RELATFAC      18         19         20
```

All three exogenous factors are correlated.

```
PSI

            USAGE    SATISFAC
            -----    --------
             21         22


THETA-DELTA

  PRODQUAL   INVACCUR   TECHSUPT   NEWPROD   DELIVERY   MKTLEADR
  --------   --------   --------   -------   --------   --------
    23         24         25         26        27         28


THETA-DELTA

  PRDVALUE   LOWPRICE   NEGOTIAT   MUTUALTY   INTEGRTY   FLEXBLTY
  --------   --------   --------   --------   --------   --------
    29         30         31         32         33         34


THETA-DELTA

   PROBRES
   -------
     35
```

'CAUSAL MODEL WITH MULTIPLE INDICATORS'
Number of Iterations = 23

LISREL ESTIMATES (MAXIMUM LIKELIHOOD)

LAMBDA-Y

	USAGE	SATISFAC
USAGE	1.000	- -
SATISFAC	- -	1.000

LAMBDA-X

	FIRMPROD	PRICEFAC	RELATFAC
PRODQUAL	1.000	- -	- -
INVACCUR	0.994 (0.077) 12.855	- -	- -
TECHSUPT	0.866 (0.084) 10.297	- -	- -
NEWPROD	0.880 (0.083) 10.550	- -	- -
DELIVERY	0.905 (0.082) 11.020	- -	- -
MKTLEADR	0.931 (0.081) 11.524	- -	- -
PRDVALUE	- -	1.000	- -
LOWPRICE	- -	2.010 (0.481) 4.181	- -
NEGOTIAT	- -	2.032 (0.487) 4.169	- -

475

MUTUALTY	--	--	1.000
INTEGRTY	--	--	1.209
			(0.194)
			6.216
FLEXBLTY	--	--	1.303
			(0.202)
			6.447
PROBRES	--	--	0.838
			(0.175)
			4.786

BETA

	USAGE	SATISFAC
	-------	--------
USAGE	--	--
SATISFAC	0.411	--
	(0.078)	
	5.241	

GAMMA

	FIRMPROD	PRICEFAC	RELATFAC
	--------	--------	--------
USAGE	0.065	0.095	1.020
	(0.104)	(0.221)	(0.204)
	0.621	0.428	4.987
SATISFAC	--	--	--

COVARIANCE MATRIX OF ETA AND KSI

	USAGE	SATISFAC	FIRMPROD	PRICEFAC	RELATFAC
	-----	--------	--------	--------	--------
USAGE	1.000				
SATISFAC	0.411	1.000			
FIRMPROD	0.307	0.126	0.744		
PRICEFAC	0.111	0.046	0.124	0.163	
RELATFAC	0.395	0.162	0.242	0.086	0.364

> *USAGE* is a significant predictor of satisfaction.

> Only *RELATFAC* is a significant predictor of *USAGE*.

PHI

	FIRMPROD	PRICEFAC	RELATFAC
	--------	--------	--------
FIRMPROD	0.744		
	(0.121)		
	6.159		
PRICEFAC	0.124	0.163	
	(0.045)	(0.074)	
	2.724	2.209	
RELATFAC	0.242	0.086	0.364
	(0.065)	(0.035)	(0.103)
	3.746	2.489	3.521

Correlations among exogenous constructs. All are significantly correlated.

PSI

	USAGE	SATISFAC
	--------	--------
	0.567	0.831
	(0.082)	(0.101)
	6.897	8.216

SQUARED MULTIPLE CORRELATIONS FOR STRUCTURAL EQUATIONS

USAGE	SATISFAC
--------	--------
0.433	0.169

Coefficient of determination for two structural equations.

SQUARED MULTIPLE CORRELATIONS FOR Y - VARIABLES

USAGE	SATISFAC
--------	--------
1.000	1.000

Note: recall that the single indicators for the two endogenous constructs were set to 1.0.

THETA-DELTA

PRODQUAL	INVACCUR	TECHSUPT	NEWPROD	DELIVERY	MKTLEADR
--------	--------	--------	-------	--------	--------
0.256	0.265	0.442	0.424	0.390	0.355
(0.041)	(0.042)	(0.060)	(0.058)	(0.055)	(0.051)
6.171	6.267	7.337	7.269	7.127	6.948

THETA-DELTA

	PRDVALUE	LOWPRICE	NEGOTIAT	MUTUALTY	INTEGRTY	FLEXBLTY
	--------	--------	--------	--------	--------	--------
	0.837	0.342	0.327	0.636	0.469	0.382
	(0.107)	(0.104)	(0.106)	(0.089)	(0.077)	(0.073)
	7.843	3.273	3.092	7.179	6.104	5.220

THETA-DELTA

	PROBRES

	0.744
	(0.098)
	7.600

SQUARED MULTIPLE CORRELATIONS FOR X - VARIABLES

	PRODQUAL	INVACCUR	TECHSUPT	NEWPROD	DELIVERY	MKTLEADR
	--------	--------	--------	--------	--------	--------
	0.744	0.735	0.558	0.576	0.610	0.645

SQUARED MULTIPLE CORRELATIONS FOR X - VARIABLES

	PRDVALUE	LOWPRICE	NEGOTIAT	MUTUALTY	INTEGRTY	FLEXBLTY
	--------	--------	--------	--------	--------	--------
	0.163	0.658	0.673	0.364	0.531	0.618

SQUARED MULTIPLE CORRELATIONS FOR X - VARIABLES

	PROBRES

	0.256

GOODNESS OF FIT STATISTICS

CHI-SQUARE WITH 85 DEGREES OF FREEDOM = 178.714 (P = .12407733D-07)
ESTIMATED NON-CENTRALITY PARAMETER (NCP) = 93.714

MINIMUM FIT FUNCTION VALUE = 1.324
POPULATION DISCREPANCY FUNCTION VALUE (F0) = 0.694
ROOT MEAN SQUARE ERROR OF APPROXIMATION (RMSEA) = 0.0904
P-VALUE FOR TEST OF CLOSE FIT (RMSEA < 0.05) = 0.000388

EXPECTED CROSS-VALIDATION INDEX (ECVI) = 1.842
ECVI FOR SATURATED MODEL = 1.778
ECVI FOR INDEPENDENCE MODEL = 7.927

A measure of the amount of variation accounted for each variable by its particular factor.

Overall model fit statistics.

478

CHI-SQUARE FOR INDEPENDENCE MODEL WITH 105 DEGREES OF FREEDOM = 1040.194

INDEPENDENCE AIC = 1070.194

MODEL AIC = 248.714

SATURATED AIC = 240.000

INDEPENDENCE CAIC = 1128.883

MODEL CAIC = 385.657

SATURATED CAIC = 709.519

ROOT MEAN SQUARE RESIDUAL (RMR) = 0.0759

STANDARDIZED RMR = 0.0759

GOODNESS OF FIT INDEX (GFI) = 0.865

ADJUSTED GOODNESS OF FIT INDEX (AGFI) = 0.810

PARSIMONY GOODNESS OF FIT INDEX (PGFI) = 0.613

NORMED FIT INDEX (NFI) = 0.828

NON-NORMED FIT INDEX (NNFI) = 0.876

PARSIMONY NORMED FIT INDEX (PNFI) = 0.670

COMPARATIVE FIT INDEX (CFI) = 0.900

INCREMENTAL FIT INDEX (IFI) = 0.902

RELATIVE FIT INDEX (RFI) = 0.788

CRITICAL N (CN) = 90.318

CONFIDENCE LIMITS COULD NOT BE COMPUTED DUE TO TOO SMALL P-VALUE FOR CHI-SQUARE

'CAUSAL MODEL WITH MULTIPLE INDICATORS'

FITTED COVARIANCE MATRIX

	USAGE	SATISFAC	PRODQUAL	INVACCUR	TECHSUPT	NEWPROD
USAGE	1.000					
SATISFAC	0.411	1.000				
PRODQUAL	0.307	0.126	1.000			
INVACCUR	0.305	0.125	0.739	1.000		
TECHSUPT	0.266	0.109	0.645	0.641	1.000	
NEWPROD	0.270	0.111	0.655	0.651	0.567	1.000
DELIVERY	0.278	0.114	0.673	0.669	0.583	0.593
MKTLEADR	0.285	0.117	0.693	0.688	0.600	0.610
PRDVALUE	0.111	0.046	0.124	0.123	0.107	0.109
LOWPRICE	0.223	0.092	0.249	0.247	0.215	0.219
NEGOTIAT	0.226	0.093	0.251	0.250	0.218	0.221
MUTUALTY	0.395	0.162	0.242	0.241	0.210	0.213
INTEGRTY	0.477	0.196	0.293	0.291	0.253	0.258
FLEXBLTY	0.514	0.212	0.315	0.314	0.273	0.278
PROBRES	0.331	0.136	0.203	0.202	0.176	0.179

FITTED COVARIANCE MATRIX

	DELIVERY	MKTLEADR	PRDVALUE	LOWPRICE	NEGOTIAT	MUTUALTY
DELIVERY	1.000					
MKTLEADR	0.627	1.000				
PRDVALUE	0.112	0.115	1.000			
LOWPRICE	0.225	0.231	0.328	1.000		
NEGOTIAT	0.228	0.234	0.331	0.666	1.000	
MUTUALTY	0.219	0.225	0.086	0.173	0.175	1.000
INTEGRTY	0.265	0.272	0.104	0.209	0.211	0.440
FLEXBLTY	0.286	0.294	0.112	0.225	0.228	0.474
PROBRES	0.184	0.189	0.072	0.145	0.147	0.305

FITTED COVARIANCE MATRIX

	INTEGRTY	FLEXBLTY	PROBRES
INTEGRTY	1.000		
FLEXBLTY	0.573	1.000	
PROBRES	0.369	0.397	1.000

FITTED RESIDUALS

	USAGE	SATISFAC	PRODQUAL	INVACCUR	TECHSUPT	NEWPROD
USAGE	0.000					
SATISFAC	0.000	0.000				
PRODQUAL	-0.019	0.041	0.000			
INVACCUR	0.055	0.033	0.045	0.000		
TECHSUPT	0.003	0.032	0.032	-0.004	0.000	
NEWPROD	-0.058	-0.030	-0.074	-0.029	0.059	0.000
DELIVERY	-0.028	-0.054	-0.041	-0.026	-0.046	0.106
MKTLEADR	0.019	0.010	-0.002	-0.022	-0.049	0.016
PRDVALUE	0.217	0.087	0.169	0.140	0.229	0.181
LOWPRICE	0.044	-0.046	-0.064	-0.122	0.014	0.042
NEGOTIAT	-0.084	0.011	0.038	-0.001	0.082	-0.002
MUTUALTY	-0.066	-0.100	0.084	0.052	-0.098	0.079
INTEGRTY	0.042	-0.119	0.120	0.094	0.011	0.088
FLEXBLTY	-0.004	-0.122	0.014	-0.042	-0.081	-0.126
PROBRES	0.010	0.037	-0.049	-0.029	0.006	-0.026

FITTED RESIDUALS

	DELIVERY	MKTLEADR	PRDVALUE	LOWPRICE	NEGOTIAT	MUTUALTY
DELIVERY	0.000					
MKTLEADR	0.065	0.000				
PRDVALUE	0.095	0.059	0.000			
LOWPRICE	-0.115	0.022	-0.027	0.000		
NEGOTIAT	-0.073	0.065	-0.024	0.010	0.000	
MUTUALTY	0.107	0.027	0.093	-0.059	-0.002	0.000
INTEGRTY	-0.006	-0.010	0.243	0.016	-0.007	-0.029
FLEXBLTY	-0.076	-0.068	0.236	0.034	-0.066	0.081
PROBRES	-0.077	-0.087	0.200	-0.093	-0.053	-0.103

FITTED RESIDUALS

	INTEGRTY	FLEXBLTY	PROBRES
INTEGRTY	0.000		
FLEXBLTY	-0.041	0.000	
PROBRES	0.043	0.027	0.000

SUMMARY STATISTICS FOR FITTED RESIDUALS
SMALLEST FITTED RESIDUAL = -0.126
 MEDIAN FITTED RESIDUAL = 0.000
LARGEST FITTED RESIDUAL = 0.243

STEMLEAF PLOT
```
-12|622
-10|9530
- 8|83741
- 6|76438664
- 4|9843996211
- 2|0999876642
- 0|907644222100000000000000000000
 0|36000114469
 2|277223478
 4|1223452599
 6|559
 8|12478345
10|67
12|0
14|0
16|9
18|1
20|07
22|96
24|3
```

STANDARDIZED RESIDUALS

	USAGE	SATISFAC	PRODQUAL	INVACCUR	TECHSUPT	NEWPROD
USAGE	0.000					
SATISFAC	0.000	0.000				
PRODQUAL	-0.542	0.546	0.000			
INVACCUR	1.526	0.436	3.138	0.000		
TECHSUPT	0.052	0.409	1.430	-0.154	0.000	
NEWPROD	-1.196	-0.384	-3.423	-1.292	1.839	0.000
DELIVERY	-0.600	-0.693	-2.039	-1.233	-1.495	3.569
MKTLEADR	0.437	0.124	-0.120	-1.117	-1.724	0.559
PRDVALUE	2.972	1.040	2.293	1.887	2.985	2.363
LOWPRICE	1.402	-0.593	-1.454	-2.736	0.255	0.757
NEGOTIAT	-2.788	0.147	0.870	-0.013	1.469	-0.034
MUTUALTY	-1.582	-1.347	1.396	0.851	-1.468	1.199
INTEGRTY	1.385	-1.704	2.357	1.830	0.188	1.492
FLEXBLTY	-0.189	-1.794	0.310	-0.900	-1.450	-2.287
PROBRES	0.214	0.485	-0.742	-0.436	0.085	-0.370

STANDARDIZED RESIDUALS

	DELIVERY	MKTLEADR	PRDVALUE	LOWPRICE	NEGOTIAT	MUTUALTY
DELIVERY	0.000					
MKTLEADR	2.499	0.000				
PRDVALUE	1.243	0.780	0.000			
LOWPRICE	-2.176	0.438	-1.103	0.000		
NEGOTIAT	-1.383	1.287	-1.058	3.810	0.000	
MUTUALTY	1.641	0.427	1.174	-0.941	-0.035	0.000
INTEGRTY	-0.096	-0.181	3.186	0.308	-0.128	-0.847
FLEXBLTY	-1.416	-1.323	3.150	0.735	-1.478	2.956
PROBRES	-1.105	-1.271	2.467	-1.343	-0.775	-1.977

STANDARDIZED RESIDUALS

	INTEGRTY	FLEXBLTY	PROBRES
INTEGRTY	0.000		
FLEXBLTY	-2.310	0.000	
PROBRES	1.063	0.836	0.000

SUMMARY STATISTICS FOR STANDARDIZED RESIDUALS
SMALLEST STANDARDIZED RESIDUAL = -3.423
MEDIAN STANDARDIZED RESIDUAL = 0.000
LARGEST STANDARDIZED RESIDUAL = 3.810

```
'CAUSAL MODEL WITH MULTIPLE INDICATORS'
MODIFICATION INDICES AND EXPECTED CHANGE

        MODIFICATION INDICES FOR LAMBDA-Y

                    USAGE    SATISFAC
                   --------  --------
        USAGE        - -      2.729
        SATISFAC     - -       - -

        EXPECTED CHANGE FOR LAMBDA-Y

                    USAGE    SATISFAC
                   --------  --------
        USAGE        - -      0.210
        SATISFAC     - -       - -

        STANDARDIZED EXPECTED CHANGE FOR LAMBDA-Y

                    USAGE    SATISFAC
                   --------  --------
        USAGE        - -      0.210
        SATISFAC     - -       - -

        MODIFICATION INDICES FOR LAMBDA-X

                 FIRMPROD   PRICEFAC   RELATFAC
                 --------   --------   --------
    PRODQUAL       - -        0.040      2.224
    INVACCUR       - -        1.574      0.690
    TECHSUPT       - -        2.009      0.872
    NEWPROD        - -        0.543      0.276
    DELIVERY       - -        3.565      0.570
    MKTLEADR       - -        1.294      0.589
    PRDVALUE      6.242       - -       15.289
    LOWPRICE      3.907       - -        0.000
    NEGOTIAT      0.489       - -        3.916
    MUTUALTY      1.094      0.107       - -
    INTEGRTY      2.959      0.574       - -
    FLEXBLTY      3.484      0.003       - -
    PROBRES       0.778      0.766       - -
```

Estimates of the reduction in chi-square
obtained from estimation of the parameters.

485

EXPECTED CHANGE FOR LAMBDA-X

	FIRMPROD	PRICEFAC	RELATFAC
PRODQUAL	- -	0.030	0.162
INVACCUR	- -	-0.192	0.091
TECHSUPT	- -	0.258	-0.122
NEWPROD	- -	0.132	-0.068
DELIVERY	- -	-0.328	-0.094
MKTLEADR	- -	0.191	-0.093
PRDVALUE	0.267	- -	0.637
LOWPRICE	-0.217	- -	-0.002
NEGOTIAT	0.077	- -	-0.333
MUTUALTY	0.113	-0.075	- -
INTEGRTY	0.179	0.165	- -
FLEXBLTY	-0.197	0.012	- -
PROBRES	-0.098	-0.207	- -

STANDARDIZED EXPECTED CHANGE FOR LAMBDA-X

	FIRMPROD	PRICEFAC	RELATFAC
PRODQUAL	- -	0.012	0.098
INVACCUR	- -	-0.078	0.055
TECHSUPT	- -	0.104	-0.074
NEWPROD	- -	0.053	-0.041
DELIVERY	- -	-0.133	-0.057
MKTLEADR	- -	0.077	-0.056
PRDVALUE	0.230	- -	0.384
LOWPRICE	-0.187	- -	-0.001
NEGOTIAT	0.067	- -	-0.201
MUTUALTY	0.097	-0.030	- -
INTEGRTY	0.155	0.067	- -
FLEXBLTY	-0.170	0.005	- -
PROBRES	-0.085	-0.084	- -

MODIFICATION INDICES FOR BETA

	USAGE	SATISFAC
USAGE	- -	2.729
SATISFAC	- -	- -

EXPECTED CHANGE FOR BETA

	USAGE	SATISFAC
USAGE	- -	0.210
SATISFAC	- -	- -

STANDARDIZED EXPECTED CHANGE FOR BETA

	USAGE	SATISFAC
USAGE	- -	0.210
SATISFAC	- -	- -

MODIFICATION INDICES FOR GAMMA

	FIRMPROD	PRICEFAC	RELATFAC
USAGE	- -	- -	- -
SATISFAC	0.016	0.026	3.249

EXPECTED CHANGE FOR GAMMA

	FIRMPROD	PRICEFAC	RELATFAC
USAGE	- -	- -	- -
SATISFAC	0.013	-0.036	-0.373

STANDARDIZED EXPECTED CHANGE FOR GAMMA

	FIRMPROD	PRICEFAC	RELATFAC
USAGE	- -	- -	- -
SATISFAC	0.011	-0.015	-0.225

NO NON-ZERO MODIFICATION INDICES FOR PHI

MODIFICATION INDICES FOR PSI

	USAGE	SATISFAC
USAGE	- -	
SATISFAC	2.729	- -

EXPECTED CHANGE FOR PSI

	USAGE	SATISFAC
USAGE	- -	
SATISFAC	0.175	- -

STANDARDIZED EXPECTED CHANGE FOR PSI

	USAGE	SATISFAC
USAGE	- -	
SATISFAC	0.175	- -

MODIFICATION INDICES FOR THETA-EPS

	USAGE	SATISFAC
USAGE	2.729	- -
SATISFAC	2.729	- -

EXPECTED CHANGE FOR THETA-EPS

	USAGE	SATISFAC
USAGE	-0.425	- -
SATISFAC	0.175	- -

MODIFICATION INDICES FOR THETA-DELTA-EPS

	USAGE	SATISFAC
PRODQUAL	4.073	1.409
INVACCUR	1.902	0.007
TECHSUPT	0.180	0.240
NEWPROD	1.177	0.071
DELIVERY	0.034	1.156
MKTLEADR	1.035	0.016
PRDVALUE	0.927	0.001
LOWPRICE	5.155	2.285
NEGOTIAT	7.247	2.411
MUTUALTY	1.926	0.104
INTEGRTY	2.884	2.232
FLEXBLTY	0.230	1.506
PROBRES	0.018	1.408

EXPECTED CHANGE FOR THETA-DELTA-EPS

	USAGE	SATISFAC
PRODQUAL	-0.076	0.053
INVACCUR	0.053	0.004
TECHSUPT	0.019	0.027
NEWPROD	-0.049	-0.014
DELIVERY	0.008	-0.056
MKTLEADR	0.043	-0.006
PRDVALUE	0.059	0.002
LOWPRICE	0.117	-0.087
NEGOTIAT	-0.140	0.089
MUTUALTY	-0.082	-0.021
INTEGRTY	0.100	-0.090
FLEXBLTY	0.029	-0.070
PROBRES	-0.008	0.083

MODIFICATION INDICES FOR THETA-DELTA

	PRODQUAL	INVACCUR	TECHSUPT	NEWPROD	DELIVERY	MKTLEADR
PRODQUAL	- -					
INVACCUR	9.847	- -				
TECHSUPT	2.046	0.024	- -			
NEWPROD	11.714	1.670	3.382	- -		
DELIVERY	4.159	1.521	2.236	12.741	- -	
MKTLEADR	0.015	1.247	2.974	0.313	6.247	- -
PRDVALUE	0.400	0.108	2.567	0.717	0.014	4.843
LOWPRICE	1.736	5.975	0.011	5.094	0.215	1.694
NEGOTIAT	1.021	0.938	0.465	3.061	0.991	0.445
MUTUALTY	0.193	0.083	7.724	1.666	4.709	0.001
INTEGRTY	1.834	0.655	0.094	2.686	1.385	2.214
FLEXBLTY	2.335	0.305	0.071	5.620	0.084	0.000
PROBRES	0.716	0.004	1.946	0.272	0.286	0.667

MODIFICATION INDICES FOR THETA-DELTA

	PRDVALUE	LOWPRICE	NEGOTIAT	MUTUALTY	INTEGRTY	FLEXBLTY
PRDVALUE	- -					
LOWPRICE	1.217	- -				
NEGOTIAT	1.120	14.514	- -			
MUTUALTY	0.704	2.260	1.902	- -		
INTEGRTY	1.182	0.108	0.020	0.718	- -	
FLEXBLTY	1.044	2.474	2.451	8.738	5.335	- -
PROBRES	2.178	2.377	0.137	3.910	1.129	0.699

MODIFICATION INDICES FOR THETA-DELTA

	PROBRES
PROBRES	- -

EXPECTED CHANGE FOR THETA-DELTA

	PRODQUAL	INVACCUR	TECHSUPT	NEWPROD	DELIVERY	MKTLEADR
PRODQUAL	- -					
INVACCUR	0.110	- -				
TECHSUPT	0.054	-0.006	- -			
NEWPROD	-0.128	-0.049	0.079	- -		
DELIVERY	-0.075	-0.045	-0.063	0.147	- -	
MKTLEADR	-0.004	-0.040	-0.070	0.022	0.098	- -
PRDVALUE	0.029	0.015	0.090	0.047	-0.006	-0.113
LOWPRICE	-0.048	-0.090	0.005	0.098	-0.019	0.053
NEGOTIAT	0.037	0.035	0.030	-0.076	-0.042	0.027
MUTUALTY	0.018	-0.012	-0.141	0.064	0.105	0.002
INTEGRTY	0.051	0.031	-0.014	0.074	-0.052	-0.063
FLEXBLTY	0.056	-0.020	-0.012	-0.103	-0.012	0.000
PROBRES	-0.037	0.003	0.075	0.027	-0.027	-0.040

EXPECTED CHANGE FOR THETA-DELTA

	PRDVALUE	LOWPRICE	NEGOTIAT	MUTUALTY	INTEGRTY	FLEXBLTY
PRDVALUE	- -					
LOWPRICE	-0.096	- -				
NEGOTIAT	-0.093	1.191	- -			
MUTUALTY	-0.057	-0.080	0.073	- -		
INTEGRTY	0.067	-0.016	0.007	-0.054	- -	
FLEXBLTY	0.060	0.074	-0.074	0.194	-0.172	- -
PROBRES	0.105	-0.087	0.021	-0.133	0.068	0.054

EXPECTED CHANGE FOR THETA-DELTA

	PROBRES
PROBRES	- -

MAXIMUM MODIFICATION INDEX IS   15.29 FOR ELEMENT (7, 3) OF LAMBDA-X

'CAUSAL MODEL WITH MULTIPLE INDICATORS'
STANDARDIZED SOLUTION

LAMBDA-Y

	USAGE	SATISFAC
USAGE	1.000	- -
SATISFAC	- -	1.000

LAMBDA-X

	FIRMPROD	PRICEFAC	RELATFAC
PRODQUAL	0.863	- -	- -
INVACCUR	0.857	- -	- -
TECHSUPT	0.747	- -	- -
NEWPROD	0.759	- -	- -
DELIVERY	0.781	- -	- -
MKTLEADR	0.803	- -	- -
PRDVALUE	- -	0.404	- -
LOWPRICE	- -	0.811	- -
NEGOTIAT	- -	0.821	- -
MUTUALTY	- -	- -	0.603
INTEGRTY	- -	- -	0.729
FLEXBLTY	- -	- -	0.786
PROBRES	- -	- -	0.506

BETA

	USAGE	SATISFAC
USAGE	- -	- -
SATISFAC	0.411	- -

GAMMA

	FIRMPROD	PRICEFAC	RELATFAC
USAGE	0.056	0.038	0.615
SATISFAC	- -	- -	- -

CORRELATION MATRIX OF ETA AND KSI

	USAGE	SATISFAC	FIRMPROD	PRICEFAC	RELATFAC
USAGE	1.000				
SATISFAC	0.411	1.000			
FIRMPROD	0.356	0.146	1.000		
PRICEFAC	0.275	0.113	0.355	1.000	
RELATFAC	0.655	0.269	0.465	0.353	1.000

Standardized coefficients. Note that the three exogenous construct indicators set to 1.0 now have estimated coefficients.

PSI

	USAGE	SATISFAC
	-------	--------
	0.567	0.831

REGRESSION MATRIX ETA ON KSI (STANDARDIZED)

	FIRMPROD	PRICEFAC	RELATFAC
	--------	--------	--------
USAGE	0.056	0.038	0.615
SATISFAC	0.023	0.016	0.253

THE PROBLEM USED   26496 BYTES (= 2.5% OF AVAILABLE WORKSPACE)

TIME USED: 1.4 SECONDS

492